Pro[...]

Informal Empire in [...]
Culture, Commerce and Capital

The *Bulletin of Latin American Research* Book Series

The *Bulletin of Latin American Research* publishes original research of current interest on Latin America, the Caribbean, inter-American relations and the Latin American Diaspora from all academic disciplines within the social sciences, history and cultural studies. The BLAR/SLAS book series was launched in 2008 with the aim of publishing research monographs and edited collections that complement the wide scope of the Bulletin itself. It is published and distributed in association with Wiley-Blackwell. We aim to make the series the home of some of the most exciting, innovatory work currently being undertaken on Latin America and we welcome outlines or manuscripts of interdisciplinary, single-authored, jointly-authored or edited volumes. If you would like to discuss a possible submission to the series, please contact the editors at blar@liverpool.ac.uk

Informal Empire in Latin America: Culture, Commerce and Capital

EDITED BY
MATTHEW BROWN

BLACKWELL PUBLISHING
350 Main Street, Malden, MA 02148–5020, USA
9600 Garsington Road, Oxford OX4 2DQ, UK
550 Swanston Street, Carlton, Victoria 3053, Australia

First published 2008 by Blackwell Publishing Ltd

Library of Congress Cataloging-in-Publication Data

Informal empire in Latin America : culture, commerce and capital / edited by Matthew
Brown. p. cm.

Includes bibliographical references and index.

ISBN 978-1-4051-7932-4

1. Great Britain–Relations–Latin America. 2. Latin America–Relations–Great Britain.
3. Great Britain–Commerce–Latin America. 4. Latin America–Commerce–Great Britain.
5. British–Latin America–History. 6. Imperialism. I. Brown, Matthew.

F1416.G7I54 2008
303.48′28041–dc22

2008006997

A catalogue record for this title is available from the British Library

Set in 10 on 13 pt Palatino
by TnQ, India
Printed and bound in the United Kingdom
by Page Brothers, Norwich

For further information on Blackwell Publishing, visit our website:
http://www.blackwellpublishing.com

Contents

Informal Empire in Latin America: Culture, Commerce and Capital

EDITED BY MATTHEW BROWN

University of Bristol, UK

Bulletin of Latin American Studies Book Series: Interdisciplinary Approaches to Latin America

SERIES EDITORS: NICOLA MILLER, JEAN GRUGEL, DAVID HOWARD, GEOFFREY KANTARIS AND TONY KAPCIA

The *Bulletin of Latin American Research* (BLAR) has a distinguished history of publishing primary research from a range of disciplines in Latin American studies. Our readers have long been able to draw upon ideas from History, Geography, Politics, International Relations, Anthropology, Sociology, Gender Studies and, increasingly, Cultural Studies. Many of our articles have addressed thematic topics and debates of interest to all Latin Americanists, such as mestizaje, populism or the politics of social movements. This is one of the great strengths of being an area studies journal rather than a discipline-based one. We now hope to complement the multidisciplinarity of the journal with this new book series, which will have an explicitly interdisciplinary focus. We will publish innovative work from scholars who are working across disciplines, raising new research questions and developing new methodologies. The series aims to develop into a major forum for interdisciplinary work in Latin American studies.

This first volume of the series arose from a conference held at the University of Bristol, UK, in January 2007 on the theme of informal empire. The conference and the book both build upon recent advances in the historiography of imperialism and studies of the nineteenth-century modern world, most obviously the work of Ann Laura Stoler, Catherine Hall and C. A. Bayly. The aim of the conference was to consider these new approaches to informal empire alongside the many still-unresolved questions raised in the debates conducted by Latin Americanists first during the 1970s and again in the 1990s. By juxtaposing political economy and cultural studies, this book breathes new life into the concept of informal empire. It both illuminates the study of British imperialism, from which Latin America is usually conspicuous only by its absence, and provides a sound basis for interpreting the complex processes of nation-building and state-formation in Latin America.

Acknowledgements

The international conference from which this volume springs was an expensive undertaking. It was generously funded by the British Academy (Conference Grant BCG-44027), the Society for Latin American Studies, the Bristol Institute for Research in the Humanities and Arts, the Arts and Humanities Research Council, the British Empire and Commonwealth Museum and the University of Bristol's Centre for the Study of Colonial and Postcolonial Societies, its School of Modern Languages and its Faculty of Arts Research Director.

I would like to thank Caroline Williams, David Hook, Rebecca Earle and Rory Miller for their support of the project from the very beginning. Thanks to Sam Barlow, Andrew Redden and Alastair Wilson for their peerless administration which ensured the event ran smoothly. Papers were also given at the conference by Leslie Bethell, Alistair Hennessy, Joseph Smith, Felipe Támega Fernández, Michael Costeloe, Paul Garner, Jonathan Curry-Machado, Margarita Díaz-Andreu, Stephen Howe, Adrian Pearce, José María Aguilera Manzano and Luis Fernández Martínez. They all made excellent contributions to the dialogue that informed the revisions of the conference papers into the published chapters of this book. John Darwin, David Brookshaw, Emily Walmsley and Robert Bickers chaired panels and guided our discussions towards comparison with other regions and experiences of empire. I thank David Brown, Natasha Carver, Jo Crow, Lorraine Leu, John MacKenzie, Nicola Miller, Andrew Thompson and Rhiân Williams for their comments on earlier drafts of my Introduction.

Thanks to Nicola Miller and the BLAR Series Editors. It is an honour and a privilege to form the first imprint of this series. Thanks to Rita Matos and Blackwell for their work in making the project a success. I am very grateful to Martín Alonso Roa Celis and the Museo Nacional de Colombia for permission to use their images in the wonderful cover illustrations.

The following abbreviations are used throughout the text:

AGI	Archivo General de Indias, Sevilla
HMG	His/Her Majesty's Government
FO	Foreign Office Papers
TNA	The National Archives (formerly the Public Record Office, Kew)

All translations are by the chapter authors unless otherwise stated.

About the Cover Images

'Banco de UKarib'
Photomontage
2007

This book's cover images place nineteenth-century European travellers' illustrations upon Colombian banknotes from the same period in order to explore the theme of informal empire. The travellers used include Auguste Le Moyne (Untitled image of soldier, 1835) and Jules de Crévaux ('La bella popula', published in *América pintoresca*, 1884). The photomontage explores

the multiple physical and cultural presences in America and the Caribbean: aboriginal, black and British imperialist. The title plays upon the conception held by some indigenous groups, in which cannibals are referred to as 'Caribs'. A 'Carib' could be anyone who participated in the slave trade, including

European people, on the basis that the men and women who were deported during the slave trade never returned. Thus they deduce that these people were devoured by the white men in a cannibalistic process. This photomontage is a meditation on the consumption of natural resources, and the increasing economic and cultural integration of the people and lands of the Americas into a world market. It forms part of a wider project to be exhibited later in 2008, and draws on images held in the collections of the Museo Nacional de Colombia.

Martín Alonso Roa Celis, Bogotá, August 2007

Contributor Biographies

Matthew Brown is a Lecturer in Latin American Studies at the University of Bristol.

Malcolm Deas is a Fellow of St. Antony's College, Oxford, UK.

Jennifer L. French is Assistant Professor of Spanish and Comparative Literature at Williams College in Williamstown, Massachusetts, USA.

Louise Guenther has held visiting appointments at the Centre for Brazilian Studies and St Antony's College at the University of Oxford, UK. She has held MacArthur and Fulbright fellowships, and received her PhD from the University of Minnesota, USA in 1998.

Charles Jones is Reader in International Relations at the University of Cambridge, UK.

Alan Knight is Professor of the History of Latin America at the University of Oxford, UK.

Colin Lewis is Senior Lecturer in Latin American Economic History at the London School of Economics, UK.

Fernanda Peñaloza is a Lecturer in Latin American Cultural Studies at the University of Manchester, UK.

Karen Racine is an Associate Professor of Latin American History at the University of Guelph, Ontario, Canada.

David Rock is Professor of Latin American History at the University of California at Santa Barbara, USA.

Andrew Thompson is Professor of Commonwealth and Imperial History at the University of Leeds, UK.

Introduction

MATTHEW BROWN

The compromised nature of national sovereignty remains a recurrent feature of political rhetoric in Latin America into the twenty-first century. Radicals, populists and revolutionaries denounce foreign intervention to mobilise support for their causes. In Venezuela, Hugo Chavez (2007) repeatedly lambasts the USA's 'imperial agenda' in Latin America. In Mexico, Subcomandante Marcos rails against the way that 'imperialism has changed its mode of attack, but [...] continues its struggle against us' (Marcos, 2007). Multinational businesses such as Coca-Cola and Dunkin' Donuts are the targets of groups seeking to 'resist imperialism' in a variety of ways (Suescun Pozas, 1998: 540–555). Permanent US military posts in Manta, Ecuador and Comalapa, El Salvador give credence to allegations of a strategic network of covert interventionism across the region (Lindsey-Poland, 2004; Golinger, 2007). Protesters in Cochabamba, Bolivia, lament the unsympathetic and imperialist nature of International Monetary Fund and World Bank prescriptions for economic growth in Latin America (Crabtree, 2005). Even human rights and development organisations, including Human Rights Watch and Amnesty International, are accused of infringing national sovereignty in Peru and Colombia (e.g. Conaghan, 2005: 279). These debates and struggles revolve around the extent to which limits should be set on foreign intervention in supposedly sovereign nation-states. When the Argentine footballer-turned-celebrity-radical Diego Maradona protested (2005) about the Free Trade Area of the Americas, calling it an affront to Argentine 'dignity', and resenting that US President George W. Bush came to Buenos Aires to 'treat us like his subjects, because we are not his subjects nor anyone's subjects', he hit the nail on the head about the cultural underpinnings of informal empire. Such anguished calls for respect and sovereignty make clear the need to address the historical resonances of the contemporary situation, and to interrogate more closely and more analytically the history of 'informal empire' in Latin America. Commerce and capital provide the framework, but it is in the relationships between individuals, and the perceptions of these relationships, where difference and inequality are marked out, and where the asymmetry of power is made explicit, is resisted and is addressed.

Gallagher and Robinson's (1953: 13) assessment that nineteenth-century British policy towards the rest of the world was 'trade with informal control if possible, trade with rule if necessary', has long been a central reference point of historical studies of British–Latin American relations. Gallagher and Robinson powerfully described the 'informal empire' as the part of the impe-rial iceberg that was hidden below the water-line (Gallagher and Robinson, 1953: 1), and urged scholars to consider a hypothesis that included 'informal as well as formal expansion, and [that] must allow for the continuity of the process'. Their work 'set the agenda for the study of imperial history' (Cain and Hopkins, 2002 [1993]: 26) for several decades, particularly in the field of British activities in Latin America. Yet now one of the most influential schol-ars of empire, Ann Stoler (2006a: 136), has dismissed 'informal empire' and 'indirect rule' as 'unhelpful euphemisms, not working concepts'. For Stoler informal empire is a euphemism for imperialism, part of a 'scholarly vocabu-lary [that] defers to the terms of empires themselves'.

This book sets out to test Stoler's concerns by means of an interdisciplinary and comparative study of British interactions in Latin America in the conven-tional age of 'informal empire', roughly 1810–1940. If 'informal empire' is go-ing to be a 'working concept' again, then it will have to be re-defined, re-contextualised, and re-tested. That was the task set for the contributors to this volume, who adopted a range of approaches and methodologies, and who came to divergent conclusions. In this introduction, I provide a working defi-nition of the general concepts in use; I lay out the context of British involve-ment in Latin America in the nineteenth century in the form of a brief historical narrative for non-specialists; I summarise the historiographies upon which the project builds; and, finally, I suggest how the new studies of the problem pre-sented here can suggest new approaches towards Informal Empire. In his Af-terword, Andrew Thompson explores some of the conceptual and comparative conclusions of the analyses featured in the volume, with particular reference to other areas of the British Empire.

Informal Empire: Existing Concepts and New Directions

Gallagher and Robinson's (1953) hypothesis on the 'imperialism of free trade' came to dominate the study of British involvement in Latin America for half a century.[1] Launched in the 1950s, it became increasingly contentious

---

1　The 'informal empire' debate remained largely one that took place in Britain. Spanish historians of Latin America were occupied with other issues. For a dis-cussion of why and how, see Josep Fradera's comments in an interview with Christopher Schmidt-Nowara, in Schmidt-Nowara and Nieto-Phillips (2006: 160–163). With some exceptions, historians in Latin America found dependency theory more relevant to their own concerns than 'informal empire'. On the ap-peal of the 'dependency' thesis, and the problems it faced, see Haber (1990: 8–15).

in the 1960s and 1970s as it coincided and sometimes clashed with structuralist and Marxist interpretations of Latin America's dependency on external economies, with Platt (1967, 1968a, 1972) arguing vociferously for the weakness of informal empire in Latin America. As Wm. Roger Louis put it, by 1975 a 'controversy' was raging around the degree of change and continuity that there had been in British policy, and around its practical effects 'on the periphery', an area that included Latin America (Louis, 1976: 235–237; also Jones, 1980). A second stage of debate took place in the 1990s between Thompson (1992) and Hopkins (1994) and was subsequently concluded and wrapped up into surveys and summaries by Miller (1993, 2001) and Knight (1999). The study of Britain's 'informal empire' in Latin America could, therefore, be seen today as a moribund subject to which most scholars are, or should be, indifferent. So why turn to informal empire again? In the next section, I set out three reasons why we should examine the informal empire debate from new perspectives.

The first and most simple reason for returning to informal empire is that the debate left many unsolved questions that still need answering. Eugênio Vargas García's recent historiographical summary focused on the effective political control that Britain exerted over areas of Latin America, looking 'under the orbit' of British power for evidence of influence (2006: 381). It raises several new questions: for example Vargas García is still not quite sure whether Britain actually wanted to exert influence in Latin America, or to what extent metropolitan impulses were effective on the ground. Clearly there is more to be done on these subjects by returning to the existing documentary sources and by expanding the range of materials for study, particularly with evidence from within Latin America itself in addition to the British diplomatic and commercial archives drawn on by earlier studies.

The second reason to turn to informal empire relates to the persistence of the term in academic circles. The debate about whether British–Latin American relations are best characterised as imperial exploitation or mutual advantage has been going on for so long that the concept has managed to remain current despite widespread and repeated critiques. Informal empire has acquired a broadly recognised meaning that can encourage interdisciplinary and comparative dialogue. This meaning, in its simplest form, evokes a powerful nation managing to control a territory over which it does not exercise sovereignty. This makes it a form of imperialism, if we follow Cain and Hopkins's definition that 'the distinguishing feature of imperialism ... is that it involves an incursion, or attempted incursion, into the sovereignty of another state' (Cain and Hopkins, 2002: 54). Yet a broadly understood meaning is not the same as a 'working concept'; to arrive at such an object we need to examine the nature of the incursion and the resultant control that is exercised – be it political, or economic, or cultural, or military – and the extent to which this control does or does not affect or infringe sovereignty. This means reconfiguring 'informal empire'. Trends in scholarly research in recent years – particularly but not exclusively post-colonialism and the 'cultural turn' – open up new avenues (discussed below) for investigation, comparison and discussion.

The third answer to the question 'Why informal empire again?' is that scholars have begun to employ it already in a quite different sense from the conventional usage. Literary scholars and cultural historians have turned to 'informal empire' influenced by Said (1978) and Pratt's (1992) work linking travellers, culture and imperialism. Ricardo Salvatore talks of the USA's 'informal empire' being built in Latin America between 1890 and 1920 on 'a collection of diverse discourses, multiple mediators or agents, and, at times, contradictory representations' (Salvatore, 1998: 70). It is the interdisciplinary recognition of the relevance of culture to discussion of imperial and colonial encounters that explains the recent convergence between British imperial studies and Latin Americanism (e.g. Gallo, 2001b; Fowler, 2004; Aguirre, 2005; Brown, 2006; Ramirez, 2007). This volume hopes to clarify and build upon these developments.

Before we can move down the new, tree-lined and welcoming avenues of culture and comparison, however, it is essential to define our terms. Gallagher and Robinson (1953: 1) recognised this dilemma themselves, observing that the imperial historian was 'very much at the mercy of his own particular concept of empire'. Or, as A.J.P. Taylor (1976: 197) dismissively put it, 'nineteenth-century imperialism had many strands, so much so that all the theories about it are true within their terms of reference'. An updated definition of 'informal empire' is offered at the end of this introduction; contributors to this volume (in particular Alan Knight) work towards their own, sometimes divergent, definitions.

If 'informal empire' is a problematic concept, then the other words in our book's title also carry their own issues. As Mignolo (2005) has argued, 'Latin America' was a nineteenth-century Parisian construct to denote the independent republics who had cast off colonialism, and one that was used by Creole elites to exclude indigenous and Afro-American peoples from their respective nations and publics. Moreover, 'Latin American Studies', the discipline within which many of this volume's contributors make their living, can itself be seen as 'a kind of cultural neo-colonialism' (Beverley, 2003: 49). This book itself of course, forming as it does part of a British body of knowledge 'about Latin America', including contributions from scholars working at British universities – regardless of their own national origins –, and growing out of a conference paid for by the British Academy and other British societies, can be seen within this tradition.

The meaning of 'culture' has occupied better minds than mine. Here I follow Raymond Williams's tripartite definition: (a) 'the best that has been thought and written in the world'; (b) 'the body of intellectual and imaginative work, in which, in a detailed way, human thought and experience are variously recorded'; and (c) 'a description of a particular way of life, which expresses certain meanings and values not only in art and learning but also in institutions and ordinary behaviour' (1961: 57–58). For our purposes of examining informal empire this definition of 'culture' can be summarised as a patchwork of 'values, beliefs, practices and discourses' (Dirks, 1992: 3–5), where those discourses are the linguistic means in which 'ideas organise and regulate social and institutional worlds' (Hall, 2000: 11). In this our understanding of culture follows closely that set out by Gilbert Joseph where culture is 'the symbols and meanings embedded in the daily practices of elite and subaltern (or foreign and local) groups', with culture seen as flexible, processual and 'constantly being refashioned' (Joseph, 1998: 8). As such, this interpretative field builds upon work on travel and 'cultural encounters', and highlights the role of migrants and sojourners in determining the meanings of informal empire. It will quickly become clear to the reader that contributors have their own views on the relative usefulness of 'culture' as an analytical category in assessing informal empire. Some but not all follow Hunt's (1988: 7) hypothesis that 'economic and social relations are not prior to or determining of cultural ones; they are themselves fields of cultural practice and cultural production'.

Commerce and capital should be less problematic terms, constituting as they do the principal means employed towards the gaining of influence in the historiography on British informal empire in Latin America (Lynn, 1999: 101–121). Lord Palmerston indicated that 'it is the business of government to open and secure the roads for the merchant' (Palmerston, 1841: 297), and in this sense commerce and capital were empire's end as well as its means. Capital, as Adelman (1999: 283) has noted, was also central to the construction of states in Latin America. Capital was the bedrock of 'proprietary transformations' and capital interests were 'anything but static' as they sought to 'stabilise market relations through the daily management of conflicts over debts, failed contracts, and the status of money. Private claims over valuable assets – and the ability to enforce them – animated personal interests and shaped what capitalists wanted and expected from public rulers' (Adelman, 1999: 4). As we see in the chapters by Colin Lewis and Charles Jones in this volume, the distinction between 'national' capital and 'foreign' capital was often extremely difficult to discern. A reconfigured 'informal empire' revolving around culture, commerce and capital – roughly correspondent with Adelman's Ideas, Interests and Institutions in which 'none are reducible to the other, but each is patterned by other fields of social life' (Adelman, 1999: 4) – can, it is suggested, continue to provide analytical rigour to a popularly understood concept.

Assessing Cultural Encounters

In reconfiguring 'informal empire', we draw upon the valuable work on 'cultural encounters' or 'contact zones' that appears in the work of Pratt, Salvatore and Aguirre. This body of work emerges out of the increasing confluence between the theoretical inspirations of literary and cultural critics, and those of imperial historians. Drawing on these advances, Burton (2003), Hall (2002) and others persuasively argue that in order to ascertain the real nature of imperialism and its consequences, scholars should turn even further away from their previous reliance on metropolitan archives and the 'imperial mind', and move towards the often ignored, day-to-day relationships formed between colonised, colonisers and their many mediators. Stoler (2006b: 3) has worked through the 'tense and tender ties' of colonialism, arguing that 'intimate relations' shape, determine and define colonial relations: 'these ties are not microcosms of empire but its marrow'. In order to understand colonialism and imperialism, therefore, scholars need to examine the day-to-day experiences of ordinary people, as well as metropolitan laws or the presence of gunboats.

As part of her project of reconfiguring how we understand colonial and imperial relationships – what Cooper (2005: 1) calls 'unbounding colonialism' – Stoler has redefined empire itself. She exhorts scholars to 'identify those gradations of intervention and sovereignty that call themselves by so many nonimperial names' (Stoler, 2006b: xvi), and argues convincingly for the study of 'imperial formations ... states of becoming rather than being, macropolities in constant formation' (Stoler, 2006a: 135–136). If the map painted red to denominate the British Empire was an inaccuracy, then Stoler argues that the entire world should be painted in shades of red, blue and green to reflect the shifting boundaries and composite quality of all imperial formations.[2]

This is persuasive, yet it still leaves us with the difficulty of knowing how to distinguish between different manifestations of 'imperial formations'. The question of what to call British activity in Latin America in the long nineteenth century remains moot. Indeed, some recent work on the cultural aspects of informal empire can be critiqued on the grounds that

---

2   Taking 'informal empire' out of the equation can have other consequences, of course; as in Samson (2007) who suggests that '"formal Empire" is a strangely narrow definition of British colonialism'.

their definitions are vague or slippery. Salvatore (1998), for example does not define 'informal empire' at all and neither does he cite Gallagher and Robinson or make any reference to the British historiography. In contrast, Robert Aguirre does define his term, yet he bases his analysis of British travelling, collecting and writing about nineteenth-century Central America on the premise that 'informal imperialism' was a 'political and economic strategy' that 'carved out an area of competitive advantage based largely on trade and economic policy but buttressed strongly by myriad cultural activities on the ground' (Aguirre, 2005: xv). He argues that 'cultural forms ... – travel narratives, museum exhibitions, panoramas, diplomatic correspondence, ethnological freakshows, and adventure novels – lent crucial ideological support to the work of informal imperialism, shaping an audience receptive to the influx of British power in the region' (Aguirre, 2005: xvi). All of which presupposes that 'informal imperialism' *was* a policy – which has been vigorously disputed by many critics, including Charles Jones in this volume – and that informal empire was a reality on the ground across Latin America – a contention rejected by many of the contributors to this book. The supposition that cultural forms 'buttressed' political and economic strategy, and 'supported' the work of informal imperialism, seems rooted in rather conventional interpretations of 'informal empire'. The continent's political independence in the nineteenth century is widely agreed to have been compromised by the influence of more powerful regions. But did the apparently omnipresent threat of direct intervention constitute 'imperialism'? Was the widespread cultural respect, if not veneration, for Great Britain, part of a 'neo-colonial' mindset? To what extent does the concept of 'informal empire' capture the relationships that existed between Britain and various Latin American countries?

Reconfiguring Informal Empire

This book arose out of my attempt to understand the nature of British involvement in nineteenth-century Latin America. It initially seemed to me that 'informal empire' was too strong a term to describe the particular situation that I was studying – the involvement of around 7,000 British and Irish adventurers in the independence of Colombia, Venezuela and Ecuador (Brown, 2006). These adventurers were variously too headstrong, too incompetent, or too inebriated to be accused of operating on anyone's instructions, let alone forming part of a coherent imperial project directed from London. Further consideration of the literature on informal empire suggested, however, that this might be an apt description of the way that informal empire worked in Latin America, where its 'agents', if we can call them that, were neither committed to the cause nor interested in promoting its values, yet were often perceived as imperialists by the locals they encountered, and in some way, therefore, their decisions and actions did shape society in the lands where they lived. The gap between the production of British policy, and the reception (or not) of practices 'on the ground', meant that it was hard to reconcile even with 'absent-minded' imperialism, following Rivière (1995) and Porter (2004b), or empire by accident or improvisation.

Bringing scholars together to address the subject both conceptually and comparatively seemed the best way to get closer to an answer to the question. We aimed to get a broad view of how 'informal empire' worked, with contributors on the most commonly identified areas of strong British influence – Brazil and the River Plate – as well as less obvious regions, such as Colombia and Patagonia. The discussion was explicitly interdisciplinary, including several scholars trained or influenced by Robinson and Gallagher themselves, but also a younger generation of researchers who feel that they owe more to postcolonialism and subaltern studies. One result is a clearer picture of the gradations and varieties of informal empire across the region, emphasising that these were largely determined by local conditions and mores. We hoped to build on the work on US–Latin American relations that cast foreign-local encounters 'as complex affairs involving multiple agents, elaborate cultural constructs and unforeseen outcomes' (Coronil, 1998: ix). We wanted to prove the validity of Stephen Howe's claim that 'studies of culture, discourse and worldview, of indigenous resistance and adaptation, can happily and creatively co-exist with work on colonial high politics or political economy, (Howe, 2001: 135).

The result of our encounter, which took place during two cold, windy and wintry days in Bristol, is this book, and it represents a resounding vote in favour of retaining and clarifying 'informal empire' as an analytical tool.

The Rise of British Informal Empire in Latin America

British involvement in Latin America has its roots in the adventures, lootings and 'discoveries' of Walter Ralegh and then Francis Drake – imperialists and pirates who sought to extract gold and riches from the Spanish empire during the long colonial period when it was often supposed, though not entirely accurately, that Spain had closed the doors of its empires to other Europeans (O'Phelan Godoy, 2002; Herzog, 2003).

This book focuses on the long nineteenth century, yet the decline and fall of British informal empire in Latin America could be convincingly presented as spanning a much longer period, from 1762 to 1965. This *longue durée* begins with what might be cast as episodes of formal imperialism – the successful occupation by British forces of Havana and Manila (1762–1763) in the Seven Years War. On these occasions, and later in 1806–1807 when British forces led by Sir Home Popham occupied Buenos Aires and Montevideo, geopolitics and local resistance dictated that the British abandon formal imperial involvement within a year. Elsewhere, the British continued to occupy and collect formal colonies in Latin America, over which Great Britain exercised formal sovereignty. Trinidad was taken from Spain in 1797, the Malvinas/Falklands were occupied in 1833, British Guiana was expanded territorially (at the expense of Venezuela) through the explorations of the Schomburgk expedition in 1840, and British Honduras (today Belize) was formally established through treaty negotiation with Guatemala in 1859.

British commercial involvement in Latin America was on the rise even in the eighteenth century. Adrian Pearce has shown how British penetration of neutral trade, and the contracts signed with Spain before Independence, reveal considerable British dominance of external trade and much political influence well before Napoleon Bonaparte's decapitation of the Spanish Empire in 1808 (Pearce, 2007). During the Independence period, the Spanish American rebels consistently appealed for British support, dedicating great efforts to securing British recognition of their independence from Spain, with emissaries living and lobbying in London (Racine, 1996). In turn, Britain sent merchants, diplomats, commissioners and consuls – as well as mercenaries, adventurers and chancers – who lived in South America and represented their country's interests (Brown, 2006). These permanent and temporary migrants represented a mixture of British commerce, capital and culture. Later it was the indentured labourers who travelled from the Asian colonies to work in Peruvian guano and other industries, who linked formal to informal empire (Northrup, 1995).

After Independence, and with Spanish influence in the former colonies waning and often completely rejected by new nation-builders, informal empire could grow in strength in areas where the legitimacy of popular sovereignty constructed around new 'nation-states' was often weak. British recognition of Independence in the 1820s was the 'highpoint' (Smith, 1978: 7) of British informal political influence in Latin America, where the treaties of recognition were specifically designed with British interests in mind, such as the prohibition of the slave trade and guarantees of beneficial British trading rights. As Nicola Miller has summarised, Latin America's relatively 'early decolonisation [in comparison with other world regions] result[ed] in a lengthy experience of formal political sovereignty being compromised by economic dependence' (Miller, 1999: 3). Yet until the 1860s, the volume of Britain's trade with Latin America remained relatively low. 'Official' British interest in the region, for what it was worth, was strategic rather than commercial in a region that was still felt to be 'far away and [that] lacked political or strategic importance'; indeed 'the over-riding aim of British foreign policy in the nineteenth century was the preservation of an ill-defined and vague status quo throughout the world' (Smith, 1978: 3). British power revolved around naval bases and coaling stations, such as the Falklands/Malvinas, which became what Lord Curzon referred to as the 'tollgates and barbicans' of empire. These colonies, growing out of an original strategic function, then became the 'bridgeheads of trade' (Darwin, 1997) into the informal empire as the nineteenth century progressed.

With the technological innovations of this period – the telegraph, the transatlantic steam ship, and the railway – importing and exporting to and from Latin America became less burdensome. The 1870s and 1880s saw trade between Britain and Latin America boom, as the latter became fully incorporated into the Atlantic economy, principally in the subordinate position of an exporter of raw materials to the industrialising powers of Europe and North America (O'Rourke and Williamson, 1999). In the view of many scholars, it was in this period that British interest, influence and commerce combined to make informal empire a reality in many areas of Latin America until the First World War. At this time, therefore, 'Britain still exercised considerable sway over much of Latin America' through the 'competitive weight of its inexpensive manufactures, abundant capital and ubiquitous navy' (Kennedy, 2002: 17). The 'imperial fabric' was 'held together by an almost invisible web of connecting forces and influences, of which the Royal Navy was one of the most important' (Gough, 1999: 80). Yet even then, 'British' power was variant along its own national or regional lines – as work on the Welsh in Patagonia, the Scottish in Venezuela or the Irish in Brazil and Argentina has shown (Rheinheimer, 1988; Williams, 1991; Murray, 2004; Marshall, 2005).

The Fall of British Informal Empire in Latin America

From its height in the 1890s–1910s, concentrated primarily in the Atlantic seaboards of Argentina, Uruguay and Brazil, British informal empire faltered at differing rates according to the type of influence being exerted. The *strategic* dimension to British imperialism in Latin America had already begun to diminish after 1850, as other areas of the world assumed more problematic and more pressing characters (Vargas García, 2006: 377). In that year, the Clayton–Bulwer Treaty represented a political accommodation with the USA over Central America, which was a 'step in Britain's political disengagement from Latin America' (Smith, 1978: 23). In 1869, the opening of the Suez Canal cut the journey time from South-east Asia to Northern Europe by two-thirds. For Great Britain, the Western hemisphere suddenly seemed a lot further away, in comparison to the apparently increased proximity of its Eastern Colonies. British lobbying on the construction of a canal in Panama – part of Colombia until 1903 – continued but was superseded in this period by French and then US projects.

In terms of *economics*, the Barings collapse of 1890, discussed in David Rock's chapter, had more effect on Argentina than it did on Great Britain, and revealed the markedly different weights of informal empire on centre and periphery. As Colin Lewis shows in his contribution to this volume, the role of British capital in Argentina's continuing 'weak institutionality' and 'incomplete capitalist modernisation' by the late nineteenth century 'remains a matter of debate'. But while British influence on Argentine economic policy may have decreased, the actual volume and profits of trade and investment actually continued to increase. The First World War was a period of increased competition over scarce resources for the 'great powers' in Latin America (Dehne, 2005).

By the late nineteenth century, British *diplomatic* influence on Latin American politics was also on the wane. British diplomats in Brazil and elsewhere realised that they had little tangible to offer beyond vague threats and promises (Smith, 1979). This often led to frustration and helplessness on the part of diplomats who had specifically chosen to serve in out-of-the-way stations where they hoped and expected to enjoy a relatively high social status and freedom from undue worry regarding the protection of British interests. By the early twentieth century, British officials in Latin America 'demonstrated neither the will nor did they possess the means to bring about a Latin America resolving around a British orbit' (Smith, 1978: 24).

The decline in *political* influence was accelerated during and after the First World War, after which the USA replaced Great Britain as the hegemonic power in Latin America. In the inter-war period, Britain's economy declined, the US economy surged and Latin American nationalism started to affect its external commercial relations to a greater extent. After 1914, modernity and the liberal model of trade were ever less frequently linked to Great Britain in the minds of Latin American elites. The Second World War is often held to mark the end of British interest in Latin America, with the nationalisation of the British-owned railways in Argentina marking the end of a long period of interest and influence. Nevertheless, this is not to say that British influence in Latin America ended in the 1940s. Indeed, in many ways the decline in 'informal empire' and British control in the inter-war period took place at the very same time at which British trade was at its highpoint. In the 1930s, British trade and influence in Argentina remained considerable. Rory Miller (2006) has argued that British economic activity continued to be vigorous, flexible and voluminous in the two decades after the Second World War. There were more 'joint ventures' with local firms, merchant houses remained active and investment in the booming oil industry provided generous profits. But after 1945, this British involvement was part of a general pattern of European investment, 'of which Britain was an important but not dominant part' (Miller, 2006).

The supposed 'fall' of British informal empire must also be qualified by recognition of the existence of multiple competing imperial and national projects against which it was pitted. In the period discussed above, Latin America never formed part of a hegemonic 'informal empire', but rather it existed in the shadow of several empires. The 'close encounters' (Joseph, LeGrand and Salvatore, 1998) of US–Latin American relations began in 1823 when President James Monroe issued his famous doctrine warning Great Britain, Russia and other European powers that 'the American continents ... are henceforth not to be considered as subjects for future colonization by any European powers' (Monroe, 1823). It moved on through such well-known incursions as the United Fruit Company enclaves and CIA support of coups and civil war (Joseph, LeGrand and Salvatore, 1998). German, Italian and other European influences were also strong during the period of British dominance. This was regionally varied and locally moderated, of course, but strong in areas as diverse as opera, car-manufacturing, tango and aviation (Archetti, 1999: 3–7; Dávila and Miller, 1999: 13–16; McBeth, 2001; Aguilar, 2003; Hiatt, 2007: 335–338). In his contribution to this volume, Alan Knight suggests that the cultural influence of Italians in Argentina was much greater than that of Britons.

Britain's cultural influence in Latin America was heavily circumscribed by other more resonant traditions. The principal external cultural references in nineteenth-century Latin America came from France, not Britain or the USA. The 1789 and 1830 French Revolutions were an aspiration or warning to Latin American elites; the writings of Rousseau, Voltaire and Montesquieu were the required reading of those who imagined themselves to be Enlightened nation-builders. The canonical text for Latin American continental identity, José Enrique Rodó's *Ariel* (1900), was inspired more by Ernest Renan's work on the dichotomy between Caliban and Ariel than it was by Shakespeare's *The Tempest*. Rodó's *Ariel* warned against the encroaching power of the utilitarian and materialistic USA – by 1900, for Rodó, Britain's power was not even worth warning against.

Spain retained a residual influence in Hispanic America in the nineteenth century, as did Portugal in Brazil. Most Spanish attention became focused on the metropole's internal crisis, and then on a reorganised and strengthened colonial settlement in Cuba, Puerto Rico and the Philippines (Fontana, 1979, Fradera, 2005). In Hispanic America an initial wave of revulsion for things Spanish, taken up by some of the most fervent rebels in the Independence period, was replaced by a more tolerant regard for *hispanismo* and expressions of gratitude for the Spanish language and Hispanic culture. The work of Andrés Bello on grammar and culture was but the most notable example (Jaksic, 2001). Later in the nineteenth century, *hispanidad* became an ideology to be exported by Spain to its former colonies in a fashion that

Hennessy (2000) has suggested calling 'surrogate imperialism', with references to the proposals of the Spanish writer Ramiro de Maetzu in the promotion of *hispanidad*.

Competition and cooperation between rival powers meant that any empire in Latin America had to operate with incomplete, contested and improvised authority. In this context, it is useful to note Frederick Cooper's thoughts about 'layered' colonialism. Cooper uses the example of late-nineteenth-century Sudan, 'which was colonised by Egypt, which was part of the Ottoman Empire but itself experienced heavy British intervention' (Cooper, 2005: 11). Late-nineteenth-century Panama, early-twentieth-century Argentina or mid-nineteenth-century Mexico would be similar Latin American examples where rival imperial projects competed with, and sometimes defeated, the nation-building and state-building efforts of local elites. The expeditions of archaeologists to Latin America revealed these rivalries, where French, German, US and British researchers vied with each other for the best 'discoveries' and for the best local staff, translators and guides (Díaz-Andreu, 2008; although for an interpretation stressing cooperation over competition, see Botero, 2007). These imperial projects sometimes employed the threat of outright force – gunboat diplomacy or invasion, as used by Britain, Germany and France in Colombia, Venezuela and Mexico respectively – and sometimes used culture and ideas. Together they show that 'informal empire' was continually contested by other foreign powers.

The narrative of British and other foreign influences provided above, however, forms no more than one side of the story. It privileges the role of external actors as agents of change in Latin America, and neglects the variety of external as well as internal references that shaped Latin American societies. Nation-building, state-building, cultural production and economic activity in Latin America were local processes that drew on external examples and influences, to be sure, but which were primarily founded upon local and national necessities and reactions to local circumstances. It is easy, but inaccurate, to call the period 'neocolonial' (Pratt, 1992: 147), which implies that Latin America's relationship with Britain was colonial in all but name. Such a term precludes the many ambiguities of power relationships that form the crux of all imperial and geopolitical relationships. As Simón Bolívar noted in 1830, writing just a month before his death, Latin America's problems were largely internal, meaning that 'once we've been eaten alive by every crime and extinguished by ferocity, the Europeans won't even bother to conquer us' (Bolívar, 1830: 146). Latin American leaders such as Bernardino Rivadavia perceived a difference between the British people and the British government, and tailored their strategies accordingly (Rivadavia, 1817: 17). Latin Americans perceived British 'informal empire' in ways that were starkly different to how it looked from Whitehall, and how it was presented in adventure stories or travel memoirs (Forman, 2000b). Savvy leaders often used the threat of foreign intervention as an opportunity for rhetorical pronouncements on national sovereignty. Cipriano Castro's famous declaration, in response to the unsubtle gunboat diplomacy of Great Britain and Germany, that 'the insolent foreigner's footprint has profaned the nation's sacred soil' (Castro, 1902), was as much designed to re-enforce his own precarious hold on power by emphasising his role as the saviour of the sacred national soil, as it was to warn the foreign power away from a sovereign state (McBeth, 2001). As Andrew Thompson shows in his Afterword to this volume, the rhetoric of infringed sovereignty became a key element of nationalist discourse in later nineteenth- and twentieth-century Latin America.

Filling the Latin-America-Shaped-Hole in British Imperial Historiography

The discussion, above, of the historiographical trends in British Imperial History and in Latin American Studies, suggest a growing convergence of thematic interests coupled with a divergence of methodological approaches. This volume attempts to take advantage of the former and to overcome the latter. It is worth remembering that Gallagher and Robinson (with Denny, 1961) wrote on Latin America before the Parry Report (1965) encouraged a generation of historians of Latin America in the UK away from British imperial history and into Area Studies. This was in many ways a good thing. The work of Abel and Lewis (1985), Miller (1993), McFarlane (1994) and others laid much more emphasis on 'Latin America's external connection' than on Britain's expansion into Latin America and, consequently, their work became increasingly divorced from interpretations of British imperialism (e.g. Cain and Hopkins, 2002: 4–5) that retained a British narrative over the Peruvian, Mexican and Uruguayan particularities. On the other side of the disciplinary fence, the Latin American experience remains absent from the colonial studies literature associated with Stoler, Burton and Cooper that emphasises the importance of focusing on the gritty details of colonialism and the more 'nebulous aspects' of imperialism. They 'blur the boundaries' of the paradigms of the discipline of imperial history (Ward, 2003: 47), but Latin America remains absent from the grand narrative.

The blurring of boundaries has been coupled with a corresponding movement away from methodological homogeneity, and much consequent disagreement over approaches and terminology. In this volume alone, some contributors use the Gramscian concept of 'hegemony'; others talk of Foucaultian power dynamics. Some commentators at the conference, most notably Stephen Howe, suggested that 'semi-colonialism' might be a more useful way of thinking about Latin America's relationship with Britain in the nineteenth century. Gott (2007) draws on the work of Quijano (2001) on *colonialidad* or coloniality, where societies retain or assume the characteristics of colonialism, even when they have become nominally independent. The chapters that follow are explicitly diverse in their subject matter and in their methodologies. All, however, take a comparative approach that acknowledges the divergent manifestations of 'informal empire' across Latin America and across the globe; and all take an interest in the meanings and consequences of this coloniality, or neocolonial attitude, towards a diverse range of European cultures. Contributors are united by their efforts to relate 'informal empire' to other terms of analysis.

The present volume seconds Gott's call for comparison (Gott, 2007: 270), and follows Richard Price's plea for imperial historians to look beyond the 'British World' or the 'British Atlantic' and into more complicated waters of the 'fragilities of empire' (Price, 2006: 612). It adheres to John Darwin's view of 'the British world-system' as a 'cumbrous amalgam of empires formal and informal' (Darwin, forthcoming), and it stresses the connectedness of the nineteenth-century world, with social, political and commercial networks stretching across national and imperial boundaries. As such, it is a meeting between British 'imperial history' and Latin American Studies, even though it is debatable how many of the contributors would choose to position themselves in the former rather than the latter camp. The book takes a 'broad-angled and eclectic vision' and tries to be 'sensitive to and willing to investigate the manifold, often paradoxical connections that have operated between different territories and peoples over time, and acknowledge as well the full diversity of power systems and actors involved' (Colley, 2002a: 144, 134). It accepts Catherine Hall's observation that 'different colonial projects give access to different meanings of empire. The [British] empire changed across time ... each [manifestation] with the different preoccupations of those specific temporalities, places and spaces' (Hall, 2002: 15). One measure of the success (or otherwise) of this volume will be if it contributes to the mapping of the changes that occurred in British imperialism when it encountered Latin America.

Another measure of success, though perhaps a more idealistic one, would be if scholars of British Empire began to take more than token notice of Latin America. At present, much of the best work on Britain's nineteenth century is dismissive, ignorant or inaccurate about Britons' involvement in Latin America. Perhaps this is a result of the historic 'insularity' and 'political and methodological conservatism' of the historiography of British imperialism (Kennedy, 1996: 345). Perhaps it is more simply a problem of linguistic ability, with scholars of British imperialism lacking the language skills to engage with documents in Spanish and Portuguese; as Aguirre observes, a variety of factors have coincided to 'skew our understanding of British imperialism and obscure the importance of Britain's engagement with Latin America' (Aguirre, 2005: xv). One of these factors has probably been the inability of Latin Americanists to successfully scale the walls keeping them enclosed within Area Studies boundaries.

Even the work produced and inspired by 'new imperial' scholars such as Stoler, Burton and Hall, who repeatedly call for scholars to take greater account of peripheral and marginal historical actors, almost entirely neglects the Latin American dimension of European colonialisms right through the eighteenth and nineteenth centuries. Some have representative Latin American chapters (Burton, 2003; Lambert and Lester, 2006) and some include the region with cursory mentions, for example of 'Argentine beef' (Kennedy, 2002: 5). Others reduce the region to a footnote. Stoler acknowledges, in one such aside, that 'when Spanish empire and US intervention in Latin America are brought back into the colonial studies equation, the multiplex arrangements of empire and their genealogies look very different' (2006a: 136). Burton recognises, also in a footnote, the 'apposite' work of Latin Americanists who have been 'doing what has come to be called "postcolonial critique" for a long time ... [because] the empires with which they engage do not necessarily follow the models laid out as implicitly British and putatively universal in some postcolonial studies scholarship' (Burton, 2003: 10). Yet the July 2007 'British World' conference had just one paper dealing primarily with Hispanic or Lusophone regions out of 25 panels and six keynote speakers.[3]

Bayly's (2004) *The Birth of the Modern World* is a case in point. It is, overall, an admirable, scholarly and sophisticated interpretation of imperialism and state-building that becomes stereotypical and indeed inaccurate when it deigns to mention Latin America. Here we try to build upon Bayly's broader analysis, drawing upon his advances in methodology and conceptualisation of the long nineteenth century, learning from the moves towards a real comparative history of connections and consequences within and beyond the Area Studies framework.[4] This volume tries, like Schmidt-Nowara and Nieto-Phillips (2006) and Thurner and Guerrero (2003) before it, to begin to fill in the Latin-America-shaped hole in the fields of 'new imperial' and 'postcolonial' studies.

It seems to be stating the obvious to record that Latin America was an integral, if peripheral, part of the British world that was created by the

---

3 See programme posted at http://www.uwe.ac.uk/hlss/history/britishworld2007/pro_programme.doc [accessed 19 June 2007].

4 At the Society of Latin American Studies 2004 Annual Conference, at the University of Derby, there was a useful and productive panel debating Bayly's treatment of Latin American themes. My thanks to the participants, upon whose insights I have drawn here.

expansion of British industrial society, as is shown in the work of Cain and Hopkins (2002). In a rare example of scholars of British Empire taking Latin America seriously, they used Argentina as one of their examples to demonstrate the way that British commercial expansion was predicated upon an 'extended network of personal contacts based on mutual trust and concepts of honour' (Cain and Hopkins, 1986: 507). These commercial networks evolved, with investment and time, into social and cultural networks, based not just on trust and honour, but also on family, kinship and the shared experiences of collaborative elites (Knight, 1999: 124–125) in education, commerce and culture. These networks of 'gentlemanly capitalism' (Cain and Hopkins, 1986) spread throughout and beyond the formal empire, linking back to the metropole and its hub, the City of London. Networks of commerce, capital and culture also linked periphery and informal empire, and the many colonial centres that formed 'imperial networks' that often had only minimal contact with England (Lester, 2001). The Cain and Hopkins model of 'gentlemanly capitalism', and the ideas of 'imperial networks' or 'imperial careers' formulated by Lambert and Lester (2006) provide a good formula for incorporating Latin America, and 'informal empire' more generally, into an understanding of British imperialism. As Charles Jones shows in his contribution to this volume, the networks and trajectories of Latin American businessmen and politicians were not unconnected from those of British diplomats, bankers and traders. The encounters of informal empire were many faceted and personal as well as public. Louise Guenther's chapter shows how gender shaped these meetings and relationships, often with profound long-term consequences. To re-state: formal and informal empire were interconnected and to some extent interchangeable. Often there was only a 'slender imperial veneer' of 'control' that separated formal from informal empire (Price, 2006: 608).

Hall (2002) and Lester (2001) have persuasively argued for the staging of British metropole and British colonies within one analytical theatre. But there is little point in seeing British metropole and British colony as 'terms which can be understood only in relation to each other' (Hall, 2002: 12) or 'mutually constitutive' (Price, 2006: 603) and part of shared dramas and 'imperial networks', if doing so means that supposedly peripheral areas of British power, such as Latin America, drop off the back of the stage. Informal empire was part of the imperial project, but one that differed in practice from the policy dreamed up by imperial guardians and colonial officials, and even from the plans and aims of diplomats given relatively free rein in their dealings with local citizens in Rio, Caracas or Patagonia. Fernanda Peñaloza's chapter in this volume argues, through a focus on the aesthetics of the sublime, that European travellers attempted to make Latin America intelligible according to their own preconceptions and desires that they brought with them from other imperial spaces.

The task therefore remains to attempt to study, as Bayly does, all imperial worlds within the same analytical frame – rival metropoles, interconnected colonies and the informal empires that shaded between them. Cultural influence was sometimes the flipside, sometimes the counterpoint of commercial predominance (Hennessy and King, 1992). Culture, commerce and capital must be recognised as three sides of imperial formations that were neither predetermined projects nor wholly independent factors.

An Interdisciplinary and Comparative Approach to Empire and Sovereignty

Interdisciplinarity, in Felipe Fernández Armesto's formulation (2002: 153), means 'pursuing one's specialism in the conviction that it is permeable, and that it overlaps with others, and that it is very much the richer for it'. This volume was designed with interdisciplinarity in mind. This was timely because, as disciplinary boundaries became blurred in the 1990s, scholars working on British involvement in Latin America in the nineteenth century – whether from desks in History, Hispanic Studies or Literature departments, or in Area Studies Institutes – all found themselves engaging, to a degree, with the subject of informal empire. This project sought to overcome interdisciplinary divides or antagonisms, and to avoid the 'ill-tempered disputes between schools and paradigms' of the past (Howe, 2001: 140), but if this were not possible, then to create a dialogue of shared experience in a common project. It seemed at the time that much could be gained if the attempt was successful.

Thinking comparatively remains key to such an endeavour. John Elliott's comparative history of the Spanish and British empires in the Americas (2006) sets the standard for approaches to this subject. No longer can we be content to study Europe's empires in isolation from each other. Elliott demonstrates that a single analytical field that crosses imperial frontiers is essential if we are to comprehend any individual colonial experience, and imperative to understanding the legacy of colonialism in Europe itself. Similarly, Jeremy Adelman (2006) has provided the crucial comparative approach to the Iberian Atlantic in the Age of Revolution. Comparing the disintegration and reconstitution of the Hispanic and Lusophone imperial worlds in the Americas from 1770 to 1830, Adelman demonstrates how the 'revolutions' for Independence were as much about sovereignty, and defined by local, regional and social competitions for the control of the meaning and reality of that sovereignty, as they were about collective identities. For Adelman, commerce was as integral to these changes as was culture. At the end of his book, Adelman leaves us with a picture of imperfectly formed and competing structures of sovereignty. Informal empire, carrying with it an innate capacity to slip into gaps and grooves in national sovereignties, was as such the natural continuance of the disputed sovereignties of the late-colonial period. In Brazil, the process was less obtrusive than in war-torn Spanish America, and it showed more continuity with the immediate post-Independence period, but formal commercial treaties were still signed and Britain exerted considerable influence over Brazil at some key moments of Brazil's nineteenth-century history. As Leslie Bethell argued at the Bristol conference, gradations of informal empire were the result in relatively peaceful Brazil just as they were in regions where Britain exploited post-conflict instability.

Disputed sovereignty provided the framework for national political projects during the nineteenth century in Latin America, and beyond. One unanticipated by-product of the approach of this book – the focus on the local manifestations of British 'informal empire' in Latin America, whilst keeping in sight the comparative examples of France, the USA, South Africa or Shanghai – is that we can approach what Gallagher and Robinson called 'the broad notions, the illusions and apprehensions, the tone and spirit of the collective mind' in British policy-making back in London (Gallagher and Robinson with Denny, 1961: 25) with a healthy scepticism. We can recall Lord Palmerston's utterance that:

> these half-civilised governments, such as China, Portugal, Spanish America, require a dressing-down every 8 or 10 years to keep them in order. Their minds are too shallow to receive an impression that will last longer than some such period, and warning is of little use. They care little for words and they must not only see the stick but actually feel it upon their shoulders before they yield to that only argument which brings them to conviction, the *argumentum Baculinum* [the argument of the big stick]. (Palmerston, 1850: 199)

and see his words as a rhetorical display of imperial fantasy rather than an actual account of reality in the periphery. Through considering British economic and political policy alongside the cultural representations and encounters, we can move towards a better idea of the levels of ignorance and disdain, and the barriers to communication and education, that disguised Latin American reality from the men charged with British relations with Latin America. We can thus better assess the extent to which competing ideas of sovereignty were imagined, compromised and asserted.

Towards a Reformulation of Informal Empire

This book suggests that by introducing culture into the concept of 'informal empire' we can reformulate it and revitalise it. Following Fernando Coronil's observations on US imperialism in Latin America in the twentieth century, we can observe that 'the traditional focus on political economy entails a neglect not only of domains outside the economy, but also of the cultural dimension of economic practices themselves' (Coronil, 1998: xi). Dane Kennedy's analysis of British imperial historiography, that 'any assessment of [the mutual interaction of imperialism] which ignores the cultural dimension – that is the realm of mutual representations of the self and the other – is one that misses what may well be the most persistent and profound legacy of the imperial experience', may be more debatable (Kennedy, 1996: 359). Cultural encounters were the basis of 'the 'collaborative bargain' on which all kinds of empire – formal or informal – almost invariably depended' (Darwin, forthcoming).

Rather than following Stoler's (2006a: 136) dismissal of 'informal empire' as a working concept, or attempting to 'theorise a new interpretative framework' (Joseph, 1998: 5), our dialogue has veered towards reformulating 'informal empire' with a cultural bent and a postcolonial eye whilst keeping it anchored in its political economy roots. Andrew Thompson, in the Afterword to this volume, argues that we must reformulate 'informal empire' to make it workable and useful – 'fit for purpose' in the current civil service jargon.

Drawing on Vargas García's analysis of the political economy literature (2006: 383–384), we can see Great Britain seeking, exerting and eventually relinquishing control over regions of Latin America in accordance with commercial and/or strategic imperatives. But in moving towards our definition of 'informal empire' we must also find an element of political control, and the presence of asymmetrical power relations. The constant hypothetical presence of the threat or use of force must be there too, even though the actual implementation of the threat was markedly infrequent and often rather unsuccessful. The use of force was often discarded even as an expensive 'last resort' (Smith, 1978: 23), 'from a desire to abstain from having a resource to forcible means, so long as there appeared a possibility of obtaining redress by any other' method (Palmerston, 1832: 561).

Stoler's dismissal of the concept of informal empire is premature. It can and must 'work' as a concept precisely because, as Cooper argues, 'if every form of asymmetrical power is termed empire, we are left without ways of distinguishing among the actual options we might have' (Cooper, 2005: 15). The concept of 'informal empire' reminds us of the many restrictions placed on imperialism, restrictions that arose from local resistance and geopolitical strategy as well as from the 'imperial mind' and the workings of metropolitan power, yet an understanding of informal empire that fails to bring out the underlying unity between it and the formal empire is sterile.

But in this sense we might be entitled to ask just how far we have come since Gallagher and Robinson first posed the question (e.g. Gallagher and Robinson, 1953: 3–5). Approaches to Latin America's nineteenth century – those that focus on economic dependency, the Age of Revolution, nation-building, state-building, colonial legacies – all deal with similar questions to our discussions around 'informal empire'. All these works are concerned with ascertaining the point at which sovereignty can be said to have existed, or to have been compromised, or to have been accepted and supported.

So if 'informal empire' is to function as a 'working concept', then it must rest upon a three-dimensional framework that posits commerce, capital and culture as three interdependent and mutually reinforcing influences that limited local sovereignty. Different contributors to this volume ascribe greater or lesser value to each of these factors according to their disciplinary background and the region, subject and period under study. Nevertheless, for 'informal empire' to exist, there must be evidence of commerce and investment which shape political and diplomatic relationships, and there must be a demonstrable role for culture, either in supporting those relationships (as per Aguirre, 2005) or as an independent variable (as in a local consciousness of asymmetrical power relations). Where one of those three conditions is lacking, no informal empire can be said to exist. The tentacles of informal empire must be found on the ground and in the mind. They must have an empirically demonstrable reality of asymmetrical power and of a measurable control being exerted; but also a cultural underpinning in the minds of the citizens and nations whose sovereignty is being compromised. Informal empire must be lived, and known, if it is to exist.

Each of the following chapters goes beyond informal empire to investigate the limits of sovereignty and nation- and state-building in Latin America.[5] For clarity and coherence, the analysis focuses on South America at the expense of Mexico, Central America and the Caribbean islands.[6] Alan Knight suggests an alliterative typology of imperialism around God, glory, gold and geopolitics, and compares British activity in Latin America, particularly Argentina, against these standards. David Rock weighs up the competing merits of 'informal empire' and postcolonialism as prisms through which to view Argentina's relationship with Britain in the long century after independence from Spain. Karen Racine explores the religious underbelly of British

---

5   In this sense, our project shares the concern of going 'beyond' established concepts in Latin Americanism in recent years, such as Chasteen and Castro-Klarén (2003), Naro (2003) and Davis (2006).

6   At the Bristol conference, Paul Garner, Michael Costeloe, Jonathan Curry-Machado, Luis Fernández-Martínez and José María Aguilera all spoke on these regions, which clearly have a lot to add to our understandings of the way European informal empires worked, or did not work, in Latin America. Karen Racine's paper was not presented at the Bristol conference.

informal imperialism through a study of the British and Foreign Bible Society. Colin Lewis measures the weight of foreign and local investment and influence in Argentine railways. Charles Jones explores the interstices between commerce, capital and culture, focusing on personal correspondence, literary writings and the career trajectories of the protagonists of informal empire. Fernanda Peñaloza explores the relationship between informal empire, travel writing and the sublime, arguing that Patagonia's unknown geography was at once desired and feared by British travellers. Malcolm Deas assesses the levels of British influence in Colombian society, economy and culture. Jennifer French's discussion of postcolonial analysis allows her to read Benito Lynch's novel *El inglés de guesos* as a fiction about informal empire in multiple senses. Louise Guenther analyses the gendered nature of informal empire, focusing on archival sources relating to the British merchant community in Bahia as well as on later fictional renderings of relationships between British men and Brazilian women. The contributors show that 'informal empire' can be used in cautious, creative and critical ways as a means of comprehending the encounters between societies in the long nineteenth century. It is up to readers to decide how useful they find it.

1

Rethinking British Informal Empire in Latin America (Especially Argentina)

ALAN KNIGHT

St Anthony's College, Oxford, UK

I

General concepts are useful and sometimes essential in history (i.e. histori-ography), even though historians are usually less concerned about concep-tual precision and definition than their colleagues in the social sciences. Plenty of good history can be written without elaborate conceptual discus-sion; but history can also be vitiated if concepts are used casually or un-thinkingly. This applies most obviously to grand and general concepts (such as imperialism or hegemony),[1] although it sometimes also applies to decep-tively concrete or 'commonsense' concepts (e.g. monarchy, government, family, peasant). The test of a 'good' concept is that it helps us understand history: it 'fits', informs, provides insight and understanding. To do this it must (a) be reasonably clear, (b) display some congruence with 'reality' and (c) conform to standard usage.[2] A 'bad' concept, in contrast, muddies the waters and distorts clear thinking. Concepts – like theories – are good or bad to the extent that they enlighten or obscure. While 'facts' may be readily seen as 'right' or 'wrong', concepts are better seen as useful or useless (or, worse, counterproductive). Utility rather than truth is the touchstone.[3]

---

1 Dumett (1999: 19) issues a stern exhortation 'to re-examine basic definitions in history (particularly those surrounding imperialism), to call for clear-cut speci-fication of issues, to make firm distinctions between various categories and sub-types and, above all, to be cautious about accepting new or radical conceptual frameworks without solid grounding in the evidence'.

2 Criterion: (a) is obvious, though nevertheless frequently flouted; (b) assumes there is a reality out there that we can – partially and imperfectly – grasp and (c) prevents us from making up idiosyncratic definitions or models that, how-ever precise and logical, depart from reasonable usage and thus impede communication.

3 Utility may allow – or even encourage – the co-existence of competing defini-tions/models, as I go on to suggest.

In this pragmatic spirit, let me briefly address imperialism and empire. First, I equate the two: imperialism is the practice (or ideology) associated with building and maintaining an empire.[4] An empire involves the sustained, asymmetrical exercise of power and influence by one group of people over another; the groups in question being defined according to some combination of spatial, ethnic and political origins/allegiances.[5] While the threat or use of force is common, I am not convinced that coercion should be a required diagnostic feature of imperialism.[6] We might, for example settle on a formulation that states that coercion – actual or feared – is commonplace within empires; but that imperialism (empire-building and -maintenance) involves much more than coercive relations; and that some variants of imperialism (thus, of asymmetrical relations of power and influence between groups defined according to their spatial, ethnic and political origins/allegiances) may exist in the absence of coercion. This is the view I would take. However, whether we choose to call non-coercive imperialism 'imperialism' or something else ('hegemony' would be the obvious choice)[7] is really a matter of heuristic and discursive strategy; it is a question – yet again – of whether to 'lump' or to 'split', whether to aggregate in larger, looser categories or to disaggregate into smaller and more discriminating ones;[8] and the decision may depend on the particular context. Did, for example the resolution of the Baring crisis of 1890 depend to any degree on the threat of force and, if not, is the Baring crisis off-limits as an episode in the history of British informal imperialism?[9] A consensual solution might be to envisage both a strong and a weak, a thick and a thin, definition or model of imperialism, the first *requiring* coercion as a *sine qua non*, the second

---

4 Compare Hopkins (1994: 483): 'imperialism suggests a process whereby elements of sovereignty were being eroded; empire implies a stage of completeness comparable to the status of colonies in a formal empire'; or Doyle (1986: 12): 'imperialism is ... the actual process by which empires are formed and maintained'; or Howe (2002: 22): 'if an empire is a kind of object ... then imperialism is a process'.

5 For comparable definitions, see Doyle (1986: 12, 19, 30): 'I favor the behavioral definition of empire as effective control, whether formal or informal, of a subordinated society by an imperial society'; and Howe (2002: 14–15).

6 Davis (1999: 83): 'An empire without coercion is hardly an empire at all'.

7 Keohane (1984: 32, 45) proposes that 'the key distinction between hegemony and imperialism is that a hegemon, unlike an empire, does not dominate societies through a cumbersome political superstructure'.

8 'Lumping' and 'splitting' are usually attributed to Hexter, who (1979: 241–242) credits Donald Kagan.

9 Ferns (1992: 242) maintains that the British Government 'refused to consider any political intervention in Argentine affairs' and that therefore 'the resolution of the Baring crisis was a business deal, not an exercise in imperialism'.

regarding coercion as a common but not universal feature of the phenomenon.[10] So long as we are reasonably clear about both definitions or models, it does not too much matter that two remain in play; as historians we may well agree on the events and processes at work (e.g. the role of coercion in a particular relationship, like the Anglo-Argentinian, or at a particular conjuncture, like 1890), but we may choose to conceptualise or describe them differently. This is a fairly common historiographical outcome.[11]

In addition, some would wish to make 'exploitation' a touchstone of imperialism (Davis, 1999: 83). Here, I think, the case is much weaker. There are two main reasons for thinking this. First, while there have been plenty of reputable historians who have regarded moralising (making value judgements) as a vital part of their trade,[12] I think that such a stance is inadvisable and should fall victim to Hume's 'guillotine', which requires a robust separation of 'is' and 'ought' statements (thus, statements of fact and value judgements, Nowell-Smith, 1961: 36–37). In my view, historians are not hanging judges and, if 'exploitation' is taken to be a normative concept (as I think it must), then its use involves us wading into the muddy waters of morality. Since the criteria of morality – of what is right and wrong, what is exploitative or non-exploitative – cannot be empirically determined, we will find it difficult to debate the issue, let alone reach conclusions.[13]

Of course (my second point), some would say that exploitation *is* an objective or scientific concept; that it can be readily detected and measured (like, e.g. coercion, which certainly can be detected and even measured and which, therefore, can be 'amorally' analysed). But I find this unconvincing.

---

10   Here we enter the rarefied world of 'conceptual stretching' and 'classical' versus 'radial' categories: Collier and Mahon (1993: 845–855).

11   Thus, the extensive literature on comparative revolutions regularly throws up a distinction between 'revolutions' and 'revolts'; analysts differ regarding both the criteria of differentiation and the allocation of particular cases; but this absence of conceptual consensus is, in my view, neither surprising nor alarming.

12   Notably Acton (1975: 40–41) who, citing Froude, declared that 'history ... does teach that right and wrong are real distinctions. Opinions alter, manners change, creeds rise and fall, but the moral law is written on the tablets of eternity' (and it was the historian's duty to read the tablets and declare the law).

13   I have made the same point (Knight, 2006: 351–358) in the context of recent Latin American historiography, where normative judgements have been both made and eagerly advocated. It is not, of course, an original point: Butterfield (1951 [1931]: 1) starts with a vigorous critique of 'the historian ... (as) avenger and ... judge', 'moral indignation' being 'a dispersion of one's energies to the great confusion of one's judgement'. Unfortunately, Butterfield then resorts to a rambling diatribe against so-called 'Whig history' (which is never defined).

Some forms of exploitation, it is true, are so egregious that, by almost any (modern) standard, we would not hesitate to use the term: for example chattel slavery. Here, modern Marxists and neoclassical economists would be in broad agreement.[14] There were, of course, plenty of apologists of slavery in the past. The issue remains one of morality; it so happens that, on this particular question, modern morality is broadly consensual, hence Marxists and neoclassical economists find themselves in agreement, if for rather different reasons. Empire, however, is another matter. It has plenty of modern-day apologists and boosters; indeed, the recent resurgence not only of imperialist studies but also of imperialist advocacy – and, we might add, imperialist policy – is striking (Dumett, 1999: 1–2, and, more polemically, Ferguson, 2004a, 2004b; see also Lal, 2004; we might wish to ponder if there is a connection here). But this resurgence precisely demonstrates that there is no consensus regarding the exploitative nature of empire. For some scholars, empire was and is a Good Thing (Ferguson, 2004a: 365–366, 2004b: 2).[15] It provided order, stability, infrastructure and development (among other 'public goods'). For other scholars, it was and is synonymous with exploitation. Again, my approach would be to ditch overtly normative concepts such as exploitation (which I take to be, by definition, bad) and to reformulate the question in normatively neutral terms. These could be summed up in the perennially useful tag: *cui bono*? Who benefitted (and who lost) from empire? The question is, of course, deceptively simple. It involves asking: whose blood and whose treasure was expended? Who profited and who paid the bill? Who got the plum jobs and the associated prestige and patronage? Who basked in imperial peace and prosperity and who were the victims of a Roman peace?[16] Often, I think, the answers are complex and not entirely one-sided: thus, it was not just a question of imperial metropolises exploiting colonial dependencies (such as India), still

---

14 See Fogel and Engerman (1976: 16) where the authors, stung by (ill-informed) allegations of callous racism, are at pains to point out that the slave system, whose economic performance they cliometrically evaluated in positive terms, was both 'a bad social system and a reprehensible moral system'.

15 While recent advocacy of empire is beyond the scope of this chapter, I admit to being puzzled how a self-proclaimed liberal and Thatcherite can applaud a system which, by definition, denies individual choice and self-determination. Empires may promote economic integration (as did Stalin); they may – sometimes, not always – promote free trade; but they necessarily deny civil equality and political representation, egregiously in formal empires, more evasively in informal empires. Empires may, of course, experience liberalisation and even a measure of democratisation; but such processes are not their basic theme tune, but rather their swansong.

16 'They create a desolation and call it peace' (Tacitus, 1964: 80).

less 'informal' clients (such as Argentina), but rather one of winners and losers on both sides of this divide; which is why the maintenance of empire – especially informal empire – involved a good deal of peripheral collaboration, collaboration that was often rational and voluntaristic.[17] While the class relations of a unitary 'social formation' (usually a nation-state) may embody forms of structural exploitation (that, at least, would be the classic Marxist formulation, premised on the labour theory of value), imperial relations are not so theoretically clear-cut. The *cui bono* question is therefore essential to ask, but not easy to answer. And answers are likely to spread the benefits (and costs) of empire across the metropolitan/peripheral divide.[18]

When we think of empires, we – including most of the contributors to this book, I suspect – probably tend to think of sprawling sea-borne empires, such as the Spanish or British, where the contrasting groups, the metropolitan rulers and the peripheral people subject to imperial rule, were separated not only by ethnic make-up and political allegiances, but also by huge tracts of ocean ('the seams of Pangaea', in Crosby's (1996: 10) arresting phrase).[19] Land-based territorial empires (Rome, Tsarist Russia or, perhaps, the 'imperial republic' of the USA) also fit the definition, in that their expansion involved the subjugation of (neighbouring) peoples, of different ethnic background and political allegiance. It is a quirk of history, however, that thalassocracies have invariably split apart as imperial bonds frayed, while territorial empires have occasionally consolidated into more durable nation-states (albeit states bearing the scars of ethnic discrimination). The Tsarist/ Soviet empire has partly collapsed; but the USA has transmuted, more or less, into a viable nation-state.[20] Indeed, we could go further and suggest

---

17 Here, Hopkins (1994: 475) and Thompson (1992: 422) are in agreement. The notion of the 'collaborating elite' was, of course, central to the Gallagher and Robinson thesis: see, in particular, Robinson (1972: 120–124).

18 Such cost-benefit analysis is likely to differ as between formal and informal empires: in the first, metropolitan (as well as peripheral) tax-payers may incur heavy costs; in the second, empire comes cheaper, but may be more vulnerable, hence the metropolitan beneficiaries receive a less effective subsidy. In times of war, when blood rather than treasure is expended, the contrast is even clearer: no Argentinians died at Gallipoli or Vimy Ridge. For an incisive analysis of the British imperial balance-sheet, see O'Brien (1988: 163–200).

19 For a useful depiction of Pangaea, its seams and successors, see Winchester (2006: 51).

20 For the time being. Some observers (such as Huntington, 2004) discern a progressive splintering of American national culture, chiefly as a result of (Latino) immigration. We should remember, too, that the USA came close to break-up in the 1860s.

that a good many long-lived nation-states have grown out of older mini-empires, the product – in the case of Europe, for example – of that phase of late medieval expansion that has been analysed by Bartlett (1994). Thus, Spain, England and France were built, under dynastic auspices, on the basis of military and demographic expansion, which subjugated – that is subjected to asymmetrical authority – a swathe of ethnically distinct peoples (Welsh, Scots, Irish, Bretons, Occitanians, Catalans, Basques, *moriscos*), thus leaving a legacy of 'internal colonialism' (Hechter, 1975). In Britain's case, the eighteenth century – roughly, where we come in – witnessed a reinforcement of the 'British Empire in Europe', as Chris Bayly (1989: 77ff.) appropriately calls it. Recently, however, these ancient processes have been reversed, as supposedly unitary nation-states have gone the way of devolution, notably in Spain and Britain.

Thalassocracies, however, have rarely if ever made the transition to nation-statehood. (Indeed, non-contiguous states, such as Pakistan, are rare and do not have an encouraging record.)[21] The two empires that putatively encompassed Latin America – first the Iberian,[22] then, perhaps, the British – were maritime, in the sense that metropolis and 'colony' were separated by the Atlantic, a formidable barrier, especially in the days of sail. But they differed in an obvious and crucial sense, in that Spain's American empire was 'formal', while Britain's was 'informal'. Their extraction of 'surplus' – the way they made the empire pay – was correspondingly different, in that Spain relied on direct extraction by the Crown, while Britain was prepared to commit public money (e.g. the Royal Navy) for the benefit of private initiative and profit-making (Ferns, 1960: 14). The formal/informal distinction requires some brief clarification since, while it is certainly useful and – which is not the same thing – widely used,[23] it is not as straightforward as sometimes assumed.

Conventionally, 'formal' empire involves direct rule by the metropolis, while 'informal' empire depends on a repertoire of informal pressures and influences (which may include coercion and the threat of coercion). Both relationships imply the asymmetrical exercise of power by one group over another, as previously defined. As is often the case in these broad

---

21 Which brings us back to the USA again, which has been a rare case of a successful non-contiguous state since 1867. But, compared to Pakistan, the (Alaska–Washington State) gap was about half as big; it crossed a more friendly neighbour; and it linked kindred populations.

22 I use 'Iberian' as shorthand for Spanish-and-Portuguese, while recognising that these were somewhat different variants of imperialism. Most of the analysis that follows concerns Spanish rather than Portuguese America.

23 As an example, Aguirre (2005) is an interesting but odd book, not least because it focuses on museum exhibits and freak shows in Britain, and says very little about British 'informal empire' as conventionally understood.

discussions, the formal/informal distinction has been captured in alternative terminology: for Keohane (1984: 45), formal empire denotes 'imperialism', while informal empire suggests 'hegemony'.[24] One simple rule of thumb would be: if the subordinate region is painted red (or whatever is your chosen colour) on the map, it is subject to formal empire, if not, not.[25] In fact, however, the formal/informal dichotomy conceals, I think, at least two different elements that, since they can be permutated, give rise to four distinct outcomes. Furthermore (another familiar consideration), the dichotomy – or dichotomies (plural) – are not black-and-white alternatives, but rather contrasting ends of continua. First, formal/informal refers to *direct* rule as against *indirect* rule. In some imperial contexts, authorities are imposed by the metropolis and consist of 'metropolitan' personnel: Roman proconsuls, Spanish (i.e. *peninsular*) *virreyes*, British viceroys and district commissioners. In others, indirect rule is preferred: authority is vested in co-opted members of the host society: 'puppet' kings (such as Herod the Great), Indian caciques and kurakas in Spain's American dominions, Indian princes or northern Nigerian emirs. In fact, most empires contain elements of both. As the above examples suggest, Rome, Spain and Britain all combined direct and indirect rule; the pattern varied by time and place. Informal rule – as I go on to suggest – was cheaper and perhaps less provocative; but it carried risks (of dissent and disobedience) and created a veil of ignorance that masked the host society from the metropolitan power, impairing the latter's 'cognitive power' and making effective social engineering difficult.[26] (Hence, for example, the Bourbons' decision to impose tighter direct control

---

24 Domínguez (1978: 19, 54–55), offers a good 'operationalisation' of this usage, in discussing the USA's role in Cuba: 'imperialist' between 1898 and 1934; 'hegemonic' from 1934 to 1959.

25 I recognise that maps reflect power and ethnocentrism and are not objective guides to reality, especially when it comes to political coloration (see, e.g. Black, 1997: Chapter 1). But then imperial and international relations in general are similarly subjective.

26 'Cognitive power' denotes the authorities' ability to collect information about subjects or citizens and the territory they inhabit; I borrow the term from Whitehead (1994: 46–47). Informal imperialists have to rely heavily on 'native' collaborators for their information and intelligence, since they cannot engage in systematic information- and intelligence-gathering themselves, in the way that formal imperialists can (e.g. William the Conqueror and the Domesday Book or the British Raj and its decennial censuses in India). A collaborationist bias was therefore inevitable: in Argentina, for example British representatives in the late 1820s were strongly critical of Governor Manuel Dorrego, though they never 'formulated any grounds for disliking the Governor except that he was disliked by the majority of the respectable class' (Ferns, 1960: 197). Much the same happened during the Mexican Revolution a century later.

over Spanish America in the later eighteenth century, in a bid for more effective social engineering and economic exploitation of the colonies).

In addition, however, the formal/informal dichotomy denotes *de jure* as
against *de facto* authority. By *de jure* I mean authority that is generally recognised
as legitimate, which endures and which determines the colours on maps. In
contrast, *de facto* authority exists (perhaps transiently) by virtue of *force majeure*.
Successful wartime *coups de main* (I apologise for the unplanned proliferation of
foreign phrases) bring direct rule: for example, the British in Havana in 1762 or
Montevideo and Buenos Aires in 1806–1807. These seizures of power did not
result in permanent colonisation: the invaders were repulsed, or induced to
leave. No durable colonisation ensued. (Compare Gibraltar, where it did.
Menorca was a half-way house.) A good many colonial or imperial relationships
begin with *de facto* occupation and acquire *de jure* validity only with the passage
of time; some – such as Puerto Rico or the Falklands/Malvinas – never acquire
unimpeachable validity. More commonly, at least in Latin America, the British
used *de facto* power and influence without choosing to exercise – even briefly –
the sort of direct rule that was associated with military occupation. Force might
be used – or threatened – but it formed part of a broader repertoire of non-violent pressures and influences, which might have included economic sanctions
or rewards, diplomatic support or opposition, and, perhaps, more diffuse cultural affinities. Thus, in the case that concerns us, Britain's supposed 'informal
empire' in Latin America (especially Argentina) involved no sustained direct
rule (1806–1807 was a blip), but rather depended on this repertoire of pressures
and influences, among which force was but one element and, many would say,
an element of declining importance. Thus, Britain's 'informal empire' in Argentina grew stronger as the threat of force receded.[27] Given these two dichotomies,
and the fourfold typology that results, the options, and the potential for shifts
between them, can be depicted graphically (see Figure 1).

Britain's 'empire' in nineteenth-century Latin America – including Argentina – fell squarely in the top right quadrant (B) of Figure 1. There were some
pockets of formal empire, recognised as such by most international observers
and mapmakers (Belize and, more contentiously, the Falklands/Malvinas),
which fell into the bottom left (C). Brief British occupations of, for example

---

27   On the recession of force, see Ferns (1992: 49–61). The Argentine case thus
      seems to confirm Robinson's rule that, as peripheral integration into world
      markets advances, the 'need' for external coercion usually recedes. Compare
      Smith (1981: 16–17, 35), which lumps Latin America along with Africa and Asia
      and (wrongly, at least for Latin America) sees a liberal imperialist – that is
      peaceful commercial – form of mid-Victorian expansion give way after 1875 to
      a more aggressive territorial form.

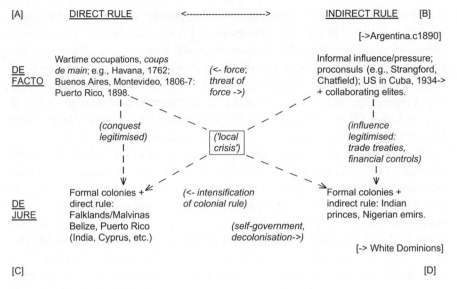

Figure 1. Categories of Empire

Havana in 1762 and Buenos Aires and Montevideo in 1806–1807, did not endure and become legitimated as bits of formal empire (i.e. they did not track from A to C, following the path taken by Belize or the Falklands/Malvinas). More interestingly, British 'informal' dependencies (B) did not track into either C or D. They did not, in other words, follow the path taken by Egypt or Zanzibar. Imperialism remained resolutely informal and was not 'formalised', that is, did not acquire *de jure* status. (There were, perhaps, modest steps in that direction with the trade treaties that codified British access to Latin American markets, to a degree constraining Latin American economic sovereignty; but these, however objectionable to nationalist opinion, fell far short of *de jure* imperial control, Miller, 1993: 43–44.) Given that a good many areas of informal empire, especially in Africa, were converted into formal colonies (most of them directly ruled, some, such as northern Nigeria, subject to indirect rule), this is something worthy of consideration and explanation.

In one sense, the durability of informal rule is not surprising, since it offered benefits to both sides of the asymmetrical equation (hence my reluctance to stress exploitation). As Gallagher and Robinson – whose perspective strongly influences this analysis – pointed out, informal control (or 'paramountcy', as they sometimes called it, further expanding the conceptual options on offer) was cheaper and less problematic, since it avoided the costs, in blood and treasure, of direct rule (Gallagher and Robinson, 1953: 13). The Whig poet James Thomson concurred: Britain's 'Empire of the deep' (i.e. thalassocracy) represented 'inexpensive power' that, unlike the major territorial empires of history, was 'unencumbered with the bulk immense of conquest' (Koebner, 1965: 82). Certain domestic consequences followed: territorial empires, requiring large standing armies, often seem to have bred authoritarian regimes and praetorian politics; an informal maritime empire could more happily co-exist with a liberal, commercial and civilian polity, at least at home. Of course, what a 'polite and commercial people' like the British got up to once they were overseas was another matter.[28]

Why, then, was preferred informal rule sometimes replaced by the costly alternative of direct formal rule? (Or, to phrase the question more relevantly, why was informal rule maintained in Latin America at a time when it was being replaced by formal rule in Africa?) It was a question of priorities and trade-offs;[29] but to appreciate this we have to pause for a moment to consider the basic rationale of imperialism (British or any other). The establishment and maintenance of the kind of asymmetrical relationship that constitutes empire may respond to one or more of several goals, but in turn requires two basic strategies, which serve these (several) goals. The goals vary according to the empire and metropolis in question. However, for the sake of simplicity they can be summed up under a fourfold alliteration: God, glory, gold and geopolitics. Thus, empire-builders build empires for the sake of saving souls and bringing the light of the gospel to heathen parts; in pursuit of individual or national glory; for profit (whether by trade, investment, or downright plunder); and in order to further the power and security of the

---

28   William Blackstone, quoted in Langford (1989: 1). For this reason, the notion that a distinct form of 'gentlemanly capitalism' diffused from Britain to the empire – especially the informal empire – seems rather whimsical. True, the British – unlike many of their Latin American collaborators – tended to favour sound money and balanced budgets and, if these are the criteria of gentlemanliness, the point is valid, albeit hardly revelatory. However, such preferences did not prevent them supporting, for example, the sanguinary and drunken Mexican dictator Victoriano Huerta (1913–1914), who had little of the gentleman about him (and who, incidentally, presided over hyper-inflation). See Knight (1986: Vol. 2, Chapter 1).

29   It is worth making the point that, as I understand the Gallagher and Robinson principle (informal empire if possible, formal empire if necessary), it represented less a firm and codified official prescription than an *ex post* explanation of how the British Government (and its 'official mind') worked in practice, over time, through a long sequence of events and crises. The decision-makers themselves responded and acted under the pressure of events, sometimes inconsistently, and may well have been utterly unaware of the principle (to use linguistic/anthropological jargon, it was an 'etic' not an 'emic' principle). See Robinson and Gallagher with Denny (1961: 9–10, 19–20); also MacLean (1995: 190).

metropolis. (There is a further complication that involves, not some radically alternative motive, but rather the espousal of these goals by colonial authorities and semi-autonomous subjects, even in defiance of metropolitan wishes: this has been termed 'sub-imperialism'. Examples would include Sir Home Popham, who conceived the *coup de main* against Buenos Aires in 1806; Sir Lionel Carden, Britain's maverick minister to Mexico during the Mexican Revolution; and powerful proconsular representatives such as Lord Strangford in Rio and Frederick Chatfield in Central America (Manchester, 1933: 57–135; Ferns, 1960: 17–45; Rodríguez, 1964; Calvert, 1968: Chapter 7). Though we need to bear this in mind, it does not fundamentally affect the present analysis.)

In respect of these goals, Spanish imperialism oscillated between all four. British imperialism in Latin America, however, was relatively simple: compared to, say, sub-Saharan Africa, there was scant missionary activity (inverting Spinoza, we might say that God was nowhere); glory counted for little, since British military interventions in Latin America were few (and rather inglorious, as it happened); and, while geopolitics counted for something (hence, for example the Clayton–Bulwer Treaty of 1850, establishing joint Anglo-American control of a putative Isthmian canal), over time even this secondary consideration faded and Britain increasingly deferred to the USA, especially in the circum-Caribbean region (Calvert, 1968). There remained gold, the pursuit of profit through plunder (Drake and Morgan), trade (hence the slave *asiento*, the commercial treaties and burgeoning textile exports of the early nineteenth century), and later investment (loans, railways, mines, public utilities, especially in Argentina). Thus, compared to Spain, Britain was largely motivated by economic motives, by the pursuit of profit. 'The policy of Great Britain in Latin America', a US diplomat concluded in 1913, 'is purely commercial and forms of government matter little to her; (and) she has no missionaries in Latin America'.[30]

This does not mean, however, that British policy was necessarily pacific and Cobdenite, least of all in the early nineteenth century. Dr Johnson's famous observation – 'there are few ways in which a man can be more innocently employed than in getting money' – is, like a lot of the sayings of the sage of Lichfield, more clever than convincing, certainly when it comes to British overseas policy. Rather, as Bayly (1989) argues, British policy, prior

---

30 Calvert (1968: 235) quoting Nelson O'Shaughnessy, US Chargé (and acting Ambassador) in Mexico City in 1913. Church of England ministers had long lamented the 'failure of the true church to bring the light of their witness into the many dark places of South America': Ferns (1960: 236), citing the Rev. John Armstrong (1829).

to *c.*1840, tended to be aggressive, coercive, and still strongly mercantilist. And forms of government did matter, inasmuch as they promoted or obstructed commercial penetration.

We might note, by way of passing comparison, that US informal imperialism, deployed in Latin America in the twentieth century, was, like Spanish but unlike British imperialism in the region, more diversely motivated. Though gold remained crucial, God – or, at least, a sense of providential mission and superior morality – also re-entered the equation, while geopolitics counted for much more (especially in the circum-Caribbean and following the onset of the Cold War). Furthermore, geopolitical priorities afforded some opportunities for glory (e.g. Teddy Roosevelt charging up San Juan Hill during the Spanish–American War), while they also projected Latin American issues into US domestic politics, thus generating, perhaps, a fifth motivation – which, in an effort to sustain the alliteration, I am tempted to call the *gusano* factor.[31] The British, of course, had no *gusano* lobby, no Latin American tails that wagged the British dog; furthermore, nineteenth-century British politics was neither as democratic nor as demotic as twentieth-century American politics and British elites, possessed perhaps of a shared 'official mind',[32] could therefore formulate policy relatively autonomously of partisan and populist politics. Not so their American counterparts during the Cold War.

These four – or five – *motivations* are in turn served by two basic *strategies*, which seem to be common to all forms of imperialism. If metropolitan powers are to serve God, get gold, win glory and pursue their geopolitical interests (while, perhaps, also securing the *gusano* vote), they have to do two things: (a) bend the peripheral or dependent society to their will, obliging it to worship, work, trade and generally behave as the metropolis wishes, and (b) keep out rival metropolitan powers who seek to muscle in and prevent these things from happening. Thus, successful metropolises – whether practitioners of formal or informal imperialism – must undertake a measure of socio-political engineering, while throwing a kind of *cordon sanitaire* around their dependencies. Formal empire, though it involves heavier commitments of blood and treasure, offers a surer guarantee of these goals: the metropolis

---

31   *Gusano* (worm) refers, unflatteringly, to the Cuban exile community in the USA, especially Florida, which exercises a powerful influence on US policy towards the island.

32   Robinson and Gallagher with Denny (1968: 21–22), where the authors go on to note (1968: 23–25) that, for British policy-makers, 'the mass voter was still an enigma'; that public opinion paid little attention to Africa; and that 'the electorate's indifference and zeal for retrenchment' gave policy-makers considerable freedom of manoeuvre.

can rule, police, educate and acculturate, while throwing up military and economic ramparts around their protectorate. Informal empire comes relatively cheap, because the task of political control is largely carried out by agents in the host society – Gallagher and Robinson's famous 'collaborating elites'. But control of this kind, though cheaper, is less secure (as we shall see in the case of Argentina): sooner or later it faces challenges both from within (domestic discontent) and from without (the pressure of rival metropolises); and, in the absence of formal control, these challenges cannot be confidently beaten off.

It is precisely challenges of this sort, therefore, that, in the form of Gallagher and Robinson's 'local crisis', bring about conversions from informal to formal empire. That is to say, confronted with either peripheral protest and/ or rival metropolitan challenges, the threatened metropolis decides that it must pay the price of formal empire, assume direct rule and thus parry the threat. In schematic terms, we get a shift from B to C or D (see Figure 1). (C implies a thorough imperial takeover; D involves converting collaborating elites into the instruments of indirect colonial rule.) The classic case was Egypt in 1882. In Latin America, however, no comparable transition occurred under British auspices; the closest regional parallel would be the US intervention in Cuba and Puerto Rico in 1898 which, motivated by a prolonged 'local crisis' and US fears of European intervention, led to the assumption of a 36 year protectorate in the case of Cuba and permanent colonial status for Puerto Rico. As we consider mainland Latin America, especially Argentina, we may pause to consider why no such outcome threatened (e.g. at moments of crisis such as 1890).

II

If India was the jewel in Britain's imperial crown, Argentina was the prize possession within her informal empire. By 1914, Argentina stood alongside Canada, South Africa and Australia as a trade partner and recipient of British investment.[33] This fact alerts us to an obvious (yet perhaps neglected) conclusion: on the eve of the First World War, Britain's overseas economic links were – with the major exception of India – skewed towards temperate

---

33 British investment in Argentina in 1913 stood at £358 million, compared to £370 million in South Africa, £380 million in India and Ceylon, and £415 million in Australia and New Zealand. If Uruguay (£46 million) is added, the 'River Plate' figure rises to £404 million. Argentine trade with Britain (imports + exports) stood at £48 million, compared to £70 million for Australia and £79 million for South Africa. See Denoon (1983: 50–51).

regions of recent settlement (Crosby's 'neo-Europes'), where societies of 'prefabricated collaborators' had been established, on the basis of agrarian/ pastoral economies whose comparative advantage neatly meshed with that of the mature British industrial economy.[34] Britain's tropical possessions were much less important, in economic terms. (Gallagher and Robinson, of course, argued (with Denny, 1961) that Britain's tropical empire in Africa was created primarily in response to geopolitical concerns regarding the route to India.) In this, Britain differed from the USA – itself a temperate region of recent settlement – which, in its links to Latin America, was more interested in Cuban sugar, Brazilian coffee or Mexican minerals, than in Argentine grain and beef. Hence, Argentina's snug fit with the British economy contrasted with its awkward incompatibility with the US economy.

However, the achievement of this Anglo-Argentine economic nexus was a slow and at times painful business (Ferns, 1960: 18–19, 23, 36–37). Several factors delayed its consummation. First, Spanish mercantilism barred the entry of (legal) British trade until 1810. True, Britain enjoyed the questionable benefits of the *asiento* and, in addition, could count on a good deal of contraband penetrating the porous frontiers of Spain's American empire. However, smuggling imposed heavy transaction costs and could not provide the basis for extensive and profitable trade. Hence, the British government hatched hare-brained plans to crack open the tempting Spanish empire (which shimmered on the horizon rather as the mythical China market would a century later. We might note that scheming Spanish-American activists such as Miranda played a part in prompting these plans and visions: Britain, like the USA, was always at risk of being suckered into Latin American ventures by plausible characters who traded on metropolitan gullibility).[35]

However, British policy was compromised by the vicissitudes of the revolutionary and Napoleonic Wars: it was one thing to subvert an enemy's colonial dominions; but when in 1808 Spain became an ally, plans for invading the Americas had to be shelved. Hence, fortunately for his career, Wellington was sent to Spain, where he won the Peninsular War, rather than to Mexico, his original destination, where his troops and his reputation would no doubt have been decimated by Mexico's most effective generals, yellowjack and malaria. Nevertheless, throughout the period of imperial expansion and aggression that stretches from the Seven Years War to the 1840s (and which

---

34   Crosby (1996: 2). The 'prefabricated collaborator' term comes from Robinson (1972: 124).

35   Politeness aside, it would be wrong to call Miranda a *gusano* (see note 31 above), since he was a transient visitor (not a resident) and he did not command a mass lobby.

reached a crescendo during the revolutionary and Napoleonic Wars), Britain repeatedly deployed force against Spain's American possessions; and such policies did not abruptly halt with Spanish American Independence. Following Havana in 1762 and Buenos Aires and Montevideo in 1806–1807, the British installed the Braganzas in Brazil and obliged them to sign a controversial trade treaty (1808, 1810), intervened to support Uruguay as a buffer state in the 1820s, blunted the French offensive against Rosas in 1840, deployed the Royal Navy in order to defend Montevideo and coerce Rosas in 1843–1847 and used force or the threat of force on numerous other occasions in Mexico, Peru and Venezuela (Miller, 1993: 34–35, 43, 50–56, 59; Graham-Yooll, 2002: Chapters 1–7). Meanwhile, 'proconsuls' such as Strangford (Brazil) and Chatfield (Central America) intervened in local politics and used threats – the use of force and/or the withdrawal of armed support – to promote British policy (Manchester, 1933: 94–101; Street, 1953: 477–510; Rodríguez, 1964; note also Ponsonby's swaggering conduct in Buenos Aires, in Ferns, 1960: 169–170; and compare Bayly, 1989: 194ff).

Such interventions were not necessarily successful, as Gootenberg (1989: 18–19) reminds us, but they constituted a policy of threat, pressure and influence entirely appropriate for a great power as yet uncommitted to free trade and *doux commerce* and still wedded to 'militaristic and monopolistic' ways, reminiscent of 'continental neo-absolutism' (Bayly, 1989: 162). As a result, the Spanish American reaction to British initiatives was often lukewarm. The Braganzas might self-interestedly welcome British protection, but the British invasions of Buenos Aires provoked strenuous and effective – perhaps 'proto-patriotic' – resistance. The *porteños* might chafe under Spanish rule, but they had no desire to exchange one imperial master for another, especially when the new master, during the brief British occupation of Buenos Aires, behaved as a ruthless monarchical mercantilist. Beresford came less as a liberator than a colonial satrap; hence only 58 creoles signed the oath of loyalty to the British Crown (and that in secret); and the British, far from promoting commerce, made off with the viceroyalty's stock of bullion (Ferns, 1960: 26, 29). Like other hegemonic powers, the British launched their invasion in the belief that 'all rightminded people want to be British' and were taken aback when the natives proved ungrateful (Ferns, 1960: 39). (Compare American interventions from Veracruz in 1914 to Somalia in 1993 and Iraq in 2003.)

The experiences of 1806–1807 were an exemplary lesson for both sides. Castlereagh relinquished the 'hopeless task' of conquest in mainland Spanish America, opting instead for the 'silent and imperceptible' path of commercial penetration (Ferns, 1960: 47–48, 86). Not all British statesmen followed suit, however. As for the Argentines, the patriotic *levée en masse* of 1806–1807 left an important legacy of 'newly born national pride' that could be celebrated on suitable anniversaries and be drawn upon in times of crisis

(Ferns, 1960: 186, 259–260; see also the useful historiographical resumé in Gallo, 2004: 167–238). The same was true, if to a lesser degree, elsewhere in Spanish America. The ex-colonies-turned-republics, fragile though they were, did not represent easy targets for renewed colonial takeover. Spanish and French aggression was successfully resisted. This perhaps confirms a general historical rule-of-thumb: colonies that have attained independence rarely succumb to renewed colonial rule.[36] One bout of colonialism, it seems, inoculates the body politic against a second subjection. Thus, attempts at a renewed colonialism in the Americas failed: most dramatically with Maximilian in Mexico in the 1860s.

British efforts to supplant Spain as a formal South American colonial power, though consonant with British policy during the 'imperial meridian' (Bayly, 1989) of 1780–1830, came to nothing. (The seizure of the Falklands/Malvinas in 1833 was, at best, a minor consolation.) Castlereagh's hopes of peaceful commercial penetration were also disappointed. Trade briefly boomed in the 1810s, then stagnated (in monetary terms). The British came to realise that, even if an independent republic was preferable to Spanish colonial rule, it still fell far short of expectations (Ferns, 1960: 66, 75). First, the primitive economy of the Río de la Plata generated only limited exports and foreign exchange.[37] Demand was low, depressed by the lack of currency, the high cost of transport and the strength of the subsistence economy. Gauchos and peons could live a viable if basic existence on the pampas, eating meat, drinking *mate*, dressing in leather, comfortably seating themselves on the skulls of steers. These obstacles to trade limited British commercial penetration; hence, in terms of value, British exports to the Río de la Plata remained roughly static, in monetary terms, from the 1820s to the 1840s and Anglo-Argentine trade remained 'marginal' to the British economy (Ferns, 1960: 132–133, 167, 195; Miller, 1993: 72–73).

---

36   Of course, colonies have regularly been swapped between imperialist powers. However, once an independence struggle – a war of national liberation – has been fought and won, renewed (formal) imperial rule rarely occurs.

37   Compared to what? The Brazilian empire for one, see Manchester (1933: 96–98). The relative success of Brazil as an early field for British trade can be attributed to several factors: Britain already had a foothold in Brazil thanks to the slave trade and the old Anglo-Portuguese alliance; the transition to Independence was relatively smooth and pacific; the Brazilian monarchy provided a fairly stable regime, congenial to British interests; and Brazil had a viable export sector (chiefly sugar, later cotton and coffee) that earned foreign exchange, thus facilitating imports (e.g. of British textiles). Finally, production for export was concentrated on or near the coast, hence transport bottlenecks were less acute than in many Spanish American countries.

These economic obstacles were compounded by political, social and cultural barriers to British trade. Though Buenos Aires was a lively market society, open to world trade (Adelman, 1999), the interior (relatively larger than in later times, of course) was leery of foreign imports; hence, here as in Peru, Mexico and Colombia, protectionist artisans and merchants blocked the British advance. Even *porteño* caudillos such as Rosas saw the political wisdom of pandering to the protectionist sentiments of the interior (Ferns, 1960: 251; Lynch, 1992: 172). Conscious policy conspired with cultural prejudices ('a jealous and xenophobic public temper', as Ferns puts it, in his best Dickensian turn of phrase).[38] Were not the British irreverent heretics who refused to bow to the host and who, it was said, had tails tucked inside their trousers? (The proof was the way they sat in the saddle (Ferns, 1960: 84, 153); see also Gregory, 1992: 35, 142). The inexorable pressure of 'events' also took its toll. Recurrent warfare, both within Argentina and between Argentina and Brazil and Uruguay, hampered trade, imposed added transaction costs, undermined business confidence and brought about a default on the Barings loan of 1824. The British, frustrated, tried to enforce a more congenial regime, in the Río de la Plata, as in China. In the 1840s, the Royal Navy blockaded the Plate, in a futile attempt to browbeat Rosas and force him to open the waterway to commerce. Whitehall churned out copperplate memoranda that lamented the obstacles to trade, the chronic upheaval and the missed opportunities that afflicted South America, and proposed more radical action (Ferns, 1960: 74, 83, 164, 219).[39] In the depressed 1840s, with European markets apparently contracting as a result of industrialisation, the British scouted the possibilities of a forward policy in South America, which would bring a degree of order, an increase in trade and a more secure British commercial presence.

Eventually, these desiderata were met, as a result less of British policy than of trends within Argentina.[40] Rosas, whom the British had fruitlessly blockaded, finally proved an adequate, if not ideal, collaborator: 'I dislike

---

38   Ferns (1960: 68); and, for further examples of cultural prejudice and xenophobia, Ferns (1960: 85, 145–146, 151–153, 259–260, 265–266). Lynch (2001) illustrates the continuance of xenophobic violence, at least on the frontier; by the late nineteenth century, however, British interests in Argentina were pretty securely integrated; soon, it would be Eastern European Jewish immigrants who would feel the force of 'native' prejudice.

39   On the Murray Memorandum, see Miller (1993: 51, 55). Platt (1968b: 321–322) seems overly keen to downplay the Murray Memorandum (and the policies it reflected).

40   So my explanation of change is, it seems, 'pericentric' (to be found in the periphery, i.e. in Argentina, rather than in the metropolis, Britain) (Doyle, 1986: 25).

and condemn the System of Rosas, as all liberal Men must do', Captain Gore wrote to Palmerston, 'but I conceive it would be a great Evil should he be vanquished, as this system gives protection to life and property, more particularly that of Foreigners, and it is based on Order' (Ferns, 1960: 288). Thus, 'the regime of General Rosas presented itself as a working alternative not to good government, but to no government at all' (Ferns, 1960: 216). Rosas's nemesis and successor, Urquiza, was also keen for British endorsement and proved an acceptable collaborator (Ferns, 1960: 288). When the representative of Barings arrived in Buenos Aires in 1852, bearing a brace of pistols for whichever caudillo warranted British/Baring cajolery, he decided that they were better delivered to a Royal Naval officer, since, he concluded, 'things have changed exceedingly in this Country ... all the ... dignitaries and officials I have had to deal with are learned Doctors of Law and peaceful Civilians. The era of the caudillos has passed away: thank God' (Ferns, 1960: 283).

The judgement was somewhat premature, but showed which way the wind was blowing. The chronic instability of the post-Independence period was abating. Rosas's Roman peace began to transmute into a more organic stability. Rough-hewn caudillos now seemed to share Rivadavia's erstwhile concern for trade, stability and economic development (Ferns, 1960: 289). The 1860s were a key decade: Argentina's credit was re-established, the Treaty of Free Navigation (1863) opened the River Plate to trade, and the London and River Plate Bank and the Buenos Aires and Great Southern railway were launched.[41] Stability fostered trade, trade generated revenue and both in turn fostered stability. Argentine exports began to grow, facilitating imports from Britain. As the first railways snaked their way across the pampas, they attracted British investment, boosted exports and, the British Minister observed, brought the benefits of 'civilization and business' (Ferns, 1960: 324, 388). This scenario was not, of course, confined to Argentina. Brazil and Chile had already shown how stability and *desarrollo hacia afuera* [outward-oriented development] could be combined; Mexico and Peru would later follow suit. While British trade and investment were crucial – Britain, now ideologically committed to free trade, was by far the world's leading commercial power and source of capital – the timing and modalities of this new virtuous circle of political stabilisation and economic growth depended

---

41   Ford (1962: 86); Joslin (1963: 31), which notes how the infant London and River Plate Bank recruited Norberto de la Riestra, formerly the Minister of Finance of Buenos Aires, whose role was 'to advise ... on local banking matters and to be the main intermediary between the bank and the high political circles where favours were granted'. Welcome to the collaborating elite.

greatly on peripheral – or what Robinson (1986) called 'excentric' – factors.[42] Mexico, for example, lagged behind Chile, Brazil or Argentina, because its cycle of civil wars and foreign invasions was more severe and protracted, while its economy and topography were more resistant to commercial penetration.

Peripheral/excentric factors were also crucial in determining the form of political stability achieved and the nature of the collaborative relationship established between Britain and the Latin American republics. Given their 'unashamedly economic' priorities (Ferns, 1960: 164), hence their narrow-minded concern for profit (gold) and their relative indifference to God, glory and geopolitics, the British took a tolerant view of Latin American politics. Pope's famous couplet (1763: III, 303) summed it up: 'For forms of government let fools contest/Whate'er is best administered is best'. So long as certain basic needs were met – stability, a respect for contracts, the protection of life and property (e.g. not being beaten to death for dishonouring the host) – the British would do business with anyone (recall Captain Gore's judgement on Rosas, above p. 40). Unlike the USA in later decades, the British government did not peddle any political panaceas (Britain, of course, was not locked in a global Manichaean struggle with an ideological opponent). Democracy, civil rights and social justice were not at issue. Britain itself was no model of democracy in those days; and British views of Latin America were frequently coloured by racist and quasi-colonialist prejudices (Ferns, 1960: 270, describes those of the egregious William Gore-Ousely). 'Gentlemanly capitalism' did not require any commitment to gentlemanly politics (Cain and Hopkins, 2002; also note 28 above); away from home, in their 'informal empire', the British were prepared to tolerate slavery, disliked social subversion and favoured strong, and if necessary authoritarian, government. They applauded repressive dictatorships, such as that of Porfirio Díaz, which they saw as the sole means of disciplining the feckless Indians and mongrel mestizos of Mexico (Knight, 1995: 275–278). After all, Díaz was doing roughly what the European powers were doing in Africa: bringing peace, order and (though they did not use the term) development.[43]

---

42 Joslin (1963: 6–9), gives a good resumé of what might be (very tentatively) called the mid-nineteenth-century 'take-off' of Latin America.

43 Egypt was a favourite country of comparison for the British in Latin America. 'Mexico', observed the British Minister, Thomas Hohler, 'is frequently termed the Egypt of America': Hohler to Grey, 11 November 1914, TNA FO 371/2032/79839. In conversation with President Woodrow Wilson, Hohler likened Mexican peons to Egyptian *fellahin* (Hohler memo., 11 February 1914, TNA FO 371/2025/8667). Note also Arnold and Frost (1909).

Hence, British enthusiasm for Díaz's would-be authoritarian successor, General Victoriano Huerta (1913–1914), whose vain efforts to hold back the Mexican Revolution won British plaudits (Calvert, 1968: 220, 227, 235–237). Hence, too, there was no 'scramble for Latin America': compared to Africa, Latin America was of less strategic significance (there was no Suez, no Cape) and 'collaborating elites' could usually be relied upon to exercise control in satisfactory fashion.[44] In addition, Britain was by now a 'weary Titan', leery of assuming further global commitments, especially in defiance of the United States.

Argentina, of course, was a cut above the 'Indoamerican' republics to the north: by the 1880s it had achieved stability under oligarchic and largely civilian auspices; it had 'conquered the desert' and thus solved its Indian problem; and it was experiencing a dynamic process of export-led growth, in which Britain was a major player (in 1889 nearly 50 per cent of British overseas investment went to Argentina, Ferns, 1960: 397).[45] Argentina's resemblance to the White Dominions, already noted, meant that it could, to an extent, be treated as a mature, self-governing, economic partner. The narrative of great men and dramatic events that had thus far characterised Anglo-Argentine relations now gave way to a more humdrum story of commercial activity and market actors. Bankers and entrepreneurs replaced the caudillos, proconsuls and naval captains of the previous generation. Threats of force – which would be deployed and carried out against the 'rogue state' of Venezuela in 1902 (see Hood, 1977) – were now redundant in Anglo-Argentine relations. The British could count on their loyal collaborators to maintain the necessary desiderata. As President Pelligrini – a Harrow-educated distant relative of John Bright – put it, at the time of the Baring crisis, 'rather than suspend service on the debt, I would renounce the presidency' (Miller, 1993: 154).[46] And, in consequence, Lord Salisbury could confidently inform his Mansion House

---

44   Of course, the USA took a different view: the Caribbean was *mare nostrum* and the Panama Canal was a vital strategic asset (the American Suez). So, beginning in 1898, the USA embarked on a series of interventions in the circum-Caribbean; American motives were chiefly strategic (not directly economic); and the interventions – a kind of unilateral mini-scramble – were designed both to both fend off rivals and to engineer congenial collaborating regimes in key countries, including Cuba, Haiti, Nicaragua and the Dominican Republic.

45   Of course, the Baring crisis of the following year put an end to this boom. For aggregate figures see note 33 above.

46   Note the similarly compliant tone of Uruguay's president described in Winn (1976: 115).

audience that, although 'we have been earnestly pressed ... to undertake the regeneration of Argentina finance ... Her Majesty's Government [is not] in the least degree disposed to encroach on the function of Providence' (Ferns, 1960: 465). Even after the political shake-up of 1916, when the Radicals took power amid the economic uncertainty engendered by the First World War, the collaborative bargain held, and it received a kind of official, if controversial, imprimatur with the Roca–Runciman treaty of 1933 (Alhadeff, 1985: 367–378).

What underpinned the Anglo-Argentine relationship during its heyday (c.1880–1945)? And was it a case of 'informal imperialism'?[47] The driving force was clearly not fear and coercion, but perceived mutual self-interest. (We should note in passing that other Anglo-Latin American relationships *were* occasionally tainted by (asymmetrical) fear and coercion: the 1902 Venezuelan blockade has been mentioned.) Like the White Dominions, Argentina economically complemented Britain.[48] It made sense, as the later slogan would have it, to sell to those who buy from us. Britain remained, at least until 1914, the world's greatest source of capital, and – the Baring crisis notwithstanding – Argentina offered a safe and profitable haven for overseas investment (Ferns, 1992a: 271–272).

Did 'culture' – the great explanatory variable of today's historiography – count for much? It no doubt helped that Argentine leaders such as Sarmiento were confirmed Anglophiles, or that English mores and institutions

---

47 Here we get to the nub of the debate between Thompson (1992) (who, following Platt and Ferns, says no) and Hopkins (1994) (who, echoing Gallagher and Robinson, says yes). Like many such debates, this one involves both conceptual/theoretical differences (such as the role of coercion and exploitation) and empirical disagreements (how far Britain could exercise power over Argentina). It also involves a good deal of mutual incomprehension and muddied water. For the sake of brevity and clarity, I will not wade into the debate; my own position – which an Argentine might qualify as *ni fu ni fa* [neither one nor the other] – should become clear in the pages which follow.

48 There is a large and illuminating literature comparing Argentina to the White Dominions; much of it adopts a twentieth-century slant and asks why (in comparison to Canada or Australia) Argentina failed to sustain its previously impressive economic growth. Perhaps paradoxically, a major factor appears to have been the Dominions' participation in a formal empire and the interests and policies which, in contrast to the independent republic of Argentina, were thereby fostered – for example by way of land and land settlement policy (see Solberg, 1987). Note also Denoon (1983), Sheinin and Mayo (1997), and Fogarty, Gallo and Diéguez (1979).

(governesses, public schools, football, department stores) came to exercise influence – though not thanks to any deliberate policy on the part of HMG. (We could compare the active cultural diplomacy of the USA in the later twentieth century, when the combination of mass culture and Cold War elicited a proactive response.) But before stressing 'culture' overmuch, we should ask whether, as an explanation, it generates much 'value-added'. Is it really an 'independent variable' and, if so, how important a variable is it? After all, some English mores and fashions had been in vogue long before – even when British prisoners-of-war were languishing in captivity after the abortive invasions of 1806–1807. Decades later, when British trade and investment had mounted, it made sense to buy British goods: either because they were good value, or because exports generated pounds sterling that could be spent in the British market. When new mass-produced US goods came on stream in the 1900s, Argentine consumption patterns soon changed (MacDonald, 1992: 85; Rocchi, 2001). The trading nexus, of course, was associated with a flow of people who played polo or football (they also played cricket, which did not catch on: my hypothesis would be that it requires at least a century of formal colonial rule to inculcate the rules of this most peculiarly imperial pastime). Thus, while the cultural contact between Britain and Argentina was surely significant, I would see the logic of economic collaboration as paramount; culture trailed economics, and, perhaps, gave a civilised veneer to material relationships. Pelligrini may have gone to school in Harrow, but did that affect his conduct during the Baring crisis? And was his going to Harrow not itself a product of the prior economic liaison between Britain and Argentina? At any event, the British cultural impact was sketchy: food, religion and language (football terminology apart) were largely untouched. The mass migration of Italians had a much more profound cultural influence than the commercial hegemony of Britain.

Given that the Anglo-Argentina relationship was largely consensual, could it be qualified as imperialism? It is worth stressing the (ostensible) paradox in this story. In the early nineteenth century (and before), Britain had readily, if usually unsuccessfully, deployed force in the Río de la Plata. Yet, after 1820, British trade and investment had tended to stagnate. The paradox is only ostensible because, of course, force (such as the blockade of the Plate) was largely designed to open the way to trade. In the later nineteenth century, as trade and investment forged ahead, force receded. The British could confidently rely on collaborating elites to mind the shop, even in moments of crisis, such as 1890. The parallel with the White Dominions again springs to mind: thus, in Figure 1, Argentina and the Dominions, though occupying separate quadrants (since the Dominions were part of the formal empire and being part of the formal empire mattered),[49] are both to be found on the far-right end of the 'in-direct rule' axis.

Furthermore, whereas in some Latin American countries the threat of force remained long after the last gunboat had sailed over the horizon, it is hard to believe that Argentine governments behaved the way they did out of fear of British reprisals. If imperialism requires coercion, or a lively fear of coercion, then this was a pallid imperialism at best. However, if we return to our broadbrush definition – the sustained, asymmetrical exercise of influence and authority by one group of people over another, etc. – then it is clear that the Anglo-Argentine relationship involved an asymmetry of power and influence. The economic figures speak for themselves: the Argentine economy depended heavily on foreign trade; a fraction of Britain's trade was with Argentina, but a large slice of Argentina's trade was with Britain;[50] the share of Britain's overseas investment located in Argentina, though significant, was dwarfed by the share of foreign investment in Argentina that came from Britain. The Baring crisis, though a serious tremor for the City of London, was a major financial and economic earthquake for Argentina, bringing in its wake 'the imposition of unpopular austerity measures, a striking reduction in real wages, and the sale of state enterprises to foreign bankers'; it represented, Carlos Marichal concludes, a 'capitulation to the dictates of the international banking community in almost every sphere of the economy' (Marichal, 1989: 152).[51] Hence, Lord Salisbury's relaxed good humour contrasted with Pelligrini's white-knuckled resolve. Again, if Argentina went to war, as in 1865, Britain scarcely noticed; but 1914 – and the ensuing conflict – had dramatic effects on Argentina (compare Ferns (1960: 423–424) with Albert (1988: 38–41, 51–52)). And, of course, no Argentine fleet had ever sailed up the Thames, blockaded

---

49 Not least when it came to war, as in 1914. But official (*de jure*) membership of the Empire may also have conferred long-term advantages in political-economy terms (see previous footnote).

50 As British diplomats liked to remind their Latin American interlocutors: in 1827 Ponsonby, the British representative in Buenos Aires, having listed British interests in the Río de la Plata, pointedly asked President Rivadavia 'if he [Rivadavia] could believe [that] the Government of the richest Country in the Universe [*sic*] could be influenced in their counsels by such trifling pecuniary concerns, not so great as many of the private merchants of England were in the daily habit of transacting with disinterestedness [*sic*] and almost indifference' (Ferns, 1960: 187).

51 See also Jones (1980: 440–443). Some might wish to qualify Marichal's robust conclusion; however, the chief point is not the Argentine experience per se, but the contrasting experiences (indicative of asymmetry) of Argentina and Great Britain.

London or engineered the creation of Belgium as a convenient buffer state.[52]

This comparison is pitched at the national level, where the asymmetry is obvious. If, however, we 'unpack' the two nations then the evidence becomes more ambiguous and the *cui bono* question requires a measured answer. The Anglo-Argentina liaison greatly benefitted pampas landlords and exporters (and, perhaps, workers and consumers in the littoral more broadly); meanwhile, it prejudiced British farmers, stockraisers and rural workers who, according to the remorseless logic of free trade, went to the wall. Ferns eloquently captures the contrast: 'derelict fields in Cambridgeshire existed in part because fields in the Argentine Republic were heavy with cheap cereals, and Argentine *estancieros* have wintered on the Riviera while herdsmen in Shropshire went bankrupt' (Ferns, 1960: 488). The respective Gross National Products (GNPs) no doubt benefitted – thus helping to elevate Argentine into the top ten of global economies in respect of per capita income – but the sectoral impact varied. There were winners and losers, although the former appreciably outnumbered the latter (a rather different conclusion would emerge if, for example, we unpacked the Anglo-Mexican economic liaison). In economic terms, therefore, Argentina's relationship to Britain loosely resembled that of the self-governing Dominions. Britain exercised a form of economic hegemony, characterised by asymmetrical influence, but this was not maintained by force; it generated genuine benefits, and it elicited collaboration that was rational and self-interested. Comparative advantage worked and was seen to work. Since this was a relatively 'pure' economic relationship, uncontaminated by geopolitical concerns, religious proselytisation or the quest for glory, it remained highly informal, securely lodged in the top right quadrant of Figure 1 (B). In its heyday, there was no need for British intervention either to fend off competitors or to shore up the structure of collaboration. The Baring Crisis bore little resemblance to the Egyptian crisis of ten years earlier.

---

52 This may seem like stating the obvious. But it is a feature of imperialism, broadly defined, that some actions seem natural or run-of-the-mill (such as Britain despatching ships to the South Atlantic or the USA invading Iraq), whereas reverse counter-factuals appear bizarre or unthinkable. The same is true (if less dramatically) in the economic realm: the USA runs trade and budget deficits far in excess of those of lesser economies that have been sternly chastened for their supposed profligacy. One does not have to be a loopy postmodernist to recognise that it is an attribute of power – of 'structural power', as Susan Strange calls it – to set the frame of reference, even to 'naturalise' certain unequal relationships (see Strange, 1988: Chapter 2). As a recent US spokesman (allegedly) said: 'we are an empire now and when we act we create our own reality' (Suskind, 2004). Up to a point, one might add.

However, the consolidation of this relationship – and the 'path-dependency' it established – had consequences for the post-1914 period, when the pre-war economic order crumbled, and could be only partially and imperfectly restored. By then, British interests in Argentina were facing both a domestic challenge from Argentine critics and opponents (nationalist intellectuals and politicians; new leftist parties; incipient trade unions; and querulous consumers) and also an external challenge from foreign rivals, especially Americans and Germans, who could out-compete Britain in the new environment of the 'second industrial revolution'. Indeed, this battle was well on the way to being lost elsewhere in Latin America. In confronting the domestic challenge, Britain had to rely on Argentine collaborators – a strategy that lost some of its cogency as the oligarchs of the Partido Autonomista Nacional (PAN) gave way to Yrigoyen and the Radicals. The latter did not fundamentally challenge Argentina's economic model or Britain's place within it; but they pandered, populist-style, to trade unions and consumers. Increasingly, therefore, the British found themselves in the reactionary camp of, say, Colonel Varela, the 'hyena of Patagonia', or the conservatives who ruled during the 'infamous decade' and who signed the controversial Roca–Runciman treaty in 1933 (Hennessy, 1992: 18).

In the formal empire, where Britain faced similar challenges from nationalist parties (e.g. the Indian National Congress), and labour unions (Australian stevedores and sheep-shearers), a range of political responses was available, ranging from repression to reform. In the informal empire, Britain had no overt political role; at best – and at some risk – Britain had to lobby behind the scenes.[53] And, unlike the USA during the Cold War, Britain lacked the resources or the commitment to undertake sustained interference in the rumbustious politics of Argentina. (And if Argentina was difficult, revolutionary Mexico was impossible.) At the same time, in the informal 'empire', foreign competition could not be systematically countered by tariffs or imperial preference. Roca–Runciman represented a negotiated deal between elites, not an outright British imposition; and it came with a political pricetag for both sides (Alhadeff, 1985: pp. 367–78; MacDonald, 1992: 83–85). Having relinquished political ambitions decades earlier, Britain could not compensate for economic decline by pulling political levers, for no such levers existed. There remained only the mutual interest of British and Argentine elites, sanctioned by history and, perhaps, seasoned by a degree of common culture. But the latter served little purpose as the world moved on,

---

53 For example, during the period of serious labour unrest in Argentina in 1917–1922: Mallet, Buenos Aires, to FO, 29 December 1919, 26 January 1920, with enclosures, TNA (National Archives) FO 371/4408/A377, A1210.

as Britain declined and as Argentina's oligarchic elite was first challenged, then deposed, by a populist-nationalist movement dedicated to the destruction of British imperialism. The irony was that, by the 1940s, there was little left of British imperialism to destroy. Not only was British power and influence moribund; a new hegemon had appeared on the horizon, committed to the creation of a new, different, and more enduring 'informal empire'.[54] But that is another story.[55]

---

54   Hence the 'Anglo-North American War of 1941–1947' in the Americas, described in Jones (1992: 206–212).
55   With apologies for the final cliché. I address the USA's 'informal empire' in a forthcoming chapter, 'US Hegemony in Latin America' (provisional title) in Rosen, *Hegemony and Resistance in Latin America* (Knight, forthcoming).

2

The British in Argentina: From Informal Empire to Postcolonialism

DAVID ROCK

University of California, Santa Barbara, USA

Three major schools, Marxist, nationalist and liberal, have dominated traditional debate about imperialism (for these distinctions, see Cain and Harrison, 2001). The two former approaches became the most potent when they promoted anti-colonial and anti-imperialist revolutionary movements. The liberal variants included 'informal imperialism', also known as 'the imperialism of free trade', inspired by British policy towards the non-European world during the nineteenth century. Gallagher and Robinson (1953) argued that the adoption of free trade by Britain after the Napoleonic wars, and an apparent disdain at that time for imperialist expansion, did not inhibit the British government from using force to expand commerce and to prise open foreign markets. They defined such policies as informal imperialism – a system in which one nation restricted the sovereignty of another for commercial or financial profit without imposing direct political control. Informal imperialism implied political domination but fell short of colonial rule.

From 1978, the study of imperialism changed profoundly on the publication of Edward W. Said's *Orientalism* (1978), the work that launched 'postcolonialism'. Said and his successors repudiated all the earlier approaches to colonialism and imperialism, including informal imperialism, on the grounds they had failed to analyse the 'ideological, cultural and political dimension of the colonial encounter' (Naregal, 2001: 2). The postcolonial writers argued that the work of Michel Foucault, which defined power in new cultural forms, rendered the old theories of imperialism obsolete. They fostered a concern with colonialism and imperialism as 'discourse' and provoked interest in their psychological aspects. 'Colonialism is a state of mind in the colonizers and the colonized', proclaimed Ashis Nandy, observing that 'the crudity and inanity of colonialism are principally expressed in the sphere of psychology' (Nandy, 1983: 1). On such foundations came ideas like 'hybridity' and 'mimicry' made famous by Homi Bhabha to denote the complex psychic entangling between colonizers and colonized. Mimicry, for instance, created 'a colonial subject who will be the same as the colonizer but still different: "white but not quite"'; likewise, hybridity (or hybridisation) 'undermines colonial authority because it repeats it differently'

(Young, 1990: 187,189; see also Young, 2001). As explained by Parry (2004: 76), 'the oppositional conceptual categories of colonizer and colonized have been displaced by categories of complicity, mutuality, and reciprocity'.

At the Bristol conference in January 2007, we were invited to consider whether informal imperialism remains of any value in defining imperialist interactions between Europe and Latin America. Alternatively, should we opt for postcolonialism and follow its directions into culture and psychology? Both sides are open to some basic objections. Despite their heterogeneity, the older writers on imperialism confined the discussion to narrowly economic, political or diplomatic channels, and had nothing to say about cultural and subjective elements. For their part, the postcolonial writers were guilty of eso-teric and jargon-ridden writing, and of static or 'essentialist' modes of analy-sis. They were held to be insensitive to diachronic process and change and were accused of reducing historical actors to stereotypes. Frederick Cooper, an historian of Africa, demanded much more 'rigorous historical practice' and far less 'homogenized coloniality'. He complained that Bhabha, for instance, left 'the two stick figures of colonizer and colonized interacting with each other (Cooper, 2005: 13, 16, 49). Strong on culture, the postcolonial writers appeared weak in social science as well as history. Howe (2000: 130) held that the post-colonial writers were deploying some highly sophisticated theory 'in the ser-vice of a fairly crude and Manichean politics'. 'In focusing attention on the colonial psyche', warned Sara Mills, 'we risk ignoring the political and eco-nomic basis on which these psyches were constructed' (Mills, 2003: 193).

Gallagher and Robinson applied the idea of informal empire primarily to Egypt and superficially or incompletely to Latin America. Postcolonial-ism too inflected Latin American studies more slowly and less completely than those of other parts of the world. The movement's precursors – Frantz Fanon, Albert Memmi, and Aimé Césaire – had few Latin American con-nections, while its principal figures – Said, Bhabha and Gayatri Chakra-vorty Spivak – originated in the Middle East and South Asia. Collectively, their writings mirrored conditions in decolonizing and recently decolo-nized regions. They were more concerned with colonialism – direct foreign rule and its aftermath – than with imperialism, a more opaque phenome-non and all too often synonymous, in Cooper's words, with almost 'any form of asymmetrical relationship' (Cooper, 2005: 29).[1] It was difficult to

---

1   In *Culture and Imperialism*, Said (1993: 9) used a very broad definition of imperi-alism taken from Michael Doyle: 'a relationship formal or informal, in which one state controls the effective political sovereignty of another political society. It can be achieved by force, by political collaboration, by economic, social, or cultural dependence'.

impose postcolonialism directly onto Latin America, which had experienced colonial rule quite differently from other parts of the non-European
world and much longer ago. Latin America differed from Asia and Africa
because of the chronic struggles following Independence between modern-
izing creole elites, the agents of coercive westernisation and popular indigenous resistance. Latin American postcoloniality went far beyond the
conventional binary relationship between European colonizers and the indigenous colonized and extended to the multiple ties between Europeans
and Europeanising creoles. Not only victimised by external imperialism,
Latin America long endured the onslaughts of internal colonialism (for one
account, in a very large literature, see Rock, 2002).[2]

The postcolonial approach might therefore be applied to post-Independence Latin America making the nineteenth- and early-twentieth-century
liberals into the centrepiece of analysis. In liberalism, the imperialist voice
could often be heard in its most strident and least equivocal forms. Canonical
liberal texts such as *Facundo* by Domingo F. Sarmiento invite the testing of
postmodern and postcolonial concepts like Foucault's discursive formations
or the idea, fundamental to *Orientalism*, of 'a form of representation that mis-
represents what is actually there' (Young, 2001: 399). In liberalism, the postcolonial definitions of culture as a mechanism of repression resonate in the
liberal state, which became a conspicuous example of 'the political institutional regime of the production of truth'. The liberals created paradigms of
Said's 'Other' when they launched their campaigns against the rural masses
they were attempting to subdue. Bhabha's 'mimicry' or his 'returning the
Gaze' provide striking analytical models to the ways in which the subjugated
peoples learned to contemplate and to accommodate their liberal conquerors.
In many parts of Latin America after Independence, foreign imperialists became redundant as the indigenous liberals pursued imperialist agenda with
uncompromising zeal and conviction (for a seminal discussion, see Mehta,
1996: 59–86).

Nevertheless, as Coronil (2004: 221–240) emphasised recently, many
strands of postcolonial analysis – mimicry, travel writings, the notion of
the 'Other' developed by Said – had other potential applications to Latin
America. In a noted study, Mary Louise Pratt pointed to one of the ways
forward. Her interests lay in the Latin American contact zones, 'where

---

2 In *Postcolonialism. An Historical Introduction* (Young, 2001: 193–206) and in *Post-
   Colonialism. A Very Short Introduction* (Young, 2003: 122–128), Robert J. C. Young
   linked José Carlos Mariátegui with Latin American forms of postcolonialism and
   'Che' Guevara with Frantz Fanon. The comparisons are loosely explored and
   unconvincing.

disparate cultures meet, clash and grapple with one another, often in highly unsymmetrical relations of dominance and subordination'. She focused on transculturation: 'how subordinated or marginal groups select and invent from materials from a dominant or metropolitan culture'. She examined the works of European travel writers. She perceived them as 'the vanguard' of the railway builders and the mining entrepreneurs because their principal role lay in assembling a picture of primeval backwardness and laying the preconditions for capitalist and imperialist intervention: 'Ideologically, the vanguard's task is to reinvent America as backward and neglected, to encode its non-capitalist landscapes and societies as manifestly in need of the rationalized exploitation the Europeans bring' (Pratt, 1992: 4, 6, 151).

In this chapter, I probe imperialism in Latin America by drawing on recent research on interactions between Great Britain and the Argentine Republic. The analysis divides into two sections, which deal with informal empire and then address postcolonial themes. The informal empire approach highlights the importance of the British in the Rio de la Plata despite the absence of a colonial administration. Gallagher and Robinson, however, created a very general hypothesis, which, as it changed over time, became vague and inconsistent. On Argentina, their data were weak and led them – along with their critics – into historical misinterpretations. They applied the idea of informal empire only to the free trade era before 1914, when it obviously works much better during the postliberal era of the First World War and after.

The value of the postcolonial perspective lies in its flexibility as a set of 'discursive formations' addressing the multiform aspects of cultural power (on the absence of uniformity in postcolonial perspectives, see Loomba, 2000). In this chapter, I explore briefly several topics along the lines of a postcolonial approach. First, British visitors to Argentina provided many illustrations of the ethnocentric outlook characteristic of imperialism that dismissed anything 'native' as corrupt and inferior. Using portrayals of the Argentine gauchos, however, I also display British attitudes that became less exclusionary and more transactional. Acknowledging local liberty and independence, and based on interaction rather than blind assumptions of dominance, they represented more attenuated forms of imperialism. Second, selecting another area popular among postcolonial writers, I examine the attempts to inculcate pro-British attitudes in Anglo-Argentine private schools in Buenos Aires. Like the discussion on the British travellers, the analysis of the schools marks no more than a beginning of a potentially much larger study following the lead of writers such as Stoler (2002). Finally, I illustrate the way the British promoted the Anglophile liberal version of Argentine history in their efforts to colonise the Argentine elite culturally. The issues of who writes history and whom its writers represent are topics of widely recognised importance among postcolonial writers starting with Fanon himself. As he declared, colonialism 'turns to the past of a people, and distorts, disfigures and destroys it' (in Said, 1993: 237). The Argentines recognised the importance of this 'power to narrate' soon after the beginnings of the republic. The three themes touched on here all denote various forms of cultural imperialism, although Argentina never became an arena of uncontested British hegemony. The British had to compete with other Europeans led by the French and with Americans for cultural status and influence. Soon after the First World War, they also faced a challenge from Argentine nationalists.

The Applications of Informal Imperialism

Gallagher and Robinson claimed that when the British failed to conquer the Rio de la Plata in the two military invasions of 1806–1807, they turned to techniques of indirect control. First, the Anglo-Argentine treaty of 1825 enabled British merchants to dominate Argentine trade. Later, in the mid-1840s, when General Juan Manuel de Rosas challenged their commercial leadership, the British countered with gunboat diplomacy. In the 1860s and later decades, the British-built railways and many other investments in Argentina reconsolidated British dominance. Finally, Gallagher and Robinson cited the Baring crisis of 1890 as another illustration of British financial and political power over Argentina.

In the early nineteenth century, the ties between Britain and Argentina were mainly commercial (an exchange of cattle goods for textiles and hardware), although small British and Irish sheep-farming and landowning communities formed near Buenos Aires. The British and Anglo-Argentine merchants, along with a few landowners of British origin, created a web of contacts with the Argentine elites that grew more extensive with the rapid expansion of railways in the 1880s and the modernisation of the cattle industry around 1900. By the late 1920s, the British and Anglo-Argentine community, at possibly 60,000 strong, became the largest group of British expatriates outside the British Empire with the exception of the USA (see Rock, forthcoming).

British economic imperialism, as defined by Argentine Marxists and nationalists, derived from the salience of the British in sectors headed by banking, transportation and urban utilities. From around 1880, the Anglo-Argentine community disseminated British ideological and cultural models through associations, schools, customs and sports in ways that promoted the prestige of Britain and enhanced the standing of British businesses. Having survived the financial crises and the economic depressions of the 1870s and the 1890s, and then the shocks of the First World War, the British occupied a prominent position in Argentina until the 1940s. Decline, however, had started as early as 1913, when British investment ceased and accelerated in the 1920s, when British trade lagged. Finally, Britain's longstanding position disintegrated after 1948, when Argentina nationalised the railways.

Although Gallagher and Robinson (1953) included Argentina in their list of countries subject to informal empire, they provided only a few illustrative incidents as proof: their article mentioned the commercial crash of 1827 in Buenos Aires, the shipping blockade of the mid-1840s and the pressure allegedly exercised by Britain during the Baring crisis. Ferns (1953) also used the expression informal imperialism in his article on Anglo-Argentine relations. He abandoned it in *Britain and Argentina in the Nineteenth Century* (1960), which viewed the ties between the two countries in very different terms as models of comparative advantage. His position had shifted radically: 'If we accept the proposition that imperialism embraces the fact of control through political power', he wrote, 'then the verdict for Britain is unanimously "Not Guilty"' (Ferns, 1960: 487). E. J. Hobsbawm applied the term to Argentina (1969: 121–124) but very loosely alongside rival formulations such as 'dependent economies' and 'honorary dominions'. Informal imperialism achieved maximum influence in the essays in Louis (1976) but thereafter lost eminence and adherents. On Argentina, a concluding debate took place in the articles by Thompson (1992) and Hopkins (1994), in which the former made a spirited attack on informal imperialism that the latter sought to refute.[3]

Cain and Hopkins (2002: 26) noted that 'the controversy [on informal empire] has flagged in recent years, not least because of the admitted difficulty of giving precision to such a broad concept'. Robinson, for instance, developed several views of the imperialist 'threshold' – the point at which the interactions between Britain and other nations veered into imperialism. In the 1950s, he mentioned the 'economies which could be made to fit best [into the British economy]', suggesting a form of hyper-agency on the part of Britain as the necessary condition of informal imperialism (cited in Mommsen, 1980: 90). He then defined imperialism in contrasting minimalist terms as 'a sufficient political function of integrating some countries at some times into the international economy' implying that a mere nudge from

---

3   A more recent study, with a thesis illustrating 'the limits of British international authority', is McLean, 1995. In this author's view, the British learnt that 'influence in South America was not readily attainable by the coordination of diplomacy and naval power' (McLean, 1995: 2, 206).

Britain towards open trade qualified as imperialist intervention. Another Robinson definition of the 1970s appeared even more malleable:

> Imperialism in the industrial era is a process whereby agents of an expanding society gain inordinate influence or control over the vitals of weaker societies by 'dollar' and 'gun-boat' diplomacy, ideological suasion, conquest and rule, or by planting colonies of its people abroad. The object is to shape or reshape them in its own interest and more or less in its own image. It implies the exertion of power and the transfer of economic resources. (Robinson, 1972: 117–118)

Following this definition, Robinson would claim that Argentina met the test of informal imperialism because Britain's commercial and financial influence became powerful enough 'to reshape [the country] in its own interest' by developing an agrarian export economy. His analysis remained strikingly ethnocentric: it attributed agency to Britain alone, forgetting that much of the impulse for transformation came from Argentina itself. Inadvertently, Robinson was subscribing to the same view as the old imperialists themselves, who had argued that 'Argentines rule the country, foreigners develop it' (Every, 1933: 15).

In Robinson's brand new 'excentric' theory of imperialism published in the early 1970s, imperialist domination was 'not simply something that Europe did to other countries, but also something they were persuaded or compelled to do to themselves' (Robinson, 1986: 271). His theory of collaboration (or collaborative elites) strayed far away from his original emphasis on British political intervention and gunboat diplomacy. With its connotations of psychological control and its shift away from a metropolitan focus, the new approach became an important way-station towards 'hybridisation' and 'mimicry'. As Peter Cain noted recently (2006: ix), 'the distance between Ronald Robinson's idea of collaboration and Homi Bhabha's notion of hybridity is rather less than champions of either approach have been prepared to consider'.

The original defining feature of informal imperialism lay in the use of force by the British government against a weaker extra-European polity for purposes of political domination and then economic gain. D. C. M. Platt emerged as the trenchant critic of informal imperialism conceived in these terms. In his writings on Argentina after Independence, Platt emphasised that Britain applied force against mainland Argentina on one occasion alone in the mid-1840s during the shipping blockade on Buenos Aires ordered by Lord Aberdeen, which included an Anglo-French naval assault against Argentine fortifications on the Río Paraná. With this one exception (apart from the annexation of the distant Falkland Islands in 1833), the British practised the policy of non-intervention laid down during the era of Lord Castlereagh and George Canning in the 1810s and 1820s. That policy enjoined British diplomats to promote trade and to protect the property and the lives of British subjects but to abstain from political involvement. Platt cited the Treaty of Amity, Commerce and Navigation of 1825, which defined the status of the British in Argentina as equal, but never superior, to that of other foreigners. Against Gallagher and Robinson's claim that in the period 1830–1860 Britain practised an 'imperialism of free trade' in Argentina, Platt argued that Anglo-Argentine trade remained too small to justify the heavy expenses of an interventionist policy. For the late nineteenth century, he rejected the collusion between the British and the Argentine ruling class, as elaborated by Robinson's idea of the collaborating elites.[4] Platt referred to the Baring crisis to emphasise that the British government rejected demands for intervention by British bondholders.[5]

Platt drew extensively from British official publications headed by the Parliamentary Papers, which offered a selective vision of British policy and led him into a very rigid interpretation of 'intervention'. By confining the discussion to literal manifestations of British 'control', he ignored the nuances of informal imperialism – its invisible character and the robotic, self-programming behaviour of those caught in its snare – as emphasised by Robinson's later work. On Argentina, Platt delved more deeply than Gallagher and Robinson, but not far enough. He too misinterpreted important points of detail and weakened his critique. In the early nineteenth century, he underplayed the disruptions occasioned by British commercial penetration as illustrated in well-known sources such as *Letters on South America* by Robertson and Robertson (1843). They described the introduction of a cash

---

4   Platt reiterated his views in several books and articles, all focused on the nineteenth century until 1914. He included parts of Latin America, Asia and the Ottoman Empire in his analysis but concentrated increasingly on Latin America, extending his chronological range from the mid-Victorian into the Edwardian era. In later years, his sources included works in Spanish although the general argument remained much the same throughout his writings. See Platt (1968a, 1968b, 1972: 192, 1973).

5   Ferns (1960: 465) provides details to illustrate Platt's argument that Lord Salisbury refused to intervene in Argentina to support British bondholders. Ferns later returned to the issue: 'Salisbury refused to consider any intervention in Argentine affairs. The resolution of the Baring crisis was a business deal, not an exercise in imperialism'. Also: 'The evidence in the archive of the Marquis of Salisbury further confirms that the British government from first to last refused to consider political action'. Throughout the period 1890–1893, the pressure for intervention remained weak and ill-concerted (Ferns, 1992: 242, 273).

economy that overturned the social hierarchy and led to the formation of a virtual British trading monopoly (Robertson and Robertson, 1843: 53–54, 176). Platt ignored cultural themes relating to inter-denominational marriages between British merchants and upper-class Argentine women. Such marriages met opposition from Catholics in Buenos Aires that evolved into a powerful anti-imperialist discourse: 'foreigners brought to this country had drained all its immense riches … and thus the country is reduced to its present state of poverty'.[6] Platt exaggerated the weakness of British trade in Argentina before 1860, which he had cited to suggest British indifference towards the Rio de la Plata. Woodbine Parish, the first British consul in Buenos Aires, noted that in the 1820s British trade with Argentina grew much larger than with the rest of Spanish America combined. Trade then declined later that same decade, although Buenos Aires always remained an important market for British manufacturers. Parish's work on the public debt of Buenos Aires for the year 1837 showed that the markets of the Rio de la Plata still exceeded those of the rest of Spanish America (Parish, 1839: xix, 337, 340, 352). Platt ignored the development of British beef salting plants, British estancias and Irish sheep-farming in the province of Buenos Aires from the mid-1820s. He omitted to note that Anglo-Argentine trade surged during the Crimean War and the American Civil War, which boosted Argentine wool exports.

Finally, Klaus Gallo has provided new data from the last years of the eighteenth century that strengthen the Gallagher and Robinson approach but undermines Platt's. Gallo showed that powerful members of the British government and the armed forces already recognised that the policy later pursued by Canning in the 1820s – a treaty protecting the British but granting them no extraordinary privileges against other foreigners – held the key to stable British economic dominance. In 1798 or 1799, Sir Ralph Abercrombie, who had recently conquered the island of Trinidad, proposed British military expeditions for the liberation of Spanish America:

> [They] should be undertaken without any view to conquest, to exclusive commerce or to plunder. Every port in Spanish America, and the whole trade of that extensive continent, should be declared free and laid open to every nation of the world. Every country should feel interested in it, Spain and Portugal excepted: Great Britain, however, from her enterprise, from her capital, and from her industry, would in reality possess nine parts in ten of this great enterprise. (in Gallo, 2001b: 23)

---

6 Quoted and translated in *The British Packet*, 6 April 1833.

Supported by political figures led by Henry Dundas, Secretary of War under William Pitt the Younger, Abercrombie's scheme anticipated the Gallagher and Robinson model of the imperialism of free trade. It proposed military and naval intervention in Spanish America, particularly in the Rio de la Plata region, in order to secure access to markets. In conferring on other nations the same commercial rights as their own, the British could disclaim any charge of 'imperialism' but exercise economic hegemony by virtue of the higher productivity of British industry and commerce (Gallo, 2001a).

Nevertheless, so far as Argentina went, both sides of the informal imperialism debate had serious weaknesses. On one hand, Gallagher and Robinson overrated the power of British merchants in Buenos Aires in the late 1820s; they exaggerated the impact of Aberdeen's blockade in the 1840s and the extent of British intervention in the Baring crisis. On the other, Platt properly criticised the sketchiness of the Gallagher and Robinson thesis, but it is not difficult to expose the inadequacies of his own data and interpretations. Robinson's most important contribution lay in the idea of the collaborating elites, which steered him away from his former ethnocentricity. The nineteenth century provided multiple examples of the willingness with which Argentine political leaders collaborated with the British. One famous occasion occurred on St George's Day 1823, when chief minister Bernardino Rivadavia toasted Great Britain 'as having the most adept government and as the nation with the greatest decency and enlightenment' (Wilde, 1960: 149).[7]

Informal imperialism seemed much more applicable to the twentieth century than to the nineteenth, although, as free trade began to vanish, it could no longer be equated with the 'imperialism of free trade'. Studies by Gravil (1985) and Albert (1988) documented British efforts to control Argentine foreign trade and exchange rates during the First World War.[8] In 1914–1915, British control over shipping contributed to an eightfold leap in shipping rates that prolonged a commercial recession in Argentina. In 1918–1919, the

---

7   The original reads 'por el gobierno más hábil ... y por la nación más moral e ilustrada'.

8   Gravil notes (1985: 60) that 'in wartime, Britain demanded that Argentina's entire foreign trade should be reserved for the Allied nations'. In Albert's view (1988: 119), the war became 'a convenient pretext for holding down commodity prices by creating and enforcing monopsonies and using blacklists ... so as better to control Latin American trade in the post-war period'. A recent study stressing anti-German pressures within the British expatriate business community is Dehne (2005).

British cajoled the Argentine government into purchasing agreements for Argentine farm products that provided supplies at below market prices. The First World War transformed the role of the British diplomats in Buenos Aires, rendering obsolete Platt's portraits of the nineteenth-century diplomats as leisured patricians. The consular staff worked exhaustively on the 'black lists', which developed into an effort to destroy German commercial competition permanently. As minister plenipotentiary, Sir Reginald Tower intervened with the Argentine government to protect British companies when the shortages of imported raw materials and the complaints of belligerent workers exposed them to public criticism. Tower led the campaign to enlist British and Anglo-Argentine volunteers for military service on the Western Front. His task involved thousands of medical inspections, numerous fund raising events, organising transportation to Britain, and setting up pensions in Argentina for war widows and returning wounded soldiers.

In the 1920s, Anglo-Argentine trade failed to recover its pre-war levels as US competition mounted. The British government then swung towards an interventionist commercial policy, initially by exhortation but then by pressure. First, a ceremonial visit by the Prince of Wales to Argentina in 1925 sought to rekindle pro-British sentiment in Buenos Aires to help British exports. Second, while serving as the first British ambassador in Buenos Aires, Sir Malcolm Robertson urged the Argentines to 'buy from us that we may buy from you'. Third, the 1929 D'Abernon trade mission organised by the British Board of Trade won major preferences for British at the expense of American exporters, although the Argentine congress failed to ratify them. By the late 1920s, the British sought the support of elite associations headed by the *Sociedad Rural Argentina* as a lever against American competition by threatening to exclude Argentine exports to Britain by Imperial Preference (as noted in the best account of the treaty, Gravil and Rooth, 1978: 360–364).

The pressure mounted in the early 1930s with the onset of bilateral trade. The Roca–Runciman treaty of 1933 restored the flow of remittances from British companies during the Great Depression and lowered Argentine duties on goods imported from Britain. In return, the British allowed beef exports from Argentina as an exception to the recently adopted system of Imperial Preference. Overall, the 1933 treaty dictated the terms, the volume, the content and the relative prices of Anglo-Argentine commerce; it protected British companies in Argentina headed by the railways. Argentina's concessions to Britain included a preferential lowering of duties on British goods and the allocation of scarce foreign exchange for purchases of British goods. Britain now exercised a form of power over Argentina that resembled the aggressive economic imperialism depicted by Rudolf Hilferding. The British were using a 'politically powerful state [able to] pursue its own commercial policy regardless of the conflicting interests of other states. [That state could] assert its financial interests abroad and exert political power on smaller states' (in Mommsen, 1980: 37). 'One reason', noted Sir Walter Runciman, the leading British negotiator, 'why nothing came of the [D'Abernon Mission] was that we had no means of exercising any pressure. We are now in a position to do that' on the adoption of Imperial Preference (in Rooth, 1993: 146). Arturo Jauretche, a nationalist publicist and agitator, described the Roca–Runciman treaty as 'the legal statute of colonialism'. Displays of British economic power in Argentina recurred in 1936, when a government-controlled system of public transportation in Buenos Aires protected British-owned tramways against competition from locally owned buses. British exports to Argentina leapt from a low point of £10.7 million in 1932 to £20 million in 1937 (Gravil and Rooth, 1978: 365). When the influence of the USA expanded throughout Latin America in the 1940s, the British lost the extraordinary power they had wielded in Argentina in the 1930s. Nevertheless, during the war, Britain imported large quantities of beef from Argentina under the system of the blocked sterling balances allowing payment for Argentine goods to be postponed indefinitely.[9] During the allied naval blockade against continental Europe, Britain exerted great economic power over Argentina in the form of monopsony when it became the latter's single remaining major European market (Fodor, 1986: 154–182).

Postcolonial Perspectives

In Halperín Donghi's memorable phrase (1987: 141), Argentina was 'born liberal' during Independence and remained liberal except during the hiatus of 1829–1852 under Governor Rosas of Buenos Aires. Liberalism became the chief funnel for external influence as it promoted selective cultural borrowings throughout Western Europe and the USA. Among the mass of cultural imports from abroad, British models predominated in notably few instances. Jeremy Bentham during the Rivadavia era of the 1820s became the only British intellectual to command any direct influence; his solitary eminence among the British compared with the French luminaries, from the Marquis de Condorcet to Ernest Renan and beyond, who were numbered in dozens over many decades (Ingenieros, 1961). Even when the *porteños* [inhabitants of Buenos Aires City] adopted British habits such as taking afternoon tea, they would sometimes arrive as Parisian re-exports, as suggested by one of the

---

9   The 'blocked sterling balances' refer to earnings in pounds sterling during the Second World War that were held on account in the Bank of England at a nominal interest rate and were due for payment after the war. For discussion, see Rapoport (1981).

early-twentieth-century cafés on calle Florida called 'Le Five O'Clock'.[10] Around 1880–1910, British merchants and *estancieros* [ranchers] helped to develop high-quality livestock in Argentina and, as Hora (2005) has shown, they influenced the farming practices and the lifestyles of the rural gentry. Prominent Anglo-Argentines helped found several patrician associations linked to the landed interest headed by the Sociedad Rural Argentina and the Jockey Club. Anglophile attitudes existed among powerful sectors, but as innumerable anecdotes showed, they always remained secondary to the Francophiles. Thomas George Love, the founder of *The British Packet* in the 1820s, the first English-language newspaper in Buenos Aires, vented his ire at having to watch Shakespeare's *Othello* in Spanish taken from a French translation, an insipid version of the play shorn of all its dramatic content (Wilde, 1960: 50). Manuel A. Montes de Oca (1867–1934), an influential lawyer and landowner, helped found the Asociación Argentina de Cultura Inglesa (AACI) as a way of bringing British 'culture' to the Argentine elite, but admitted that he felt more at home reading his favourite works by Oscar Wilde in French rather than English (Ottino, 2003: 14). In the early 1850s, when Juan B. Alberdi sought constitutional models abroad, he looked at countries that had written constitutions, and therefore not at Britain. In his work *Recuerdos de Provincia*, Domingo F. Sarmiento recorded how he had once devoured the novels of Sir Walter Scott but he took his blueprints for popular education from the USA, a nation of immigrants like Argentina, not from Britain.

The Argentine liberals were always looking overseas for inspiration, but they rarely looked at Britain alone. Several late-nineteenth-century political figures – Bartolomé Mitre, Julio A. Roca, and Carlos Pellegrini – collaborated overtly with the British, but others – including Sarmiento, Adolfo Alsina, Carlos Tejedor, and later Roque Sáenz Peña and Estanislao Zeballos – had few British connections and no discernible British loyalties. General Agustín P. Justo, president in 1932–1938, stood out arguably as the most pro-British of all the Argentine presidents, but leaders indifferent to the British (some of whom had remote Irish connections) superseded him following the military coup of 1943. The British had no influence on presidential elections or on Congress and no particular standing in the Argentine press except at times perhaps in *La Nación*, the distinguished newspaper founded by Mitre. On occasion, as during the Boer War, the British faced strong criticism. 'A barely manifest ill-will is rampant in our press and the crowing outcry of the newsboys "la derrota de los ingleses" received with an appreciative

---

10 See the advertisement in *Standard*, 6 January 1906.

smile by eager buyers', observed the *Standard* of Buenos Aires in 1900.[11] The British had no contact with any of the political parties; like the other European communities in Argentina, they prided themselves on remaining apolitical. No Anglo-Argentine, (unless Pellegrini, who was half Anglo-Argentine on his mother's side, were defined as such), made a career in the top tier of Argentine politics.

The British commanded great importance in Argentina but enjoyed no precedence in the eyes of the Argentines. The 1825 treaty allowed the British to worship separately and to bury their dead in non-Catholic cemeteries, but they had none of the other extraterritorial privileges they staked out elsewhere such as in nineteenth-century Bahía or in twentieth-century Shanghai, where in both places they enjoyed separate courts. Their efforts to win more concessions, most notably the exemption of their local-born sons from military service, failed consistently. Periodic disputes erupted over the rights claimed by consuls to settle the property of Britons who died intestate, but this issue was never resolved conclusively to the consuls' advantage. If the consuls prevailed, the estates usually found their way back to relatives in Britain but when they failed, the heirlooms would pass to Argentine spousal partners and offspring.

A humorous illustration of the status of the British compared with other Europeans appeared in 1862, a year that marked the inception of large-scale British private investment. One day that year, President Mitre and his leading associates, (among them Carlos Pellegrini's father), were attending a ceremony to open a suburban railway in Buenos Aires. Addressing this gathering, Foreign Minister Rufino Elizalde spoke first:

> The history of the human race teaches us that to some nations is given the heavenly mission of reforming and civilising others. Foremost in every impulse is Great Britain, for she has awakened the energies of the world. She it was who cherished in the country aspirations for Liberty and fanned the flame of our independence. We entered into the struggle poor; she lent us money; we were unable for a long time to pay the debt; she treated us with the noblest generosity. England is our best friend. At first we vainly fancied that Argentine capital could make railways, but soon we were undeceived. English gold came to the rescue; English intelligence will perfect the work and guarantee the triumph of the arts of peace. ...

> Sr. Pellegrini on rising charged Sr. Elizalde with partiality, in not having coupled France and Italy with Great Britain as the friends of the country and the pioneers of civilization ...

---

11   *Standard*, 24 April 1900.

[Mitre himself then declared], let us remember how much Great Britain and North America have done [to develop railways]. Nor is France in the background ... If we take Europe for our preceptor, France will guide us with her genius, England will animate us with her capital and energies, and Italy inspires us with her noble sentiments.

Sr. Elizalde next made some apologetic remarks, confessing that we are indebted to France and Italy almost as much as to England.

Dr. Acosta continued in this vein: to France we owe our fashions and literature, to England our imports, yet more are we indebted to Italy. That noble country lent us the blood of [Giuseppe] Garibaldi. Let us drink to the Italian nation, for blood is worth more than imports and fashions and books.[12]

The Argentines thus assigned a form of contested division of labour and a graduated status to Europeans and Americans. France usually came first as the great source of 'culture' and style, and Italy second (at least during the 1860s) because of the ties between Italian and Argentine liberalism forged by Garibaldi when he fought against the allies of Rosas in Montevideo; Britain provided money and know-how but little of value beyond; at that time too, the USA enjoyed favour for showing how to tame a wilderness and to settle the land, embodying Alberdi's dictum: *gobernar es poblar*. As one of the smaller Western European communities in Buenos Aires during the late nineteenth century, the British occupied an inconspicuous position. They claimed a reputation for business honesty and punctuality but set a bad example for drunkenness, which provoked the cliché *el borracho inglés* [translated as 'drunk as a lord' or literally, 'the sozzled Briton']. Prominent pre-war Argentine liberals who later became nationalists remained pro-British until the First World War. 'Until 1908–1910', wrote the economist Alejandro E. Bunge in 1921, 'our policies, which were adapted to British policies, were beneficial in every respect. Our economic progress has been due largely to our strong commercial links with Britain and other European states' (in O'Connell, 1986: 75). Afterwards, a steady decline in Britain's standing supervened. Labour turmoil during and after the Great War – the port and railway strikes in 1916–1918, the infamous *Semana Trágica* of January 1919, and rural strikes in Patagonia of 1921–1922 – irrevocably damaged the British, whose reputation sagged further in the 1930s following the Roca–Runciman treaty (Rock, 1975).

The standing of the British in nineteenth-century Argentina, closer to one among near-equals than of *primus inter pares* with other Europeans, found

---

12 *Standard*, 27 February 1862.

some reflection in the style and content of British writing about the country. The absence of any conscious imperial mission and of an imperial administration induced interactions with the Argentines often more reminiscent of the USA than of the British Empire. The British added profoundly to knowledge about this region of South America, particularly of the pampas and the littoral areas, and of Patagonia and the Chaco, the northern and southern extremes. Their rich published accounts included the memorable book by the Robertson brothers, which provided a fascinating glimpse of the littoral and its melange of local and foreign denizens in the early years of Independence. The 1820s marked publication of Thomas Love's portraits of Buenos Aires, which became in translation one of the main sources on the early British community (Love, 1942). Major works by Woodbine Parish came a little later and, of course, Charles Darwin's 'Beagle' diary (1989).[13]

Among the British writings on Argentina, the most obdurate and insensitive stereotypes came from officials: the ministers plenipotentiary, the consuls and the clergymen. Sir Richard Burton, the Anglo-Irish explorer, (famous in the annals of 'Orientalism' for his clandestine visit to Mecca), provided one conspicuous example. Burton served for a period as British consul in Rio de Janeiro and, in 1866, he travelled to Buenos Aires and thence to the Upper Paraná as an observer during the war of the triple alliance against Paraguay (McLynn, 1991). He provided numerous representations of the type of imperialist outlook commonly identified in postcolonial literature as the 'imperial gaze' and 'the discursive mechanism of the colonial "Other"'. An example was his racialised and pseudo-anthropological representation of the Paraguayan soldier:

> He is, as a rule, far more Indian than Spanish. Most of the prisoners with whom I conversed were in fact pure redskins. The figure is somewhat short and stout, but well put together, with neat, shapely, and remarkably small extremities. The brachycephalic head is covered with a long curtain of blue-black hair ... (Burton, 1870: x)

Burton became a prototypical 'vanguard' figure identified by Pratt (1992: 140, 151). Burton viewed the war as a mission of redemption and civilisation

---

13   Later on, the celebrated accounts included Seymour (1869), where the author crossed the pampas into Córdoba bearing a prefabricated metal hut made in England. Another recently published account of sheep-farming, (brought to my attention by Rory Miller), is Boyle (1999).

that would open up Paraguay to progress and capitalist development. Its aim was:

> to unlock the Southern Mississippi [meaning the Rio Paraná, and to destroy] the batteries and ridiculous little stockades which served to keep its waters comparatively desert and to convert a highway belonging to the world into a mere monopoly of Paraguay. (Burton, 1870: 11)

Burton deployed the imperialist trope of the white woman at risk of kidnap and ravishment by native savages. He mentioned 'the wife of an English colonist, who being remarkably handsome requires as much protection as a twenty carat diamond. Sundry gauchos have sworn to carry her off, and if they can they will' (Burton, 1870: 134).[14]

Sir Horace Rumbold, the British minister in Buenos Aires in 1880–1881, exemplified a similarly blinkered imperialist mentality. In *The Silver River*, he recalled how he used to linger at the site of the surrender by Sir John Whitelocke, the military commander during the British attack on Buenos Aires in 1807. He claimed that Whitelocke had surrendered for no reason, because his forces remained undefeated – a view that very few other people shared:

> Often have I sat on one of those benches and pictured to myself the sullen retreat of the victorious and unbroken battalions, and have dreamed of what might have been had they only been allowed to hold what they had taken. Consider only what might have been the results. The treasures of these vast regions wrested for good from the blighting influence of Spanish misrule, the quick impulsive colonial race steadied and energised by the infusion of English blood, trained from its infancy to English habits of thought and action, and nurtured in rational English notions of freedom; the grateful soil enriched and fertilised by British wealth and industry; in short, a second and fully bounteously endowed Australia started on her career within three weeks of England. (Rumbold, 1890: 18)

In a book published in the early 1930s, Edward Every, who served for 30 years as the Anglican bishop of South America, made some extraordinary statements of British exceptionality among the allegedly polluted human species of South America. Every disliked all South Americans, partly because he viewed them as colonised culturally by the French:

> Culturally the British and Latin Americans are not drawn to each other; it can only be the few who become our warm friends and take their ideals from

---

14 On this issue, see Colley (2002b: 69), who stresses captivity in a context of 'deals and compromises constantly going on in European and non-European cultures'.

England; to the great majority Paris will always be their intellectual and spiritual home. (Every, 1933: 18)

Every caricatured the imperialist mentality. As he saw it, the inability of South Americans to meet British standards had its roots in 'moral reasons: our sturdiness of character and racial superiority – the superiority of our civilisation'. He exhorted local British men never to marry Argentine women, although unfortunately 'some would succumb'. He noted that the Argentines played a lot of English games, often quite well, but with a 'deplorable lack of the sporting spirit … They have yet to learn to accept defeat'. He was horrified by a visit he had once made to an Anglican mission in Paraguay because:

> Never before had I faced so large a purely heathen congregation and spellbound I watched the inscrutable dark faces, wondering reverently what the Holy Spirit was effecting with them, as the missionary delivered his message. What point of contact did he find with them? How far were these dull minds capable of understanding? (Every, 1933: 119)

Doubts about the future of the British in Argentina suffused the book. Every's exaggerated sense of cultural superiority and his disparaging attitudes towards the Argentine society and its people – considerably in excess of the nineteenth-century models – were juxtaposed against paranoia about Argentine nationalism and an unwelcome awareness that British prestige in Argentina was waning. 'We have passed', he wrote, 'From the position of being easily first to being obliged to fight hard to hold any place at all' (Every, 1933: 179).

Some of the Britons who arrived as tourists and sojourners adopted more neutral viewpoints less redolent of imperialism or colonialism, although usually infused with paternalism. Thomas Hinchliff, who visited in 1860–1861, became one of the many who wrote rapturously about riding out in the pampas: 'Away and away again, with a fresh sweet breeze and a rising sun, the most delicious combination of elements that a mortal man could desire; away over the springing turf. It seemed as if a few sweet weeks should add something to a man's life' (Hinchliff, 1863: 134–135).[15] Books like Hinchliff's addressed a British (and often American) audience among the rural gentry and focused on topics appealing to people with equestrian interests. These writings invariably contained a long excursus on the Argentine gaucho. The officials such as Burton and Rumbold had little positive to say about the gauchos – they were violent, indolent, superstitious and

---

15   Hinchliff journeyed in a private capacity, but had some official connections in Buenos Aires through his cousin, Frank Parish, the son of Sir Woodbine Parish, who was currently serving as British consul.

slovenly – but the tourists often took a different view. Typically, they viewed the gauchos as admirably free spirits who possessed classic Hispanic virtues such as strong personal loyalty, dexterity with horses, gallantry and infallible courage. Hinchliff considered one peon he met on an estancia as typical of:

> A certain class of the gauchos of the country. He had the full upright figure of a European and his movements showed an activity and elasticity which would make a formidable enemy in a struggle; his complexion was swarthy, and his straight black hair and low forehead showed the remains of Indian blood in his veins. His bearing was bold and reckless and I think he was rather proud of being pointed out as celebrated for concluding personal quarrels by taking the life of his foes. (Hinchliff, 1863: 170)

Hinchliff's outlook recalled Pratt's concept of transculturation. He perceived the gauchos as a primeval native people destined either for taming or for extinction as Argentina modernised its economy and transformed its society through railways and European immigrants. As he saw it, the future and survival of the gauchos depended on their willingness to accept subordination to the Europeans. He thought well of the gauchos who adopted this course. He visited a sheep estancia in Uruguay owned by a Scot:

> [Whose] sole companion was a peon of very unprepossessing appearance, but of staunch fidelity, who having distinguished himself in quarrels by generally killing his man, now determined to devote all his energy and talent to the service of his gallant young master. (Hinchliff, 1863: 161)

In 1878, the youthful Lady Florence Dixie spent six months roaming through southern Patagonia on horseback with her husband and brother, and afterwards wrote a classic book about her adventures (Anderson, 2006). She wrote at some length about one young man she met named Isidoro:

> As he rode away, I could not help admiring his manly bearing and his perfect seat on a splendid well-bred horse, which seemed not unworthy of its master. He wore his guanaco *capa* with a certain foppish grace – every article of his accoutrements from his perfectly coiled *lasoo* to the brightly coloured garters round his new *potro* boots, were perfectly finished.

Dixie found the young man attractive partly because he was independent and therefore unavailable for imperialist subjugation. She depicted him, despite his typically South American garb, as a person akin to a Spanish *hidalgo*: a European and thus close to an equal. Her favourable view of Isidoro contrasted with some very distasteful remarks she made about the black porters on the dockside at Rio de Janeiro and about some of the Tehuelche Indians she encountered in Patagonia (Dixie, 1881: 214).

A generation later, the influence of the British public schools and the development of British schools in Buenos Aires revealed some other facets of British cultural imperialism in Argentina. In the early 1900s, a few members of the ruling liberal oligarchy argued for the introduction of British-style schools to teach the male children of the elite. They hoped to inculcate among young Argentines of high social class the personal virtues – so-called character building – commonly proclaimed as uniquely British. At the time of his death in 1906, ex-president Carlos Pellegrini, who was a graduate of Harrow School near London (a so-called old Harrovian), was planning to establish a college modelled on the English public school. It would be easy to imitate here a type of English school', he had written, 'In which, far from the great centres of population, with extensive grounds favourable to health and physical education, and in a kind of paternal boarding house, the young men may receive the intellectual and moral education to make them worthy citizens of a liberal cultured democracy'.[16] Admiration for English public schools had a long standing in Argentina and the practice of sending a few children to school in England began soon after Independence. Bernardino Rivadavia, the great admirer of Bentham, went to London in 1824 not only on state business, but also to visit his two children at school there. During Rivadavia's period of office in the 1820s, Love (1942: 144) mentioned that Argentine schoolboys were being sent to Stonyhurst College, a Jesuit school in the north of England. More than a half-century later in the 1880s, Miguel Alfredo Martínez de Hoz, who became one of the greatest of the Argentine landed estate owners, was sent to another Catholic school in England at the age of eight. Twenty-five years later, two of the sons of Martínez de Hoz attended Eton College. Miguel Alfredo headed the Anglophile faction of the Argentine landed elite. His education and aristocratic tastes marked him out as an embodiment of cultural mimicry and hybridisation. He bred English thoroughbred horses on his famous stud farm at Chapadmalal (near the coastal resort of Mar del Plata) and raced them in England from a base in his luxurious mansion in Eaton Square, London. At Chapadmalal, wrote an observer in 1911, 'the visitor might easily imagine himself in England, as, from master to man, nothing but English is spoken; the hours of labour, the cooking, even the making of bread, are all on the English style' (in Lloyd, 1911: 548).

St. George's College, located in the village of Quilmes about twenty miles from Buenos Aires, provided a local model of the English public school of the type Pellegrini aspired to. Established in 1897 by Canon J. T. Stevenson,

---

16   *Standard*, 11 September 1906.

a South African-born Anglican cleric, the college grew into a close imitation of the metropolitan originals. It prepared Anglo-Argentine boys to enter local business or commerce, or, alternatively, for the senior grades of the British public schools and the leading universities. St. George's emulated the mythical cult of sports and fair play, and the pursuit of moral excellence that characterised Stevenson's models. 'In our Public Schools', he wrote, 'there is a secret which other nations envy and that secret is the training of character' (Stevenson, 1936: 2). The direct impact of St. George's locally was long confined to the small Anglo-Argentine community. It sought to erect impenetrable barriers against any risk of 'going native', and resisted the admission of non-Anglos until the 1940s.

St. Andrew's Scotch (*sic*) School founded in the 1830s became another influential seat of British education in Buenos Aires following its resurgence from previous mediocrity and apparent morbidity around 1880. The pupils at St. Andrew's stood lower in the social scale than those at St. George's, but in 1910 they emerged as the top performers in an essay competition devised by the local branch of the Empire League on the topic 'Belonging to the British Empire'.[17] As the prize-winning essays showed, the pupils were ingesting the artfully constructed and benign view of the Empire of its advertisers in Britain. Their propaganda emphasised the Empire's openness and inclusiveness, and its devotion to liberty and representative government. In Buenos Aires, the term 'imperialist' developed meanings akin to 'democratic' and 'representative', as a debate illustrated among members of the British community in Buenos Aires on how to commemorate Queen Victoria's Diamond Jubilee in 1897. At the time, Canon Stevenson made a pitch for all the funds collected for the Jubilee to be given to him in order to establish St. George's College, but the Presbyterians and the Catholics demurred because his plan favoured the Anglicans alone. The non-Anglicans wanted the money to go towards a charity home for needy sailors. They described their project as 'imperialist' meaning that it would benefit men of every persuasion as opposed to the 'sectarian' proposal sponsored by Stevenson.[18]

St. George's and St. Andrew's represented small pools of imperialist sentiment in Buenos Aires, but remained bastions of ethnic exclusiveness looking inward into the local British community alone and not outward into the population at large. A third and more successful model for imperialist proselytising was the Buenos Aires English High School (BAEHS) founded in 1883 by Alexander Watson Hutton. Raised in Glasgow, educated at the

---

17   St. Andrew's Scotch School, *Logbook 1894–1924*, entry for 15 May 1909.
18   *Standard*, 13 April 1897.

University of Edinburgh (and originally contracted to teach at St. Andrew's Scotch School), Hutton embodied a brand of imperialism, perhaps typically lowland Scottish, that became populist and politically progressive. He paraded his imperialist sentiments by taking part in every imperialist commemoration held in Buenos Aires from the early 1880s on. In 1907, for instance, he stood out for establishing a local branch of the Empire League, although when it was formed he was soon accusing its leaders, who were appointed by the British Legation, for their inactivity. They had been far too slow to react to a visit to Buenos Aires by Robert Baden-Powell, the hero of the siege of Ladysmith. 'A representative body should have been at the boat', Hutton complained. 'The entertainment of one of Britain's greatest heroes was left to Argentines.[19] Hutton's progressive side became visible in one of many instances in the early 1890s when he objected to the exclusion of women from membership of the English Literary Society, then the principal British ethnic association in Buenos Aires. In 1907, Hutton founded a women's section of the Empire League.

In sharp contrast to Stevenson, Hutton was prepared to promulgate British, and thus imperialist, values among the Argentine middle class. He set up the BAEHS as a coeducational and bilingual institution, although probably not for reasons of principle but because he had to find a niche in the highly competitive market for English education. In its multiethnic guise, Hutton's school, unlike St. George's or St. Andrew's, became an institutional agency of cultural penetration and interchange between the British and Argentine populations. Already by the late 1890s, as the *Standard* of Buenos Aires reported, the BAEHS had educated a large pool of Argentines and Anglo-Argentines, women and men alike:

> Scores, nay hundreds of ladies, now comfortably settled in life, hundreds of gentlemen now independent or holding responsible positions in some of our leading commercial institutions and banks ... Many foreign and native families make use of the opportunity to let their children enjoy the benefits of a thorough English education and the EHS has done much to bridge over the chasm, which all too often separates people of different nationality.[20]

Hutton saw no contradiction between supporting imperialism and loyalty to Argentina. Addressing his old boys in 1910, he declared that 'he had done everything in his power to mould them both physically and mentally

---

19   *Standard*, 27 August 1909.
20   *Standard*, 26 November 1901. [www document]. http://www.baehs.com.ar. [accessed 22 January 2008]

fit to take their places as leading citizens of this great Republic'.[21] Long after his retirement in 1929, his former pupils honoured him with a great banquet, an event that illustrated the way Hutton bestrode and integrated two cultures. Speeches in Spanish and English flowed one after the other without distinction at the gathering. The banquet honoured the Argentine men who had ascended to community leadership in Buenos Aires and some of the Anglo-Argentine veterans who had earned medals during the First World War. The evening ended with a profusion of greetings from women Hutton had once taught. Most of the women bore English maiden names and Hispanic married names, such as Mary Kelly de Dominie and Elena Stockdale de Guerrico.[22]

Hutton built one of the first school swimming pools throughout Argentina, but won greatest renown as the founder of organised football. He promoted the game initially at the BAEHS and then among his old boys, whose long invincible team became the 'Alumni'.[23] The explosive growth of many English sports around the turn of the century illustrated the development of an affluent and leisured urban society in Buenos Aires, but it also provided the foremost example of British cultural influences seeping into *porteño* society. Men such as Hutton had made Buenos Aires 'thoroughly sportive', a local journalist noted. 'Everywhere we see that the Englishmen are the organisers, promoters, or the chief factors in the sport'.[24] Football's earlier days in Buenos Aires marked the forging of still closer links between the British and the Argentine elite, which the former encouraged to patronise the game. Martínez de Hoz himself served a stint as president of the Argentine Football Association. He declared himself happy to perform this duty, which included sponsoring a visit to Buenos Aires by Nottingham Forest Football Club, in order to keep the young from vice and gambling.[25] As occurred in so many parts of the world, English sports became the covert arm of British imperialism. Pellegrini illustrated how sport and imperialism became linked. He argued that the Argentines should practise sports like the

---

21 *Standard*, 21 April 1910.
22 *Standard*, 22 September 1929.
23 In 1909, the visiting Everton team played the English High School 'where Argentina's best footballers learnt to play the game (*Standard*, 22 June 1909). The reputation of the BAEHS 'as an educational establishment is only equalled by that of the famous Alumni team who learnt to play the game on the campus of their alma mater' (*Standard*, 16 December 1909). On British sports in Argentina, see Raffo, 2004.
24 *Standard*, 12 November 1896.
25 *Standard*, 25 June 1905.

British, because they had made Britain into 'a manly nation that everywhere gives proof of its extraordinary strength'.[26] The *Standard* echoed his view: in Britain, sports had helped to develop a 'virile race, whose energy, resolute character and spirit of fairness had enabled the creation of the British Empire and to secure the willing obedience of subject peoples in all parts of the world'.[27]

By the 1920s, the British schools totalled around 50 in Buenos Aires and 80 throughout the country; in all, they educated around 2,500 children per year. Most of the schools enrolled small numbers of children, compared with the largest such as St. Andrew's, the BAEHS and Northlands (a leading girls school established in the early 1920s), whose pupils climbed to about 200 boys and 100 girls.[28] Despite the activities of leaders such as Hutton, the schools overall remained too disparate and uncoordinated to become the agencies of a consistent or standard imperialist ideology. Many were financially weak, having to compete not only against each other for Anglo-Argentine pupils, but also against numerous European rivals, French, Italian, even at times Irish schools, for a share of the Argentine pupils with Europhile parents. The British schools contrasted with their numerous German peers, which received government subsidies and promoted an extreme and more uniform sense of ethnic solidarity known as *Deutschtum* (Herwig, 1986: 45). In 1926–1927, Ambassador Robertson made a brief effort to replicate the German model. He tried to standardise the schools while he sought to unify the British community as part of his larger mission of restoring British trade. He argued that schools, education and British 'culture' held the key to the survival of British economic interests. His attempts to reform the schools failed when the entrepreneurs who controlled them refused his calls for consolidation. The fragmentary structure persisted. The British schools taught British and imperialist values, but their governing bodies refused to bow to metropolitan supervision.

Finally, the strands of British imperialism became entangled with the way history was being written and taught in Argentina. Bartolomé Mitre (1823–1906), who served as president during the 1860s, founded the so-called liberal school of history in which all Argentine children were indoctrinated following the development of the public education system in the 1880s. Mitre's elegant and extensively documented multi-volume work, *Historia de*

---

26 *Standard*, 20 November 1897.
27 *Standard*, 12 July 1902.
28 On the schools, see F. R. G. Duckworth, 'The British Schools in Argentina. Report on Visit of Inspection May 2nd–July 13th, 1927'. Typescript copy enclosed in TNA FO 118/595.

Belgrano y de la independencia Argentina, the fruit of decades of research, included tales of heroic local resistance to the British 'invasions' of 1806–1807. Nevertheless, Mitre and many succeeding historians always presented the British in a very positive light, crediting them with stirring the *porteños* into an awareness of liberty and a desire for freedom from Spanish colonialism (Mitre, 1947 [1857]: 252–253).

The Anglophile interpretations of history grew particularly strong in the early twentieth century. In 1905, shortly before his death, Mitre embellished his earlier views of British influence by asserting that 'the name of Great Britain will figure in the story [of Argentine Independence] as the principal factor of its progress'.[29] Pellegrini authored another panegyric, which he read in public. In 'The Influence of the English People on the History and Development of Argentina', he listed the British 'contributions' to the Republic. He reaffirmed the beneficial consequences of the 'English invasions'. He congratulated the early British *estancieros* for their contributions to stockbreeding when they imported pedigree livestock. He saluted the gigantic railways and all the other constructions of British capital. He urged his countrymen to assimilate Britain's 'virtues' – an idea that led him to support the creation of British-style public schools.[30] In 1910, Joaquin V. González, a noted writer and politician, wrote a paean to King Edward VII. On his accession in 1901, wrote González, the king had abandoned his former sybaritic lifestyle:

> He entered into a halo of the most absolute silence and austerity. He spoke no more except in the language of all the great kings of England. His language echoed with the simple grandeur of hundreds of his ancestors. They had imposed a weight of traditions of unsurpassed glory and responsibility. They represented the vastest government ever known to man, at the side of which the Roman Empire was merely a poor province. In this immense machinery, which bewilders, dazzles, electrifies, and captivates one with its majestic order, the only person not seen is the artificer, the man at the wheel, [namely the king himself], whose steady and imperturbable hand wavers not one instant from its directive position.[31]

During this pinnacle era of Anglo-Argentine trade and investment, the highblown rhetoric flowed in the reverse direction from Britain towards Argentina. A banquet held in London in July 1906 attended by 264 British business leaders to honour ex-president Julio A. Roca provided an outstanding illustration. In the keynote speech, Lord Lansdowne, the former Foreign Secretary, fed the

---

29 *Standard*, 3 August 1905.
30 *Standard*, 1 December 1905.
31 Purportedly a private letter by Gonzalez, but quoted in *Standard*, 12 March 1910. I have embellished the translation to make it more intelligible.

self-esteem and the self-image of the Argentines. He declared that 'among the younger nations of the world, there is none that appeals more to our imagination or inspires us with a brighter anticipation than the Argentine Republic'. He sought to draw the Argentines still closer to Britain when he congratulated them for modelling their constitution on that of the USA, a nation he described as Great Britain's greatest offspring.[32]

The attempt to puncture this mythical edifice finally began in the 1930s, when the burgeoning nationalist movement in Argentina sought to discredit the imperialist and Anglophile discourses. In *La Argentina y el imperialismo británico: Los eslabones de una cadena, 1806–1933* (1934), Rodolfo Irazusta, a right-wing nationalist journalist, denounced the interpretations of British influence as indoctrination that aimed to construct modes of ideological domination over the Argentine governing class. He claimed that a psychic virus had become entrenched in the so-called oligarchy, which induced degrading dependence and subservience. As his main example, Irazusta cited the submissive statements of the Argentine trade delegation in London during the negotiations over the Roca–Runciman treaty in the previous year. During their stay in London, the members of the delegation affected a close personal tie with Edward, Prince of Wales that had begun during the prince's two visits to Argentina in 1925 and 1931. In 1933, the Prince's welcoming speech to the delegates – to which they had replied with appropriate obsequiousness – depicted their ties with him as emblematic of a wider, and similarly hierarchical, link between Great Britain and the Argentine Republic. The Prince illustrated his assertion with an anglicised potted version of Mitre's history: The relationship between Britain and Argentina, he declared, had arisen during the wars of Independence when the former supported the latter in the struggle with Spain. He suggested that independence could not have been won without British assistance and that the British had infused the Argentines with the commitment to liberty, which had since guided the country's development. Afterwards, for more than a century, British benevolence towards Argentina underlay the latter's progress and prosperity. The Prince suggested that Argentina could now pay back some of its moral debt by accepting the commercial concessions being sought by Britain. Meanwhile, behind the scenes, the British government reinforced the Prince's message by threatening to apply Imperial Preference against Argentina, which would mean closing the British market to Argentine meat and grains.

Irazusta attacked the Prince's bogus version of Argentine history. He stressed the way historical interpretations of the Anglo-Argentine tie were

---

32   *Standard*, 12 August 1906.

being used to reduce the Argentine Republic to subordination. The liberal school of history had thus become a tool of British empire-building. Irazusta scorned the claim that Britain had 'won' the independence of Argentina: Canning had afforded diplomatic recognition to the United Provinces of the River Plate, but that hardly made him a liberator. According to Irazusta, the Anglo-Argentine ties constructed during the Independence era represented merely the first link in the long chain ('los eslabones de una cadena') of an Anglo-Oligarchic entente that, to Argentina's detriment, had persisted until 1933. Irazusta challenged the view that the notion of liberty in Argentina derived from the British; (indeed its main European roots lay in post-Enlightenment Spain and revolutionary France). He interpreted a remark by a British official in 1933 that 'from an economic point of view, [Argentina formed] an integral part of the British Empire' as an insult – it was intended in fact to favour concessions to Argentina and to override Imperial Preference. In an expression foreshadowing the thesis of the British historians of informal empire led by Gallagher and Robinson, he proclaimed that 'free trade means British dominion and Argentine slavery' (Irazusta and Irazusta, 1934: 24–54).[33] Irazusta threw down the gauntlet to the liberal historians, the so-called *historia oficial*, and helped launch its nationalist challenger dubbed *el revisionismo histórico*. He seized upon an objectionable speech by the Prince of Wales to launch a critique of the Argentine governing class and its conception of the nation's history. He wanted a new outlook, a new language and an alternative history – a new set of discursive formations – in order to destroy British dominance and the domestic interests that supported it.[34]

Conclusion

The Anglo-Argentine connection provides only broad heuristic support for the idea of informal imperialism presented originally by Gallagher and Robinson. Britain played an all-important role in Argentina after Independence through its preponderance in commerce and investment, but it is difficult to demonstrate during the period 1810–1933 that the British infringed Argentine national sovereignty in any regular or prolonged fashion. Arguably, Argentina's only justified claims against British 'imperialism' occurred with

---

33   Julio Irazusta's contribution to the essay was a juvenile historical critique of the policies of Castlereagh and Canning.

34   Irazusta founded a new discourse that came to dominate Argentine politics. As used by Eva Perón, for example 'More abominable than the imperialists are the national oligarchies, who sell off the future contentment of the people for mere pennies' (see 'Mi mensaje', cited in *Clarín*, 19 November 2006).

the capture of the Falkland Islands in 1833 and during the shipping blockade ordered by Aberdeen of the mid-1840s. Platt's critique of Robinson and Gallagher (partly based on the work of Ferns) provided a more accurate picture of the Anglo-Argentine tie, but questionable interpretations and data impaired Platt's views too. The case for informal empire (although not, of course, for the 'imperialism of free trade') is most evident in the Roca–Runciman treaty, when the British grasped a plethora of new powers over Argentine trade and monetary and tariff policies.

Postcolonial analysis affords new insights on the way the British exercised forms of cultural power in Argentina. It allows for a multivariate approach beyond the confines of high politics and narrowly conceived economic relations. The postcolonial approach enables British influence in Argentina to be weighed and measured against that of other European nations. If 'imperialism' afflicted nineteenth-century Argentina, it was more accurately designated 'Western European' to include the French and the Italians. Regardless of their commercial and financial power, the British hardly shone forth as the 'dominant' external power except in the early 1930s. No foreign power or foreign powers collectively, however, could be said to 'control' Argentina. National sovereignty remained real and visible in multiple ways, such as in the workings of the legal system or economic policy. Brief instances in the nineteenth century, such as the early 1890s, of attempts by British interests to control economic policy were unsuccessful. Striking illustrations of local sovereignty occurred during the First and Second World Wars, when Argentina remained neutral (in the latter case until the eve of the German surrender in 1945). Overall, postcolonial approaches leave an impression of British imperialist *aspirations* in Argentina rather than of consummated imperialist hegemony. An unbalanced and asymmetrical relationship always prevailed between the two countries, but 'imperialism' (like 'liberty' as Cain observed, 2006: ix), remains an ambiguous and elusive category.

Among nineteenth-century British visitors to Argentina, some striking differences of attitude became observable between the official mind, as represented by Burton and Rumbold, and the travellers and tourists such as Hinchliff and Dixie. When measured by Every's extraordinary ethnocentricity, the imperialist gaze grew more intense in the twentieth century, but that occurred when British influence came increasingly under threat. A probing of the period 1896–1910 illustrates some of the ways in which the British, helped by local collaborators, enhanced their status. One technique lay in endorsing the liberal school of Argentine history, which incorporated pro-British myths in the narratives of national emancipation and development. On other occasions, as the citation from González's writings illustrated, the British exported the mystique of monarchy and the veneration for imperial institutions. Finally, the British schools in Buenos Aires diffused British values. Their different approaches included the elitist and ascetic model of St. George's and the polyethnic style promulgated by the BAEHS. Sport, initially led by football, became a vehicle to disseminate British concepts of leadership and personal integrity, and to promote the energy and the virtues that were said to have created and upheld the British Empire. Such were a few of the variants of British 'imperialism' at work in Argentina. They affected some segments of the elite and the upper middle class far more deeply than others, but hardly touched the population at large.

3

Commercial Christianity: The British and Foreign Bible Society's Interest in Spanish America, 1805–1830

KAREN RACINE

University of Guelph, Canada

A Bible and a newspaper in every house, a good school in every district – all studied and appreciated as they merit – are the principal support of virtue, morality, and civil liberty. (Attributed to Benjamin Franklin)

If it is true, as the saying goes, that nineteenth-century England was a nation of shopkeepers, it would follow that commercial transactions dominated interactions between people of different economic class, social status, religious creed, ethnic origin, and region of residence. It would also make sense that Britons approached citizens in the rest of the world with a transactional attitude. And, although religions cannot be considered commodities exactly, Britons were as keen to export their Christian faith abroad as they were to sell manufactured bolts of cotton and sets of porcelain china. The British and Foreign School Society undertook its operations in Spanish America much as a secular business would: it assessed its products' market potential, it gauged the receptivity of its projected client base and it targeted particular demographics to receive its advertisements. Its agent James Thomson travelled through Spanish America with a case full of translated New Testaments, always ready to make a sale and win a convert. He had a capitalist's heart, believing that objects that were purchased would be valued more than those which were donated. In many ways, early nineteenth-century Christian evangelisation assumed characteristics more commonly associated with commercial activity, its proponents adopting some of the structures and processes of commercial enterprises, and their rhetoric borrowed from the language of Adam Smith and other free market economists.

In one small corner of a much larger cultural transformation that was occurring throughout Spanish America in the early decades of the nineteenth-century, the agents of the British and Foreign Bible Society (BFBS) and their local enthusiasts joined forces to propagate a type of spiritual exercise that not only reflected early nineteenth-century democratic practices, but also indirectly sought to instill them in Spanish America. The BFBS offered Bibles and New Testaments direct to the citizenry, and encouraged the lower classes both to read the Scriptures for themselves in Spanish translation (and later in indigenous American languages as well) and to ascertain their own lessons for living a moral life. The whole undertaking reflected a spirit of individualism, optimism, entrepreneurial energy and pedagogical innovation that characterised many Spanish American patriots' vision for the future. For a short time in the 1820s, the BFBS enjoyed the patronage not just of important government officials such as Bernardino Rivadavia in Argentina, Bernardo O'Higgins in Chile, José de San Martín in Peru, Vicente Rocafuerte in Mexico and Pedro Gual in Colombia, but also of many local bishops and Catholic priests who one might have expected to be their opponents. Nevertheless, James Thomson's impolitic praise of the benefits of religious pluralism wherever he went, added to the Church's suspicion of the Bible Society's Protestant-inspired non-annotated Testaments, helped sharpen some of the deepest cleavages in early national Spanish American political life.

James Thomson's energetic dissemination of Spanish Testaments carried contradictory messages. Although his work implied that individuals of all classes, including women and indigenous people, possessed the ability to read and interpret important material without an interlocutor (something that could be extrapolated outward into dangerous political territory), his Christian message also affirmed the more traditional paternalistic authority of a sacred text and the mode of life it prescribed. Therein lay the central question for the Spanish American elites during the Independence era, and the one that linked them so closely in spirit to their British counterparts: how to educate and uplift their fellow citizens in a controlled way that would not threaten their own privileged position. One strategy, the sort of thing being held out to slaves in the British West Indies, was to create situations in which the lower classes (or, in the case of the Caribbean, the slaves) could earn their advancement through hard work, savings, and prudent behaviour. Value, it was thought, came from hard work and having to pay. Christianity, liberty, freedom, useful knowledge – everything came with a price tag attached. This chapter explores the confluence between missionary and commercial cultures in British activity in Spanish America in the first half of the nineteenth century. It brings out the oft-ignored religious component of 'informal empire'.

Contemporary anthropological studies of missionaries and missionary cultures are much influenced by the work of John and Jean Comaroff, who put forth an argument that 'quotidian practices', or the slow alteration of daily activities, and not political or military occupation, were the main inroads of acculturation. The Comaroffs described this process as 'the colonisation of the consciousness' (Comaroff and Comaroff, 1991, 1992).[1] Modern historians of the mission enterprise in the Middle East, Africa and Asia argue that, far from being the last gasps of a backward religious mentality hanging on in a secular world, the missionaries and their work were actually central to the modernising project itself. Speaking about China, Ryan Dunch described the missions as 'one element in a globalising modernity that has altered Western societies as well as non-Western ones' (Dunch, 2002: 301) and Ussama Makdisi coined the term 'evangelical modernity' to describe the fragile exchange of information, cultural practices, languages, technology and medicine that took place between missionaries and locals in Lebanon and Syria (Makdisi, 1997: 681). Andrew Porter has studied in detail the 'entanglement' of missions and empire (Porter, 2004a: 7). It is true that missionaries, perhaps more than the other branches of the imperialist project, merchants, the military and the administrative bureaucracy, worked closely and independently with colonial peoples in their daily lives and concerns, and were more affected (both positively and negatively) by the situations they encountered. The new missionary studies emphasise, quite rightly that, contrary to the blanket assertions of those who condemn a process they call cultural imperialism, in fact both the evangelisers and their audiences were affected by each other's ways and beliefs. To believe otherwise would be to reduce the local population to passive recipients who had the outside world forced upon them, rather than acknowledging that they were capable of making their own assessments about what might actually be useful to them. The philosopher Appiah makes a similar point (2006: 69–85).

Setting apart the actual goal of conversion, the major historical role of European (and later American) missionaries has been to compile dictionaries, grammars, travel accounts, descriptions of cultures and geographies, and to record the myths, fables, legends and beliefs of the people they encountered. Translations, even when flawed and partisan, are the nexus at which people start to understand (and misunderstand) each other. Yet, neither their production nor their reception is a stable enterprise; all translations are interpreted according to a particular set of needs or ontological framework. That is not to say, however, that they do not carry an original intent or have a defined value for each side. Studies of missionaries, translations and incomplete conversions among indigenous people are available for most regions of colonial Latin America, and all bear witness to a similar two-way exchange of values, daily practices and useful knowledge.

---

1   John Comaroff and Jean Comaroff's terms and ideas, as outlined in Dunch (2002: 212).

What sets apart the BFBS's activities in Spanish America in the early part of the nineteenth century, however, from nearly all other instances of the global missionary enterprise, is that its agents were Christians evangelising other Christians. Although the BFBS eventually did translate and offer New Testaments in indigenous languages such as Quechua, Aymará, Otomí and Guaraní, most of their efforts in Spanish America focused on Catholics of European ethnic origin living in an urban setting. Given the BFBS's commitment in Britain to the cultivation of a broadly inclusive, non-denominational membership (which included Catholics, Dissenters, Quakers, Evangelicals and Anglicans), and its decision to produce Bibles and New Testaments free from annotations, introductions or any authoritative interpretative apparatus – their role as propagators of a Protestant Bible in Spanish America becomes more complex.

Indeed, the BFBS agents in Spanish America were not missionaries in the standard sense of the word. Instead, they functioned more like franchisees, or capitalist entrepreneurs, who trusted that the marketplace of religious ideas would favour them once their publications were made available. In London, the BFBS founded a voluntary society with a board of directors, and took yearly subscriptions, held annual meetings, presented public accounts and clothed their entire enterprise in the language of commerce. Investments in translations would pay dividends in the form of future adherents. Spanish Americans would demonstrate the value they placed on the New Testament by buying copies rather than accepting free ones as charity. Individuals would read the book for themselves and reject the need for priestly direction. Indeed, it was less the Christian message of the Bible itself than the form the BFBS used for its dissemination that should be of interest to students of informal empire and cultural exchange. Religion and liberty were unquestionably compatible, were even mutually fortifying, and they shared the modern values associated with individualism, free choice, rationality, commerce and the marketplace. In the rest of this chapter, I provide an introduction to the workings of the BFBS, first at home and then in Spanish America, before making some tentative concluding comments on the relationship between religion and 'informal empire'.

The BFBS (also commonly known as the Bible Society) was founded in 1804, the same year that Napoleon crowned himself Emperor of France and when British patriotism began to assume a distinctly martial and middle-class character. The Bible Society was not the first organisation of its type – the Society for the Promotion of Christian Knowledge had been around since 1698 – but the establishment of the BFBS represented a new confidence and ambition on the part of its founding members. Its first president was Lord Teignmouth and members of the committee at various times included: the surgeon-editor William Blair, Zachary Macaulay,

William Wilberforce, Evan Nepean, Chancellor of the Exchequer Nicholas Vansittart and Thomas Babington. This same conglomeration of Dissenting, abolitionist, evangelical, and reformist-minded individuals was behind a host of voluntary organisations with middle-class orientations and values, including the Society for the Suppression of Vice, which was also established in 1804. These middle-class voluntary associations sought to create hard-working, self-disciplined owners of small property in a stable and legitimate political system that would leave the overall structure of power and privilege unchallenged (Morris, 1983: 115; Porter, 1985: 606). The BFBS had a simple, straightforward goal, which was to translate the Bible into as many foreign languages as possible and, through that medium, to disseminate the Holy Scriptures among foreign people abroad and poor souls at home (Cussen, 1992: 81). The emphasis was on the distribution of the Bible itself, and their editions were printed without comment, notes, religious tracts or the inclusion of the Anglican Book of Common Prayer. Although William Blair originally opposed the admission of Catholics to the BFBS, in the end, it was determined that there would be no religious test for members; all were welcome to join in the Society's common goal. Of course, issues of language, religion and political loyalty were inseparable, and many disagreements emerged around the margins of the various charities and Bible societies. For example, one subscriber threatened to resign from the Society for Promoting Christian Knowledge when its directors wanted to hold a meeting to discuss how to obstruct Catholics from forming their own group; the subscriber stated indignantly that he opposed efforts 'to convert a Religious charitable organisation into a political engine for the dissemination of causeless alarms, and for stirring up the King's peaceful subjects to animosities destructive of the tranquillity and union of the Empire'.[2] Ironically, the BFBS's agent in Spanish America, James Thomson, faced similar resistance among Hispanophile Catholics as he travelled across the continent in the 1820s.

The directors of the BFBS expressed an interest in the Spanish-speaking world almost immediately after they founded the organisation. In December 1805, William Blair announced to the Reverend William Steinkopf that the Society was about to print 2,000 copies of the New Testament in Spanish, but lamented that its text was not as elegant as an earlier edition that he had gone to much trouble to locate, the 1708 version by Sebastián Encina called *El Nuevo Testamento … Nuevamente sacado a luz, corregido y*

---

2   Dr M. Gaskin to unidentified recipient [possibly Lord Auckland], (Bartlett Building, Dropmore, n.d.), British Library, Additional Manuscripts, 34,458, ff.435–436.

previsto por Don Sebastián de la Enzina.[3] In a fit of pique, Blair scribbled on the margin of some correspondence that the newest translation was bad, faithfully rendered but obsolete and ill-adapted to the modern ear.[4] Nevertheless, Blair promised to have the proofs checked for accuracy by a Protestant Spaniard resident in London, and cautioned that 'carelessness and ignorance will corrupt the work'. Clearly, there was a booming market for Spanish Bibles in England; with BFBS sponsorship, four editions of the New Testament were published in London in 1806, 1813, 1817 and 1820, as well as a translation of William Paley's *Natural Theology.*[5]

By 1810, the Bible Society's success and rapid expansion could hardly go unnoticed. Its 1811 annual meeting, held at the Freemason's Tavern, attracted the Bishops of Durham, Salisbury, Dorwich, Cloyne and Clonfert and the general audience in attendance was estimated at 1800 persons drawn from all Christian denominations (*Morning Chronicle*, 13 May 1811). Clearly, its rapidly expanding numbers, the political implications of such an open membership policy and the Society's conscious decision not to append High Church or Anglican content or context to its editions of the Bible, were viewed as a threat by the Established Church. The BFBS's success even sparked public debates between prominent figures. For example, the Reverend Christopher Wordsworth (brother of the famous Lake Poet William Wordsworth) published two pamphlets in which he complained that by allowing Dissenters into its midst, the Bible Society was opening the door to their wider participation in public life. By allowing them to disseminate these unmediated texts, the BFBS was also indirectly undermining the Established Church and, by implication, state authority (Wordsworth, 1810). The complaints were overreaching, but their fury indicated the degree of passion aroused by the issues. Lord Teignmouth responded in a pamphlet of his own, and various other voices joined the fray, including the editors of the conservative *Quarterly Review* who reviewed the evidence and arguments of both sides, and generally saw no harm and much good coming from the BFBS activities (*Quarterly Review*, 1810; Teignmouth, 1810).

---

3 Blair to Steinkopf, 69 Great Reynolds Street, 31 December 1805, in Cambridge University Library, British and Foreign Bible Society Archives (hereafter BFBS Archives), Home Correspondence (hereafter HC).

4 Blair marginalia on a letter from Thomas Smith, Little Morefield, 31 December 1805, BFBS Archives, HC.

5 The Encina titles carried the colophons: (London: Samuel Rousseau, 1806), (Bermondsey: Diego Powell, 1814), and (P. White, 1817). The last edition emphasised that it was '*nueva edición, cuidadosamente corregida*', which is to say, 'a new, carefully-corrected edition'. Pi Sunyer (1978: 126–128).

Both sides of the debate clothed their arguments in mercantile, free-market rhetoric. For example, Wordsworth conceded that the founders of the BFBS had initially responded to a 'great demand for these Bibles' in Welsh and, after a few years of their work, 'the demand was greater than the supply' (cited in *Quarterly Review*, 1818: 70). As a result, the editors of the *Quarterly Review* invoked a *laissez-faire* approach to the dissemination enterprise: 'if there is a void in Christian knowledge not filled up by another institution, we know no law, human or divine, which prohibits an attempt to supply the defect' (*Quarterly Review*, 1818: 73). In fact, even the Anglican Reverend Wordsworth himself acknowledged that he was more appalled at the circulation of Dissenters' New Testaments at home than abroad, because the diffusion of the Bible among foreigners, no matter who exported it, offered 'good into the common-stock and treasure-house for the refreshment and relief of afflicted humanity', although he might have wished that 'the means furnished to the Bible Society had been thrown into the treasury of the other Institution' (*Quarterly Review*, 1818: 76; Wordsworth, 1818: 53). These were calculated assessments of the spiritual marketplace.

The organisation of the BFBS reflected its origins in middle-class aspirations and anxieties. *The Quarterly Review* 1818 essay included an appendix that charted how the BFBS's funds derived from their members' subscriptions, as a way to prove that the public was voting with its pocketbook for the goals, strategy and ecumenical composition of the Bible Society. In other words, the BFBS's growing riches were enough to confirm objectively that it was taking the correct tack. The more money the Society took in, the more it spent on Bibles, translation projects and shipping costs throughout the world. As its proponents observed: 'in a religious sense, it was our *riches*, but in a financial sense it is our poverty. The *greater* our "receipts" are of this kind, the *smaller* does our monied capital become. Every pound begets its corresponding loss of cash to the Society' (*Quarterly Review*, 1818: 79). A critic tried to monetise the rivalry by showing that the 'capital stock' of the BFBS represented a financial net loss to that of its Anglican counterpart, the Society for the Propagation of the Gospel in Foreign Parts, by at least £1,195 in 1809, but his apparently self-serving arguments were quickly discounted (Dealtry, 1810: 16).

Although its earliest efforts focused on Wales, Germany and India, the BFBS shared all Britons' interest in the Hispanic world in the Napoleonic era. Its interest turned to Spanish America quite soon after the first juntas arose in 1810, but did not make much concerted effort until later in the decade. Throughout the early 1810s, its most notable effort in Latin America was made in the Haitian Kingdom of Henry Christophe, formerly the French colony of Saint-Domingue. Already here one can discern a degree of entrepreneurial energy in the overseas agents of the BFBS. For example, in November 1810, its agent in Haiti reported that he had unsuccessfully sought purchasers for his translated testaments and was forced to give away three copies. Bereft of useful contacts and put off by the social conditions on the island, he informed the committee that he had left the remaining testaments with a local bookseller, M. Camille Rigail, who already had sold eleven copies at $2 each. The agent struck a deal with the entrepreneurial Haitian, whereby the latter would undertake to print handbills and advertising and for his efforts would keep 25 per cent of the sales receipts (ARBFBS, 1811: 103). Two years later, from the island of St. Thomas, the BFBS agent reported that he had received a shipment of 200 Spanish Testaments that were already gone, such was the 'real hunger and thirst after the Word of God among the Spaniards', especially those royalist refugees from Santo Domingo and the Spanish Main (ARBFBS, 1813: 439).

Perhaps not surprisingly, the BFBS unloaded its first shipments of Testaments and Bibles in those Spanish American towns that were associated with active ports, where liberal merchant communities had supported the autonomous juntas that had sprung up in the wake of King Ferdinand's captivity: Buenos Aires, Caracas and Montevideo. The Bible Society's Spanish translation was circulating in Montevideo as early as 1807. In 1810, the BFBS sent 50 Spanish New Testaments to the Spanish Main, at a cost of £5-19s-9d, a figure that represented only about 5 per cent of its total expense on Spanish language materials (ARBFBS, 1811: 181, 216). At that time, translation and dissemination in the Spanish language was receiving less attention than the Society's publishing efforts in English, French, Dutch, East Asian languages, and Bengali. Nevertheless, the first tentative connections were being made with Spanish America, usually through British merchants resident abroad. The BFBS committee was pleased to note that their books had been 'gratefully received by the Priests of that persuasion [Roman Catholic] in South America' (ARBFBS, 1811: 35). By 1812, the eighth year of its existence, the BFBS reported to its shareholders that it had circulated the Scriptures in Chile, Buenos Aires, Cartagena, Demerara, Suriname and Honduras, and congratulated themselves 'both as Christians and Britons' for promoting 'the individual, society, and national happiness' among their fellow creatures across the globe (ARBFBS, 1813: 389). Once again, the Society's activities were cast explicitly as a sort of spiritual investment, a charitable act that would be repaid with interest.

In the Río de la Plata region, despite the British military occupation of Buenos Aires in 1806, sentiments generally favourable to British trade and innovations prevailed. There was a large British expatriate community who took on the informal role of distributors for the BFBS testaments, further blurring the line between commerce and Christian evangelisation. All the foreign products on offer represented a way to join oneself to modernity by embracing new material and spiritual connections to a larger, cosmopolitan transatlantic culture. A few years later, a local correspondent named Mr A. Greaves sent the committee an evaluation of the inhabitants of La Plata and their want of Scriptures, a sort of market analysis done for businesses to determine their prospects and potential. Writing in 1812, he judged that 'no people calling themselves Christians lie under a deeper religious gloom than the inhabitants of La Plata' – they know of the Gospels because they have been told of them, and received sermons from them, but 'not because the Gospel itself has been allowed to preach to them'.[6] To make matters worse, the only texts even potentially available to them were useless because they were in Latin or expensive editions far beyond the reach of the common citizen. In 1812, the BFBS sent only £18-9s-7d worth of material to Buenos Aires, 100 Spanish Testaments, 25 Portuguese ones, and 31 English texts (ARBFBS, 1812: 347).

Greaves clearly perceived a connection between the dissemination of the BFBS texts, and the twin political goals of expanding liberty and literacy among working classes, and of opening the region to British economic and cultural influence. He noted that one of the first things that the Bishop of Buenos Aires did after the British evacuated the port, was to have his staff fan out and confiscate all the BFBS testaments that were in the hands of the common folk, 'under the severest ecclesiastical penalties'. In fact, Greaves reported, there was a new breeze blowing in Buenos Aires, and men of modern minds (including American-born clergy) were aware that Catholics and Protestants could both revere the Holy Scriptures and move past their doctrinal differences towards cooperation for better material and spiritual conditions for all. Greaves then listed a series of modernising efforts undertaken by the government of Buenos Aires, including: the opening of a public library, the abolition of the Inquisition, the removal of restrictions on books, and the encouragement of foreign miners to immigrate and help build local industry (ARBFBS, 1814: 128). In all these ways, he considered that the citizens of Buenos Aires were attempting to throw off the shackles of the past and turn to a new freedom of individual enterprise and liberty. It was not entirely true, of course, but it was what he wanted to see, and it was calculated to gain further financial support from the BFBS office back in London.

The violent decade of the 1810s in Spanish America was not conducive to itinerant book selling missionary work, or to proselytising of any kind. For this reason, there were no recorded shipments from the BFBS to Spanish America in 1813 or 1814. This is in marked contrast to its success elsewhere in the world. By 1816, the Society announced that it had already circulated

---

6   'State of the Inhabitants of La Plata in South America, as it respects their want of the Scriptures, and disposition to receive them. From a correspondent lately returned from Buenos Ayres', St Paul's Church-yard, 18 December 1813', in ARBFBS, 1814: 125.

an astounding 1,557,973 copies in several languages, but a meagre proportion of those were destined for the Americas (ARBFBS, 1816: 65). As the Napoleonic wars drew to a close in 1814–1815, and King Ferdinand VII returned to power in Spain vowing to pacify the dissident provinces of America, however, Britons from all socio-economic classes, religious orientation and political conviction took up the cause of Spanish American liberty. William Walton, one of the agents who was then recruiting soldiers for the Venezuelan forces in London, had anticipated an eventual conservative counterattack from the Spanish Monarchy, its Catholic Church establishment, and the Vatican, warning in 1810 that any attempt on the part of the Bible Society to introduce translated Testaments among the American Spaniards would result in serious injuries (Walton, 1810: II, 152). Walton's warnings were prescient; the reaction came on 29 June 1817, when Pope Pius VII issued a bull condemning the activities of Bible Societies, calling them a 'pestilence' and a crafty device 'by which the very foundations of religion are undermined'.[7]

After that point, energised by its royalist competition, the BFBS activities in Spanish America rapidly picked up pace. In 1816, they sent 100 New Testaments to the Spanish Main (at a cost of £11-5s-0d) and 26 Bibles and 80 Testaments to Buenos Aires (£21-0s-4d) (ARBFBS, 1817: 336). Others had been consigned to Brazil and Port-au-Prince in Haiti. The next year, additional books were sent to Honduras and Demerara. In 1819, 1,500 Spanish and Portuguese Testaments were sent to America (at a cost of £169-11s-2d) and 800 more in 1820 (£126-5s-0d). In 1821, distribution expanded to Santo Domingo, Brazil, Argentina and Chile. In 1822, it sent 1,812 Bibles and 2,636 New Testaments (£1,127-6s-8d), moving South America into the top ranks of the Society's markets for the first time (ARBFBS, 1822: 95). There was, in fact, a broader interest in the Spanish American book market developing in London in the 1820s. As if to blur the lines between commerce and Christianity even further, Rudolf Ackermann, the preferred publisher for BFBS editions, was also the major producer and exporter of other textbooks, journals and forget-me-nots for a Spanish American audience in the 1820s (see Roldán Vera, 2001, 2003).

In London, the growth of an active community of intelligent and learned Spanish American exiles provided the BFBS with willing sources of valuable information and linguistic ability right on the doorstep. One of their most significant undertakings was the completion of a new version of Padre Felipe Scio's translation of the New Testament in 1817, which was specifically intended for Spanish America and completed under the careful guidance of the exiled Venezuelan scholar-secretary Andrés Bello.[8] Only one of thirteen

---

7   *The Complete Pocketbook for 1817.* Found at the West Yorkshire Archive Service, George Canning papers, as his almanac and yearly calendar.
8   José María Fagoaga to Andrés Bello, London (31 July 1816), in Bello (1984: 75).

major translation projects that year, the BFBS printed 5,000 copies of the Spanish American edition of Scío's New Testament (ARBFBS, 1820: xciv).[9] The work itself was a shared intellectual project based on a commitment to high-quality scholarship, Christian devotion and the preservation of Spanish culture in America. Bello had been recommended to William Blair by the eccentric Mexican liberal José María Fagoaga, who had bumped into Blair at the British Museum on a sunny summer day and discovered that the BFBS was searching for a qualified translator. Bello also benefitted from the recommendation and support of his equally religious friend, the Reverend Joseph Maria Blanco White, an exiled Spanish liberal who converted to Anglicanism upon arrival in England, and who was constantly searching for opportunities for his perpetually broke friend Bello to gain some paid work (Murphy, 1989: 224n; also Hamilton Thom, 1845; Moreno Alonso, 1998; Pons, 2006). The Scío New Testament was significant, since it was a known quantity that was approved by ecclesiastical authorities in Spanish America. Bello worked hard to produce a faithful, straightforward, useable modern translation of the standard work for the benefit of his fellow citizens back home.

The Bible Society made a decisive advance in its efforts to disseminate the Testament among Catholic Spanish Americans in 1818, when it commissioned its first dedicated agent to travel to the region and work directly on its behalf. They chose James Thomson, a Scottish doctor of divinity, who would exercise the dual role as agent of the BFBS, and its sister organisation the British and Foreign School Society (which advocated for the Lancasterian system of mutual education at home and abroad, and which often used the BFBS Testaments as its pupils' textbooks).[10] James Thomson was an indefatigable proponent of the Bible's role as a personal guide to living a moral life. He was convinced that the best way to spread the good word was by selling the BFBS's Testaments, because they would be valued more if their owners had spent money on them. He also consciously focused his efforts on the dissemination of his Bibles among young children, believing them to possess more open minds than their parents and therefore offering a better chance for a successful investment of his time and energy. Wherever

---

9   The Society noted that it had sponsored Scriptures in 120 languages to date, including Delaware and Mohawk.

10   Personally invited by Simón Bolívar, Lancaster went to Venezuela to oversee schools based on his system of mutual education. See Vaughan (1987). The BFSS, like the BFBS, faced opposition from the Established Church for its refusal to use religious tests for entrance and its decision to propagate a generic, ecumenical form of Christianity instead of using traditional Anglican theology and texts. The resulting controversy between Andrew Bell and Joseph Lancaster, and their competing school systems, mirrored Christopher Wordsworth's attack on the BFBS. See Lancaster (1833).

he went, from Buenos Aires to Veracruz, he consistently sought local merchants and highly placed political patrons, thus making good use of his savvy marketing skills.

Thomson undertook a rough, three-month passage across the Atlantic and arrived in Buenos Aires on 6 October 1818 and he remained in that region for three tumultuous years. Although Thomson reported back to the BFBS that he had not met with as much initial enthusiasm as he might have liked from Supreme Director Juan Martín de Pueyrredón, he nevertheless sought out friendly support among members of the British merchant community and other sympathetic government officials. In fact, in Buenos Aires, he had more success establishing the Lancasterian school system with the support of Bernardino Rivadavia and Father Bartolomé Muñoz (Thomson, 1827). Rivadavia, in particular, spent several months in London and had a Spanish edition of Paley's *Natural Theology* in his personal library, so he was personally attracted to issues of religious education and state-building (Gallardo, 1962: 165). With high-level government support and funds from general public subscriptions, Thomson managed to found eight schools in Buenos Aires, including one for girls, and by the early 1820s made the extraordinary claim of having a network of over 100 schools of mutual education operating throughout the region, with a total of 5,000 pupils enrolled (Browning, 1921: 69). He also met and cultivated a friendship with the exiled Chilean journalist-priest (and future director of Chile's National Library) Camilo Henríquez, who quickly became an enthusiastic supporter. Thomson then travelled to Mendoza, San Juan and to Montevideo, working on behalf of both the BFSS and the BFBS. A small auxiliary Bible Society was formed in Argentina, which periodically sent small remittances back to the head office in London, some money coming from donations, but the majority coming from the sale of Bibles and Testaments (ARBFBS, 1823: lxvi).[11]

In 1821, Thomson signed a contract with the Chilean envoy Miguel Zañartu to go across the Andes and undertake a similar mission there. According to the terms of the contract, Thomson would receive 100 pesos per month for one year (Amunátegui, 1895: 67, 73). Upon arrival in Chile, he noted a great difference. He was now received by the highest officials, and quickly received official letters directing citizens in Valparaiso and Coquimbo to give him their full support in opening schools of mutual education. He faced stiff opposition from ecclesiastical authorities, however, and neither his Lancasterian schools nor his plan to attract Protestant agriculturalist immigrants and miners amounted to much in the end. Thomson's time in Chile was

---

11   ARBFBS (1825: 50) indicated that a total of £103-10s-8d had been remitted to date. In 1824, local booksellers reported a brisk trade in BFBS merchandise. After 1826, however, the Auxiliary Society seems to have ceased existence.

significant, though, because there his energies started to turn away from his educational mission and focus more directly on his Bible Society mandate. In a letter back to the BFBS, dated 12 October 1821, one can discern a significant shift in Thomson's personal interests as he breathlessly recounted his successful catechisation of a Patagonian chief called Cualli Piachepolon. He had made a sale, and he was hooked.

Domingo Amunátegui, a sceptical Chilean critic of Thomson's mission, depicted the BFBS agent as nothing more than religious huckster, who claimed to be spreading the word of God, but who really just wanted to sell the sacred Scriptures (Amunátegui, 1895: 53). He implied that Thomson kept hidden his ultimate desire to convert Spanish Americans to Protestantism, in effect selling them a false bill of goods, by downplaying the content and context of his Testaments, and by focusing his efforts on unsuspecting and defenceless children. Indeed, there was a very bitter debate going on during his time in Chile about the advisability of introducing other religious sects and constitutionally sanctioning the right to religious freedom. Amunátegui characterised Thomson as a 'Protestant missionary' and an 'infidel' whose secret plan to alter the religious balance in the country alarmed his Catholic, patriotic supporters once they caught on to his nefarious intentions (Amunátegui, 1895: 86, 128). Thomson's brand of commercial Christianity is set out nicely in the aforementioned 8 October 1821 letter where he informed his BFBS superiors that 'in a few years from now, South America will have contracted great debts with our Society, but they will repay all your beneficences with the products of their mines'.[12] Commerce and religion were entangled in Thomson's mind. And at the same moment Antonio José de Irisarri, the Chilean agent in London and a partisan of the BFBS, was involved in similarly interlinked activities. He contracted a (disastrous) financial loan, and secured the services of a teacher of mutual education named Anthony Eaton. Irisarri and Thomson both saw education, commerce and Christianity as three pillars of their transatlantic relationships (Irisarri, 1833; see also Dawson, 1990). Others were less sympathetic to the project. Amunátegui scornfully dismissed Thomson as one who 'possessed all the gentility of a merchant' and who liked to identify himself as coming from 'the land of Adam Smith' (Amunátegui, 1895: 132, 141). In 1822, Thomson sold 146 New Testaments in Valparaiso, Coquimbo and Huasco, and remitted £19-6s-0d back to the Society's treasury in London.

Back in London, the BFBS continued to make serious investments in its Spanish American activities. In 1822, it commissioned a comprehensive

---

12   Thomson to BFBS, quoted in Amunátegui (1895: 132). Apparently, the copper-miners were particularly anxious to acquire religious instruction from the BFBS texts, see ARBFBS (1823: lxvii).

survey of the nature and quality of all previous (competing) major editions of Biblical texts available in the Spanish language. The work identified a surprisingly small number of editions, namely: the Pentateuch (1459), Pinel's *Biblia* (Old Testament, Jewish version, 1553), *El Testamento Nuevo en Romance Castellano* (1569), Cassiod de Reyna's *La Biblia* (1569), Ejusd's *El Testamento Nuevo* (1596), Cipriano de Valera's *La Biblia* (1602), Ejusd's *El Nuevo Testamento* (1625), *La Biblia* (Old Testament, Jewish version, 1646), *El Testamento Antiguo* (1661), the Pentateuch (1695), Encina's version of Cassiod de Reyna's *El Testamento Nuevo* (1708), the Pentateuch (Jewish version, 1718), *La Biblia* in 2 vols. (Spanish-Hebrew, 1762), Scío's *la Biblia* (1794), Encina's *Gospel of St Matthew* and *El Testamento Nuevo* (London, 1808), their own 1817 version of Scio's New Testament, and editions of Ejusd that came out in London in 1820 and 1821 (ARBFBS, 1822: 132–133). The obvious conclusion to be drawn from this list was that the pace of publishing interest had picked up as the centuries progressed, that there were few competing editions available in the Spanish-speaking market and that therefore there must be a massive pent-up demand in Spanish America for the BFBS's texts. That same year, an unnamed correspondent reported that all 250 Bibles sent over in the packet boat *George* had been sold and otherwise distributed in Caracas to meet the 'very considerable demand' of young and old, women and men, priests and lay people (ARBFBS, 1824: 119–120). Spanish government officials based in Spain, London and throughout the Americas had observed the growth of the Bible Society's activities with some alarm. Writing from Aranjuez, Diego Clemencín informed the Spanish Secretary of State that he was requesting their Ambassador in London to procure the Bible and Missionary Societies's statutes to see if their ultimate goals could be ascertained.[13] Acting with all speed and attention due to such a grave matter, Luis de Onís, the secretary of Spain's Embassy in London, dutifully acquired not just the statutes, but also the most recent annual reports, and sent translations through Bilbao, the most economical route.[14]

From Chile, the missionary Thomson moved northward to Peru, following the route taken by his military compatriot Lord Cochrane, who was in charge of creating a Chilean navy. He arrived in Lima and met José de San Martín, who greeted him with a warm embrace, and affirmed their shared belief that without education, there could be no society. Perhaps carried away by his own enthusiasm, Thomson reported back to London on 9 November 1822 that the prestige of the Roman Catholic Church was

---

13 Clemencín to Secretary of State, 22 May 1822, Aranjuez, Archivo General de Indias, Seville (hereafter AGI), Estado 86B, n.46 (1).
14 Onís to Clemencín, 23 July 1822, London, AGI, Estado, 86B, n.46 (2).

diminishing visibly each day. He passed on a story about a Peruvian priest who had become frightened and had burned his BFBS edition of the Scío New Testaments when he noticed that it had a small typographical error that caused it to differ from the officially sanctioned colonial Spanish version (Amunátegui, 1895: 236). Evidently, the BFBS editions circulated widely among political and learned circles in Lima; Thomson noted that at one session of Congress that he attended in December 1822, when the issue of religious tolerance and the definition of an official state religion was being debated, many members carried and quoted from BFBS Testaments as they made their arguments. In the end, Thomson regretted to report, the Congress decided to declare Peru's only constitutionally permitted religion to be officially Catholic, Apostolic and Roman.

In 1823, Thomson returned his accounts of the sale of Bibles and Testaments at Lima, and presented the Society with a bill for £299-1s-9d. He held high hopes that Peruvians who had bought or received the material would admire their British patrons and collaborate with them 'in advancing the knowledge of the word of God' (ARBFBS, 1824: 118–119). Even more pleasingly for the BFBS, who hoped to instil an individualistic, energetic work ethic among people they had assumed were left in a torpor under the Spanish monarchy's heavy hand, Thomson had made the acquaintance of a local militiaman who was undertaking a translation of the New Testament into Quechua, the imperial language of the Incas. Thomson noted that, while it was always better to give than to receive, local resources did not permit the work to be done without external support, although he was confident that '[t]he desire for purchasing the Scriptures here far exceeds any thing I have met with in other parts of South America'. He had committed the BFBS to pay for the printing of 1,000 copies when the translation was finished, and intended to circulate it widely, with a corrected second edition to follow soon thereafter (ARBFBS, 1824: 119). In Lima, he reported, 500 Spanish Bibles and 500 New Testaments were sold in just two days, and he calculated that he could have sold 5,000 had that many been available. In Buenos Aires, his BFBS colleague the Reverend John Armstrong was investigating the possibility of securing local assistance to translate their works into Guaraní, 'a language extensively spoken in Paraguay'. As the BFBS and its agents fanned out over the continent, their vision of the market potential for their productions expanded as well.

Over time, James Thomson became more and more aggressive in attempting to sell his Bibles. On 24 September 1824, as he was awaiting a boat in the port of Paita to take him northward to Ecuador, he urged his fellow passengers to purchase his wares. Once the BFBS arrived in Guayaquil, he became even more innovative (or crass, if one prefers). He hit upon the idea of advertising his New Testaments by pasting up advertisements in public places, the text of which could have been hawking any other type of product. His posters promised:

> For sale in [insert city name here], the New Testament of Our Lord Jesus Christ, in a single volume, well printed, and elegantly bound, for the small sum of *ocho reales*. This sale will only last [insert number here] days. We await those who desire to acquire the sacred code of our religion and who will seize this opportunity to do so. (Advertisement reprinted in Amunátegui, 1895: 326)

Thomson's evangelisation strategy clearly drew upon commercial language to advance his goals, and by setting out the BFBS edition as an aspirational product for middle-class displays of piety and taste, he further blurred the distinction between commerce and Christianity.

He continued on to Bogotá, where he spent a short amount of time before returning to London in 1825. While in Colombia, however, he encouraged the formation of Lancasterian schools, and also joined with local notables to found the Colombian Bible Society. Again revealing the aspirational nature of the entire enterprise, the first meetings were showy affairs, held at the Santo Domingo Chapel of the University with high government officials, ecclesiastical authorities, and the town's most respectable citizens in attendance. Minister of the Exterior Pedro Gual assumed the Presidency and they raised 1,380 pesos on the first night (Amunátegui, 1895: 360; Browning, 1921: 93–94). The BFBS sent 50 Spanish Bibles and 100 New Testaments to Thomson at Bogotá, valued at £31-15s-6d. This enthusiasm did not last, however. Three years later, Joseph Brandram, the BFBS Secretary, wrote to Thomson enquiring about the Colombian Bible Society's silence and failure to remit any money despite having accepted shipment of 5,000 New Testaments.[15]

Throughout Spanish America, BFBS merchandise found its way into booksellers' shops and into the packs of rural traders. Not all the merchants were scrupulous or devoted to the sincere dissemination of the Christian message or sensitive to local conditions. For example, Theophilius Parvin, a bookseller in Buenos Aires, wrote to BFBS Assistant Secretary John Jackson in London informing him that he was able to sell Bibles weekly at $2.50 apiece, and New Testaments at 50 cents. He was actively seeking new markets in the interior, in Tucumán, Salta and Cochabamba, and was pushing for the editions to be used as cheap texts in public schools. Similarly, reporting from Chile in 1825, a local agent wrote to Jackson that the 'inhabitants are extremely poor, yet well disposed, but from their Poverty, it was utterly

---

15   ARBFBS (1828: 56); Brandram to Thomson (1827), BFBS Archives, Foreign Correspondence (out) #1, f.183. ARBFBS (1826) indicates that 10,000 New Testaments had been shipped.

impossible to exact Money in exchange for these valuable Works', so he had used his discretion to distribute them to the Bishop of Santiago, the soldiers in the garrison and various inhabitants in the city.[16]

In 1827, controversy again assailed the BFBS, partly as a result of its expanding translation activities in Spanish America and partly because of the publicity generated by the publication of Thomson's narrative. On the surface, its rivals' critiques centred on the accuracy of the Society's public accounts of its receipt books, with the Edinburgh Bible Society calling into question the BFBS's 'integrity, good faith, and [the] discretion, with which its affairs have been administered' (*Quarterly Review*, 1827: 2). In fact, their horror had been aroused by the decision of the Society to include the Apocrypha along with the standard Church-sanctioned books, without any comment or distinction to guide the readers. This galling act was judged by the now-conservative editors of the *Quarterly Review* (1827: 3) to be 'one of the most dangerous as well as insidious corruptions of the Church of Rome', which proved 'the intellectual and moral incapacity for the discharge of the solemn duties which these gentlemen have undertaken to perform'. The *Quarterly Review* alleged that 99 per cent of contributors would be scandalised to know that their financial contributions were supporting a stalking-horse for Popery, and as proof, the opposition pointed to the BFBS's management expenses for the year 1826, a list that included money being paid to agents in Syria, Turkey and South America, all regions with a strong cultural or historic connection to the Catholic Church.[17] In a similar fashion to exposure of business scandals, the BFBS directors and agents were charged with making sweet deals to benefit themselves; for example, some altruistic agents such as Leander Van Ess in Germany claimed to refuse salaries, but later it was revealed that he was the translator of one edition that he was selling and purportedly therefore was receiving a handsome stipend for his services. Again following a business model, the editorials charged that these financial contortions were not the business of the general public, but were indeed 'the afford of the directors and the subscribers, and it is for them to settle it between them'. In fact, after twenty years, the noble goal of setting the word of God before peasants and uninitiated foreigners seemed to have become a point of minor consideration in comparison with the swelling of the Society's own coffers, alleged the critics (*Quarterly Review*, 1827: 5–6). The controversy

---

16   [Anon] to John Jackson, 12 September 1825, St. Jago, BFBS Archives, Foreign Correspondence (in) 1826/1869.

17   H.D. Lewes, the agent in Turkey, got £300 that year, Benjamin Baker in Syria received £300, and James Thomson and the Reverend John Armstrong split £300 in South America.

even spilled over to the Spanish American book market; in Buenos Aires a local book-dealer confided to the BFBS that he was sometimes able to unload a Bible that did not yet have the Apocrypha printed in it to unsuspecting folks who had never seen a Bible before.[18]

The opposition's wrath knew no bounds, and it claimed that the newest translations, those undertaken in the mid-1820s, 'without one single exception ... have been either executed by incompetent translators, or printed without having been subjected to a proper translation' (*Quarterly Review*, 1827: 7). The Earl-Street committee (a derisive term used for the BFBS directors) had permitted the Bible to be rendered into Mohawk, Bengali, Chinese, Georgian and many other heathen tongues by native speakers who had not been properly trained in the Greek and Hebrew versions, and who did not have certified credentials. Furthermore, there was no way to check these local translations for accuracy since no one on the committee or in England possessed sufficient language abilities to do so. In other words, proponents of the Established Church's view were beginning to see the wisdom in the Catholic Church's long-standing opposition to the circulation of the Bible, believing that the evil manifested in these translations 'exposes the unlearned reader to the danger of misunderstanding the Scriptures to his own destruction' (*Quarterly Review*, 1827: 26). The care and precision made in creating the authorised English translation meant that it possessed a fidelity and divinity not to be found in the recent, more casual and careless vernacular editions. Echoing the position taken by CEOs everywhere when trouble arises, the critics exempted the 'high and exalted personages who lend their names for the purpose of patronising such establishments' because they 'seldom enjoy the leisure required for the superintendence of their affairs'. Instead, the blame fell squarely on the shoulders of the 'busy, incompetent, and interested retainers who commonly swarm about the purlieus of such associations' (*Quarterly Review*, 1827: 28).

Nevertheless, the BFBS continued to take an interest in the indigenous languages of South America as the decade drew to a close. James Thomson had donated several books to the Society's library, including grammars, sermons and catechisms in the Quechua, Moche and Araucanian languages. In 1828, a British medical doctor who was resident in Bolivia forwarded a copy of the Lord's Prayer translated into 'the Indian language spoken between Lima and Guayaquil', which he also asked to be placed in the BFBS's library. The Reverend Mr Hannah of London donated a grammar of the Quechua language that had been printed in Lima in 1754, and a Mr Salazar deposited

---

18 Theo. Parvin to John Jackson, 19 January 1825, Buenos Aires, BFBS Archives, FC (in) 1825/1893, and Robert Hudson to John Jackson, 2 January 1826, Buenos Aires, BFBS Archives, FC (in), 1826/1839.

a seventeenth-century lectionary in Nahuatl and Spanish (ARBFBS, 1828: 60).[19] The Society itself continued to sponsor translations into indigenous languages. In 1828, they undertook Arawak and Basque editions. Vicente Pazos Kanki, a native of Bolivia, had met James Thomson in a Paddington stagecoach and agreed to translate the Gospels of St Luke and St. Matthew into Aymará for £400 over two years, plus another £300 for travel expenses. Pazos Kanki only completed the first task, however, with a book titled *El Evangelio de Jesu Cristo según San Lucas en aymará y español* (J. Moyes: London, 1829).[20] In the year of its appearance, the BFBS printed 1,014 copies of Vicente Pazos Kanki's Aymará translation of the Gospel of St Luke which were eventually destined for La Paz (ARBFBS, 1830: 121). The next year, they published a Nahuatl Gospel of St Luke, translated by Mariano Paz y Sánchez, 'a priest of Santa María Chichimecatitlán'.[21]

Oddly, Mexico was the one place that the BFBS never made much effort to penetrate. It had close commercial connections with British mercantile houses, and its archaeological past had already begun to captivate the British imagination following William Bullock's wildly popular panoramas and ethnographic displays (Aguirre, 2005). James Thomson asked to be allowed to travel to Mexico in 1827 to initiate BFBS activities there, but his journey did not amount to much. He had an influential supporter in the person of Vicente Rocafuerte, an Ecuadorean who had resided in London for several years before relocating to take up a government post in Mexico, and who was a passionate proponent of religious tolerance. Rocafuerte had long provided financial support for the BFBS's activities in London, subsidised many of their translations and enjoyed close ties with the Quaker prison reformer Elizabeth Fry. He was an active proponent of religious toleration, and produced an erudite pamphlet on the subject, the *Ensayo sobre la tolerancia religiosa*, in which he praised the idea of children being able to study the Bible for themselves, as they did in England and the USA. Rocafuerte drew a clear connection between the conditions that permitted free study of the Bible and those nations that were the richest and most powerful (Rocafuerte, 1831: 19). Tellingly, in a sharply argued booklet devoted to expounding the benefits of religious tolerance, Rocafuerte also considered it relevant to include a section on savings banks, and the principle of economy and prudence that he implied would be desirable values that would follow in train with religious

---

19 Also in 1828, the Spanish liberal exile Joaquín Lorenzo Villanueva donated a manuscript translation into Catalan of the Gospel of St Matthew. BFBS Archives, Manuscript 375.

20 The book is very rare, but copies can be found at the BFBS Archives, and at the Biblioteca Nacional in Madrid. It was based on Scío's version.

21 BFBS Archives, Manuscript 376.

tolerance, as he had seen in action in England (1831: 69). Commerce and Christianity had become intermingled in his mind too.

Soon after James Thomson arrived in Mexico City in 1827, he was able to persuade the liberal thinker José María Luis Mora to become a corresponding member of the BFBS, and to donate a copy of his three-volume work on Mexican history and some pamphlets for their library in London. Mexican booksellers did remit approximately £500 in both 1828 and 1829 as the results of the sales of New Testaments, but these were small returns on shipments of 7,100 books valued at £1,651-11s-4d (ARBFBS, 1829: 54). When Thomson returned to Mexico for a second time in 1830, the eight cartons of Bibles that he brought with him were seized in the Veracruz customs house and his friend Rocafuerte was no longer able to help him. The powerful Foreign and Interior Minister Lucas Alamán, who was a strong voice for the conservation of Hispanic culture in republican Mexico, interceded to prevent the distribution of books he considered to be dangerously Protestant in content.[22] Alamán's suspicions were not entirely without merit. Although the BFBS consistently stuck to a non-political, non-dogmatic position in its public pronouncements and in its business meetings, the editorial press adopted a more partisan position. For example, in an article called 'Bible Societies', *Blackwood's Edinburgh Magazine* (Blackwood's, 1825: 633) pronounced its great joy that:

> [t]hese religious discussions ... may not draw a single Catholic to Protestantism, but they must utterly destroy the worst parts of Catholicism. They must abolish its pernicious laws, beat down its mischievous dogmas, overthrow the despotism of the priest, and give freedom and religion to the laymen.

The BFBS's expanding interest and range of activities in Spanish America in the 1810s and 1820s developed alongside British commercial domination of the region. Since the sixteenth century, England and Spain had been imperial and cultural rivals in the New World, a competition that carried religious undertones as well. In the early nineteenth century, Spain and England joined together to fight for the banner of freedom against the French despot, two monarchies united in liberty, tradition, constitutionalism and commercial interests. So, when the Spanish American colonies broke away, a whole new continent presented itself as fertile ground for British investment, trade and cultural outreach. James Thomson, John Anderson, Theophilius Parvin and the dozens of other nameless local agents who appeared in Spanish

---

22   Lucas Alamán to Cabildo de esta Sta Yglesia Metropolitana, 11 September 1830, Mexico, Archivo General de la Nacion – México, Bienes Nacionales, Vol. 406, exp.72; see also Rodríguez O (1975: 195).

America with Bibles and New Testaments in hand were quite sure that they were working for God's Empire, spreading His Word to the spiritually oppressed and the uninitiated. These commercial Christians measured their success in inventory distributed and in funds remitted back to London. They utilised their unique access to the various national Lancasterian school projects throughout Spanish America to have their own religious books adopted as mandatory texts, thereby gaining a monopoly on that market. The activities of the BFBS and its agents represented just one small episode in a much larger, and continent-wide, Spanish American debate about the structure of their post-Independence nations. The BFBS and its agents tried to persuade Spanish Americans to buy into informal empire through the medium of religion. Their Protestant, and proto-democratic, vision of one person, one Bible, coupled with the desire to create value through the marketplace, meant that they were not just disseminating religious texts, they were selling a wholesale shift in culture. There were many Spanish Americans who were anxious to buy it.

4

Britain, the Argentine and Informal Empire: Rethinking the Role of Railway Companies

COLIN M. LEWIS

London School of Economics, UK

This chapter examines the position of railways during the period of British commercial and financial dominance in the River Plate in order to reassess ongoing debates about informal empire and economic imperialism. It argues that the hegemonic status often attributed to railways in the British–Argentinian equation is misplaced, and certainly misunderstood. This misconception derives in part from a projection back into attitudes and antagonisms prevalent in the 1930s. For good or ill, by the 1930s London-registered railway companies had come to assume an emblematic status in the British–Argentinian relationship. The conjuncture was unfortunate: heightened volatility and structural change in the international economy highlighted flaws in the liberal, export-led growth model of the *belle époque* just as rail technology was reaching the end of its natural shelf-life. This combination of circumstances undermined earlier, broadly positive, contemporary evaluations of railways. Negative misconceptions, which came to the fore in the 1930s, had (and continued to have until quite recently) a pernicious impact on subsequent writing about the British–Argentinian relationship.

The chapter opens with a brief survey of the literature on economic imperialism. This is followed by a stylised account of changing attitudes to British investment in railways. The third and fourth sections explore specific events in the history of British–Argentinian railways, events and processes that may shed new light on debates about the 'imperialism' of railways. These include the nature of ownership and funding, railway policy and the railway boom of the 1880s, and conflict between 'London' companies and domestic interests in the period around 1900. The final section revisits these events in the light of new contributions to the railway historiography.

It is worth recording at the outset that the history of the British–Argentinian railway connection opened in the 1850s and closed in the 1940s. The longevity of the relationship, as much as the position of railways as a prime example of social overhead capital, allowed ample opportunity for controversy.[1]

Informal Empire, Economic Imperialism and the British–Argentinian Connexion

The debate about the 'imperialism of free trade' (Robinson and Gallagher, 1953) entered the Argentinian historiography earlier, and with greater force, than writing on many other parts of the continent. Some contributors date British financial and commercial imperialism in the Argentine from the Baring Loan of 1825, tracing a design that culminated in the 1933 unequal trade pact (Halperín Donghi, 1970: 75–76, 84–92; Alhadeff, 1985: 367–368). The emphasis on *economic* imperialism is reinforced by the bizarre episode of unsuccessful British military adventurism in the River Plate 200 years ago. Two invasions in 1806 and 1807 were repulsed by largely national forces. The defeat and expulsion of British troops, and robust responses to subsequent Anglo-French naval blockades, put paid to any formal imperial designs on the Argentine – if such there were – but did not inhibit the growth of increasingly close trading and investment relations between the Argentine and the UK. Was this relationship exploitative of the Argentine, or mutually beneficial? As Ferns argued in 1960, it is possible to make a strong case for the benefits accruing to the Argentine from the relationship with the UK.[2] Of critical importance are the dynamics of the relationship and the extent to which mutual advantage, or an exploitative arrangement that was adverse for the Argentine, changed over time. Thompson (1992: 421–422) has constructed a useful template for 'measuring' British informal imperialism in the Argentine. That is: did Britain exert indirect power over foreign policy, internal politics

---

1　Because of its special characteristics, economists distinguish between 'enabling' social overhead capital investment in such projects as transport, communications and power generation, and directly productive investment in agriculture and manufacturing. These characteristics include a particularly long gestation period (the length of time between the planning and full operation of a project) and the nature of the returns that accrue not only to the owners of enterprises but to society as a whole.

2　Amongst the British beneficiaries of the relationship, Ferns identifies the Anglo-Criollo business community, shareholders of some banks, railway companies, meat-processing plants and mercantile enterprises, and consumers, especially the 'wage working class' whose standard of living was considerably enhanced by cheap River Plate commodities. In the Argentine, Ferns specifies land-owners (including immigrants), workers (whose wages and employment prospects widened considerably) and the Argentinian state – although Ferns does not use this term (Ferns, 1960: 487–491).

and domestic economy? Did Britain obtain rents from an asymmetrical relationship; was the landed elite an independent actor, or did it serve as an intermediary of imperialism – in short, was it a collaborating elite?

There is a paradox. The period broadly addressed by the 'economic imperialism' strand in the historiography was one during which the country experienced spectacular rates of growth. Or it may be that the frustration of expectations aroused by economic performance during the era of export-led growth, the so-called *belle époque* (c. 1870–1914), after the 1920s accounts for the tenacity of the imperialism of free trade thesis: only foreign manipulation could explain why that early development trajectory was not sustained. It is widely acknowledged that income levels in the Argentine were substantially greater than in neighbouring areas around 1880 and similar to those in Western Europe and the USA (Coatsworth, 1998: 24–27; della Paolera and Taylor, 2003: 2–3). A hundred years later, while the Argentinian position had slipped against the USA, the 'growth gap' with the rest of Latin America and with Mediterranean and Latin Europe (particularly those countries that accounted for the largest proportion of emigrants to the Argentine) had widened considerably.

Table 1 shows that Argentinian per capita income was high by European and Latin American standards in 1913, and was gaining relative to those in other areas of recent settlement such as Australia and Canada. Indeed, even as late as the post-Second World War period, despite some slippage, the economic trajectory of the republic continued to shadow that of other 'new' settler countries, rather than that of neighbouring republics and 'Latin' Europe.[3]

Table 1.   GDP Per Capita (1990 International $US)

Region	1820	1870	1900	1913	1950
Latin America					
Argentine	1300	1311	2756	3797	4987
Brazil	646	713		811	1672
Mexico	759	674		1732	2365
'New Countries'					
Australia	517	3645		5715	7493
Canada	893	1695		4447	7437
USA	1257	2445	4096	5301	9561
Europe					
Italy	1117	1499		2564	3502
Spain	1063	1376		2255	2397
UK	1707	3191	4593	4921	6907

Sources: Maddison (2001: 185, 195), della Paolera and Taylor (2003: 8).

---

3   For a definition of 'new' countries, the economics of settler capitalism and comparisons between the Argentine and other new countries, see Denoon (1983), Platt and Di Tella (1985) and Sutch (2003).

During the classic age of British hegemony in the River Plate, the economic transformation of the Argentine was impressive by any standard.

The comparative growth of the country between 1880 and 1938 is startling even when account is taken of the more sluggish performance of Australia. Having exhibited particularly high rates of growth of gross domestic product (GDP) per capita in the middle decades of the nineteenth century, the Australian economy entered a long recession in the 1890s. As the record of the other countries in the set indicates, it is difficult to envisage a counterfactual that would have yielded a better result. Between 1869 and 1914, annual rates of economic growth per capita averaged 3.9 per cent (Díaz Alejandro, 1970: 3; Rapoport, 2000: 101).[4] Few economies have sustained such a high *average* rate of growth for almost two generations. If this was economic imperialism, it was hardly bad for growth.

Perhaps growth of this order accounts for the limited attention given to economic imperialism, or even the British connection, in historical writing before the 1930s. Mainstream writing addressed themes that were principally concerned with state-building, a process considered essential for 'progress', and founded on integration into the liberal capitalist order of the period. Process and progress were depicted in terms that were distinctly whiggish and triumphalist (Halperín Donghi, 1980: 829; Moreyra, 2003: 68). And the role of British capital was considered to be both instrumental and benign: 'British capital became so routine an element of administrative life that municipal and provincial governments vied with the national state for funds in the London stock exchange' (Halperín Donghi, 1993: 189). Contemporary opinion similarly regarded railways as crucial to state formation and nation-building.

Before the 1920s, there were few sustained criticisms of the liberal project of political modernisation and social progress underpinned by export-led growth. *Entreguismo* and *vendepatria* were words that would only enter the literature with force some time later (Oszlak, 1982: 148).[5] Arguably, the more articulate contemporary reservations about the liberal model were those of the 1920s that specifically questioned its economic outcomes, concerns that

---

4   Estimates of growth per capita vary considerably. Calculations by Cortés Conde for 1875–1912 cited above by Rapoport (2000: 101), namely 3.9 per cent, are substantially above estimates provided by others, for example, 2.5 per cent (Maddison, 2001: 196). Halperín Donghi (1986: 27–28) shows aggregate growth averaging 3.7 per cent per annum between 1875 and 1896, but falling by more than a third to 2.3 per cent from 1896 to 1912.

5   *Entreguismo* and *vendepatria* were terms applied to both process and to individuals or groups, that is, a betrayal of national interest by the elite, and opportunists who either failed to defend the nation or 'sold out' to foreigners.

prefigured new currents in the historical writing of the 1930s and after. Although of only limited impact at the time, a new conservative, nationalist political economy was articulated by the *Revista de economía argentina*, whose columns advanced the case for protectionism and natural industrialisation while stressing the limits of export led-growth (not least international economic volatility), regional and sectoral imbalances resulting from the liberal model, and structural constraints associated with concentrated patterns of land and 'excessive' urbanisation (Falkoff, 1981: 57–75). The questioning of liberal economics, and prevailing theories of comparative advantage, which first appeared in the pages of the *Revista* would shape late thinking about unequal exchange.

The *Revista de economía argentina* apart, most of the contemporary revisionist historiography focused largely on the political. Revisionist texts questioned both social and political transformations vaunted by earlier writing. A substantial proportion of this reinterpretation of the process of nation-building, ranging from the right to the left, addressed the pernicious consequences of the British–Argentinian relationship and, by association, export-led growth.[6] Revisionist texts, especially those produced in the 1930s focusing on the British connection, constituted some of the first contributions to the economic history literature about the Argentine, as well as to the historiography on economic imperialism. It was at this point that left-wing authors began to describe the landed oligarchy as decadent and anti-national, as conspiring with foreign capital to exploit the country and subvert an alternative political-economic model that would have yielded a more dynamic and equitable socioeconomic order (Moreyra, 2003: 81–82). Collectively, the *Revista* and the revisionist literature of the 1930s had a profound influence on later schools: structuralism, popularised after the late 1940s, and dependency, prevalent in the late 1960s and the 1970s. Whereas pre-1930s historical writing had been largely 'political' in focus, much of the new writing was concerned with the

---

6   While revisionist writing of the 1930s to the 1960s ranged from the anti-imperialist right to the nationalist left, there were several tensions. Almost all contributors agreed on the negative influence of Britain on the Argentine – from Independence until the Second World War – and extolled the Rosas regime as a defender of national interests. Beyond these themes, there was less common ground. Some applauded the catholic, conservative values of segments of the traditional landed class – who offered an authentic national project that had been undermined by a liberal internationalist commercial oligarchy. Others saw latifundistas as a check on development (Halperín Donghi, 1970: 9–24, 36–54). Key contributors of the 1930s include the brothers Irazusta, protagonists of an alternative to the liberal, internationalist project, and Scalabrini Ortiz, who took a negative view of the commercial and financial relations with the UK.

economic and the social, borrowing substantially from the social sciences. Studies that reflect the structuralist and dependency traditions include Ferrer (1967) and Dorfman (1983).

Not all the new literature of the 1960s and 1970s peddled a pessimistic assessment of the functioning of the international economic order before and after the 1930s, but much of what may be broadly described as the new historiography did. The Instituto Torcuato Di Tella was associated with a body of writing on Argentinian economic and social history that presented a more measured assessment of the period of export-led growth.[7] Nevertheless, the dominant currents of structuralism and dependency were largely negative in their portrayal of the British–Argentinian relationship, and although not directly writing from the standpoint of proponents of the economic imperialism thesis, they produced work that was in sympathy with it.

From the 1950s to the 1980s, structuralism and dependency were the dominant paradigms. A challenge – this time radical and neoliberal – to negative assessments of the *belle époque* only began to re-surface in the 1990s. Re-vindicating the welfare gains of economic internationalism, and stressing the importance of property rights for economic growth, this writing is inclined to dismiss the dependency and structuralist theses and, by implication, approaches that emphasise the 'imperialism of free trade'.[8] Firmly linked to the new institutional economics school observable elsewhere in the economic historiography of Latin America, proponents of this approach point to the high cost of economic isolation, even during the problematic 1930s, and mistaken assumptions (and policy recommendations) associated with structuralism and dependency. Applauding the saliency of contributions by Díaz Alejandro to the study of the economic history of the Argentine, this new writing also implicitly acknowledges the persuasiveness of the Ferns take on the British–Argentinian commercial and financial relationship before 1900, and has had an impact on the railway historiography – as discussed below.

---

7   The first generation of scholars associated with the Di Tella who contributed to the economic history literature include Roberto Cortés Conde, Guido Di Tella, Ezequiel Gallo, Túlio Halperín Donghi and Manuel Zymelman. Equally authoritative work about the *belle époque*, and earlier periods, that sustained the modernisationist thesis was produced by authors such as José C. Chiaramonte and Vicente Vázquez Presedo. Much of this writing was indebted to the seminal scholarship on growth economics by Carlos F. Díaz Alejandro.

8   The principal exponents of the 'new economic history' are Gerardo della Paolera and Alan M. Taylor. Together and individually they have produced a body of work that offers a persuasive new institutionalist take on Argentinian economic history. For a measured attempt to integrate neostructuralist and new institutionalist approaches see Winograd and Véganzonès (1997) and, possibly, Gerchunoff and Llach (2003).

'British' Railways and Argentinian Development: Contemporary Perceptions and the Historiography

By the 1930s, railways had come to epitomise the UK–Argentinian commercial and financial relationship. Demonstrably, they constituted a very large proportion of the total stock of British investment in the republic, and were viewed as 'London' enterprises. Yet the characterisation of railways as the prime expression of British business in the republic is flawed in several respects. As will be argued in this section, assumptions of hegemony derive from a period late in the history of the relationship, and ignore domestic managerial and financial involvement in the railways sector during formative phases and an enduring 'Buenos Aires' presence in some companies until around 1900. In addition, these characterisations are based on assessments of corporate consolidation that underestimate the degree of rivalry among foreign firms, and largely ignore the supervisory capacity of the state.

Conventional images of a dual or double primacy – railways as the principal expression of corporate Britain and of a sector dominated by London companies – took concrete form only in the inter-war period. After the 1920s, broadly favourable assessments of the 'railway connection' were overwhelmed by increasingly sophisticated radical and nationalist criticisms (flagged in the preceding section). Until the 1920s, fairly positive contemporary opinions about the British companies were sustained by a revival of railway construction, by investment in technical upgrading, and by largely successful corporate propaganda that emphasised a community of interest between investors and consumers, and between the companies and rail workers. Discordant, negative assessments of the London–Buenos Aires axis gained currency only around the time of the negotiation of the Roca–Runciman Pact in 1933. These presented British companies as technically and managerially bankrupt mechanisms of exploitation, and the landed oligarchy as the supine agent of voracious foreign capitalists.[9] It was at this point that the image of the 'English octopus' (*el pulpo inglés*) took root. The image and the term were persuasive. Cartoons depicted a greedy consortium of British railways, centred on Buenos Aires with tentacles spreading across the country, in control of natural resources and national assets, tenaciously constricting and suffocating Argentinian development. The double-hegemony misconception lends weight to this simple but effective depiction of British exploitation.

---

9   For a pioneering example of contemporary radical revisionism, see Irazusta (1934 and 1963) and Irazusta and Irazusta (1934). For an informative, critical contemporary British diplomatic assessment, see J.V. Perowne, Foreign Office, F.O. Minute on British Presence in the Argentine, 11 September 1939, TNA FO 371/22765: A6503/6503/51.

This is not to say that, by the early twentieth century, railways were not a prominent feature of the British–Argentinian connection. They were. Around 1910, most Argentinians experienced almost daily contact with 'London' enterprises. In the pampas, though not necessarily in such outlying regions as the north-west, consumers of rail services shipped produce – or travelled – on lines that often displayed English names. Telegrams were sent and received at telegraph offices located at railway stations built in the 'English' style. In a number of up-country townships, centrally located railway depots (often carrying name boards such as 'City Bell', 'Durham', 'James Carik', 'Henderson', 'Keen', 'Lincoln' or 'Roberts') appeared to be more permanent architectural features of the urban landscape than the police *comisaría* (if one existed) or chapel. By the 1920s, commuters in greater Buenos Aires, Córdoba, Rosario and Bahía Blanca similarly travelled on 'English' passenger trains. However, daily contact did not necessarily imply antagonism. Until the inexorable deterioration that occurred in the 1930s, relations between providers and consumers of transport services were punctuated by moments of accommodation and tolerance – as well as antagonism about the price and quality of services. Indeed, as late as 1929, when such a populist figure as President Hipólito Yrigoyen (the archetypical representative of urban professional and some working-class groups) applauded the contributions made by London railways to national progress, and expressed a strong preference for a continued British (as opposed to US) presence in the sector, prospects still appeared to be bright.[10]

Allowing for the crabbed international economic and domestic political environments of the 1930s, why did such a negative characterisation of the railways, and particularly of the companies as mechanisms of British imperialism, gain ground so rapidly? Part of the answer may lie in the nature of social overhead investment and technology. Railways, like utilities, are 'natural' monopolies. They entail substantial start-up costs, which serve as a barrier to entry, and are 'lumpy' enterprises that involve a complex nexus of elements and function effectively only when complete. Railway technology is also a general purpose, enabling technology with wide scope for improvement and application, and a considerable cumulative growth impact on other sectors. This can generate distributional conflict: are owners or users of the new technology best able to capture the resulting efficiency gains?

---

10 A surge of US investment in the Argentine around 1928–1929, including the purchase of shares in several London-registered railways and utilities, occasioned unease in official circles. See Sir Malcolm Roberts, British Ambassador, Buenos Aires, to Sir Austen Chamberlain, Secretary of State, 16 May 1929, TNA FO 371/13460:A3329/52/2.

And, in common with all general purpose technologies, rail technology has a 'natural' shelf-life: as its scope is exhausted, the growth impact fades (Lipsey, Bekar and Carlaw, 1998: 15–54; Crafts, 2003). And, innovative technologies invariably triggered expectations and speculation: expectations that tended to be realised in the medium term, rather than the short, and speculation that offered opportunities for windfall gains – and losses, and disturbed financial markets.

As lumpy 'natural' monopolies, employing an expensive (and often rapidly changing) technology with wide application and a likely impact on growth, it is unsurprising that railways were franchised and regulated by the state, in the Argentine as elsewhere. Government determined the routes, chose the location of stations, set operating schedules and tariffs, and often policed construction costs, particularly when underwriting profit guarantees. Given the scale of investment and the length of time needed to bring projects to fruition, from the perspective of the companies, legislative authorisation was essential to condition the market and to promote investor confidence. For government, licensing signalled a recognition of the conflict between implicit monopoly and opportunities for rent-seeking, on the one hand, and public service functions associated with social overhead projects, on the other. And there was public safety to consider too. In these respect, the railway business was always more political than many other forms of commercial and financial activity. Consequently, suppliers of rail services were invariably subject to the laws of politics as well as to the rules of the market.

Franchising and regulation meant that price was fixed (or administered) rather than being determined by input costs or the mechanics of competition. By the turn of the century, when the principle of state supervision had become firmly entrenched, 'excessive' regulation became a source of friction in corporate–state relations. Companies were irked by the obligation to secure official sanction for what they regarded as minor operational changes, issues that should be decided by commercial considerations or management. They demanded greater freedom. Administrators, on the other hand, wished to tighten regulatory regimes, not least as ideas about the role of the state and the shape of the political universe changed. Moreover, consumers invariably had recourse to non-market forms of redress if aggrieved over the price or quality of service. In addition, railways were amongst the earliest large employers of urban labour – with a disproportionately large component of skilled workers, another feature that distinguished them from enterprises operating in other sectors. All of these factors had an impact on profits and on relations with government and society, particularly during conjunctures such as the 1930s when the innovative thrust of rail technology was fading and economics and politics became less predictable.

The 'imperialism of free trade' literature ignores – or under-plays – these operational and technical aspects of railways, while accepting uncritically the monopoly nature of public services, as will be discussed below. There is also a tendency to down-play the regulatory capacity of the state (when not depicting government as the slave of foreign interests) and to vaunt the predatory competence of British firms while undervaluing the organisational capacity of other actors in the company–state–consumer (and business–labour) equation. Arguably, local interests were both instrumental and dominant in the early history of Argentinian railways, as illustrated by the franchising of concessions and the funding of construction.

'Anglo-Criollo' or British? Agents of National Development or Vectors of Imperialism?

Most of the original railways in the Argentine emerged from concessions granted to merchants in the 1850s. Although concessions were frequently amended as circumstances changed and different groups competed for ascendancy, the mercantile connection was invariably sustained. In the early days, London finance was present but never hegemonic. Overseas interests at this stage were largely technical and subordinate, represented mainly by contractors, rarely by concessionaires. Local involvement was also signalled by the involvement of the state. This was manifest in the political contacts of franchisees and various forms of support ranging from tax waivers to capital injections. With expansion during the final third of the nineteenth century, two tendencies may be discerned: local financial participation, though not necessarily managerial control, was diluted because of a surge in foreign investment; and state involvement grew, often financed through external borrowing. Perhaps the trends were both functional and complementary. There is clear evidence that mercantile capital cast for itself a transient but not necessarily speculative role in promoting railways. Merchants envisaged their initial investments as promotional and temporary (Reber, 1979: 134–135). They sought to retain control while at the same time encouraging external funding. Businesses that proved to be moderately profitable were taken to foreign money markets directly, whilst those that were not passed to the state. Yet even when companies were registered overseas, local luminaries were recruited onto Buenos Aires boards and River Plate interests continued to be represented by directorships in London. Over time, mechanisms of official support became more formal. Profit guarantees and tax concessions were substituted for ad hoc forms of aid such as loans, subventions and land grants. The formalisation of state support undoubtedly made it easier for enterprises to raise capital in overseas markets, while at the same time enhancing potential for official monitoring and the transfer of managerial and technical skills to the government rail bureaucracy.

The 'local' character of early 'London' companies is illustrated by the diffuse interest of such merchants and landowners as John Fair, Daniel Gowland, Manuel Guerrico, Enrique Harratt, Felipe and Jaime Llavallol and David Robertson in several companies. The state – in the shape of the province of Buenos Aires and the federal government – was similarly active across the sector. Government, as much as private investors, tended to engage with several enterprises rather than sponsor a single firm. Hence, many early enterprises are better described as 'Anglo-Criollo' rather than as 'British' or 'national', a feature that much nationalist and imperialism scholarship has been reluctant to acknowledge. For example, before it was transferred to the province of Buenos Aires, the list of concessionaires and shareholders of the Ferrocarril Oeste reads like a virtual who's who of the Buenos Aires merchant community (Reber, 1979: 124–127; Lewis, 1983: 18–21; López, 1991: 37).[11] Although registered in London, the Buenos Ayres Great Southern Railway Company was no less 'Anglo-Criollo', promoted by prominent British–Argentinian and Argentinian merchants, *estancieros* and public figures (Mulhall and Mulhall, 1863: I, 106; Fair, 1899).[12] Another company floated in London, the Central Argentine Railway Company Limited, was somewhat less 'local' in the composition of its shareholders and Board of Directors, although sometime president General Urquiza took a large shareholding in the company, as did the federal government, and the associated Central Argentine Land Company Limited seems to have operated largely for the benefit of resident 'British' landowners (Reber, 1979: 126; López, 1994: 69).[13] A notable – though hardly surprising – feature of

---

11   The original documents are located at Archivo General del la Nación (hereafter AGN) 1852/10/28/2/4/Doc.1723b; 1853/10/28/3/7/3/Doc.3919. Amongst the concessionaires was Daniel Gowland, president of the British Chamber of Commerce.

12   The list of names includes Armstrong, Drabble, Elortando, Fair, Green, Lezama, Lezica, Lumb and Parish. John Fair is a typical case – shareholder, concessionaire, local representative of the BAGS in Buenos Aires and sometime Buenos Aires government agent in the UK. Frank Parish similarly acted in an official and business capacity: long-term resident and British Consul in Buenos Aires, there is evidence that the local merchant community and *porteño* officials were anxious to secure his commitment to the enterprise – see, Edward Thornton, British Minister to the Argentinian Federal Government (Paraná), to Earl Russell, Secretary of State, 19 August 1862, TNA FO 6/240: 120–121, William Doria, Charge d'Affaires, Buenos Aires, 23 August 1862, TNA FO 6/238: 37.

13   The list of land company beneficiaries includes names associated with the FC Oeste and BAGS.

almost all railways established in the 1850s and 1860s is the relatively circumscribed group of individuals involved. Key merchants and *estancieros* were connected with virtually all starter enterprises – as concessionaires, shareholders, agents and directors: their interests were spread across the sector rather than focused on a single enterprise.

The merchant community in Buenos Aires was a source of expertise and contacts for the railway business. Resident merchants had been instrumental in obtaining concessions and provided starter funding. Sometimes members of ad hoc advisory groups, more usually a formally constituted local committee, merchants retained direct links with the early railways. Another feature of the local committees was the co-option of local political talent. These bodies shadowed London boards and were useful in resolving disagreements between railway and government (Lewis, 1977: 403– 405; Reber, 1979: 125–127). Occasionally distinguished directors such as Thomas Armstrong or John Fair were normally resident in Buenos Aires or, as in the case of the Drabbles, spent part of the year in Europe and part in the River Plate (Lewis, 1983: 20–21). These men 'knew the country' and were integrated into the land-owning oligarchy. Companies founded in the 1880s did not enjoy such effective local contacts. In part, this was because 'cosmopolitan' merchants were thickest on the ground in Buenos Aires, while many companies set up in the 1880s operated in up-country provinces. Established Anglo—Argentinian merchants enjoyed less effective connections with the provincial interests who gained influence at federal government level in the 1880s. Perhaps it was also the case that the cultivation of domestic interests was less important during the railway mania. As Halperín Donghi observes, by this stage, the country was awash with money and an enormous number of projects enjoying government profit guarantees appeared to be available to all comers (Halperín Donghi, 1993: 189; López, 1994: 349–353).[14] Good contacts, it seemed, were no longer a prerequisite in order to secure lucrative concessions. Hence the pace of network growth quickened, until brought to an abrupt halt by the Baring Crisis.

Whatever the immediate adverse consequences, railway mania in the 1880s yielded a national system that underwrote frontier expansion well into the twentieth century.

---

14   In 1888, the federal congress was asked to sanction guaranteed railway concessions with a capital value of £1.5 million and in 1889, over £4 million. By 1891, had they been honoured, total annual guaranteed interest payments to federally franchised railways would have cost the Exchequer approximately £1 million (Congreso Nacional, 1891: I, 281–282).

Table 3 shows that between 1885, before the onset of the railway mania, and 1895, when the last of the projects initiated before the Baring Crisis had been completed, rail route mileage increased by more than 200 per cent, and capital investment by almost 300 per cent. Given the gestation period required to bring new land into cultivation (and the post-Crisis recession) the increase in rail freight is also impressive. It is also instructive that, with the exception of the increase in freight, which grew from a particularly low base in 1875, rates of change between 1885 and 1895 were considerably greater than between 1875 and 1885.

Railway Mania and Imperialism: Competition, Collaboration or Imperialist Consolidation

An understanding of the railway mania of the 1880s is essential to assessments of the 'imperial' nature of the British–Argentinian relationship. Several conflicting constructions can be placed on the mania and its outcome. First, it can be cast as competition: competition between established railways companies and, subsequently, between existing lines and newly floated enterprises; and competition between private and state lines (Ferns, 1960: 400; Lewis, 1983: 50–60, 64; López, 2000: 626–634). Second, it can be seen as a process of national consolidation: trunk rail construction of the order suggested in Table 3 points to an integration of the national territory and the forging of a national market (Cortés Conde, 1979: 78–89; Rocchi, 2006:

Table 2. Argentinian Economic Growth Relative to the Rates of Growth of Comparator Countries, 1880–1938 (%)

	1880–1938
Australia	122.7
Canada	9.9
USA	43.2
Brazil	60.9
Mexico	69.5

Source: Vitelli (1999: 118, 121).

Table 3. Rail Network Growth, 1875–1895

Year	Mileage (%)	Capital (%)	Passengers (%)	Freight (%)
1875	1215	£8.1	2.6 m	0.7 mt
1885	2797 (130%)	£24.3 m (200%)	5.6 (115%)	3.0 mt (329%)
1895	8771 (214%)	£96.2 m (296%)	14.6 m (161%)	9.7 mt (223%)

Key: (%) - percentage change 1875/1885, 1885/1895; m = millions of pounds; mt = millions of tonnes.
Source: Barres (1944: 70, 72, 73, 83).

135, 143). Third, there is a distinct imperialist interpretation: as a state presence in the sector was financed by foreign debt, default on which resulted in foreclosure and the privatisation of government lines, the mania may be envisaged as a debt trap designed to intensify the dependence of the country on international capital. Competition, however, was real, as is evidence of state policy designed to foster competition among private lines and to diversify sources of capital.

Between approximately 1867 and 1887, the federal government authorised route studies and granted franchises for competitive construction in the west and north-west (Ferns, 1960: 411–412; Fleming, 1977: 375, 376–379; López, 2000: 51–57). For example, in the 1880s, the federal government issued concessions to a new company, the Buenos Ayres and Rosario Railway Company Limited, to build from the national capital to Rosario and on to the north-west. At much the same time, extension concessions were granted to the Central Argentine, which linked the cities of Rosario and Córdoba (where it connected with a state line to the north-west), to build south to Buenos Aires. In part, the proliferation of franchises was designed to effect connections between the then separate networks that radiated, respectively, from Rosario and Buenos Aires. But, having been in dispute with the Central Argentine for some years, the sanctioning of competitive concessions can also be seen as a mechanism applied by the federal government to tame the Central Argentine (Ferns, 1960: 402, 404–406; Lewis, 1983: 53, 61–64; López, 1994: 84–88). The result of this war of concessions was that, by 1896, there were two routes not only between Buenos Aires and Rosario, but also two linking the federal capital with such cities as Villa María, a key junction in northern *pampa húmeda*, Córdoba, the most important city of the interior, and Tucumán, the regional capital of the north-west.

New concessions on the borders of the provinces of Buenos Aires and Santa Fé, and an aggressive construction policy pursued by the province of Buenos Aires state railway, the FC Oeste, represented another challenge to 'British' companies, particularly the long-established Buenos Aires Great Southern and a newer enterprise, the Buenos Ayres & Pacific Railway Company Limited (López, 1991: 137–143, 2000: 54–56). The flotation of new enterprises, the licensing of trunk and branch line construction by private companies and pressure on the 'zones' of London companies by the FC Oeste changed the configuration of the rail network of the province of Buenos Aires, as well as extending it. By 1886, the north and centre of the province could boast a fairly extensive system with parallel lines running on east–west and north–south axes. In the south, key settlements and ports such as Azul, Bahía Blanca, Maipu, Mar del Plata and Tres Arroyos were already connected to the city of Buenos Aires, though the rail system here still exhibited a developmental, radial configuration rather than the denser, grid-iron pattern observed further north.

The state presence in the sector grew in absolute terms, although the proportion of the network represented by federal and provincial lines declined from around 50 per cent in 1875 to about 40 per cent by 1890, such was the volume of private construction during the mania. Competitive construction of this order, as implied by the trends observed in Table 2, questions long-held views in the traditional railway literature of concerted action by a monolithic bloc of foreign companies '... to dominate the Argentinian economy ...' (López, 1994: 98). Most established companies accepted that there was nothing they could do to prevent the franchising and building of competitive lines by the new enterprises, by the federal government or by provincial administrations. The best defence was to apply new funds to enhancing services and consolidating their position, and to avoid antagonising government and public opinion (Ferns, 1960: 411).

Competitive construction in the 1880s, and again during the surge in international liquidity immediately before the First World War, also corresponded with a diversification in sources of state borrowing and private company funding. Regalsky argues that this was both an object and function of official policy, and explains the massive surge in the franchising of guaranteed railways between 1887 and 1889. During these years, concessions for more than 16,000 miles of new lines were published, all with profit guarantees. 'Without doubt, the government looked to promote the entry of new investor groups into the railway business so that they would compete with established interests ...' (Regalsky, 2002: 240). This policy appears to have worked, and not just in attracting British investment. In the 1880s, the Argentine was unique in Latin America, alone attracting important flows of investment from Paris into the railway sector, a success repeated some years later. Between 1900 and 1914, French investment in Argentinian railways increased from 22 million gold pesos to 130 million – a near sixfold increase when total investment in the sector grew by a factor of 2.5 (Regalsky, 2002: 105, 325).

Regalsky is not alone in pointing to the effectiveness of official railway policy. Others have argued that the Argentinian state had a clear railway strategy, that it consciously engaged with foreign capital and was far from naive or impotent in its dealings with London-registered companies, and that there was a direct and conscious link between railway policy and state-building. Contemporaries viewed railways as the principal means of developing the country, as a device to consolidate and secure the national territory, and as essential for the application of the writ of the central government in the provinces (Lenz, 2004: 87). Oszlak and Roccatagliata similarly argue that railways served to organise the national economic space: railways were

instrumental 'in the conquest, occupation and colonization and development of the national territory' (Oszlak, 1982: 141–148; Roccatagliata, 1987:
50). Referring to the system of profit guarantees, Oszlak also maintains that
the arrangement was not designed simply to serve the needs of concessionaires and investors. The guarantee system provided the state with powers
of inspection and regulation, which were deployed to good effect. In addition, when the state acquired shares in a private company (as did the federal authorities in the Central Argentine), government became a direct
stakeholder with such additional rights as representation at company meetings and at board level (Oszlak, 1982: 149–150). Similarly, López argues the
case for the coherence of national rail policy, and robustness in dealing with
foreign capital. There was a national project that, as acknowledged at the
time, could only be implemented by calling on overseas capital (López,
1994: 92–99). This does not mean that foreign investors did not seek to exploit dependence on the London or Paris money markets to implement national strategy. On the contrary, they often did. But neither does it imply
that government was always subservient, invariably the weaker party in
dealings between the state and foreign capital. If railway policy was endog-
enously determined and the state largely effective in enforcing an independent, national rail strategy, this would imply little capacity on the part of
British interests to extract rents by exerting indirect power over internal
politics.

The revisionist literature discussed above asserts that the state was able
to articulate an effective railway policy, and capable of adopting a 'national'
stance with regard to foreign-registered companies. There is also evidence
that *estancieros*, the principal early beneficiaries of overseas-funded rail construction, were no less capable of independent action. Two examples involving the Buenos Ayres Great Southern (BAGS) may serve to illustrate this
point, while shedding new light on the debate about economic imperialism
and the balance of interest between foreign capitalists and local interests. In
the late 1860s, having observed the phenomenal increase in land values occasioned by the first wave of railway investment in the north and east of the
province of Buenos Aires, landowners in the centre-south were exercised by
the sluggish pace of rail construction in their region. At this point, local
estancieros had two important weapons in their arsenal when dealing with
'foreign' enterprises: the provincial state and the state railway, the FC Oeste.
(Perhaps there was also a third, the desire by the still fledgling BAGS to
demarcate its zone of operations.) In 1866, the provincial administration
required the company to honour its original concession by pushing the trunk
line southward from Chascomús to Dolores. The BAGS, however, preferred
to build a branch line west from Altamirano to pre-empt the FC Oeste, which
was threatening to construct south from Merlo to Azul (Lewis, 1983: 34–36;

López, 1991: 51–53, 115–125). The ensuring flurry of protests and applications for concessions provoked complaints of unfair competition and threats of expropriation. In the final event, the BAGS formally recognised the right of the government to nationalise the company and agreed to harmonise new construction – and establish junctions – with the FC Oeste, but also obtained the desired concessions, plus a state subvention for the construction of priority routes. Arguably, the effectiveness of this strategy by local landowners to increase the pace of new construction derived from the Anglo-Criollo character of the BAGS, as well as the company's anxiety not to miss out on lucrative new opportunities for investment. Local shareholder-directors were able to convey to their colleagues in London the substance of threats (expropriation and competition), as well as the business sense of responding positively to pressure to build in regions of the province that were being rapidly transformed by wool production – the 'greasy gold' of the period (Sabato, 1990: 25–27, 34–38). There was as much a correspondence as a clash of interests among *estancieros*, foreign capitalists and the state, but deals had to yield mutual benefits for all parties, not disproportionate gains for some. Government and *estancieros* were anxious to promote an increase in the stock of social overhead capital that would facilitate a rise in production, tax receipts, land values and rural incomes; BAGS directors and investors sought to ensure that they obtained a reasonable share of the resulting gains in the form of profits and dividends.

Another spat occurred around the turn of the century, approximately a decade after the privatisation of the FC Oeste, which had been acquired by a new London company, the Buenos Ayres Western Railway Company Limited. On this occasion, the conflict was as much about rail freights and local anxiety about a London monopoly as about sluggish construction. The result, however, was similar, namely a re-balancing of interests and benefits among contending parties. Until the Argentine returned to the Gold Standard in 1900, the BAGS had linked freight rates to the gold premium, adjusting charges to movements in the exchange rate. While this practice was applauded by overseas shareholders as a rational response to inflation and monetary instability in the host economy, it outraged producers and exporters. Hence, first the provincial authorities, and later the federal authorities, were pressed by landowners to play the concessions game. Numerous franchises for 'economic' railways (basically metre gauge lines) inter-spaced between the main trunk lines of the BAGS and Buenos Ayres Western were issued around the turn of the century. Subsequently, additional concessions for broad gauge cross-country routes, intersecting with BAW and Great Southern railheads, were published (Regalsky, 1989: 425–452, 2002: 327–331). Despite the bluster from the London enterprises, the strategy worked. A surge in lending from Paris and London gave substance to the strategy.

New companies were franchised. The Great Southern and Western raised additional funds to build extensions in defence of their zones, and to modernise equipment in order to reduce costs and freights. While the success of these measures was contingent on international liquidity, evidence of the willingness and capacity of local interests to act cautions against glib assertions of British hegemony.

Although these events confirm the ability of local interests to manipulate foreign capital, the early-twentieth-century tariff dispute involving *estancieros* and the BAGS also points to a critical change in the railway sector. Both boom in the 1880s, and bust in the 1890s, served to dilute the *anglo-criollo* character of the rail sector. First, massive expansion, much of it by new companies and state lines, diminished the presence of pioneer Anglo-Criollo enterprises such as the BAGS. Second, the Baring Crisis triggered greater control from London. This took various forms. Privatisation led to the transfer of state lines to overseas creditors, while even successful companies that had emerged from the crisis largely unscathed were subject to close scrutiny by jittery London interests. Taken together, these processes explain the increased 'Britishness' of the sector by the early twentieth century, in contrast to the Anglo-Criollo character of previous years.

These developments (the investment boom of the 1880s and the denationalisation of the 1890s) seem to support arguments advanced by conspiracy theorists and exponents of the imperialism of free trade hypothesis. Whether contrived or due to the mechanics of the global capitalist system, the result was the same: rail denationalisation and a further strengthening of international finance's stranglehold. But such an interpretation does not convince. Competition in the 1880s, manifest in the scramble for concessions and a pre-emptive construction of trunk routes fits ill with depiction of the British railway interests as a monolithic bloc. In addition, while Anglo-Criollo merchant financiers who underwrote earlier railway initiatives could be presented as a collaborative elite, their behaviour challenges such a facile depiction. As argued above, the dealings of the likes of Fair, Robertson and Armstrong with the Argentinian federal government and provincial administrations suggest less a capacity to capture the state than an ability to negotiate with it. Their engagements with the London money market were not dissimilar. Based on privileged knowledge of two universes, a comparative advantage that allowed them to mobilise contacts and resources both in Britain and the River Plate, they advanced an independent project rather than function as *compradores*, junior partners of international finance. Merchants did not fit neatly in a cat's paw of global capitalism or *comprador* categorisation. The local state and landowners also demonstrated a robust capacity for independent action vis à vis 'London' railway enterprises.

Revisiting the Railway Literature

Given that railways feature prominently in the research agenda and analyses of all the schools cited above, this section offers an assessment of the railway historiography that seeks to further highlight the nature of misconceptions that surfaced in the 1930s, that is, misconceptions that came to underpin negative assessments of the British–Argentinian relationship in general. A précis of late-nineteenth-century opinion encapsulates the idea of railways as public goods: Chapter II of the 1853 Constitution obliged the state to foster railways as a means of promoting national and provincial development. By 1913/1915, the Argentinian railway network ranked tenth in the world: it was the most extensive in Latin America, the third largest in the Americas (Bunge, 1918: 145–147; Tornquist, 1919: 122). Beyond these facts, however, there is little agreement. The controversy about British investment in railways in the Argentine has stimulated the production of a body of critical work that is far from finished – debate continues about the feasibility of domestic funding, the regional configuration of the network, and much more (Zalduendo, 1975: 44).

Díaz Alejandro offers a succinct modernisationist take on railways and growth which, un-apologetically, devotes little attention to questions of funding and ownership, features prominent in other discourses. For Díaz Alejandro, railways were critical as social overhead capital formation. The surge in railway investment signalled the potential of the pampas, as well as facilitating an outward movement in the frontier of production (Díaz Alejandro, 1970: 3–5). Echoing Díaz Alejandro, others have observed that 'In the Argentinian case, it is beyond doubt that the railway was an indispensable component for growth …' (Gerchunoff and Llach, 2003: 28–29; see also, Rapoport, 1988: 179–182). Underpinning this approach is the sense that rapid, sustained extension of the rail network was either beyond local savings capacity, or that the cost of tying up scarce local capital in overhead projects would have been extremely high – and was unnecessary given prevailing international levels of liquidity (López, 1994: 93–94, 96–97). Clearly, this interpretation undermines the proposition advanced by nationalist pro-*dependistas* such as Scalabrini Ortiz (1958: 17–23) that national funding was a feasible option, and that a significant proportion of domestic savings was devoted to railway finance in the form of indirect subsidies – for example profit guarantees, and direct funding, namely, government investment in private companies and state enterprises.

Accepting the thrust of the argument that reliance on external funds to finance railway construction was logical does not, however, close debates about the cost of external finance nor, indeed, the specific model. What was the real (or comparative) cost of overseas investment in the rail sector?

What was the alternative to direct investment by London-registered free-standing companies? The cost of direct investment can be assessed from several perspectives. According to official, federal data, from the 1850s to the 1940s, annual yields on capital invested in the railway system rarely exceeded 5 per cent, and were usually considerably lower (DGFFCC, 1913, 1938, 1947).[15] Dividends declared by private companies constitute another means of assessing the 'cost' of direct foreign investment, albeit a very rough proxy. Equity shareholders of premier London companies such as the BAGS often received substantial dividends. For example, between 1883 and 1887, the average nominal dividend declared on ordinary shares was 10 per cent, and from 1899 to 1913, ordinary shareholders consistently received 7 per cent. Of course, holders of preference and debenture stock received much less. Annual average yields on recognised capital invested by the BAGS usually fluctuated between 5 and 6 per cent in good times, and below 4 per cent during less fortunate years. And few companies could match the nominal dividend record of the BAGS. At the other end of the spectrum, ordinary shareholders of the Argentine North Eastern never received a dividend, save between 1904 and 1907, when they obtained an average barely above 2 per cent; the net yield on total recognised Argentine North Eastern capital touched 3 per cent on only two occasions between 1893 and 1947, and was usually below 2 per cent. These yields and dividends hardly bear comparison with returns obtained in other sectors of the Argentinian economy such as land and manufacturing. On the other hand, for British holders of BAGS equity, average nominal dividends were usually a couple of points higher than those paid by the Great Western Railway or the London & North Western Railway, but Buenos Aires was not Bristol or Birmingham (Lewis, 1968: 402–404). Perhaps the differentials between yields on railway capital and returns available in other sectors of the Argentinian economy, as much as international liquidity per se, explain why interests in the republic were largely content with the 'model' of funding railway construction and operation, that is, a reliance on foreign capital. Until the 1930s, the system seemed to be working. There was little incentive to change the model.

---

15   The Dirección General de Ferrocarriles (DGFFCC) calculated global yields on recognised capital. Annual rates of return applied to the system as a whole, that is, federal, provincial, and privately owned lines (domestic and foreign). For most of the period, London-registered companies accounted for approximately two-thirds of the Argentinian rail network. Average annual yields above 5 per cent were registered in 1869–1875, 1880–1885 and in 1905. Of course, yields varied considerably across the sector: state-owned metre gauge lines operating in the north usually recorded negative yields; high, positive yields were typical of private, pampean broad-gauge enterprises.

As suggested above, network configuration and 'London monopoly' loom large in the nationalist-cum-imperialist literature: foreign ownership was responsible for 'capricious breaks of gauge' that limited competition and British companies dominated the productive pampean region, locking the country into pattern of agro-export production (Ortiz, 1958: 19–36; Scalabrini Ortiz, 1958: 17–23). Geographers and historians have therefore revisited the debates about the determinants and consequences of network configuration. Factors shaping the location and growth of the early lines, and the emergent structure of the rail system, have received considerable attention.

Pioneering work provides convincing evidence that early network configuration was largely shaped by late-eighteenth-century patterns of economic activity, rather than by an imperial design emanating from London (Goodwin, 1977: 613–632; Brown, 1994: 251–255). Railways were a substitute for pre-modern forms of communication, rather than a mechanism promoting new activities – or a marked re-ordering of factor allocation and distribution. Admittedly, the survival (or revival) of key sectors of the 'colonial' economy in the early nineteenth century was influenced by the legacy of Spanish mercantilism and a surge in world demand for River Plate commodities at the time of Independence – a period when the region was probably the most open, competitive economy in the international system (Halperín Donghi, 1989: 117–129; Amaral, 1998: 13–17). Others have argued that the initial layout of the system was shaped by domestic political considerations, as much as by economic forces emanating from the export sector – whether presented as a pampean collaborative elite or London financial interests (Oszlak, 1982: 146–150; Lewis, 1985: 201–205). External interests were present and may have constrained state action in some areas, but imperatives driving the pace and direction of the rail construction were largely national (Oszlak, 1982: 148).

Yet others have questioned, or qualified, the export bias and structural 'deformities' of network configuration – deficiencies that feature prominently in the revisionist literature of the 1930s. Roccatagliata is adamant and confrontational in style. He argues convincingly that, as it developed, the network was not narrowly focused on the city and port of Buenos Aires – a radial configuration designed to consolidate the political hegemony of a mercantile oligarchy committed to liberal internationalism. Some companies were floated to serve the export sector, but others lines were constructed to meet regional needs in the interior. With system expansion, particularly after the 1880s, the network became more integrated and 'national'. Lateral routes developed and various nodal centres emerged: some were ports, implying a dilution of export concentration on Buenos Aires; others were centres of production for regional and national markets

(Roccatagliata, 1987: 74–81). Although Roccatagliata is writing from the perspective of an economic geographer, his interpretation chimes with that offered above derived from a revisionist assessment of competitive rail construction by 'London' companies, and the capacity of landed interests and the state to stimulate foreign investment in the financing of social overhead capital formation.

Directly and implicitly, much of the traditional and revisionist growth-economics/modernisation scholarship attributes the relative performance of the country, charted in Table 1, to the dynamic impact of railways. Pointing to the contribution of railways to industrial growth, Cortés Conde offers an interesting statistic about rail freight in 1914: exports, imports and domestic-use items each accounted for approximately one-third of total tonnage (Cortés Conde, 1979: 5; see also Vázquez-Presedo, 1971: 407–408). More recently, Rocchi also sees railways as serving the needs of local manufacturers as well as importers – while also functioning as vectors of modernity (Rocchi, 2006: 133–135, 139–140). And, as some neopolitical economists remark: 'Intuitively, transportation … must have been important …' to market integration and economic diversification (Salvatore and Newland, 2003: 40–41). These assessments accord with the 'enabling' functions attributed to such general-purpose technologies as railways and with the 'delivery' of official rail strategy. They offer a robust challenge to nationalist-cum-imperialist writing of the 1930s, and negative assessments of foreign investment in 'export railways' embedded in structuralist and dependency writing of the 1960s and 1970s. Social capital formation characterised by the national railway system brought diffuse benefits. Even if some lines were initially constructed to facilitate the growth of exports, over time, increasing network coverage and density served to integrate the national market and provide essential transport facilities for sectors and social actors beyond the agro-export oligarchy.

New assessments of federal railways strategy in the 1880s and of provincial efforts to contain 'London' companies in Buenos Aires suggest that domestic political forces played a significant role in shaping the pace and direction of the growth of the rail system. This evidence, and new analyses of state capacity, must caution against a glib acceptance of nationalist criticisms of the 1930s. State-sponsored competitive construction in the northwest, and *estanciero* efforts to enhance the density of network coverage in the province of Buenos Aires, as well as to constrain rail tariff inflation, point to considerable agency on the part of national interests. Rail construction of the order detailed in Table 3 had an integrative impact. A skeletal national network was forged as a result of the construction of trunk routes that joined the Rosario and Buenos Aires systems. Subsequent building, largely because of international liquidity in the years immediately before 1914 and then during the 1920s, increased the density of the network and extended its outreach.

The review of the railway literature presented in this section demonstrates that the historiography is diverse and that that several questions remain unresolved. Yet the thrust of much new writing supports Thompson: namely, '... British railway companies were allowed to dominate Argentina's railway network, but the government showed itself both able and willing to intervene when this so-called "trust" overstepped the limits of government tolerance' (Thompson, 1992: 433). The position obtained by British enterprises in the railway industry was because of the acquiescence of the landed sector and the political class, rather than their manipulation by external forces. The 'collaborative elite' collaborated when it was in its interests to do so, and did not when circumstances dictated otherwise. This does not mean that London companies did not become the butt of local political groups. They did. However, charges of 'monopoly' and 'imperialism', current in the inter-war period, reflect more on the changing nature of Argentinian politics and the exhaustion of the dynamics of rail technology than the performance and position of British companies up to that point. To use the language of the new institutionalism, intuitively, there was a balance of mutual (not necessarily equal) benefit in the relationship. Broadly, foreign firms delivered what was expected of them in terms of state-building, frontier-expansion, market-integration and nation-building, and the valorisation of local assets. As Argentinian society and economy became more complex, so 'delivery' was required to meet the expectations of more regions and groups. Before *c.* 1914, disputes about detail – tariffs, network configuration, the quality of transport services – confirm rather than refute assumptions of mutual benefit. The framework of the 'contract' was rarely challenged, although some of the small print was re-examined from time to time. It is difficult to fit this relationship into the hegemonic/satellite, Gallagher and Robinson or dependency moulds.

Conclusion

It should be clear that growth neither means that 'imperialism' or 'exploitation' did not exist, nor that a different model might have yielded more growth or better 'quality' growth. Nevertheless, comparative data displayed in Tables 1 and 2 indicates that the economic performance of the Argentine was impressive in the period under consideration and that it is difficult to find a counterfactual comparator that might suggest an alternative model capable of delivering greater welfare gains. Indeed, apologists for economic internationalism maintain that growth deceleration after the inter-war period was as a result of divergence from optimal growth strategies applied during the *belle époque*, and which continued to be applied by other 'new' economies with whom the Argentine was converging between the 1870s and 1920s, but with whom a development gap opened hereafter. In this sense, these other countries offer a counterfactual of how the Argentine might have grown after the 1930s and reinforce the view that the actual growth trajectory before the 1920s, and the model applied, was probably the best (Taylor, 1997, 2003; Cavallo, Domenech and Mundlak, 1999).

With regard to railways and the market, whereas the nationalist-imperialist historiography tended to emphasise domestic market capture and distortion by external agents, the new contributions to the literature on railways and growth in Latin America argue for national market integration. 'Iron rails lay behind the appearance of more modern national textile and milling industries, and because railroads carried coal for steam engines in the new factories and mills, neither were dependent, as they had been, on hydraulic sources for power' (Bauer, 2001: 141). Bauer's consumptionist take on market integration and economic diversification chimes with analyses of new institutionalists. 'Transport investment raised incomes and output by integrating markets and providing new opportunities for specialisation in agriculture and manufacturing' (Summerhill, 2006: 293–294). These analyses vindicate an original modernisationist interpretation that railways were the most palpable form of infrastructure investment in late-nineteenth-century Latin America, were viewed as such by contemporaries and largely delivered what was anticipated of them (Cortés Conde, 1974: 156). Although these assessments relate to the continent as a whole, they can hardly fail to apply to the Argentine, which, by 1900, boasted the most extensive rail network in Latin America, and also the densest.

There is a substantial degree of agreement in new contributions to the railway historiography on the Argentine about state competence, at least regarding the effectiveness of railway strategy and regulation. Domestic interests were instrumental in network design and capable of an effective defence of national interests, even if those interests were often articulated in rather narrow sectoral terms. International liquidity gave effect to an internally conceived project to drive forward the pace of railway development: profit guarantees and supervision were mechanisms that facilitated competitive construction and offered some defence against the 'natural' monopoly intrinsic to railways and public utilities. Profit guarantees and subventions were not costless, but they were standard for the sector and the period. Regulation and state supervision may have been contested by domestic and foreign capitalists, but they were hardly non-existent and they were enhanced over time because of a process of learning-by-doing. Government survival was dependent on the ability to deliver the supply of an important public good like railways and a capacity to reconcile the conflicting interests involved.

The image of *el pulpo inglés* is plausible and persuasive, but it hardly accords with the reality of railways and railway operations for most of the period considered here. The early history of railways in the Argentine demonstrates substantial domestic ownership – 'ownership' of the project as well as an equity and managerial stake in many early enterprises. Assuming a modicum of state competence and local agency, the fact that 'London' companies survived for so long must indicate that a British involvement in Argentinian railways addressed domestic requirements and was sensitive to national – as well as nationalistic – sentiments.

5

Finance, Ambition and Romanticism in the River Plate, 1880–1892

CHARLES JONES

University of Cambridge, UK

Those who wrote about British informal empire in the third quarter of the twentieth century were intrigued by the manifold ways in which British finance and commerce shaped the world, and most of all by the constraints they placed on the governments of independent states. Christopher Platt, who was sceptical about the extent of these constraints, gathered around him a group of young researchers who, on the whole, were more willing than he had been to concede the multifaceted and diffuse nature of British power (Platt, 1977). Platt also made a signal contribution to debate by encouraging work on the archives of British firms, which often provided a quite different picture from the public archives (Platt, 1965). This was not economic history, though some thought it was and spoke of 'economic' rather than 'informal' imperialism. Economic history proper was taking a quite different turn at this time, toward quantitative work closely informed by economic theory (McCloskey, 1981). Instead, the Platt researchers and their contemporaries employed the traditional methods of the diplomatic historian, applying them now to the letters of businessmen rather than officials, in order to uncover the dynamics of political relations between British firms and their host states in Latin America and elsewhere. This yielded what may properly be called a political history of commerce. Similar techniques, employed within the area of formal British rule, helped uncover the often complex relations between commerce and officialdom – box-wallahs and the lofty chiefs of the Indian Civil Service – which were seldom anything like as simple or as comfortable as twentieth-century critics of empire assumed (Dewey, 1978).

The history cultivated behind this advancing archival frontier was largely unaffected by the revolution in social history that had already been initiated by Christopher Hill, E. P. Thomson and Eric Hobsbawm. It was history from above, not below, but now from the perspective of the commercial and financial rather than the governing elites. It was, as behoved a history fuelled by the sweat and ink of Victorian clerks, a starched-collar history. But it put wind in the sails of the term 'informal empire', a phrase far too useful long to remain the possession of a narrow group. Soon, it became a coverall for work on any and every aspect of asymmetric power relations within and beyond the limits of formal or constitutional empire.

This chapter attempts to respond to some of the historiographic twists and turns of the past 30 years. It begins with a reminder of the style and concerns of 1970s work on the political consequences of direct foreign investment outside the British empire by offering a brief account of how British commercial banks helped break the back of an incipient economic nationalist turn in Argentinian politics during the late 1880s and early 1890s. Such a policy, pursued by social conservatives drawn from traditional governing families, might have averted or at least moderated the more xenophobic and populist forms of nationalism that were to dominate and divide Argentina in the mid-twentieth-century. This is, of course, speculation (some will say mere nostalgia); what befell is what happened. Though consciously old-fashioned, this initial account differs from what might have been offered 30 years ago in according a much enhanced role to the relatively autonomous machinations of local politics, and correspondingly less responsibility to the British. This is a testament to the considerable advances in our understanding of Argentine nineteenth-century politics that have been made since the 1970s. Yet it remains starched-collar history, relying on the archives of governments and banks.

A next step is to imagine what a history of this sort might have been like had it paid more regard to the personal. Records and publications were available to disclose the character and style of two of the protagonists in the clash between British banks and Argentine governments in some detail. Robert Thurburn, who spent his entire career in the service of the London and River Plate Bank, was on the periphery of the episode described in the first section of the chapter. He took over management of the Buenos Aires branch of the bank only in 1892, when the battle was over. But we know more of his personal life than of that of any of his contemporaries, and there is no reason to think him untypical except in the sense of exemplary, judging by his professional success. The other figure to be considered, Vicente Fidel López, was by contrast at the very heart of things as Finance Minister from 1890 to 1892. Taking these two men as ideal types suggests that outcomes in the 1890s may have been the consequence not simply of conflicting market and political logics, but of deep incommensurabilities between two wholly different views of life: the one instrumental and narrow, the other lofty and even a touch febrile.

The preliminary conclusion to this excursion from the public to the private realm is that the divisions evident in the first were reinforced by those in the second. So to this extent it remains a story about political outcomes and the shaping of the Argentine state. It is still dominated, just as before, by structural considerations, since the personal account principally adds the constraints of education and family to those of the market and of Argentine political culture. A final section therefore considers the extent to which work on informal empire has and should remain state-centric and structuralist and, alongside this, mounts an attack on the term 'informal imperial-*ism*', which is doomed either to be an oxymoron or something close to tautology.

River Plate Economy and Finance: Two Protagonists

The public arena in which Robert Thurburn and Vicente Fidel López both operated between 1870 and the 1890s was the world of banking and finance. Still in his teens, Thurburn arrived in Montevideo on 10 January 1870, to take up a junior post in the local branch of the London and River Plate Bank. The next day he opened a correspondence with his father, a British naval officer, that was to continue for more than a decade. This is why Thurburn, unlike most of his contemporaries in the British banks, railways and utility companies, is not a mere signature on official correspondence.

The bank he joined had been founded in 1862 under the Companies Act of the same year, which for the first time extended general limited liability by a simple process of registration to banks. It happened that 1862 was also the year in which the Argentine provinces, long divided among themselves, finally formed a federal republic under the presidency of Bartolomé Mitre, opening the door to an expansion of trade and investment. Thurburn's association with what was soon to become the strongest of the foreign commercial banks in Argentina was to last for more than half a century. From junior clerk he had risen to the post of manager of the Rosario branch in Santa Fe province, Argentina, by 1882. In 1892, he took charge of the Buenos Aires branch. There he remained until 1909, when he returned to Britain as managing director of the bank, a post from which he retired only in 1921.

Thurburn twice came close to crossing paths with Vicente Fidel López (1815–1903). The elder of the two by some 40 years, López was living in exile in Montevideo when the London Bank opened its branch there in 1863 (Joslin, 1963). The custom at this time was for the branch manager of a British overseas bank to be overseen by a local board of directors who were also relied upon to bring business to the new institution. It was the strength of its local board, for example, that led to the Hong Kong and Shanghai Bank becoming a Chinese institution though originally registered and controlled in London (King with King and King, 1987). Usually it was otherwise, with London boards backing their appointees and the influence of local directors rapidly waning (Jones, 1987). So in Montevideo, López was appointed as one of two local directors (the other being an English merchant) in the branch that Thurburn was soon to join, only to be dismissed from his directorship before long because he was too inclined to recommend his friends as borrowers without due regard, one must suppose, for their creditworthiness.

We know this only because Thomas Hyne Jones, manager of the London Bank's Montevideo branch in the 1870s, was by 1890 manager of the Buenos Aires branch of the English Bank of the River Plate, a more recent and – as events would show – a less secure institution than the London Bank. Competitors though they might be, the private banks were at this time in league against the banking policies of the federal government. So it was that on 30 January 1890, Jones wrote to Rodney Fennessy, Thurburn's immediate predecessor in the Buenos Aires branch of the London Bank, to warn him that 'the lawyer dismissed by our bank in Monte Video [*sic*] a quarter of a century ago is now Minister of Finance of the Argentine Republic. He has a long memory', Jones lamented, 'and is of a very vindictive temper' (BOLSA D75). And the warning appeared justified, because the appointment of López marked the start of the last chapter in an assault on the private banks that had begun in 1886 and would conclude only in 1892, the year of Thurburn's appointment.

Whether the two met, how often or on what terms, is really beside the point, because they are offered here as ideal types of the two worlds that intersected in the River Plate during these years, initially embracing in liberal fellowship, clashing in the economic crises of the mid-1870s and 1890, and then yielding a period of excessive economic liberalism lasting pretty much through to 1930. It was at this point that nationalist resentments built up over four decades, no longer tempered by the liberalism of the Generation of 1837 to which López belonged, burst out in xenophobia and accusations of British imperialism. Here were two very different worlds. On the one hand stood the rule-bound world of British (as often as not Scottish) commercial banking in which profit was the objective and neither family nor acquaintance conferred advantage on prospective clients. On the other was to be found a tradition in which banking was one of the means by which the nation was to be constructed: a tradition owing much to the positivist ideals of Henri de Saint Simon and the Pereire brothers in mid-nineteenth-century France (Eckalbar, 1979). In a straight fight, well-run commercial banks without political objectives will almost certainly drive public-service oriented institutions out of business. This was what the public wrangling over banking in Argentina was all about during the 1880s and 1890s.

López himself put the nationalist view with characteristic verve in a speech to the Senate in January 1891, at the height of the crisis:

> These private banks, which claim to have done such services for the country, have not, to my knowledge, lent a single peso in our countryside or provinces. They share out their cash among those they call 'good accounts', and what they call 'good accounts' are those who place large deposits in their hands. [But] let

a middling trader, someone just starting out, [or] a farmer who needs to develop his business go asking for credit from any of these banks – be it the London and River Plate, the Carabassa, or the Anglo-Argentine – and I am sure that they'll be turned away in a decidedly unceremonious manner. (Argentine Senate, 1891)

River Plate Economy and Finance: 1880–1892

To understand how a former ally of the British had reached this opinion it is not enough to rely on Jones's suggestion of personal resentment (cited above, p. 111). López was a bigger man than that. Instead, one must do something that the British were always reluctant to do, which is to take Argentine politics seriously and integrate them with the process of economic development, starting from the election of Julio Roca to the presidency in 1880. Roca's victory has often been seen as the beginning of almost four decades of scarcely interrupted economic prosperity and political dominance by the landed oligarchy through the Partido Autonomista Nacional (PAN). This understates the precariousness of economics and politics alike during the 1880s. Roca's political fortunes depended crucially on his declared policy of modernisation and stabilisation in a country that had, ever since Independence, continued to be beset by internal conflict and *caudillismo*. Yet by 1883, European markets were already saturated with Argentine bonds and the extensive range of public works and private initiatives, to which Roca looked to modernise the country and deliver a second PAN term, was being sustained largely by insider trading as the bankers strove to maintain public confidence.

That it had come to this must be blamed almost entirely upon Roca himself, who had broken with the gentlemanly tradition whereby each country issued its external bonds largely through a single European firm: Brazil with Rothschilds and Argentina with Barings. By the start of 1884, desperate to raise more money, Roca repented of his promiscuity and assured Barings that he would once again confine his dealings to their firm. This offered them and their French competitors time to unload the unsold bonds they still held from loans of the past three years. But within weeks, Roca changed track and began negotiations with a French-led syndicate for a further external loan, appearing to believe that the willingness of marginal firms to lend to his country was unambiguous evidence of its ability to repay.

By the year's end, the position was desperate, aggravated by ham-fisted timing of the announcement of changes in import tariffs. Calculated to slow down imports and secure a trade surplus to balance the steadily rising burden of debt service, these changes had had precisely the opposite effect. Given five months' notice of the higher duties, importers not un-naturally rushed to fill the city's warehouses at the cheaper rates, putting pressure on the exchanges and bringing the government perilously close to default.

From the point of view of Roca and the PAN, the direct financial conse-quences to be expected from this sad display of ineptitude were possibly of less immediate concern than the possible effect on the forthcoming presi-dential election. Constitutionally barred from serving a second term imme-diately, Roca was anxious to ensure continuity of PAN political control. Dardo Rocha, who had been rewarded with the governorship of Buenos Ai-res for his support of Roca in 1880, harboured presidential ambitions. When Roca withheld support for his candidacy in favour of his own brother-in-law, Miguel Juárez Celman, Rocha left the PAN, and though he ultimately failed to secure the nomination of the opposition Partidos Unidos in Decem-ber 1885, he appeared a plausible candidate until that moment (Alonso, 2000: 49). For a time, therefore, continuation of the party's programme of modernisation appeared to depend crucially on averting a financial crisis capable of uniting and strengthening opposition in the run-up to the elec-tion (Alonso, 2000: 46).

The hero of the hour was Carlos Pellegrini, the old-Harrovian son of an Italian-born portrait painter. Despatched to Europe to rescue the gov-ernment, Pellegrini succeeded against all odds in persuading the seven major British, French and Belgian lenders to form a comprehensive syn-dicate and to preserve the interests of government and bondholders alike by issuing a further loan, of an unprecedented £8 million, and making an advance of £1.8 million to avert default. More than this, when nationalis-tic resistance to the harsh terms of the new loan led Congress to throw out the bill proposing it in August 1884 (the spectre of Egypt loomed large!), Pellegrini managed to persuade the bankers to step down, and the markets rallied, finally ensuring the smooth succession from Roca to Juárez Celman.

Knowing all too well how close the country and their party had come to disaster in 1885, Juárez Celman, his Vice-President Carlos Pellegrini, and Finance Minister Wenceslao Pacheco were determined to reduce the vulnerability of the economy by repatriating part of the external debt, thereby reducing the salience of debt service in the balance of payments. They hoped to achieve this by obliging banks to hold a substantial part of their reserves in Argentine government bonds, while at the same time en-couraging the creation of new banks in the provinces and injecting liquid-ity into the growing economy. The financial crisis they had hoped to avert nevertheless began at the end of 1889 as fresh lending from Europe dried up and prices for Argentine exports fell. This in turn broke the speculative boom in land, and brought down elaborate credit structures based on inflated values.

Things became considerably more serious as the year progressed. At a mass rally against the government in April, the Unión Cívica was established. This led directly to an armed revolt in July, which, though defeated, brought about Juárez Celman's resignation from the presidency early the following month. This was the moment, in the early days of August, when Pellegrini, taking over the administration, invited Vicente Fidel López to serve as Minister of Finance. The situation could hardly have been worse. Not only was the economy in critical condition, so too were national politics. As Pellegrini brought those chiefly responsible for the military defeat of the July revolution into his cabinet, including Roca, the net effect seemed, to the more explosive leaders of the revolt, to have been the confirmation in power of their opponents. In a letter that perfectly encapsulates his combination of liberal optimism and conservative caution, López wrote in strong terms to Leandro Alem, his co-conspirator of July, now fomenting opposition to Pellegrini's government:

> I am informing you of the colossal task that I have over my shoulders and ask you to stop agitating the spirits, and to wait and be cautious ... If you persist in following your passions, assume that the road had split in two; you take the one of the agitators and I will continue the one of order (Alonso, 2000: 73, citing López to Alem, 8 September 1890).

November saw the failure of Barings in London. Early in 1891, as the two major Argentine official banks, vital to government finances, were about to go under, the national government appealed to the private banks to subscribe to a new internal loan to be known, with delightful absence of irony, as the Popular Loan. A telegram from Buenos Aires to the head office of the most powerful of the private institutions, the London and River Plate Bank, starkly reveals the terms of the deal. It read: 'If loan successful promise has been given by Argentine President of Republic to cancel deposit tax' (BOLSA D75, 8 March 1891). Worse, the London bank was able to use the government's acute vulnerability at this moment to push through its acquisition of one of its leading Argentine rivals, the Banco Carabassa, in the teeth of government opposition.

The long-run significance of this episode for Argentina has been obscured by imperfect integration of economic and political histories. Contemporaries were disdainful of Argentine politics. A former *Times* correspondent, Thomas Turner, insisted that '[t]heir politics is a system of puerile personalities and orational outpourings (Turner, 1892: 34), while a British diplomat, a few years later, compared the Argentine struggle over the federalisation of Buenos Aires at some length with the constitutional issues that led to the American Civil War before taking a grip on himself and concluding that:

> [t]he comparison … if pushed too far, would turn almost to the grotesque, for in the Argentine tussle for power there was no great principle at stake such as … the prior duty of the citizen to his native State rather than to the Union. (Rumbold, 1904: 209–210)

Argentine politics was all about personalities, the British decided. Nationalism as a political force, and use of the term 'nationalist' in public discourse, did not appear in Argentina until 1930, while the most significant nationalisations of British firms took place only in the late 1940s, under Juan Domingo Peron. Because of this, historians have generally accepted that liberalism remained the dominant ideology in Argentina at least up to the worldwide economic crisis of 1930 (Rock, 1986: 205). In that year, Argentina left the Gold Standard and, within months, suffered the first of what was to prove a succession of military coups, bringing an end to seven decades of almost consistently constitutional government. So, too, the 1930s created the circumstances in which Raúl Prebisch would formulate the theoretical underpinnings of policies of import substitution, export cartels and regional cooperation that would spread across the global south, through his role in the UN Economic Commission for Latin America and, later, the United Nations Conference on Trade and Development (established in 1964), remaining influential right up to the 1980s (Jones, 1983).

This view understates the extent to which the close alliance of Argentine and British liberals had already been coming under pressure in successive economic crises from as early as the mid-1870s, when voices in support of export-oriented protection of the textile industry were first raised. Among them had been Carlos Pellegrini and Vicente F. López, who as we have seen were to emerge as President and Finance Minister respectively following the forced resignation of Juárez Celman in August 1890, in which they had been instrumental (Rock, 1986: 149, 205). Up to 1930, the 1890 crisis was to be far and away the deepest the country had suffered and it brought the most serious challenge to the Anglo-Argentine relationship; at its nadir, power fell into the hands of proven economic nationalists. Alonso (2000), her eyes perhaps a little too firmly on her topic – the origins of the Radical Party – is too ready to accuse other elements in the Partidos Unidos and the later Unión Cívica of less principled positions than those of her protagonists. In her account, Leandro Alem emerges as the most dedicated and consistent opponent of the PAN. Yet López and Pellegrini shared a history of moderate economic nationalism. López had joined Sarmiento and Mitre in voicing opposition to what they felt was an unacceptably centralised and unaccountable tendency under Juárez Celman (Alonso, 2000: 45). López, along with Mitre, had attended the inaugural meeting of the Unión Cívica in 1889 (Alonso, 2000: 192). Pellegrini, in the final days, had elected to back Roca, not Juárez Celman. In short, the Pellegrini-López partnership might be expected, on past form, to pursue the PAN's programme of national development but in a more competent manner than Roca and with more honesty and regard for national autonomy than Juárez Celman.

The course of Argentine politics in 1890 was far from straightforward. During the days following the defeat of the July 1890 revolution, Juárez Celman had cast around unsuccessfully for allies to strengthen his cabinet. Meanwhile, Pellegrini commenced negotiations with Roca and, within days, the two of them together asked Juárez Celman for his resignation. Assuming the presidency on 6 August, Pellegrini appointed Vicente Fidel López as Minister of Finance. Already 75, López was to remain at the Ministry for the remainder of the six-year presidential term, and ought certainly to be counted as among the most successful finance ministers in Argentine history. By the time he left office, recovery was already well under way, helped by buoyant export demand. Even men critical of the whole tenor of Argentine politics applauded the appointment. Thomas Turner grudgingly declared that the Pellegrini cabinet 'contained at least one honest man. ... Dr Vicente Fidel Lopez, a man of high rectitude ... a man whose services the entire nation might well be proud of securing at such a juncture of affairs' (Turner, 1892: 317). But in one important particular, López did not succeed. His attempt to curb the power of the private banks – briefly alluded to earlier – was defeated in spite of a vigorous and nationalistic campaign in which he anticipated later and more xenophobic publicists.

López firmly believed that what was at issue in the struggle over banking law and taxation was nothing less than the recovery of Argentine economic and political independence. For a short time, in the early months of his tenure, it seemed that he might succeed (Alonso, 2000: 80). The 1891 Budget, brought to Congress late in 1890, proposed annual taxes of 0.2 per cent on bank deposits and 7 per cent on net profits, and subjected the private banks to the inspectorate of companies. Pleased that the more damaging provisions of the 1886 Banking Law had been defeated by events, the bankers were grudgingly content to accept and absorb the taxes, minimising their effect by changes in accounting methods. At this point, however, the plight of the *Banco de la Provincia de Buenos Aires* and the *Banco Nacional*, the two leading official banks, deteriorated markedly (Jones, 1973: 241–266).

Pellegrini's first suggestion, early in 1891, had been that the government should offer tax concessions to the private banks on condition that they took over from the *Banco Nacional* large quantities of treasury bonds, effectively becoming creditors of the government. By March the position was critical, and López called a meeting of private bank managers, asking for a loan of $20 million gold pesos (£4 million), without which the official banks would fail. Persuaded that there was some prospect of success, the London board of the doyen of the private banks, the London and River Plate, agreed to put together a syndicate to raise the required sum on condition that the government exempted all banks subscribing to the loan from the deposit tax. The deal was struck, the loan launched, but too late. The two official banks suspended payments early in March and within a few days the London and River Plate Bank had acquired its rival, the Banco Carabassa, becoming, for a time, the most powerful bank in the country, by completing a deal first bruited in January, at which time López had made his opposition crystal clear. Together, Pellegrini and López had done what they could to sustain and redirect Juárez Celman's assault on foreign financial institutions, but events had been against them from the start. After Alvear took office in March 1892, López was replaced at the Finance Ministry by José Terry. Not wanting to take the initiative himself, Terry suggested to the banks that they petition Congress. The petition succeeded, the tax was abolished and, although proposals for its reintroduction surfaced now and then, the threat was never again serious in this period (Jones, 1973: 250–260).

The Clerk and the Statesman

The nationalist moment had passed, and the failure of Pellegrini and López in this sphere was perhaps the strongest evidence in support of their analysis of the dangers of dependency that threatened the nation. López left office, his personal as well as his political life to be clouded just two years later with the death of his novelist son, Lucio, in a duel. The same year, Rodney Fennessy gave way to Robert Thurburn. What was the temper of the man, not yet 40, who had inherited the spoils of British victory? What sort of a man was López, this elderly and defeated politician? To what extent did conflict in the public sphere reflect lack of a shared culture? It is this question, and an exploration of territory neglected by the Platt School in the 1970s, that is next to be addressed.

It has to be said that it may be unfortunate for the memory of the Anglo-Argentine banking community that the private correspondence of Thurburn, and of Thurburn alone, should have survived in the archives of the Bank of London and South America, successor to the London and River Plate Bank. There must have been more attractive and generous-spirited men working for the bank; but then they did not climb to the top of the greasy pole and Thurburn did. What is more, he was intent on climbing the pole from the outset, promotion being one of the constant themes of the correspondence he conducted with his father. This alone says something about the world in which he moved.

It was a world poised between two distinct periods of British enterprise in South America, of commercial partnerships and more capital-intensive corporations. Thurburn had links with the older milieu of merchant *estancieros* [ranchers], men who had come over to Buenos Aires soon after Independence, often as supercargoes charged by British principals with the disposal of speculative consignments of textiles or hardware. These men were often in a position to acquire land cheaply or found land on their hands in discharge of a debt; and unlike many local landowners they had access to capital with which to stock and improve the land. Such, or suchlike, was the background of the long-serving chairman (1869–1899) of the Bank of London and the River Plate, George Wilkinson Drabble, who acquired vast estates in Uruguay (Joslin, 1963: 39–42).

For Thurburn, evidence of family background is sketchy. Soon after his arrival in Montevideo, in February 1870, the young man crossed to Buenos Aires for carnival and visited his numerous uncles and aunts. Soon afterwards, he learned of the business failure and attempted suicide of his maternal grandfather, William White, a Buenos Aires *estanciero*, whose death not long afterwards was to trigger litigation of Dickensian proportions over what remained of his estate. Responses to inquiries from his father, Captain J. P. Thurburn R. N., not only about family, but about other acquaintances, together with his parents' marriage, suggest that Thurburn's father must have been stationed in the South Atlantic during the 1840s and spent long enough in Buenos Aires to court White's daughter, Margarita.

What is clear from the correspondence is that, given his connections, Thurburn might as easily have entered one of the commercial houses or gone into ranching as have taken employment in a bank. Yet if he ever contemplated ranching, he was soon put off. It was not just White's failure. Life in the camp (*campo* or countryside), in Uruguay as in the USA, was a desperately lonely one, and many were broken by it. In April 1870, Thurburn wrote to his father about Hodgkin, who had recently come out from Britain to take over his family's ranch, a son having mismanaged it. 'I believe the old man has taken to drinking', Thurburn reported, and:

> As for the young one, he has gone to the bad. The first night I saw him he was drunk and was being taken home by the *serenos* [nightwatchmen]. I always thought he was a steady fellow, but it seems that all these camp fellows take to the drink. (BOLSA, Thurburn to Thurburn, 14 April 1870).

In a rather more mature letter, written fourteen years later, Thurburn explained to his father that no one could hope to make a success of ranching without three or four years' practical experience and that it was hardly worth doing except on a large scale, considerations that would have ruled him out from entering the business himself back in the 1870s (BOLSA, Thurburn to Thurburn, 29 June 1884).

The choice between private commerce and corporation was a more difficult one. Before the advent of general limited liability, sealed by the 1862 Companies Act, British commerce overseas lay largely in the hands of small firms, and it was possible for competent clerks to make their way up and aspire to a partnership. That Thurburn rejected this path was evidence either of a conservative attitude to risk or, less probably, of foresight. For the spread of corporations and the development a little later of business machines were to lead to the bureaucratisation of commerce and a corresponding decline in the status of clerks, followed, from the end of the century, by feminisation of the profession (Anderson, 1977).

Yet in the 1880s all this lay in the future, and there was certainly one moment when Thurburn regretted his decision to stick with the Bank. This came in 1884. By now manager of the Rosario branch in Santa Fe province, he was passed over for the post of manager in Montevideo. A Pooterish self-righteousness and bureaucratic spirit creeps into his correspondence at this point. 'The injustice', he protested, 'is not only to myself, but to all the men in the service' (BOLSA, Thurburn to Thurburn, 7 September 1884). Instead, the job had gone to Henry (Harry) Anderson, who had worked alongside Thurburn in the Bank fourteen years before as a junior clerk. What hurt was that Anderson had gone into business on his own account in the meantime:

> [M]y *friend* Anderson, who has accepted the post when he knew I was entitled and looking forward to it, can hardly call himself my friend any longer, more especially as I entrusted him to use his influence … on my behalf. What claims has he to the post? Since that time he has made his fortune, and I, who have stuck to the Bank all these years, am still a poor man. … [N]othing, not even my salary, can ever compensate. And the worst feature … is that what happened today will be repeated tomorrow, and there is nothing to look forward to in the service now. (BOLSA, Thurburn to Thurburn, 7 September 1884, emphasis in original)

George Drabble, whose appointment as chairman the young Thurburn had so welcomed fourteen years before, was now 'a clown, and to be despised' (BOLSA, Thurburn to Thurburn, 31 December 1884).

What emerges strongly from the Thurburn correspondence is the jealousy with which this young man, having rejected riskier enterprises, coveted advancement, and the envy with which he regarded the promotion of his peers. Property and promotion dominate the correspondence, which has a stunningly narrow and humourless compass, dismissive of local politics as mere squabbling, notable only for its effect on business. ('We are expecting the revolution to come very soon to a head. [They] have provided me with a revolver "to take care of the Bank with"', he explained to his father in an early letter (BOLSA, Thurburn to Thurburn, 14 April 1870).)

Anderson's appointment turned out to be no more than a temporary set-back. A year later he moved on to Buenos Aires and Thurburn was duly appointed manager in Montevideo. Cooperation, if not friendship between the two men, was restored. Then, in 1892, long service and, doubtless, competence, were finally rewarded. Thurburn was appointed manager of the Buenos Aires branch, by far the largest in the London Bank's network, on a salary of £5000 a year, plus bonuses. Here was a position that allowed him the means and opportunity to operate at the highest levels of Argentine society. In today's money, the rewards were in excess of £500,000 a year, and at the dinner held when he finally left Buenos Aires in 1909 to become managing director of the Bank in London, Thurburn's health was proposed by no less a man than Julio Roca, twice President of the Republic. Surviving the acquisition of the London bank by Lloyds Bank in 1918, Thurburn continued as managing director until his retirement in 1921 (Joslin, 1963: 131, 236).

The contrast between Robert Thurburn and Vicente Fidel López could hardly be greater. It was typical of the English banking fraternity that Thomas Hyne Jones, when warning the London Bank of the likely opposition of the newly appointed Finance Minister in 1892, should have anticipated trouble on account of the 'long memory and vindictive temper' of a man dismissed from his local directorship in Montevideo almost 30 years before (see above p111). Such slights are certainly important in the formation of nationalists. One has only to think of another banker-politician, Abol Hassan Ebtehaj, refused use of the European washroom even as a senior officer of the Bank of the Middle East, who turned up six years later as a hostile governor of the Bank Melli, its chief local rival (Jones, 1986–1987: 285, 317–322). But to attribute the policies adopted by López in the 1890s simply to personal resentment is entirely to mistake the man. Though high office came late in life, he came from a political family and had pursued a political career from his youth. Moreover, he had been a consistent nationalist, although the nationalism of his youth had been directed against Spain, not Britain, and – spending much of his life in exile in Chile and Uruguay – he had embraced a Hispanic-American rather than a narrowly defined Argentine identity.

Born in Buenos Aires in 1815, the son of Vicente López y Planes, Vicente Fidel López graduated from the University of Buenos Aires as doctor of law in 1837. Among the teachers who helped form his political views was Octavio Fabricio Mossotti, a Milanese liberal forced into exile following the 1823 revolution in his home city. Like his contemporaries, López was a close observer of events in France, greatly affected by the revolution of 1830 in Paris, more aware of Michelet and other French authors, and of the *Revue de Paris*, than of work in Spanish or English (López, 1929: 38–39). These influences encouraged the Generation of 1837 to oppose the dictatorial rule of Juan Manuel de Rosas. Opposition turned out to be dangerous, however, and in 1840, López fled to Chile, where he ran a school with Domingo Faustino Sarmiento, who would go on to serve as a reforming Minister of Education and, later, President of the Republic. It was during this period, when the two exiles taught together, that Sarmiento wrote his powerful and influential anti-Rosista polemic, *Facundo: Civilization and Barbarism* (1868).

López returned to Argentina to fight alongside Justo José de Urquiza in the 1852 campaign that finally ousted Rosas following the decisive battle of Caseros. At this point, he seemed set fair for a career in law and politics. His father – briefly caretaker President in 1827, but best remembered as author of the national hymn – became Governor of the rich and powerful province of Buenos Aires, while Vicente himself was appointed Minister of Education by his father (Yaben, 1938: III, 470–472). Then things began to go wrong. In the *Acuerdo de San Nicolas*, adopted at a meeting of delegates from all the Argentine provinces after Caseros, it had been agreed that a new national constitution should be prepared. There was to be a strong federal government. Inter-provincial restraints on trade were to be lifted. There was considerable support, too, for a proposal to detach the city of Buenos Aires from its province, constituting it as a separate federal district. But the merchants and career politicians of the great port city, who had developed vested interests in political fragmentation under Rosas, now baulked at a programme to which the López family – father and son – were irrevocably committed, effectively as appointees of Urquiza.

So it was that, in September 1852, Vicente López y Planes was ousted from the governorship by a liberal coup (Rock, 1986: 121). His son fled to Montevideo. There he pieced together a living as a practising lawyer, professor of political economy, and local director of the leading English commercial bank. In the meantime, Buenos Aires and the remaining confederated provinces waged an intermittent war. But when differences were settled and Bartolomé Mitre took office as the first President of a united Argentine republic in 1862, López did not immediately return. It was only in 1871 that he finally settled once again in Argentina, now serving as deputy in the provincial chamber and as professor and *rector* (Vice Chancellor) of the University of Buenos Aires. From 1879 to 1883 he took charge of the Banco de la Provincia de Buenos Aires, the oldest and most respected of Argentine banks. National office was denied him until, as was noted at the outset, his 1890 appointment as Minister of Finance. Leaving office in 1892, he soon retired from public life, but lived on into the new century, dying in August 1903.

Exile and disruption meant that for long periods López had no way of contributing to public life besides his writing. His output was indeed considerable, and falls into at least three categories. There was a good deal of journalism, ranging from an early polemic advocating Romanticism, published in

Valparaíso in 1842 (Pinilla, 1943), to his contributions of the 1870s to the *Revista del Río de la Plata*, of which he was co-editor (Lamas, López and Gutierrez, 1871–1874). To some of the 34 issues of this journal, López contributed sections of longer historical works, eventually to be published in volumes, but he also threw in shorter pieces on language and politics, and on the public works programme of the Sarmiento administration (Lamas, López and Gutierrez, 1871–1874, II: 135–163).

After the journalism come the histories: of the Argentine revolution (1881) and of the Argentine republic (1913). While it is for these works that López is now best remembered, other shorter historical works include the early *Manual de historia de Chile* (1846) and the *Manual de la historia argentina* (1907), in which López summarised his longer works for schoolteachers and their students. Given his philosophy of history, of which more later, the novels – those he wrote and those he merely planned – might be classed as an extension of his historical writing. López himself would have accepted this classification. In *La novia del hereje* (1917 [1854]), the better known of the two published novels, he pays tribute to Scott and Fennimore Cooper and adopts a standard device of the Romantic historical novel, embedding his fictional narrative in a context of historical events and characters, complete with footnotes. The avowed intent of *La novia*, he declared, was 'to make a past way of life live once more or, to put it another way, to galvanise dead societies' (López, 1917: 13).

Third, López tried his hand at a scientific treatise on what would today be called linguistics but was still known in his day as philology. In *Les races aryennes du Perou* (1871), López provides an account of Quechua, the principal indigenous language of the *altiplano*, in which he draws on the work of Friedrich Max Müller and others to suggest that it is an Aryan language, related to Sanskrit. This, in turn, is used to support the familiar claim that South America was colonised by peoples already relatively civilised, migrating in the proto-historical past from a Central Asian heartland, allowing for a pan-South American foundational myth in which miscegenation between Iberians of Visigoth descent and pre-Columbian Americans is presented as the re-unification of a people sundered by history.[1]

Journalistic essays, scholarly histories, school and university text books, novels and a scientific treatise: López tried them all, but with a constant purpose, which was the forging of a sense of national identity calculated to stabilise Argentine society. Socially conservative and communitarian, he

---

1   López was just plain wrong on dates. He identified the campaigns of Alexander the Great (334–326 BCE) as the cause of the divisive migrations. Population of the Americas from Asia began several thousand years earlier.

developed views about society, language and history that drew deeply from the wells of European Romanticism and French pre-Marxist socialism. So, classical theatre, derived from French eighteenth-century models through metropolitan Spain, 'appeared among us together with the revolution' (Pinilla, 1943: 18). This was no accident. With its emphasis on strong individual passion, French classical theatre appeared to López to be a preparation for revolution: for destruction, not organisation (Pinilla, 1943: 15). By contrast, Romanticism emerged from the reaction of French society against the excesses of revolution, a reaction that had centred upon the attempt to rehabilitate family and church as much as monarchy, and which found its leading cultural expression in a cult of the Middle Ages (Pinilla, 1943: 21). Romanticism was able to flourish in Argentina in the 1830s, in what might be thought very different conditions, because it had a foundation there in reaction against the excesses of the attempt by the first president of Argentina, Bernardino Rivadavia (1780–1845), to impose a rigid Benthamite form of government upon a society quite unprepared for it during the previous decade.

The remainder of the analogy between Europe and Argentina is not spelt out by López, though he can hardly have been blind to it. In Europe, Romanticism began as a reactionary force. Young minds seized upon it to authenticate the new nationalisms of Greece, Italy, and the rest, in which it became for a time inextricably bound up with Liberalism. For every monarchist Walter Scott there was a Byron; for every Chateaubriand, a Mazzini. So, surely, in Argentina the reactionary phase was represented by the dictatorial rule of Rosas with its attempt at legitimation through a cult of the gaucho and traditional rural life. Sarmiento, in all probability, must serve as the Byron of Argentina. But just as in Europe, at the point of equipoise between these two politically opposed Romanticisms, López detected solid achievement in the revival of scholarly study of Dante, Calderón and Shakespeare, and of medieval history, so – in Argentina – there was ... López himself, of course. And if, as he suggested, changed social circumstances meant that Romanticism was a spent force after 1830, and that a new literature was coming into being, based neither on Antiquity (Classicism) nor on the Middle Ages (Romanticism), but on contemporary society – preoccupied with the present and the future rather than the past, and with humanity rather than with individual nations: if *this* was the order of the day, then it must surely be seen as the yardstick by which López intended his own work to be judged. For he was quite explicit in his view that aesthetic value lay in being in tune with one's own age, and not in approximation to some universal goal. To say that Virgil was to be preferred to Statius 'because he wrote better verses – he insisted – is a puerile nonsense; it reveals a failure to understand that this superiority depended upon deeper, more social causes ... Virgil triumphed because he was more progressive' (Pinilla, 1943: 52).

The political purpose of all this is clear enough. López, remember, admired the function that French Classicism had performed under the *Ancien Régime* as critique of a static system. Its ultimate failure arose out of its inability to legitimise a truly novel social order. To achieve this in postcolonial South America was precisely his own mission, and provides the context of all his writings. For lack of such legitimation, his native Argentine was adrift. Sketching what he would have hoped to achieve by a further historical novel (one he never wrote), López referred explicitly to the Argentine nation, 'stunned by the excesses and calamities of incessant war', and to the need to recall it to 'the healthy path of its nationality, its only possible development' (López, 1917: xii).

Hence the attempt, through so many genres, to build a strong national myth of reconciliation between Creole and aboriginal populations, consistent, it should be noted, with dreams of a greater Argentina and the recovery of lost territory in the north (Escudé, 1988: 152ff). Elevation of the indigenous peoples of the *altiplano* to the status of foundational Aryans, a straight borrowing from Fennimore Cooper that dates back to an early point in López's career, serves the purpose of ennobling the historical division between First Nations and Creoles and, hence, the wished for reconciliation (Cooper, 1992 [1826]: 34).[2] What is to be attempted in the modern world of South America is no less than a healing of the struggles that defined Europe and separated it from a broader original culture. 'Fugitives from the hosts of Alexander, [the Americans to be] came to the land of their exile condemned to be devoured by Pizarro and Cortes, heirs to the task begun by that destroyer of the Ancient World' (López, 1917: 22). Nicolas Shumway has claimed that one source of Argentine failure in the twentieth century has been the failure of liberals and nationalists ever to settle on a single founding fiction (Shumway, 1991: 299). López represents this path not taken, the middle way. It is an appropriately nostalgic destiny for a self-confessed

---

2   The link between López and Cooper is stronger than this mere detail might suggest. There are features of Cooper's background and career with which López may have empathised. Like López y Planes, Cooper's father was a politician, a Congressman, with some claim to be among the founders of the nation as the pioneer settler of the area around what became known as Cooperstown, NY. Cooper, like López, tried his hand at polemics as well as novels. Also, Cooper deals, in *The Last of the Mohicans*, with the theme of miscegenation, which lies at the heart of *La novia*. Cora Munro is part Afro-Caribbean (p. 187). There is an interesting foreshadowing of the kind of racial reconciliation sought by López (though in this instance of Afro-Caribbean and indigenous Americans) in the doomed relationship between Cora and the eponymous Uncas (p. 406). What dies with the last of the Mohicans is not just his line, but the possibility of racial harmony and integration in the independent republic that lay just around the corner.

Romantic who conceived of Romanticism precisely as a compromise between revolution and restoration: a Janus figure uneasily positioned, throughout his life, between the thoroughgoing liberalism of Sarmiento or Mitre and the social conservatism of Urquiza or Rosas, his ambivalent relationship with English capitalism just one aspect of his greater self-imposed mission.

Of Thurburn and López it would be rash to say that the two men could not have worked together, but it is hard to imagine their having much conversation over the dinner table and little wonder that Thurburn should have warmed, instead, to the military man, Roca. More generally, it is an awakening of these personal dimensions of the history of capitalism, missing from so much of the first-phase work on informal empire a generation ago, that veterans of that period owe to those who have expanded the study of empire into consumption, visual culture, gender relations and literature following the cultural turn in history more generally. Moved to English ground, the differences between the two men suggest a meeting between Disraeli and Dombey. Structure, in the form of class, education and interest, much more than mere nationality, sets their worlds irretrievably at odds with one another; but any regrets that the acutely self-aware and social-constructivist Argentine may have felt at this turn of events would hardly have crossed the lightly stocked mind of the plain English banker. That nothing short of agency would justify the step from informal empire to informal imperialism was entirely absent from the mind of the putative imperialist and no more than evanescent in the overheated subaltern imagination.

Empire and Imperialism; Structure and Agency

In discussion of relations between Britain and Argentina, especially when they are broadened in the manner suggested here, there is an overwhelming case for dumping the phrase 'informal imperialism'. 'Informal empire' is less problematic, referring to the extent to which a complex and extensive polity may be held together by other than constitutional, legal and military means. It is in this sense that the UK has formed part of the informal empire of the USA since the 1940s, notwithstanding the presence on British soil of sovereign US bases. What constitutes that somewhat ragged contemporary informal empire, in which Australia and Canada are also to be counted, are shared language, culture and history together with trade and investment. But this is not the result of any process deserving the name of imperialism, because it came about without any very clear intention to create or reinforce the authority of the Union.

In much the same way, British 'informal empire' makes perfectly good historical sense as something of which Argentina was a part; and the British Empire was indeed – though to a lesser degree than its US successor – held together by informal structures and institutions. The literature on this subject that emerged during the Cold War was overly concerned with economic relations to the neglect of other sources of authority. This was natural enough, because in Britain this literature reflected, sometimes openly and sometimes subliminally, the process of British absorption into the US realm and a concurrent and rather painful exposure of the informal skeleton of British global power as the flesh-and-blood empire was dissolved in the acid of nationalism; and in these processes trade and investment were very prominent. This gap has since been thoroughly and inventively plugged by a wide range of studies of relations between Europe and the wider world, and of the impact of the wider world on Europe, in which the term 'informal imperialism' has at times been loosely used (see Brown's introduction to this volume, p. 7–8). More important than any semantic objection, however, is the fact that much of the original literature on informal empire has been left high and dry by the cultural turn in history generally and in imperial and colonial studies more specifically. The empirical core of this chapter has therefore been calculated to throw a couple of rope bridges across the historiographic chasm separating first-phase and second-phase literatures on informal empire by exploring the private lives of Thurburn and López, who offer contrasting ideal types of two worlds that lived cheek by jowl in Argentina and Uruguay for more than a century, intimately connected at first, then steadily more distant from one another. There is a case for attempting a new print of informal empire in Latin America that splices in some of what was left on the cutting-room floor three decades ago and even adds some new footage. So why the objection to imperial-*ism*?

Imperial-*ism* implies agency; empire, merely structure. If it is anything at all, the first is a policy or a doctrine; the second, a constitutional order. There have been vast, more or less enduring, ethnically diverse polities for many centuries, although the term empire dates back no more than 2,000 years, to the time when the Latin title *imperator*, meaning commander-in-chief – alongside the family name Caesar – emerged foremost among the many titles gathered by Octavian and his successors as Rome slid from republic to monarchy during the last century before the common era.

In their origins, therefore, the terms empire and emperor had more to do with military and legal supremacy and undisputed authority than with the composition of a polity, let alone a policy of expansion. So when the preamble to the 1534 Statute of Appeals famously declared England to be an empire, this had nothing to do with the heterogeneous nature of the Tudor realm, with its subject princedom of Wales, its Irish settlements, its residual enclave of Calais, and the wider territorial ambitions of the Tudor dynasty. It had everything to do with excluding the papacy from English affairs by forbidding appeals by subjects of the Crown within England to courts in Rome (Elton, 1960: 344).

The fact that 'empire' antedates 'imperialism' in English by more than three centuries bequeaths an interesting problem, which is that while part of the customary meaning of 'imperialism' is undoubtedly 'a national policy of territorial conquest and annexation', the term only began to be applied with any frequency to British (as distinct from French) policy retrospectively, shortly *after* a wave of new annexations in the 1880s (Porter, 2004b: 8). There was a British empire long before anyone began to speak of imperialism. The term 'new imperialism' was used by contemporaries in the last quarter of the nineteenth century not only to refer to a perceived acceleration in the extent of formal British and European rule, but also to capture the deepening of control over an *existing* empire made possible by new technologies of transport and communication, and made necessary by local resistance and heightened Great Power rivalries. Indeed, after breaking down the claim that British expansion was quiescent during the middle decades of the nineteenth century and establishing the continuous reluctance of British governments to expand the formal empire in a manner calculated to deny a burst of late-Victorian imperialism, Gallagher and Robinson concluded that 'the late-Victorians were no more "imperialist" than their predecessors, [but] *were driven to annex more often*' (1953: 13). Yet it was to precisely this drive to annex that contemporaries were referring when they adopted the term 'imperialism'.

Early-twentieth-century Marxists followed contemporary usage. For Lenin, imperialism was a process that began once the scramble for colonial territories had been completed, during the 1890s at the earliest, and which ought properly to be dated from 1900. This was because he saw the onset of imperialism as a qualitative change in the mode of competition between states, in which re-division within a closed frontier replaced competition for territories lying beyond the frontier of European dominion. At the height of the Great War of 1914–1918, Lenin could famously regard rivalry between France and Germany over Alsace and Lorraine as just as much a symptom of imperialism as any confrontation between European powers in Africa or Asia.

In a rather similar manner, contemporary British debate about imperialism in the early twentieth century dealt not simply with annexations and the forces impelling them, but with the deepening and reinforcement of the empire. A painful and costly British victory in the South African War of 1899–1902, for example, which prompted Hobson's celebrated essay on imperialism (1902), did not expand the British empire by a single square mile; since the Orange Free State and the South African Republic had, following the first South African war (1880–1881) been granted self-rule under British suzerainty, and not, as is often claimed, full independence. Indeed, constitutional developments in southern Africa during the closing years of the nineteenth century and the first quarter of the twentieth perfectly illustrate the contemporary sense of imperialism, as the status of the Afrikaans-speaking republics moved from self-government, to occupation, to annexation, and finally, in 1910, to federation in the new dominion of South Africa. Further north, meanwhile, the lands that now form Zimbabwe and Zambia were governed by a chartered company – the British South Africa Company of Cecil Rhodes – from 1889, and then incorporated formally into the British Empire in 1923 as, respectively, the self-governing colony of Rhodesia and the protectorate of Zambia (Gallagher and Robinson, 1953: 3). When annexations took place to secure vital trade routes or to block the expansion of rivals; when Whitehall demanded that the empire should not become a greater financial burden on the Treasury, inadvertently forcing the expansion of primary commodity exports as sources of currency with which to pay the new taxes needed to support growing colonial administrations; when surveyors mapped the new possessions and cheap colour printing finally allowed the coastal fringes of the nineteenth-century atlas to be superseded by the cartographic equivalent of fully fitted carpets from the 1880s: in each and every case imperialism was at work, integrating, ordering and regulating an empire that had formerly displayed much more the character of an early-modern composite monarchy, such as the Habsburg realm, than of a modern nation-state (Porter, 2004b: 66). In short, imperialism – as a British policy after 1890 – was about consolidation, not expansion; it was the re-branding of an approach to government that seventeenth-century Britons had referred to, disparagingly, as 'thorough government'; it was, in a word, about formalising the empire.

This is why the phrase 'informal imperialism' has always threatened to collapse into an oxymoron. So long as 'imperialism' is loosely defined, 'informal imperialism' can be used to describe the exercise of state-like power or power over states by non-state actors, the shoving and shaping effects of corporate power and market on peripheral states, and the development of forms of domestic and cultural regulation calculated to withstand the tensions of extreme disparities of power and wealth. But when 'imperialism' is used in the narrower sense identified here, it is clearly a nonsense to speak of 'informal imperialism'.

It was with such thoughts in mind, close to 30 years ago, that I insisted that 'there was no British imperialism in Argentina', before qualifying this bald statement by borrowing from Platt (1977) a phrase I now regret (Jones, 1980). This was 'business imperialism' (an aspect of informal empire), defined as the more or less deliberate use of market power by metropolitan corporations to circumscribe and shape the power of peripheral states without resort to appeals for support from their parent states. While recognising the value, to historians, of the narrower usage of 'imperialism', I also appreciated at this time that impatience with constitutional niceties and sensitivity to the gross asymmetries of power they sought to regulate, brought to crisis point by the final constitutional trick of de-colonisation after the Second World War, had encouraged an extension of the common usage of 'imperialism' to embrace virtually all aspects of asymmetric power, centring on the unequal relations prevailing between large and wealthy countries on the one hand, and smaller, weaker countries on the other. Indeed, I shared in that impatience; only three years later, I was to publish a history of the ongoing struggle between so-called North and South (Jones, 1983) that encouraged this semantic extension by stressing the *political* basis of the ostensibly economic contest being conducted in multilateral institutions such as the United Nations (UN) Conference on Trade and Development and the Third UN Conference on the Law of the Sea (1968–1981) during the 1970s.

Yet seen in the long run, the empire of British business, like its formal counterpart, proved quite insecure, prompting the thought that the seemingly limitless variety of forms of subordination that constitutes imperialism may be as much a sign of weakness and entropy as of strength, as power is obliged to dodge and weave in order to avoid being overwhelmed by a multitude of Lilliputian missiles. Outside the colonial empires and, later, in postcolonial states, direct foreign investment and unequal international trade relations fomented economic nationalism and expropriations, peaking in the 1970s. At the same time, it was still routine to speak of the contradictions of capitalism, and revolution in the West seemed a possibility following the ignominious defeat of the USA in Vietnam, the fall of the dollar and the oil shocks of 1973–1974. This was the great era of publications on imperialism in English, though they were, in the manner of all academic work, the present perhaps not excluded, to drift on with a considerable lag, well beyond their time. It was brought to a close only at the turn of the decade as near-simultaneous crises in Poland, Afghanistan and Iran were met with renewed resolve by Ronald Reagan. Soon afterwards, in 1982, brilliant exploitation of a sharp rise in interest rates triggered by its own excessive borrowing and the debt crisis this caused in Latin America, allowed the government of the USA to kneecap the North–South dialogue. The next year saw Britain, in its customary supporting role, respond with unanticipated force and success to the Argentine invasion of the Falkland Islands. In this way, the Third World was brought to heel, allowing the inauguration of a neoliberal hegemony that Gramsci himself would have thought worthy of the name.

Yet for all their frailty, large corporations were one of the pillars of British power well into the twentieth century, and the continuing interaction of Creole and British elites in Latin America was one of the cultural assets that British governments sought to perpetuate and deepen through the activities of the British Council from its inception in 1934. With some reservations, then, it seems reasonable to include the work of Colin Lewis, Robert Greenhill, Rory Miller, Linda Jones, myself, and others, during the 1970s and 1980s as being concerned with informal empire and its management from the mid-nineteenth century onward, though not, I insist, with informal imperial-*ism*.

This reluctance to abandon the narrow definition of imperialism as the formalisation of empire and, paradigmatically, as its *deliberate* formalisation, stems from what, among those who write about international relations for a living, is generally termed political realism. Realists privilege the state when dealing with international affairs; they privilege conflict in social relations; they privilege coercive power as a means of conflict resolution. My 1980 stance on business imperialism was scrupulously realist (though I had not yet encountered the term in this technical usage) in the first and second of these three ways. British business activities in Argentina seemed to deserve the designation 'imperialist' because they consisted in the application of market power to resolve conflicts with their Argentine competitors in ways that had deleterious effects on the growth and orientation of the Argentine state that might reasonably have been foreseen. But, of course, this use of market power served precisely to obviate any need for the exercise of British naval or military power in this quarter of the globe, which is to say to *avoid* imperialism. As Gallagher and Robinson (1953: 13) so succinctly put it: 'trade with informal control if possible; trade with rule when necessary'. It is the latter that is properly termed 'imperialism', and to call the former 'informal imperialism' is simply to lose a useful distinction. This need not, however, rule out talk of an informal *empire*, since this is a state of affairs and not a doctrine or policy, and a state of affairs that is created by men and women engaged in the course of other activities – typically trade, settlement, investment and proselytisation – sidling only crab-like or carelessly into positions of political authority or, like Fennessy, Jones, Thurburn and the tribe of British bankers, into positions from which they were prone to disrupt the efforts of would-be state-builders such as López and Pellegrini.

Given this realist emphasis, at the heart of late-nineteenth-century discussions of imperialism, on state-formation and the impediments to it, and the general tendency to relax into a less realist frame of mind in the 1960s and 1970s, it is interesting to find that some of the leading figures in the 'new imperial history' have remained realist while vastly expanding the range of social structures and milieus relevant to the functioning of empire to include family, household, literature, sexuality and gender, as well as the market. Ann Laura Stoler, for example, is at pains to establish that her concern with parenting, servants, race and other aspects of intimacy is at least in part prompted by the question of what made these things 'central concerns of the state' (Stoler, 2002: 8). It may well be that an extensive survey would find a close analogy with the literature on security over the past twenty years, which has seen a division emerge between those soft realists who retain a central concern with the security of the state while recognising an ever growing range of threats to it, including environmental threats and terrorism, and their more idealistic opponents who aspire to extend the object of security studies from state to humankind, with much inevitable and ill-disciplined trampling upon the carefully cultivated crops of cognate disciplines.

Without sacrificing realism, it is evident with hindsight that market relations were not the only informal constituents of empire or of the distribution of power between empires in the nineteenth century. Closer still to the core of the state lay the armed services. Allowing foreigners to establish the national staff college and choosing the French rather than the Germans to do the job, or vice versa, could have incalculable effects on the ethos of the military, their view of their constitutional role and their contribution to national identity (Nunn, 1983). The residue of this aspect of formal empire is still evident not only in the beleaguered College of the Americas at Fort Benning in the USA, but also at Shrivenham and Sandhurst in the UK. It occasionally bursts spontaneously into flame as when, at the outset of the conflict in the South Atlantic in 1983, when the US government still favoured a negotiated settlement and opposed a military response, the US Navy volunteered a battleship if only the British could find a crew to take charge of it as it steamed southwards.[3] (The British either could not do so or chose not to.)

The strength of transnational links supplied by military training and alliances, higher education, professional associations, family, literary forms and custom may all act to reinforce political power and constitutional arrangements. They may, as in the case of the US battleship, provide examples of the autonomous exercise of power. Their coherence need not necessarily favour the status quo. Indeed, what prompted Gramsci's development of the concept of hegemony and his critique of commonsense was a deep concern that social revolution could never succeed at the purely formal level and therefore required a new alignment of the whole gamut of sources of social power.

Yet the recent profusion of specialist studies of social and cultural aspects of power asymmetry or informal empire has sometimes obscured their inseparability, unintentionally replicating the old structuralist error of imagining politics, society, economy and high culture as so many separate realms nested like frames in a hive. Now more like an untidy archipelago, they still

---

3   Informal address by John Lehmann, US Navy Secretary 1981–1987, Cambridge, UK, 2002; confirmed in informal conversation with British naval officers at Shrivenham, July 2007.

seem too often to be discretely dealt with, each by its own dedicated epis-temic community, echoing the more pernicious sort of multiculturalism that proceeds by first fixing communities and identities and then demanding they play nicely together. Happily, a more ambitious approach to the study of empire is now emerging, which goes beyond the mere enumeration of forms of subordination or bickering about the relative influence upon one another of metropole and colony to provide a plausible, holistic and politi-cally realist account. For only a holistic account can maintain the claim to realism by keeping the state constantly in its sights. It is in this spirit that so much of this essay has been devoted to a micro-study of the River Plate in the last quarter of the nineteenth century which relates the market logic that so fascinated my generation in the 1970s to the narrow personal ambition and wide-ranging historical imagination of two of its participants. From the slag-heaps of doctoral research and the tailings of abandoned archives come the fuel and ore with which something more like un-hyphenated, un-qualified history may be forged.

6

Appropriating the 'Unattainable': The British Travel Experience in Patagonia[1]

FERNANDA PEÑALOZA

University of Manchester, UK

Some Preliminary Considerations

In the UK academic context, British empire-centred literary and cultural analyses, largely informed by postcolonial theory and its numerous reworkings and reformulations, tend to neglect British imperial interventions in Latin America. This lack of interest derives from a tradition whereby scholars engaged with postcolonial studies have often focused their attention on geographical areas that effectively pertained to the British empire's territorial domains, such as Africa and Asia. Illustrative of such a perspective is Robert Young's assertion that British academic interest in Latin America 'tends to function rather distinctly and in isolation from much of the rest of colonial-discourse analysis' (Young, 1995: 165). According to Young this is because 'it is not an area where the English have played any great historical role' (1995: 165).

The marginal presence of Latin America in the orbit of postcolonial studies in the UK obscures the fact that there has been a long-established body of work by imperial historians on both sides of the Atlantic who, for many decades now, have thoroughly researched the economic, political and cultural dimensions of British-Latin American relations. Without doubt, John Gallagher and Ronald Robinson's thesis on the so-called informal dependencies of the British empire, developed in their groundbreaking article 'The Imperialism of Free Trade' (1953), paved the way for a significant amount of scholarly production which, more often than

---

1   Parts of this chapter were taken from my PhD thesis (Peñaloza, 2004a).

not, directly addressed the question of the extent to which the concept of 'informal empire' is suitable to describe Britain's role in Latin America.

In the specific case of Argentina, which is the focus of this chapter, the work of H. S. Ferns[2] is one of the earliest and yet still most influential attempts to challenge the implications of considering Argentina as part of an informal empire. Indeed, within the Latin American region, the British–Argentine case is one of the best researched. For many scholars, 'such had been the extent of British dominance that it has become customary to describe Argentina as part of Britain's informal empire' (Hennessy, 1992: 11). This tradition has long roots. Graham-Yooll (2002: 115) draws attention to the fact that Lenin made specific reference to Argentina by using the term 'semi-colony'. Lenin claimed 'it is not difficult to imagine what strong connections British finance capital (and its faithful "friend", diplomacy) thereby acquires with the Argentine bourgeoisie, with the circles that control the whole of that country's economic and political life' (1969: 230).

Even if one is to reject Lenin's somehow awkward term 'semi-colony' and question the influence the British might have had in domestic political affairs in Argentina, it is undeniable that throughout the second half of the nineteenth century Great Britain was the predominant foreign power in Argentine economic life.[3] British companies and investors worked with Argentine governments in close partnership for decades (particularly in the 1860–1914 period); hence many economic historians have concluded that this commercial and diplomatic relationship (together with the specificities of the financial and political outcomes) was not necessarily one in which a dominant imperial power exercised control over a subordinated

---

2   Despite its quite unbearably racist overtones, H. S. Ferns's (1960) text remains one of the most authoritative works of historical research on British–Argentine relations.

3   Britain's role as the dominant foreign power in Argentina's commercial networks underwent little criticism until the 1930s, when figures such as the writer Raúl Scalabrini Ortiz began to make negative remarks about what had been in the past regarded as a mutually convenient partnership. In 1933, Scalabrini Ortiz writes: 'The Argentine Republic is in the hands of the British capital [...] We are the slaves of the Englishmen' [La República Argentina está en poder del capital británico [...] Somos esclavos de los ingleses] (cited in Galasso, 1985: 25).

colony.[4] Exemplifying this line of argument is Andrew Thompson's analysis of the estancia ownership system, which leads him to conclude that 'Britain's "informal empire" in Argentina is in essence a myth' (Thompson, 1992: 436). Although these attempts to resolve the dilemma of whether or not informal empire is a useful concept are highly valuable, I see two major drawbacks: one of them has to do with the specific case of the colonisation process in Argentina; the second one is more general and relates to the cultural dimension of Britain's imperial project in Latin America.

I do agree with the fact that British influence in Argentina was fostered by groups of individuals who belonged to both the British and Argentine political and economic elites and, therefore, benefitted greatly from a largely fruitful partnership. This relationship was not necessarily created or even monitored by British imperial authorities, however; hence it would be difficult from this perspective to frame Argentina within the dynamics of informal empire. From this viewpoint, Argentine–British relations were formulated as a duality: an imperial power allied to a newly born republic. However, the Argentine elites were, like their British *partners*, a group of predominantly white males who were producers and bearers of power structures aimed at securing for themselves a privileged social position. Such a focus, although revealing of the texture of power relations between the hegemonic groups that constituted the estancia owner oligarchy, leaves out a very important component. What is missing here is a consideration of those groups who did not benefit from the elites' partnership: How do such groups fit within these seemingly balanced dynamics of power? One such group was the indigenous peoples south of the Río Negro, in the region known as Argentine Patagonia. Not only were the original inhabitants not

---

4   Following unsuccessful attempts to take the Río de la Plata from Spain in 1806 and 1807, Britain turned to the task of securing economic privileges in the area. After experiencing a sharp decrease in overseas trade as a result of the Napoleonic system that closed European markets to British goods, merchant and financial interests in London were inclined to view Buenos Aires as the next most suitable port for their commercial endeavours. In 1825, the British signed a treaty with the Buenos Aires government that established the legal basis for their diplomatic and commercial relationship over the next hundred years. The agreement cleared the way for British investment in the newborn republic and regulated their mutual trade. It also guaranteed the civil rights of British citizens residing in Argentina. Capital investment flowed from Britain into Argentina, aimed principally at the public and mining sectors, and especially for the livestock-rearing industry. By the second half of the nineteenth century, the considerable British capital investment began to show fruit.

invited to the British–Argentine oligarchic banquet, they were also exposed to all the effects of colonial rule: appropriation of material resources, exploitation of labour, and unwanted intervention in their political and social organisation. One should not forget that whereas Patagonia was for the British Empire a territory where the desire for possession could not be fully realised, the Argentine authorities were accomplishing the effective domination of the indigenous peoples in order to secure white settlement, a plan that, indeed, included British nationals.[5] I will deal further with this issue in the second section of this chapter.

The other point I would like to highlight here is that the emphasis on the economic–political paradigm of most studies on informal empire generates an interesting paradox. Whilst they provide a solid platform from which to understand the material grounds on which cultural hegemony was deployed, negotiated and contested, in general they underestimate the impact of the cultural dimension and therefore these perspectives leave us ill-equipped to name and interpret the less apparent interventions of imperialist power. Again, Thompson provides an interesting insight by claiming that 'there is also the further question of how the existence of cultural or ideological imperialism is established' (Thompson, 1992: 436).

Indeed, fairly recently, some scholars have been critical of the fact that the economic and political dimensions of the British–Latin America relations are not only analysed in isolation from the production, circulation and consumption of cultural forms, but also that the former are privileged over the latter (e.g. Aguirre, 2005: xxi). They suggest that a focus that neglects the various layers of British informal empire fails to acknowledge the intricate power dynamics that are established in these specific contexts. In relation to the USA and Latin America, Ricardo Salvatore observes:

> An informal empire, in order to build hegemony, requires the production and circulation of truthful representations about the regions that fall under its gaze and influence. Without reliable regional knowledge (geography, resources,

---

5   Journalist and writer Roberto J. Payró invites his readers to imagine the benefits of British ownership in the region. The following quote is very illustrative of the features – order, progress, discipline, wealth, etc – that many Argentines associated with British culture: 'Let us suppose that England has taken possession of Patagonia. This supposition evokes images of action, wealth, freedom, administration, independent government, overall, a vertiginous process of progress … Are there not after all, opposite Gallegos, the Islas Malvinas [Falkland Islands]? ['Supongamos que Inglaterra es dueña de Patagonia … Esta sola suposición evoca ideas de actividad, de riqueza, de libertad, de administración, de gobierno propio, de todo un proceso vertiginoso de adelanto….. No tenemos ahí, frente a Gallegos, las islas Malvinas?'] (Payró, 1898: 447).

production, culture, and history), the flows of investment and management that emanate from the center would have greater difficulty consolidating the center's presence, 'conquering' the region's markets, or exploiting its resources [...] These representations embody the center's will to know and, at the same time, reveal fragments of a larger project of incorporating the Other (the peripheral region) into the dominant field of visibility. (2003: 67)

In similar line, Robert Aguirre has recently argued:

The cultural forms engendered by this engagement – travel narratives, museum exhibitions, panoramas, diplomatic correspondence, ethnological freak shows, and adventure novels – lent crucial ideological support to the work of informal imperialism, shaping an audience receptive to the influx of British power in the region. (2005: xvi)

In his seminal work on the configuration of colonial discourse and its interconnections with the phenomenon of cannibalism, Peter Hulme delivers a neat definition of what it implies to undertake an analysis of this nature:

The general area within which this study operates could then be named colonial discourse, meaning by that term an ensemble of linguistically-based practices unified by their common deployment in the management of colonial relationships, an ensemble that could combine the most formulaic and bureaucratic of official documents [...] with the most non-functional and unprepossessing of romantic novels. (1986: 2)

Of course, such 'colonial relationships', which shaped and are shaped by cultural practices vary according to the historical circumstances in which the colonised/coloniser dynamics are inscribed. Anne McClintock helps us to point out this tension by asking 'Can most of the world's countries be said, in any meaningful or theoretically rigorous sense, to share a single "common past", or a single common "condition", called "the post-colonial condition", or "post-coloniality?"' (McClintock, 1992: 87) McClintock argues that the political and historical contexts of the countries within the postcolonial world have shaped different forms of colonisation and, in consequence, different forms of de-colonisation. The complexity of a postcolonial reading of power relations in the specific case of Latin America lies in the process of de-colonisation. According to Else Vieira, speaking of postcoloniality in the Latin American case is referring to 'an unfinished project' because, although Independence was 'geographical in the sense of delimiting frontiers [...] there remained an informal British economic empire and a French cultural one' (1999: 276).

I am interested in the possibilities of the concept of informal empire specifically in relation to the discursive ramifications of British imperial rhetoric in narratives on Patagonia. Hence, I situate my own interpretation of imperial knowledge production as a projection of colonial desire in agreement with the analyses of the above-mentioned scholars. I think the work of Aguirre and Salvatore introduced further challenges to those who are sceptical about the usefulness of the concept of informal empire. Indeed, in the specific case analysed here, even when the British travellers ventured to destinations that were not under British rule, such as Patagonia, their writings rendered visible discursive dynamics of power inscribed in colonial practices. In this chapter, through a reading of Charles Darwin's journal entries on Patagonia, I explore one dimension of landscape representation, that of aesthetic contemplation.[6] I argue that Darwin's engagement with the landscape and his use of the aesthetic concept of the sublime are examples of British imperialist discursive operations. Furthermore, it is my contention that the concept of informal empire not only should not be completely discarded, but also that if placed in the context of meaning-making and knowledge production, it can enable us to reflect on how certain ideologies that were produced by experiences of territorial and cultural expansion were projected over topographies – in this case Patagonia – where the metropolis–colony dichotomy cannot be applied. A critical reading from this perspective can shed some light on the colonising vision that underpinned the discursive ramifications of British narratives on Patagonia in the process of Argentina's political and economic expansion plan for the region.

The British Travel Experience and Patagonia as a Colonial Setting

In her article on nineteenth-century British travel narratives on Argentina, Kristine Jones directly links economic expansion with the act of writing the journey; in her own words, 'increased investment possibilities created increased demand for information, and travel accounts met this demand. The full commoditization of the travel account now was complete' (Jones, 1986: 199). Although British travel to Argentina, like in so many other parts of Latin America, entailed speculative economic ambitions, the experience also involved scientific inquisitiveness; ethnographic curiosity; missionary visions; self-contemplative meditations; and aesthetic quests. Even when the

---

6   Darwin's journal *The Voyage of H.M.S Beagle* first appeared in 1839 as the third
     volume of Robert FitzRoy's travelogue. Because they give a more complete view
     of his experience in Patagonia I will be quoting from two editions of Darwin's
     journal: Darwin (1989), *Voyage of the Beagle*, ed. J. Brown and M. Neve, London:
     Penguin; and Darwin (2001), *Charles Darwin's Beagle Diary*, ed. R. Darwin Keynes,
     Cambridge: Cambridge University Press.

traveller's intentions are *fully declared*, these accounts are informed by a set of discourses about the familiar self and the exotic other that also reveal the intricate processes of meaning-making and knowledge production.

Given the popularisation of the travel writing genre and the increasing British presence in the Argentine economy, it should not come as a surprise that Patagonia – where sovereignty was still disputed by Argentina and Chile – was also an object of scrutiny for a significant stream of visitors and settlers from Britain. Although not all of them left a record of their impressions of the landscape and its peoples, it is worth noting that the narratives they produced have been translated into Spanish and frequently cited in a wide range of texts. Some of the most prominent names in the British experience of travel in Patagonia are: Robert FitzRoy (1839), Charles Darwin (1839), the Anglican missionary Thomas Bridges (1856), the adventurer George Chaworth Musters (1871), the engineer Julius Beerbohm (1879), the writer Lady Florence Dixie (1880), the Welsh Reverend Abraham Matthews (1894) and the latter's countryman, the nationalist Lewis Jones (1898).[7]

The colonisation of Patagonia began with a process of territorial occupation led by the infamous Argentine ruler Juan Manuel de Rosas,[8] which guaranteed the incorporation of the region as part of the national territory. This aim was secured by a far more ambitious campaign, launched almost 50 years later, under the command of Julio Argentino Roca. In reference to this military victory against the indigenous peoples, Graham-Yooll (2002: 115) invites us to consider what he calls 'a matter of speculation', which, in his own words, is 'whether or not the massacre was a direct result of pressure from Europe – especially from Britain'. Graham-Yooll states that 'Argentina needed to show Europe that it was putting its Patagonian hinterland in order [...] The conquest of the wilderness also freed land for further European settlement and agriculture' (2002: 115). Although I do not

---

7 Two more experiences of travel could be included here, although the sense of 'Britishness' in both cases can be rightly questioned: the travelogues of the Anglo-Argentine writer W. H. Hudson who explored the area south of Rio Negro in 1870, but did not published his book entitled *Idle Days in Patagonia* until 1893; and the Welsh Patagonian Eluned Morgan, whose journey from the Atlantic coast of the Chubut province to the west took place in 1899, but the publication came out in Welsh in 1907 with the title *Dringo'r Andes* (Climbing the Andes).

8 Ferns (1960: 51) states that the British *estancieros* 'found in Juan Manuel de Rosas [...] a politician, a soldier capable of controlling the community in their interest and in the British Government a power willing and able to provide access to wider markets'.

necessarily see the colonisation process of the hinterland as a direct response to Britain's demands, I think Graham-Yooll's point is useful as it enables us to clearly establish connections between Argentina's modernisation discourse – of which foreign capital investment and immigration were key elements – and the process of territorial expansion. Hence, I am not claiming that British colonial discursive interventions in Patagonia and representations of its landscape and inhabitants were responsible for the killing and imprisoning of a large number of indigenous people. Nor am I saying that Darwin's observations and those of his successors were used as propaganda for prospective British investors or immigrants, thereby relaying Argentina's ambitions for territorial occupation of the area. After all, the British travellers' portrayal of Patagonia, as will be shown in the analysis to come, is bursting with images of death and decay, which could by no means be appealing for such enterprises. In fact, the harshness of the weather, the aridness of the soil and the threat of 'Indian' attacks – all elements present in these narratives – could raise scant hope for improvement in British citizens looking to profit.

What I am suggesting, therefore, is that the representation of Patagonia as an enigmatic, untouched, sublime territory pertains to the Western language of territorial and cultural expansion, which in turn was instrumental to the Argentine nation-building process that deliberately excluded the indigenous peoples in its vision of an economic future. Bringing 'civilisation' to 'barbarian societies' was the hegemonic model the leaders of the country envisaged. Although it was of course Domingo Faustino Sarmiento in his *Facundo* (1845) who most visibly installed the national debate on landscape, identity and culture around the civilization–barbarism dichotomy, the following statement by Juan Bautista Alberdi epitomises the ideology behind the Argentine government's colonisation plans: 'Who among us knows a gentleman who boasts of being a full-blooded Indian? Who would marry his sister or his daughter to a young man from the Araucania and not a thousand times rather to an English cobbler?' (1852: 241). Narratives such as Darwin's journal implicitly validated these ideas through a convenient view of civilisation. For example, despite his critical view of Rosas's military actions, Darwin believed that, eventually, if the aims of the war were to be achieved, its effects would be beneficial, particularly in relation to the country's economy: 'The war of extermination, although carried on with the most shocking barbarity, will certainly produce great benefits; it will at once throw open four or 500 miles in length of fine country for the produce of cattle' (Darwin, 2001: 172). These discursive intersections need to be contextualised within the framework of Victorian anxieties surrounding *otherness* that were very much correlated with the exploration of the non-European world and the consolidation of a British commercial network in Argentina.

Particularly in Patagonia, the British played a key role in securing the development of a vast and strong sheep-farming industry, which became the backbone of the regional economy.[9] According to Eduardo José Míguez, although several British land companies were established in the Patagonian region, the Argentine Southern Land Company, established in 1889, was the oldest and most important (Míguez, 1985: 254). Míguez also suggests 'the significance of this company is so great that the history of its development is highly illustrative of the process through which the Patagonian region was incorporated into the economic life of the Republic' (Míguez, 1985: 254).[10]

But the definitive incorporation of Patagonia into the national model of production became possible when British investments in the railways allowed Argentine ambitions to expand the network to the Chubut province to flourish. The idea was to connect the Atlantic coast with the Andes to strengthen the region's commerce. Although these plans did not materialise until 1889, the early investment of British capital for purchasing land in the region had provided a stable financial climate for the railways' expansion to turn into reality. A number of companies such as the already mentioned London-based Argentine Southern Land Co.[11] were created for

---

9   It is important to stress that I will be dealing with the section of Patagonia that Argentina colonised and incorporated as part of its national territory (an area of about 673,000 sq km). Although in the nineteenth century the borders between the Argentine and Chilean Patagonia were still being disputed, there were military actions and immigration policies put in place in order to safeguard the Argentine Government's interests. I will avoid constantly referring to Argentine Patagonia as such in order to facilitate the readability of the present chapter. But I must highlight that by no means am I extending my observations here to Patagonia as a whole, that is to say, treating the Chilean and Argentine domains as if they constituted a homogenous whole.

10   'La historia de su desarrollo ilustra bien el proceso de incorporación de la región patagónica a la vida económica de la República' (Míguez, 1985: 254).

11   The Benetton group, which according to López (2003: 130) owns 900,000 hectares, adopted in 1991 the name of Compañía de Tierras Sud Argentino, which is the translation of Argentine Southern Land Co. Interestingly enough, the company has reprinted travel narratives on Patagonia never translated into Spanish before. Additionally, ever since the Benetton brothers bought land in Patagonia, there has been a serious conflict over land ownership led by Mapuche groups who have managed to gain support across Europe, organising a series of boycotts of Benetton products.

the purpose of investing in the region and British investors already established in the country, such as those in the Argentine Land and Investment Co., also contributed to the government's railway strategy.[12] Though relatively few in number, the British were one of the most visible and influential group of immigrants. Indeed, together with the creole elite, they constituted the oligarchic structure that ruled Argentina right up to the twentieth century.

Naturally, the British were not the only foreigners interested in the images of infinitude that Patagonia seemed to convey, but they certainly were the most influential in producing such images.[13] For instance, the Argentine explorer Francisco P. Moreno, like many of his contemporaries, confessed in his travelogue published in 1879 that his curiosity about Patagonia began after reading the copious volumes of Captain Robert FitzRoy's and Charles Darwin's accounts of the *Beagle's* voyages (Moreno, 2001: 6). Furthermore, Moreno claimed that in order to provide a faithful record of the contrasting scenery of Patagonia, 'it is necessary to have the writing talent of Humboldt or Darwin' (Moreno, 2001: 6).

The literary production from British travel in Patagonia is a significant part of the intricate layering of textuality, temporality, displacement, exclusion, inclusion and the interweaving of identities that characterises the informal empire encounter. As Simon Naylor puts it:

> As well as a site where the 'wilderness ethic' could come together with the analytical theories of the natural sciences, Patagonia also facilitated somewhat contradictory spatial fantasies. For some travellers in Argentina, Patagonia was a site of discovery and conquest, a belief that, in part, grew out of Britain's financial hegemony in the region. Meanwhile, for others it was a space of respite from the excesses of European imperialism and industrialism. (Naylor, 2001: 245)

The aestheticising drive and the intertextual map that comprise the travel writing tradition dramatises a self-interrogative consciousness that is present in the way the travellers perceived their surroundings and the

---

12   These plans were to be expanded in the early twentieth century under the leadership of Ezequiel Ramos Mexía who promoted the development of the region. In his *Memoirs*, when recalling how he introduced his project to President Julio Argentino Roca, he writes: 'The conquest of the desert that you have made with guns is not fully accomplished yet; it is necessary to undertake a conquest of the rail in order to Argentinise Patagonia' (Ramos Mexía, 1936: 205).

13   See for example the account of a French naturalist, d'Orbigny (1835).

peoples they encountered. A brief sampling of the toponymy of Patagonia demonstrates these texts' appropriative power over naming and representing the region: there is an Andean mountain chain called Darwin; many towns in the Chubut province have a Welsh origin such as Puerto Madryn, Trevelin, Dolavon or Trelew; there is a lake called Musters and a volcano called Hudson.[14] It is quite significant that, as opposed to the Welsh towns, the natural sites were not named by the British travellers themselves, but by Argentine explorers who felt the former should be honoured for their contribution to the knowledge of the area and its inhabitants. But more importantly, these writings, together with the experiences they articulate, still retain a privileged position in the official Argentine cultural memory. Because they represent the civilising force that sought to end the savagery of the so-called Patagonians, their contribution has not been forgotten. Thus, whereas Spanish translations of British travellers' texts are being reprinted,[15] and the Welsh cultural legacy celebrated, the

---

14   López (2003: 118) notes that even though these foreign place names coexist with indigenous names, it cannot be inferred that the use of the latter is a vindication of the cultural legacy of the original inhabitants of the region. In fact, many British estancias adopted indigenous names. I speculate that this practice of naming only adds an extra dose of exoticism to the landscape, in part fulfilling the expectations of colonising it. Indeed, the exotic embodied in the indigenous names dramatically confirms the illegitimate occupation of the lands as it – unwittingly – chronicles the history of dispossession.

15   In the last couple of years, publishing houses in Buenos Aires have been launching extensive collections of narratives on Patagonia, which demonstrates the growing interest in many texts that were not available in Spanish before. For example, Ediciones Elefante Blanco published several narratives on Patagonia, including translations from French and English into Spanish, as well as new editions of travelogues by Argentine explorers that had been out of print for many decades. Among their books we can find the travelogues of Auguste M. Guinnard, Estanislao S. Zeballos, all the [works] of Francisco Pascacio Moreno and a new edition of Charles Darwin's journal. In addition, another publishing house, Zagier & Urruty, launched a collection of travelogues on Patagonia in 2003 with the publication of Spanish translations of Hesketh Prichard's *Through the Heart of Patagonia* and a selection of texts under the title of *Cazadores de Huesos en Patagonia*, which groups together extracts originally published in the seven-volume narrative of Princeton University's expedition in 1896–1899. This expedition created the largest collection of photographs of Patagonian tribes ever produced.

indigenous peoples of Patagonia are still struggling to resurface from near oblivion.[16]

Although the appreciation and contemplation of landscape was not the main reason for travelling to Patagonia, contemplation did occur, and it was a vital part of the experience. The barren plains, the desert, the Cordillera, all seem to convey the masculine metaphors of power so readily. However, the sublime hyper-masculine scenery of the Patagonian landscape depicted in the male narratives has a female counterpart in the work by the British novelist, poet and travel writer Lady Florence Dixie.[17] In 1880, Dixie writes:

> For a long time after complete darkness had fallen over everything, I stood alone, giving myself up to the influence of the emotions the scene described awoke in me, and endeavouring, though vainly, to analyse the feeling which the majestic loneliness of Patagonian scenery always produced in my mind. (Dixie, 1881: 143)

---

16   Several indigenous groups were living in Patagonia by the time the travellers were undertaking their journeys. In the north-west of Patagonia were the Mapuche, and in the area between the Limay River (north Patagonia) and the Santa Cruz River (south Patagonia) were the Northern Tehuelche. In Tierra del Fuego there were the Southern Tehuelche or Aóni-kénk, the Selk'nam who inhabited the centre of Isla Grande, and the Yamana and the Alakaluf or Kaweskar, who inhabited the extreme east of Tierra del Fuego, now Chilean territory. Please note that there are many conflicting interpretations of ethnic classification of these groups, and this brief description of the main native groups of Patagonia is a rather simple sketch of the cultural diversity of the indigenous population back in the nineteenth century. For the most recent anthropological and archaeological study on the subject, see Briones and Lanata (2002). Groups of Mapuche and Tehuelche people such as the Organización de Comunidades Mapuche–Tehuelche 11 de Octubre are fighting for their territorial rights over land and for the recognition of their identity.

17   *Across Patagonia*, written by this adventurous feminist in 1880, is the only book-length published account of a nineteenth-century woman's journey from Britain to the region. Apart from Eluned Morgan's travelogue also quoted in this chapter, the other female-authored texts on Patagonia from the period I have come across are 'The Hassler Glacier in the Straits of Magellan' and 'In the Straits of Magellan', both in *Atlantic Monthly* (Agassiz, 1872, 1873). Both were written by Elizabeth Cary Agassiz who was born in Boston in 1822. She wrote those articles, among many travel writings in different parts of the world, while accompanying her husband, the Swiss naturalist Louis Agassiz, on scientific expeditions. In narratives such as Dixie's we can see how female voices frequently shift from an emancipated use of the language to a constrained use bearing conventionally masculine resonances. I have discussed this issue at length in Peñaloza (2004b).

A few years later, W.H. Hudson would claim: 'It is not the effect of the unknown, it is not imagination; it is that nature in these desolate scenes, for a reason to be guessed by-and-by, moves us more deeply than in others' (Hudson, 1893: 209). In similar vein, Eluned Morgan wrote, while galloping on horseback to the west of the Chubut province: 'Nature reigned in all the splendour of its grandiosity and we, small and fragile beings, could not do anything other than incline our heads humbly with fear and silent adoration' (Morgan, 1907: 63). The aesthetic standards of the time provided the travellers with categories that shaped their contemplative strategies and that transformed Patagonia into a scenario for aesthetic judgement. Even though categories such as beauty and taste are all at play, the aestheticised drive of narratives such as Darwin's, Hudson's, Dixie's and Morgan's is predominantly centred round the sublime.

The sublime is a canonical and imaginative construct with defined epistemological claims and conventions. The theory of the sublime not only describes the subject's diverse responses to that which arises at the very limits of representation but – as the British experience in Patagonia shows – it also defines the ways in which such responses may impact upon the subject's own sense of self. As Frances Ferguson has put it, 'Sublime objects create particular problems for the sensations – by presenting themselves as too powerful or too vast or too obscure or too much a deprivation for the senses to process them comfortably' (Ferguson, 1992: 8). Because the sublime is strongly linked with the positioning of the self in relation to what its gaze encounters, this particular aesthetic category is of key importance to understanding interconnections between the contemplative enterprise of the *disinterested* traveller and the appropriative power of colonial discourse.[18]

Inevitably, each of the aforementioned visitors articulates travel experiences that are markedly different. However, there are at least two recurrent images that traverse all of them. First, Patagonia itself as a metaphor of the unattainable, and, second, its inhabitants as a vanishing vision in the prelude to civilisation. The writers' input into the creation of these two images have differed, but these narratives have contributed to a certain extent to the creation of a territory devoid of historicity, and by so doing, concealed

---

18 I must strongly emphasise here that I am not embarking on a philosophical study of aesthetics; therefore I will not be delivering a philosophical speculation on the sublime. Chiefly by exploring the basic theoretical formulations of Burke and Kant in this particular category, I am interested in showing how the sublime as a discourse validates European processes of constructing otherness.

the processes and consequences of territorial expansion, cultural appro-priation and, in some cases, reinforced the denial of indigenous identity. The cultural enterprise of 'representing', 'naming', and 'exploring' uttered in the texts by this eclectic group of visitors, together with the experiences their narrative voices articulate, makes visible the multiple and intricate meanings attached to the construction of spaces of otherness in imperial ventures.

In the following pages, I analyse Darwin's aesthetic response to the Pata-gonian landscape, focusing on his use of the category of the sublime in its traditional effect (awe, transcendence, elevation of the spirit); I then explore the implications of the use of the sublime for the construction of otherness in light of current debates on aesthetics and colonialism.

Darwin and the Sublime

Darwin's inland explorations in the region took place at a crucial period in Argentine history, and his insights into the political and cultural life of the time contributed to the formation of enduring British and Argentine views of the Patagonian landscape and its peoples. His diary entries de-voted to the region inaugurated a representational practice that shaped a type of narration for this territory, making it a suitable scenario for con-templation and, therefore, a vehicle of aesthetic sensibility. Often express-ing ambiguity towards the other, Darwin's voice enables us to discuss how British travellers have represented Patagonia and legitimised their own representations, and how such modes of legitimisation operated alongside the discursive agents that were at the core of the Argentine nation-building process.

Charles Darwin's desire to travel and his obsession with natural history came in part from the writings of the German naturalist Alexander von Humboldt. The two volumes of Humboldt's *Personal Narrative*, given to him by his friend and teacher John Stevens Henslow, accompanied Darwin through his 'voyage around the world'.[19] While travelling around South America, von Humboldt[20] had expressed his astonishment when contem-plating the contrasting scenery of the Orinoco region: 'From the rich luxuri-ance of organic life the astonished traveller suddenly finds himself on the

---

19   I have quoted from Henslow's inscription as transcribed by the editor in Darwin (2001: 24).
20   For a recent analysis on the work of Humboldt from a perspective focusing on the aesthetic project of Romantic travelling, see Leask (2002).

dreary margin of a treeless waste' (von Humboldt, 1850: ix).[21] The natural magnificence expected of exotic South America fades away as dreary scenes met the traveller's astonished gaze. Darwin's experience at the southern shores of the American continent is almost identical to von Humboldt's in Venezuela: 'Passing from the splendour of Brazil to the tame sterility of Patagonia has shown to me how very much the pleasure of exercise depends on the surrounding scenery' (Darwin, 2001: 107).

The passages devoted to Patagonia and its inhabitants reflect Darwin's attempts to assert his scientific aspirations over his aesthetic sensibility. However, as a great admirer of von Humboldt, Darwin could do little to help himself from succumbing to the romantic exoticism that lured the German explorer. Alongside the excitement gained from the collecting, documenting and classifying that were supposed to be his chief occupations, at the end of his voyage Darwin acknowledged that the 'pleasure derived from beholding the scenery' was one of the most delightful experiences he could recall from the voyage (Darwin, 1989: 373). According to Darwin, accurate appreciation of nature demanded knowledge of it:

> I am strongly induced to believe that, as in music, the person who understands every note will, if he also possesses a proper taste, more thoroughly enjoy the whole, so he who examines each part of a fine view, may also thoroughly comprehend the full and combined effect. (Darwin, 1989: 373)

His reasoning on contemplation leads Darwin to conclude, 'a traveller should be [a] botanist, for in all views plants form the chief embellishment' (Darwin, 1989: 343). Darwin had Humboldt, his ideal traveller, in mind; undoubtedly, one of the German traveller's most significant achievements was his research on plants in South America. It follows that the type of aesthete that emerges from Darwin's reflections is a person who is well acquainted with what he beholds – the object of contemplation is not entirely unknown to him. This aesthete is knowledgeable in other respects as well; he is a person of taste, he has been instructed in proper

---

21   Charles Darwin refers to Humboldt's influence in his autobiography: 'During my last year at Cambridge I read with care and profound interest Humboldt's *Personal Narrative*. This work and Sir J. Herschel's *Introduction to the Study of Natural Philosophy* stirred up in me a burning zeal to add even the most humble contribution to the noble structure of Natural Science' (Darwin, 2002: 36). It is in St Jago when he confirms that Humboldt's perception was worth trusting: 'Here I first saw the glory of tropical vegetation. Tamarinds, Bananas & Palms were flourishing at my feet. I expected a good deal, for I had read Humboldt's descriptions & I was afraid of disappointments: how utterly vain such fear is, none can tell but those who have experienced what I to day have' (Darwin, 2002: 23).

judgement, he is versed in the appreciation of objects, and his greater delight comes from the natural world.[22] Darwin is equating the aesthetic experience gained on contemplating nature to the pleasure that arises from *knowing* it, recognising it for what it is. In doing so, he produces an aesthetic experience consonant with his scientific enquiry, upon which he relies, to overcome the astonishment that disturbs his ideal of beauty:

> Group masses of naked rock even in the wildest forms, and they may for a time afford a sublime spectacle, but they will soon grow monotonous. Paint them with bright and varied colours, they will become fantastic; clothe them with vegetation, they must form at least a decent, if not a most beautiful picture. (Darwin, 1989: 374)

For Darwin, Patagonia sometimes looked like nothing but 'masses of naked rock'. One feels how much Darwin would have liked to transform the bleakness of the landscape into a picturesque scene. Indeed, Darwin enjoyed the beautiful, but dreaded the sublime. The astonishment that intervenes in the appreciation of sublimity was at odds with his positioning as contemplative subject. He preferred the undisturbed contemplation of beauty to the unsettling effect of the sublime. The impact of Darwin's astonishment at the Patagonian steppes and the inhabitants of Tierra del Fuego stayed with him for the rest of his life.

For example, a petrified forest in Tierra del Fuego provides an intriguing scenario: 'The entangled mass of the thriving and the fallen reminded me of the forests within the tropics; yet there was a difference; for in these still solitudes, Death, instead of Life, seemed the predominant spirit' (Darwin, 1989: 175). To Darwin's overwhelmed eyes, the Patagonian landscape is a puzzling one: the 'thriving' and the 'fallen' coexist, entwined with one another. The deathly scene that Darwin observes mirrors his understanding of nature: he sees all living creatures as components of a sequence of variations in the course of time. He meticulously collected species in order to integrate them as elements of a system of coherent classification that could help him to establish links between past and present. In other words, he saw the fossils as fragments of a complex set of connections that held the key for understanding a process that bridged the gap between death and life.

Referring to the discovery of large bones Darwin enthusiastically asserts: 'The most important result of this discovery, is the confirmation of the law that existing animals have a close relation in form with extinct species' (Darwin, 1989: 162). 'The gigantic species' of 'bygone days' (Darwin, 1989: 162) fascinated Darwin and took up much of his time during

---

22   Note that I am deliberately using the masculine pronoun here.

the inland explorations. Over the course of several weeks, Darwin found the remains of different colossal animals, which led him to think that he was dealing with an 'epoch, which, geologically speaking' was 'so recent, that it may be considered as only just gone by' (Darwin, 1989: 103). Thus, Darwin believed that at one stage the 'great monsters' of the past coexisted with the animal species he found, the latter ones being 'mere pigmies compared to the antecedent races' (Darwin, 1989: 164).[23] Significantly, 138 years after Darwin's journal publication, Chatwin (1977: 1) emphasises the links between the region and a prehistoric past not altogether gone by explaining that his curiosity for travelling to the south of Argentina and Chile had started with the belief that in his grandmother's house there was a piece of skin that belonged to a 'particular brontosaurus [which] had lived in Patagonia'.[24]

It was precisely his way of understanding nature that shaped Darwin's aesthetic gaze. Under his inquisitive eyes, the Patagonian landscape was a puzzle that he was determined to solve. Such an enterprise was not easy to carry out. The sinuous path through life and death could be equally fascinating and dull. The sense of repetition could at times be tiresome and boring. Darwin diligently explores the area hoping to find diversity, but all he sees is a sequence of repetition: almost everywhere there is 'a dry gravelly soil [that] supports tufts of brown withered grass and low scattered bushes, armed with thorns' (Darwin, 1989: 84). The monotony of the scenery, which 'deserves scarcely a better name than that of a desert' (Darwin, 1989: 84), is reflected in Darwin's writing: 'everywhere the landscape wears the same sterile aspect (Darwin, 1989: 84); or 'the land continued dry and sterile' (Darwin, 1989: 90); or 'everywhere we met with the same productions, and the same dreary landscape' (Darwin, 1989: 170). Although the sequence of repetition that Darwin encountered in Patagonia unsettled him, it also fascinated him:

> There is not a tree, & excepting the Guanaco, who stands on some hill top a watchful sentinel over his herd, scarcely an animal or a bird. – All is stillness & desolation. One reflects how many centuries it has thus been & how many more it will thus remain. – Yet in this scene without one bright object, there is high pleasure, which I can neither explain or comprehend. (Darwin, 2001: 209)

---

23 It is interesting to note that in the eighteenth century, George-Louis Comte de Buffon conceived the idea that the American continent's living species were inferior. According to E. Cassirer (1951: 77), Buffon's reflections on the differences found between similar species from Europe and the Americas opened up space for Darwin's evolutionary theory.

24 I would like to thank Matthew Brown for pointing out this link between Darwin and Chatwin.

Darwin is face to face with images of apparently uninteresting nature, yet they do give him unsettling pleasure. It is in scenery like this when the traveller's and naturalist's gazes collide. As a traveller he is well inclined to succumb to the joys of contemplation, regardless of how uninviting they might be. However, as a scientist he cannot let his senses control his mind. This passage may well be read as an unintended confession: Darwin exposes his limitations as a perceiver, for it is not possible for him to comprehend why 'stillness & desolation' can awake so much pleasure. It is not difficult to see why an obsessive and passionate collector such as Darwin might have found it rather confounding, if not irritating, to derive pleasure from an empty space. Although throughout his journey Darwin seems to be in control of *what* he sees and *how* he sees it, the thrilling feeling that the Patagonian landscape inspires in him seems quite persistent. The monotonous plains embody quite extreme images. In them Darwin sees 'the great workshop of nature' (Darwin, 1989: 158) as well as 'a catacomb of extinct races' (Darwin, 1989: 93).

The haunting persistence of the Patagonian images perplexed the young naturalist. After five years travelling aboard the *Beagle*, Charles Darwin looked forward to arriving safely in England. There was plenty of time to reflect upon the impact of his long journey. On the Patagonian landscape he writes:

> In calling up images of the past, I find the plains of Patagonia frequently cross before my eyes. Yet these plains are pronounced by all most wretched & useless. They are only characterised by negative possessions – without habitations, without water, without trees, without mountains, they support merely a few dwarf plants. Why then, and the case is not peculiar to myself, have these arid wastes taken so firm possession of the memory? Why have not the still more level, the greener & fertile Pampas, which are serviceable to mankind, produced an equal impression? I can scarcely analyse these feelings. – But it must be partly owing to the free scope given to the imagination. The plains of Patagonia are boundless, for they are scarcely practicable, & hence unknown: they bear the stamp of having thus lasted for ages, and there appears no limit to their duration through future time. (Darwin, 2001: 444)

The sterile plains of Patagonia produce scenes that evoke images of emptiness (no habitations) and sterility (no water or trees). Yet, he seems to be under a hypnotic effect he can barely comprehend. Why is something so strongly linked with negativity, death, infinitude and sameness nonetheless so attractive to the mind? Darwin finds a partial explanation in the 'free scope given to imagination'. His reflection points to the apparent capacity of these deathly yet seductive images to dwell in the mind of the spectator and to force the viewer to explore beyond the limits of his imagination. A boundless landscape seems to inspire such sensations. Many years after his first encounter with the Patagonian landscape, Darwin wrote in his autobiography: 'The sense of sublimity, which the great deserts of Patagonia and the forest-clad mountains of Tierra del Fuego excited in me, has left an indelible impression on my mind' (Darwin, 2002: 44). Regarding the importance Darwin attributes to this memory, Adolfo Prieto has observed: 'Rescuing Patagonia as the most lasting memory of [his] voyage around the world, has less to do with a Patagonia still inhabited by natives of high stature than with the ambiguous feeling suggested by its vast plains to an European observer' (Prieto, 1996: 88).[25]

Like the verses of a Romantic poet, Darwin's writing embodies the exhilarating awe of the sublime. Darwin's aesthetic judgement is concerned with the imaginary exercise his mind is forced to play in an uninviting landscape that conveys equal doses of pain and pleasure. In the lengthy passages devoted to Patagonia, Darwin unfolds an aestheticising rhetoric that owes much of its power to the humane liberal spirit of the Romantic period. When analysing the sublime experience of Coleridge contemplating the incomplete shape of Gothic cathedrals, de Bolla states (1989: 47):

> on looking at the expanse delimited by the outer structure of the building and realising that the limits cannot be seen from inside – and light conspires against the visual capacity of the viewer – the mind is forced to construct the boundaries of the internal space.

So continuing with de Bolla, when confronting such a view 'the expansion of the mind to fill the void left by sight must be seen as an extension of the boundaries of the mind, so that the mind itself recedes from shape as it becomes infinite shape' (de Bolla, 1989: 47). As a result, the shapeless forms that are found in the interior of the Gothic church are an expansion of the observer's consciousness, which identifies with the object of contemplation. Just as the interior of the church challenges the visual capacity and the viewer is confronted with the eternal and the infinite, so does the uninviting landscape contemplated by Darwin. When the sense of infinity – produced by the boundless and sterile plains of Patagonia – is encountered by Darwin's gaze, his mind seeks boundaries, to construct them, and to understand their absence. His own sense of self is challenged by the void, by the blurred limits set upon his gaze.

---

25   'La del rescate [...] de la Patagonia como el recuerdo más perdurable del viaje alrededor del mundo, tiene menos que ver con una Patagonia poblada todavía por nativos de alta talla que con el ambiguo sentimiento sugerido por sus vastas latitudes a un observador europeo' (Prieto, 1996: 88).

Within the tradition of Romantic aesthetics, shaped by Edmund Burke's reflections on infinity, vastness and vagueness, the sublime is regarded as an experience that, although horrifying because the self feels threatened by it, also pleases. Burke argued that 'greatness of dimension is a powerful cause of the sublime' (Burke, 1757: 114). So is infinity because it 'has a tendency to fill the mind with a sort of delightful horror, which is the most genuine effect, and truest test of the sublime' (Burke, 1757: 115). For Burke, when the sublime is encountered in nature, the subject feels overwhelmed by a feeling of astonishment, defined as a 'state of the soul, in which all its motions are suspended, with some degree of horror' (Burke, 1757: 101). When the sublime occurs 'the mind is so entirely filled with its object, that it cannot entertain any other, nor by consequence reason on that object which employs it' (Burke, 1757: 101). Influenced by Burke, but approaching the concept of the sublime quite differently, Immanuel Kant introduced the idea that sublimity involves the elevation of reason over an order of experience that evades representation. Whereas within his aesthetic paradigm, Burke tries to scrutinise collections of objects and manifestations in nature that he identifies as sublime, and then explores their common properties, in Kant, the sublime:

> does not reside in any of the things of nature, but only in our own mind in so far as we may become conscious of our superiority over nature within, and thus also over nature without us (as exerting influence upon us). (Kant, 1978: 114)

In Kant, the experience of the sublime emerges as a feeling of the superiority of the observer's rational capacities over sensibility and, in turn, over nature itself. The triumph of rationality is the resolution of a conflict that arises from the 'inadequacy of imagination in the aesthetic estimation of magnitude to attain to its estimation by reason' (Kant, 1978: 106). Referring to volcanoes, hurricanes and the ocean, Kant says:

> we readily call these objects sublime, because they raise the forces of the soul above the height of vulgar commonplace, and discover within us a power of resistance of quite another kind, which gives us courage to be able to measure ourselves against the seeming omnipotence of nature. (Kant, 1978: 111)

According to Kant, in the process of logical estimation, which starts when the subject, for example, is confronted with vast magnitudes, 'the mind, however, hearkens to the voice of reason' (Kant, 1978: 102). This is precisely the way in which Darwin experiences the sublime in Patagonia: as a challenge to his rational ability to comprehend vastness. Hence, just as Darwin seeks to restore a sense of completeness when all he sees is perceived as infinite, Kant argues that reason demands a sense of totality and the self feels urged to comprehend the vastness in one perception. At some point, the self realises this is not possible, that no standard of sense apprehension is adequate to the infinite. This realisation, which is connected with the intrinsic limitations of our powers of perception, leads to a feeling of displeasure. This is precisely the feeling that Darwin expresses in his diary: the Patagonian landscape exerts simultaneously pleasure and displeasure. However, says Kant, the self's ability to reflect on that which is great beyond all measure portrays a 'capacity of thinking which evidences a faculty of mind transcending every standard of sense' (Kant, 1978: 98). Within the Kantian aesthetic scheme, the sublime involves a moment of blockage followed by one of finely tuned clarity of thought in which reason resists the obstructive force that challenges it. Reason overcomes the blockage by accounting for its very inability to represent the sublime, and achieves mastery over that which at first resists its control. Thus, the momentum of the sublime marks the self's newly enhanced sense of identity over nature. The categorisation of the natural sublime in a space charged by these mutually exclusive antinomies – pleasure/displeasure – makes palpable the feeling of ambivalent superiority that the experience of sublimity, as theorised by Kant, entails. It is in this polarisation of subject–object that the sublime, as a discourse grounded in categories of knowledge, intersects with colonial discourse. The theory of the sublime explains itself as the encounter of two totalities in opposition.

Thus, the Kantian sublime implies facing that which evades representation and therefore challenges the ability of imagination to make it fit into a categorisation. Regardless of the differences of theoretical approaches, the sublime as an imaginative construct stresses the identity of the self as consciously participating as a distinct opponent in the dialectic. Defining the sublime in these terms contributes to our understanding of how the imperial dimension enters in to the contemplation of landscape. It is precisely this perspective that leads William Cronon to register the concept of sublime wilderness as an overt 'escape from responsibility', a delusion that leads us falsely to believe that it is possible to 'return to the *tabula rasa* that supposedly existed before we began to leave our marks on the world' (Cronon, 1995: 80). Such an illusion might well explain the longevity of images of emptiness associated with the Patagonian region from Darwin to the present day. Cronon reassesses the concept of the sublime in the context of the expansion of the American frontier and notes how, through the intervention of this aesthetic category, wilderness is seen as 'the home of a God who transcends history by standing as the One who remains untouched and unchanged by time's arrow' (1995: 79). This discursive operation, says Cronon, demonstrates that wilderness is 'a creation of the culture that holds it dear, a product of the very history it seeks to deny' (1995: 79). Such history, in the case of the American frontier, is the expulsion of the indigenes in order to create an 'uninhabited wilderness' (1995: 79).

Cronon's assessment of the sublime powerfully exposes the way in which this aesthetic category operates as an intricate but nevertheless overt attempt at dominance. In the specific case of Patagonia and the use Darwin makes of the sublime, on the one hand we have a landscape that needs to be filled with information in order to reverse the threat that it represents, and on the other we have a landscape that needs to be wiped clean of human presence in order to exalt its wilderness.

Therefore, both the discourse of colonialism and the discourse of aesthetics produce cognitive structures of power, which present themselves as constructing identity in oppositional, epistemic and appropriative terms. They both pertain to what Foucault would call 'regimes of truth'. Both discourses construct categories – the other as landscape, the other as native – as binary opposites. But most importantly, they posit complex representational strategies that create and perpetuate irreducible differences between self and other. These two discourses overlap in the theme of travel as they provide cognitive platforms from which to create otherness.

The opportunities for self-enhancement that an empty, vast and infinite landscape creates, presuppose a subjectivity, which, like the mirror stage, operates in antagonistic conditions. Nature in the British narratives of Patagonia appears as magnificently vast and incommensurable, and its force powerfully acts on the travellers' sensibility. The sublime makes its incursion upon the travellers' own awareness of entering the scene as contemplators overpowered by the grandiosity of landscape. And yet, their narratives depict their identities emerging enhanced as a result of such an unsettling experience. Indeed, these narratives are organised around this specific type of contemplation of nature. Thus, nature itself is transformed into a self-affirmative experience, a self-identification that signals the influence of the category of the sublime in creating Patagonia as a territory of powerful aesthetic quests. From the Kantian sublime, we can see that the force of the sublime resides in what can be called a struggle for supremacy: the contemplative subject's attempt to take possession and to wield control over whatever would apparently surpass the appreciation of its judgement. In other words, what is central to the formulation of the sublime, in relation to the present work, is that its imaginative force comes as a strategy of appropriation. Indeed, from Kant's definition of the sublime we can infer that it is the will to power that drives the self in his contemplative act. And because of that, the theory of the sublime constructs an experience that apparently consolidates and preserves the self's domination over its object of contemplation.

So the sublime encodes irreconcilable differences between the object and the subject of contemplation, between the senses and reason. In their treatment of the sublime, British representations of Patagonia have created a territory that, although devoid of human presence (the natives), is the paradoxical site of human agency (the travellers). Because the only human presence that counts in the sublime moment is that of the astonished traveller who gazes at the landscape in a self-absorbing contemplative act before the 'unnameable', the 'unrepresentable', the landscape exerts images of emptiness and infiniteness. The outcome of the strong presence of the sublime in these narratives is that the indigenous peoples are de-historicised and a-temporalised, and therefore discursively erased.

Conclusion

In the case of Patagonia, it is still possible to trace the paths of nineteenth-century travellers. In a recently published travel guide book, Patagonia is described as a land of 'contrasts', where:

> thousands of handprints can be found in the Cueva de las Manos, but in most of Patagonia there's less than one person to the sq km; far from the densely wooded Andes, there are petrified forests in the deserts; and the legacy of brave early pioneers is the over-abundance of tea and cakes served up by Argentina's Welsh community in the Chubut Valley. (Box, 2003: 208)

The introductory passage of the section concludes with a sentence that summarises Darwin's aesthetic astonishment: 'Patagonia's appeal lies in its emptiness' (Box, 2003: 208). It is interesting how this travel guide book condenses into just one paragraph all the images associated with the Patagonian region: indigenous people are reduced to an archaeological site, the people who currently inhabit the area – many of whom are proud of their Tehuelche and Mapuche ancestry – are mere statistics; the landscape is depicted as promising the co-presence of life and death that puzzled Darwin; and finally the only visualised human beings are 'brave early pioneers' but their foreignness is highlighted and their cultural legacy becomes a tourist curiosity.

Not long ago, in a newspaper interview in Argentina, Jean Baudrillard spoke about the connection between the metaphor of the ultimate and exile:

> Behind the fantasy of Patagonia lies the myth of disappearance, of drowning in desolation, of the end of the world. Of course, this is just a metaphor. I can imagine that travelling to Patagonia is like reaching the limit of a concept, like getting to the end of things. I know Australia and North American desert, but

> I have the feeling that Patagonia is the most desolate of places [...] a land of exile, a place of de-territoriality. (cited in Hosne, 2001: 247)

Patagonia has itself become not only a destination for those seeking nature in a *pristine* state, but also a topography that emerges as an image constantly switching between orders of reality and fantasy. By projecting its collective anxieties and fascination with otherness upon the barren plains of Patagonia, the texts analysed in the previous chapters mapped a 'fictional' topography frequently nullifying and voiding 'reality'. In many of these texts, the myth of an untouched, unattainable, empty landscape prevails.

Conceived first as a region suitable for sheep farming, and later for oil exploration and mining, Patagonia's natural charm and promise of profit remains linked with the idea of an empty space whose sterility and isolation was heroically confronted by intrepid travellers and brave pioneers. The language of aesthetic landscape appreciation as articulated by Darwin has transformed the Patagonian geography into a sublime experience, into a space in which the lyrical evocation of an overpowering nature obscures the historical and cultural grounds of the appropriative power of colonial discourse.

This discussion of the British experience with the sublime in the Patagonian region exposes how dispossession, displacement and de-territorialisation are, in part, consequences of the great narrative of aesthetics articulated in the imaginative force of landscape contemplation posited as the encounter of two totalities. In its broadest sense, the idea of possession is incompatible with the metaphor of the unattainable that uninviting landscapes so easily convey. However, the epistemological claims of the Kantian sublime render possible the conversion of the unattainable into the attainable. The articulation of the sublime in the Patagonian landscape enables us to see how colonialism and aesthetics are conceptually and historically connected in their endeavours to posit the colonised and the coloniser as neat binaries. In this sense, the self-exploratory imperatives, which are at play in the configuration of the exotic landscape as a sublime scenario, are authentications of the legitimacy of colonial expansion, be that the result of formal imperial administration or of what Aguirre (2005: xvi) calls 'other forms of (softer) domination'. Invested with the travellers' anxieties and desire for the unknown, the dialectic between the self and the sublime, in narratives on the exotic, pertains to the epistemologies of colonial discourse which in both imperial and informal imperial settings are moulded – and were moulded by – histories of contact.

7

'Weapons of the Weak?' Colombia and Foreign Powers in the Nineteenth Century

MALCOLM DEAS

St Antony's College, Oxford, UK

This chapter aims to provide a series of reflections on whether the notion of informal empire is useful in analysing Colombia's relations with foreign powers in the nineteenth century.[1]

Colombia was certainly not a powerful nation. From a formal military and naval aspect, she was almost pathetically defenceless, with a miniscule army and virtually no navy. She was diplomatically feeble as well, scantily, sporadically and not always skilfully represented abroad. From time to time she was subjected to indignities by stronger countries, diplomatic pressure for debt payments and other claims, demands for apologies for insults to consuls or outrages committed on resident foreigners, backed up by the visits of warships and the occasional blockade of a port or ports.

Her dominant trading partner was Great Britain until the First World War, and the chief item in that trade was British textiles. The culture of the Colombian upper classes, an eclectic Creole culture, shows a number of British influences.

Colombia also suffered one major imperialist humiliation, the loss of Panama, which the USA fostered in 1903. That was in part the inspiration for Joseph Conrad's *Nostromo*, one of the earliest and subtlest books about 'informal empire' (Deas, 2006 [1993]: 271–284). Might there not be antecedents to the loss of the isthmus?

So a case might be sketched out for the presence of Britain's informal empire in Colombia in the nineteenth century. Yet I do not think that Colombia for that century, or for the greater part of the last one, can usefully be

---

1 As most readers will be aware, what has since 1886 been Colombia went under a number of names after emerging as an independent nation as New Granada in 1830. In this chapter, I have generally called the country Colombia.

considered to be part of anyone's informal empire. It might be best not to encourage this particular form of the culture of complaint and lament.

First, let us look at foreign trade, investment and debt.

Trading with a richer nation does not in itself make a country part of an informal empire. Colombia's trade with Great Britain was carried on within the framework of the Treaty of 1825, an unexceptional accord. The Colombians complained in a desultory way that the shipping provisions prevented them from discriminating in favour of a national merchant marine, but that was hardly a realistic prospect (Restrepo, 1956: I, 1). Tariffs were under Colombian control. Although what determined their level for most of the century was the government's need for revenue, tariffs did vary: protectionist arguments did from time to time carry the day, both early and late in the first century of the republic's independent existence (for fiscal problems see Deas, 1982; also Bushnell, 1956; Deas and Sánchez, 1991). The issues were freely debated in Congress and in the press. Certainly, English free trade theory found many followers, most often through Spanish translations from the French of Jean Baptiste Say or Frédéric Bastiat, but there were plenty of sceptics as well (Safford, 1988). There is no evidence to show that any foreign government had a significant influence on tariff policy.

Colombian foreign trade was for the most part carried on by Colombians. As elsewhere in Latin America, there was an influx of British merchants and speculators with Independence in the 1820s, and a brief and intensive bout of Anglomania, but it did not last (Deas, 1994: I, 38; also Deas, 2006 [1993]). Despite the country's impressive size and the Humboldtian splendours of landscape and nature, it was not much of a market, and it turned out to have little to offer that the world or the British economy at that time desired. The rich were few, turnover was sluggish, transport costs were enormous, there were few return cargoes to be had, and ships did not want to lose time and money by waiting around for them on a barren and, in the days of sail, relatively inaccessible coast. Most of these traders soon left.[2]

They had not been popular. There were moves to restrict their operations to wholesale only, and they were blamed for draining the country of specie and for the problems that resulted. Several Scotsmen who had a contract for working the salt mine of Zipaquirá were murdered for attempting to stop the old customs of pilfering, and on one occasion the small British community in Bogotá met to discuss whether threats were so serious that everyone should leave (Restrepo, 1956: II, 183, 101, 194).

---

2   It is worth noting that the first published account of the Colombian economy and assessment of its potential was by the englishman William Wills, his invaluable *Observaciones sobre el comercio de la Nueva Granada, con un apendice relativo al de Bogotá*, Bogotá, 1831, reprinted in Deas (1994: II, 13–82).

Although some stayed, this was never an economy dominated by foreign merchant houses. They were never so prominent there as in Buenos Aires, Chile or Lima, and there is no single British merchant house that survives in the national memory.[3] Even before Independence, native Colombians were accustomed to trade with Jamaica, and this trade carried on after Independence until it was replaced with trading direct with British and other European manufacturing centres. This was a relatively simple matter: Colombia did not require the presence of foreign traders, and did not offer them much either. The number of foreigners who established themselves in Colombia was always small, so small that it is not difficult to establish the identity of most of them from the consular records and the nineteenth-century directories. The presence of British goods did not imply the presence of British traders – all merchants dealt in them where they were the most suited to the market. There was never any mass immigration from any country, and no large fortunes were made. Colombians could establish their credit with correspondents abroad without great difficulty, and these could learn the rhythms and characteristics of the Colombian market and proceed accordingly. These contacts were sometimes made and reinforced by travelling to Europe, and commercial travellers occasionally visited Colombia. Some surviving correspondence shows a high level of trust.[4]

The volume of trade was not great, especially when the transit trade of Panama is omitted. It was not such as to excite much official interest in the Board of Trade or the Foreign Office. Colombia was simply not important enough to attract regular attention, and hardly ever were interests in Colombia important enough to attract expensive attention. For interests to be defended they usually have to have a substantial existence, and in Colombia they were not substantial.

---

3   The one possible exception is perhaps Frühling and Goschen, an Anglo-German house that was prominent in the tobacco trade in Tolima after taking over the interests of Montoya, Saenz y Cia, which went bankrupt in the crisis of 1857–1858. At least the *Casa inglesa* is still to be seen, the finest building in Ambalema. Geoorge Goschen, later Chancellor of the Exchequer and first Viscount Goschen, spent a couple of years in his youth in Ambalema. He must rank with the engineer Robert Stephenson, son of George, as the most eminent Englishman to have been acquainted with Colombia in the nineteenth century.

4   For a marvellously detailed description of the Colombian market after a century of independence, see the guide by the US Department of Commerce commissioner Bell (1921). For trust, see the Vargas correspondence in Safford (1965); the same note of mutual confidence appears in the correspondence of Roberto Herrera Restrepo, coffee exporter and occasional importer, with his agents, cited in my 'A Cundinamarca hacienda' in Deas (2006 [1993]: 235–265). In Conrad's phrase from *Nostromo*, 'the conditions of civilized business were not unknown' (Conrad: 1994 [1904], 43).

Investments were likewise unspectacular. The early boom in mining investment in the 1820s was not sustained. Results were mostly disappointing, and though some operations persisted, dividends were notoriously rare. Some foreign mining engineers did well for themselves and acquired local fame, but foreign companies did not dominate mining.[5] There was some foreign capital invested in steamboats on the Magdalena, in tobacco (the export mainstay from the 1850s until the 1880s) and at the end of the century in railways, but Colombian railways were few and short and did not attract first-rank construction companies. One or two were British, but they were in no way outstanding. One, the La Dorada Railway Company, was so scandalously inefficient that the Legation thought that the less said about it, the better.[6]

There remains in this brief survey of interests the question of the foreign debt. Colombia had raised large sums – the largest raised by any nascent Spanish American republic – on the London market before the crash of 1826, and there followed a long history of defaults and renegotiations, which did not reach a stable point until early in the next century (Junguito, 1995).[7] Colombia did not return to borrowing abroad on any significant scale until the twentieth century. It is hard to conclude that the debt was good business for anyone. The nineteenth-century equivalent of debt relief was default, a base form of extended credit, and the country had repeated recourse to it. This is not the place, nor am I the author, to attempt an advanced calculation of loss and gain, and who exactly lost and who gained. An unknown but perhaps substantial quantity of the debt may have been 'repatriated' into native hands and in that sense ceased to be foreign, as it always had some value for a proportion of customs payments and for speculation, and there were periods when interest and amortization payments were kept up. Colombians were those best placed to speculate. The question here is the place of the debt in any scheme of 'informal empire'.

It was well known at the time that the doctrine of the British government was to regard such lending as private business that the government was not concerned with unless it could be shown that British subjects had been unfairly discriminated against. Diplomats and consuls were from time to time

---

5   For mining, see Deas (1994: I), which covers the operations of the Colombian Mining Association from the 1820s until its demise. As always, gold and silver mining were highly speculative ventures, frequently fraudulent. The best source on Colombian mining history in general remains Restrepo (1885). For the British (and other Europeans) see Gartner (2005).

6   For a graphic description of its services see Restrepo (1942: Chapter 7).

7   See also Avella Gómez (2003), which has useful comparative statistics for British lending and investment.

authorised to use their 'good offices' in assisting representatives of the bond-holders to reach agreements with the foreign governments concerned, and in doing so some were probably more vigorous than others.[8] But the record shows that the doctrine was generally adhered to. In the case of Colombia, there is an apparent exception in the case of the *Deuda Mackintosh*, the 'Mackintosh Debt', where the protracted failure of successive Colombian governments to settle did eventually result in a brief and effective blockade of Cartagena in 1853. It was however a special case, and it was considered that James Mackintosh had not been fairly treated.[9] The British government was prepared, usually reluctantly, to direct the Royal Navy to protect British lives, but it distinguished clearly between British lives and British property.[10] By contrast, US doctrine was to protect both lives and property.

As far as their interests were concerned, the holders of Colombian bonds cannot have felt that the debtor country was part of an informal empire. The long-standing secretary of the Committee of Spanish American Bondhold-ers, John Diston Powles, had been a leading figure in the Colombian mining and colonization speculations and government loans in the 1820s, and had subsequent interests in the tobacco business in Ambalema – he was among the victims of the crisis of 1857–1858. A tireless promoter and projector, he does not seem to have had much success in furthering the interests of these particular bondholders (Deas, 2004; also Deas, 1994: I, 24 *et seq.*).

In 1895, the British Minister reported the views of the late President Rafael Núñez, the dominant political figure of the last two decades of the century: 'It was a favourite theory of his that "these republics" should only

---

8   Daniel F. O'Leary, when Minister in Bogotá, tried to disabuse the Colombian gov-ernment of the conviction that the British government would always take the line that the loans were a private affair. He hinted that its patience was not inexhaust-ible: 'I thought it expedient to use language which while it admits of a double construction, implies a contingency unfavourable to a belief entertained by the Government and those who support them, that your Lordship under no circum-stances will interfere in behalf of the Bondholders otherwise than by friendly counsel'. Later in conversation with the Minister of Foreign Affairs he referred to 'cases like the present where justice was denied for a long course of years' (O'Leary, 1 May and 1 July 1844, TNA FO 55/48).

9   Some of the Colombian documentation is in *Cuestión Mackintosh*, Bogotá, 1857. Mackintosh's brother was his representative in Bogotá in pursuit of this inter-minable claim, where he appears to have temporarily lost his reason.

10   A note on slavery: Colombia passed a free womb law in the 1820s, and finally abolished slavery in 1853. There was no significant import of slaves after Inde-pendence. The scheme of some Cauca slaveowners, including the prominent Conservative politician Julio Arboleda, to sell their slaves in Peru to escape the loss threatened by final emancipation, drew British protests.

think of their debts after everything else that the country required had been amply provided for', for capital would come for railways and the rest anyway if the returns looked high enough.[11]

The small British community in Colombia can be described in some detail. For diplomats, Bogotá was a notoriously unattractive posting. It was extraordinarily remote, even more remote than La Paz.[12] It was expensive, lonely and held out no prospect to the ambitious – for long it was a Foreign Office joke. The Foreign Office had no interest in any sophisticated reporting of the local scene, and complained if despatches were too long, as postage was also expensive. It was not easy to find men prepared to accept the post, and the archive contains a passport or two turned in by nominees who preferred to resign. Hence, it was a relief to find available the former aide-de-camp of Bolívar, Daniel Florencio O'Leary, a Jesuit-educated Irish catholic, to fill the post in the 1850s, and later Robert Bunch, the son of an English merchant long established in the republic. Bunch himself had a number of local business and agricultural interests, which would normally have disqualified him from a full consulship, let alone from serving as Minister, head of the Legation; the Foreign Office chose to turn a blind eye. These might be able men – O'Leary was the most distinguished veteran of the Legión Británica and Bunch was a cultivated and well-read man, one of the promoters of what was to become the Universidad Nacional – but they were all far away from the mainstream of Foreign Office life.[13]

Some found the other members of the small British colony uncongenial. Mr Turner, Minister in the early 1830s, did not like receiving persons in trade socially, which virtually excluded all his compatriots. He does not seem to have minded entertaining Colombians in trade, however, as many upper-class and official Colombians were: trade did not at all demean in Colombia.[14] O'Leary seems to have kept a wary and dignified distance.

---

11 Jenner, 3 January 1895, TNA FO 55/366: it was the view of the Legation that it was an open question whether Núñez was a great man, but that in matters of the debt he was certainly 'great repudiator'.

12 Stendhal, in *De l'amour*, chose Santa Fe de Bogotá as his ideal of the remote.

13 A smug Foreign Office official described Bunch as 'a man spoilt by being raised beyond his proper sphere, and consequently too much impressed with the sense of his own dignity', in TNA FO 55/196, cited in Smith (1979: 15). For O'Leary see Brown (2006).

14 For Turner's somewhat sour despatches, particularly his views on the impossible social pretensions of English merchants in Bogotá, see Deas and Sánchez (1991: I, xxxiv).

Mr Philip Griffith, Minister during the civil war of 1859–1862, reached a pitch of exasperation that he finally expressed in a long and frenzied list of the intolerable nuisances to which his fellow countrymen subjected him. His own sympathies were entirely with the Colombian government. His *bête noire* was the long-term resident William Wills, who insisted on his right as a free-born Englishman to enjoy the protection and support of the Legation, while constantly and polemically involving himself on the rebel side in the country's politics. At one and the same time, a Palmerstonian jingo and a vicariously patriotic *neogranadino*, Wills threatened to denounce Griffith's passivity by writing to old Oxford friends of his in the House of Commons. As Griffith himself wrote to his superiors, the worst of it was that although Mr Wills had had the education of a gentleman – he had gone to Rugby School and had spent some time with a tutor in Oxford, although he had not matriculated – Colombia had corrupted him and he had become as passionate and hot-headed as a native, and no longer amenable to reason. All Englishmen, according to Griffith, should make a point of refreshing their sense of proportion by regular return visits to the home country, a practice Wills had neglected.

British diplomats in Bogotá always tended to side with the party in power, from the days of Bolívar onwards. When it came to claims from British subjects for damage or loss of property in civil war, the Legation frequently agreed with the Colombian authorities that the claims were exaggerated and told the claimants that they would not be supported unless the amounts claimed were reduced. They deplored the practice of lending the flag to cover the property of natives.

Wills's modest Oxford connections were exceptional. Few of the English in Colombia had any influential friends in England. As Griffith complained, they tended to go native, more or less decorously. One reason was that there was never a large enough English community anywhere for them to have led a social life apart. Another was marriage, and quiet conversion to the Roman church. Currents of xenophobia always existed, but violent outbreaks were rare. The total number of foreigners was small – in 1844 the Minister of the Interior reported that there were only 1160 in the entire country.[15] Skilled foreigners enjoyed a higher status than they would have had at home and many enjoyed this. It was best to adapt to the local milieu, and it is clear that even in difficult circumstances many

---

15   A recent addition to the literature on this subject is García Estrada (2006).

were reluctant to call on diplomatic protection, or the supporting presence of the Royal Navy. It might make things worse. Blockades were not welcomed by traders, for reasons obvious enough.[16]

And all of this does not provide, of course, such good evidence for informal empire. An effective informal empire, one might argue, should not have to have recourse to blockades, or at least only in its initial stages. It does, however, provide interesting evidence for other conclusions.[17]

Lord Palmerston famously thought that some such demonstrations should be mounted from time to time to keep the newly independent republics in their place, and that it did not matter much which republic it was or what the pretext was. Others disliked the expense of blockades – Victorian government favoured strict economy, and few shared his occasional enthusiasm for them. The occasions were not always related to trade: two blockades suffered by Colombia in its early decades were the result of quarrels with – and supposed insults to – consuls, Vice-Consul Russell in Panama and the French Consul Barrot in Santa Marta.

The British were not the only blockaders. As well as Great Britain and France, the fleet of Italy appeared at the end of the century, on the eve of Colombia's last formal civil war, to enforce the Cerruti claim by closing Colombia's ports.[18] The USA a number of times sent warships and landed marines in Panama. Germany exacted reparations, material and symbolic, for the murder in 1879 of a number of German merchants in Bucaramanga.[19] If these episodes, some of which were certainly high-handed, are to be considered imperialistic, then obviously more than one imperialist power must be held to blame. There was also at times some

---

16   José Manuel Restrepo (1956: IV, 636–637) noted this in his diary entries on the Mackintosh affair: the English in Bogotá openly disapproved of a blockade 'which would much prejudice British interests in New Granada'.

17   An occasionally useful treatment of some episodes, but with a heavy patriotic bias, is Lemaitre (1974).

18   Cerruti was an Italian merchant trading in Valle del Cauca, much involved in the Radical Liberal politics of the region, who was forced to flee the country in the civil war of 1885. His large claim for compensation was eventually the subject of arbitration by President Grover Cleveland, and the Colombian government, then in dire economic straits from the fall in coffee prices, was forced to pay up in 1899.

19   For details see Acevedo Díaz (1978). This was perhaps the most notorious outrage suffered by foreigners in nineteenth-century Colombia, but only two Germans were killed.

rivalry between the powers: the British would not let the French appear more eager in the defence of their national honour, and there was a deal of mutual suspicion between the British Minister and the US Minister (Smith, 1979).

These *démarches* were naturally much resented. Armed with Andrés Bello's *Derecho de gentes*, the bible for the statesmen of young republics, the Colombian government made the arguments in the country's defence, and also employed another weapon of the weak, inordinate delay in responding to diplomatic notes.[20] In diplomatic terms, however, it was often not an even match, and mistakes and false moves were not always avoided even when the country had a deal of right on its side, which was sometimes not the case.

The accounts of the blockades are also revealing of the national temper, and show a healthy degree of Colombian nationalism. The attitude of Colombians in general was far from being reliably deferential. General Carmona, the Cartagena *Supremo* of 1840, had the following vigorous exchange with the English merchant Watt, as reported by Consul Kelly in Cartagena:

> So you are English, goddamit, then you goddam Englishman I'll have you know that I will have you shot if you say to me another word, understand that I would have an Englishman shot, goddamit, with the same indifference and as easily as I would have a Turk shot, or the vilest black. You are an Englishman, no goddamit, you shit of an Englishman, then I'll have you know that I shit on you (this word he repeated each time with more emphasis) I shit on all the English, on the whole Nation, on your Consul, on your Admiral, on your Squadron, goddamit and on your Queen Victoria herself! I shit on them just like I now shit on you, goddamit, and I stamp on them (stamping on the ground) like I stamp on a dog and that is how I would treat and shit on your Queen Victoria if I had her here, and the same for your Consul, goddamit. What are you English shits thinking of? Leave my territory this moment, goddamit, or I will have you shot, I care not what becomes of you for I hate all foreigners and shall drive you all out of the country, I shit on you all, goddamit.

---

20   Andrés Bello's *Derecho de gentes* was first published in Santiago de Chile in 1832, and reprinted in Bogotá a couple of years later. There are a number of other nineteenth-century Bogotá editions. An exceptionally able and lucid book, it was for long the essential manual of Latin American diplomacy and it remains a classic text in the history of public international law.

Though the Minister sent in this verbatim report from Consul Kelly he was not anxious to support Watt's complaint or to take the matter further, and hinted that Carmona had been needlessly irritated.[21]

The Colombian government usually stood on its dignity, pictured the confrontation with a degree of pathos in David and Goliath terms, and took what steps it could to resist. This can be seen in the case of Vice-Consul Russell.

A confused brawl in Panama involving this British Vice-Consul led to Palmerston ordering a blockade of Cartagena in 1837.[22] Thirteen warships appeared before the port, with a total of 249 cannons and 1,645 men, a force the local forces would find it very hard to resist: as one Colombian wrote at the time:

> The position of England with respect to ourselves is as I see it the same as that of a giant in front of a dwarf, who to exhaust him, ruin him, destroy him, needs to make no effort beyond just lifting his arm threateningly, without even having to let it fall.[23]

The government of President Santander made strenuous and expensive efforts to put the coast in a posture of defence, and to rouse the patriotic

---

21   The original conversation in Spanish was recorded in his notes by Consul Kelly: 'Usted es Inglés, que carajo, pues sepa usted Inglés de carajo, que le haré tirar cuatro balazos si me contesta una palabra más, pues entienda usted que yo haría matar a un Inglés, carajo, con la misma indiferencia y frescura que yo haría fusilar a un turco o al negro más vil. Usted es Inglés no carajo, Inglés de mierda, pues sepa usted que me cago en usted (this word he repeated each time with more emphasis) me cago en todos los ingleses, en toda la Nación, en su Consul, en su Almirante, en su Escuadra, que carajo y en su misma Reina Victoria! Me cago en ellos como me cago ahora en usted, carajo, y les piso (stamping on the ground) como a un perro y así mismo trataría y me cagaría en su Reina Victoria si la tuviera aquí ... y a su Cónsul carajo; que están pensando ustedes ingleses de mierda ... Leave my territory this moment "carajo" or I will have you shot, I care not what becomes of you for I hate all foreigners and shall drive you all out of the country, "me cago en todos ustedes, carajo"' (correspondence in TNA FO 55-30). The English translation cited above is my own. I think 'goddam', 'goddamit', have the right period flavour for *carajo*, 'goddamit' being the favourite oath at that time of the Englishman abroad.

22   The Parliamentary Paper is *Correspondence between His Majesty's Government and the Government of New Granada, Respecting the Imprisonment of Mr Pro-Consul Russell at Panama*, 1837. See also Deas and Sánchez (1991: II).

23   'La posición de Inglaterra respecto a nosotros es la misma, según lo ven mis ojos, como la de un gigante a un enano, que por cansarlo, arruinarlo y destruirlo, no necesita hacer otro esfuerzo, que levantar su brazo en amenaza, sin que tenga precisión de dejarlo caer' (Deas and Sánchez, 1991: I, xlvi).

feelings of the inhabitants. Santander's correspondence from all over the republic shows that he had some success in this, for example, in this proclamation from Santa Marta:

> GRANADANS: Counting on the courage of the inhabitants of this province, I dare to assert that if regretfully the trumpet of war should sound, proud Albion will bite the dust of these shores and will learn to respect the rights of a free people. ENGLISHMEN: The conquerors of the Iberian lion are not frightened by the neighings of sea-horses.[24]

The Mackintosh blockade produced further expressions of patriotism, including the lengthy demand for satisfaction from a citizen of Cartagena who had contracted to wash the shirts of the visiting British naval officers. Kicked out by the consul when he rushed to present his bill before the fleet's imminent departure, he wrote to the Legation protesting that this was no way to treat a citizen of a free republic. The matter, the Foreign Office dryly minuted, might well be left to the courts of New Granada.

The blockades were not violent and were usually settled fairly amicably. Commodore Peyton and his officers at the end of the Russell affair presented General José Hilario López, in charge of the Colombian defence and the on-the-spot negotiations, with a handsome sporting gun. The Mackintosh dispute was settled while the Royal Navy was en route for Cartagena, and when the flotilla arrived '... all the English officers showed themselves friends of the Granadans, and the authorities showed them every possible attention'.[25] Another of Santander's correspondents summed up the results of this sort of affair very well:

> one supposes, as we often see with governments, that is, they and their ministers commit errors and acts of vanity like this one, and although it is embarrassing they get out of it on a tangent, and are friends again as always.[26]

---

24 'GRANADINOS: Contando con el coraje de los habitantes de esta provincial, me atrevo a asegurar que si llega por desgracia a resonar el clarín de la Guerra, la soberbia Albión morderá el polvo de estas playas y aprenderá a respetar los derechos de un pueblo libre. INGLESES: Los vencedores del fierro león de Iberia no se asustan con relinchos de caballos marinos' (Deas and Sánchez, 1991: I, xlv).

25 'todos los oficiales ingleses de la escuadra se manifestaban amigos de los granadinos, y las autoridades ... los obsequiaban en cuanto les era possible' (Restrepo, 1956: IV, 678).

26 'es de suponerse, lo que vemos con mucha frecuencia en los gobiernos, esto es, que cometen por ellos y sus ministros pifias y actos de orgullo como el presente; que aunque como bochorno se salen de ellos por la tangente para quedar tan amigos como siempre' (Deas and Sánchez, 1991: I, xliv).

Nor was British naval activity always hostile. It helped to preserve government authority on the Atlantic Coast in the 'War of the *Supremos*' in 1840. There were pro-British as well as anti-British sentiments. An 'English party' after that war, led by the influential Minister of the Interior and later President, Mariano Ospina Rodríguez, for a time entertained the hope that England might make Colombia some sort of protectorate, or at least guarantee order on the coast, in return for the total abolition of slavery and some commercial privileges. Lord Aberdeen eventually minuted that no such idea could possibly be entertained.[27]

From London, the idea appeared exotic and even ridiculous. Smith (1979: 89) quotes the prevailing view:

> The interest we have in Colombia is merely indirect. For the Country, its Government and people we care nothing, and its commerce probably is very unimportant ... Colombia is valuable to us as a transit route for our commerce, and in this respect it is becoming more valuable every day; and our policy is to keep on good terms with the ruling Powers to avoid taking up occasions of quarrel, and rather to attribute to innate barbarism engrafted on Spanish absurdity, and so deal forbearingly with any proceeding which in a more civilised State of society it would not become us to pass over. A serious difficulty with such a State as Colombia, involving all the paraphernalia of War would be too ridiculous to be thought of, and too injurious to our own interests if magnified into a positive rupture. (From Hammond in London to Bunch in Bogotá, 30 April 1867, TNA FO55/195)

British interests were simply not important enough to merit any energetic defence, and as the London-based Hammond also sensed in his general wariness of the country, it was not without defences of an unconventional kind. Looking resolutely on the bright side of the republic's geographical isolation, General José María Obando outlined these defences in his *Esposición* as Minister of War in 1831:

> The strength of resistance New Granada is capable of through the obstacles of nature ... The sea, great chains of mountains, immense forests, narrow gorges, steep precipices, separate our frontiers from other nations. These advantages, reinforced by the deadly climate of our coasts, the great extent of our territory and the bad state of our roads, are so many natural fortresses superior to all works of invention and art ... nature itself is the best bastion of the

---

27   Correspondence in TNA FO 55/23-28, 34.

independence and freedom of the Granadans. (cited in López Domínguez, 1990: 85)[28]

This was the local version of the doctrine of 'natural defences' that was for long so influential in the USA.

There was an exception, a part of the nation that it did not cover, despite its *clima mortífero* [deadly climate]: Panama. The isthmus was of interest to foreign powers. The Bogotá government did not govern Panama well – sometimes it did not govern Panama at all – and to Panamanians it appeared distant and indifferent. Colombia sought to preserve her possession of the isthmus by seeking foreign guarantees and relying on the rivalries of the powers concerned: the USA, Britain and France. This strategy no longer worked by the end of the century, with the well-known result of Panamanian independence achieved with the incitement and support of the USA. Mainland Colombia figures in Conrad's contemporary *Nostromo* as Costaguana, the 'paradise of snakes', and is simply cast adrift to pursue its perverse course undisturbed by the neat little new republic of Sulaco and its neo-imperial protector the USA. Panama's independence was indeed partly owed to the ignorance, lack of knowledge of the wider world and obstinacy of the politicians of the rest of Colombia, who failed to recognise the danger and did not respond to the insinuations of the USA: not enough 'informal imperialism' being practiced in Bogotá at that conjuncture, perhaps.[29]

Finally, there is cultural influence. The culture of the higher classes of Colombia was a Creole culture, and as is often the case with such cultures it was eclectic. Foreign influences were many, and the British by no means predominated. In politics, though Bentham made a good start and Mill and Spencer later had their readers, Great Britain had little to offer South American republics: more inspiration could be had from the revolutionary, chaotic,

---

28 'La fuerza de Resistencia de que es susceptible la Nueva Granada por los obstáculos de la naturaleza ... El mar, grandes cadenas de montañas, inmensos bosques, estrechas gargantas y precisos desfiladeros, separan nuestras fronteras de las diferentes naciones. Estas ventajas, favorecidas por el clima mortífero de nuestras costas, la grande extensión de nuestra tierra y lo impracticable de nuestros caminos, son otras fortalezas naturales, superiores a todos los trabajos de la invención y del arte ... La naturaleza misma es el antemural de la independencia y libertad de los granadinos'. See also the less optimistic series of articles by P. Fernández Madrid and others that appeared in the Bogotá paper *El Día* in 1846 under the title 'Nuestras costas incultas'; Fernández Madrid feared British designs in Mosquitia, see Clemeate(2005).

29 There is a voluminous literature on the separation of Panama and its antecedents. The best two introductions are Lemaitre (1980) and McCullough (1977).

republican, Bonapartist, Catholic and violent French than from the mostly staid and inarticulate subjects of Queen Victoria. The multiplicity of cultural influences from Europe and their frequently contradictory direction is the subject of Martínez (2001): no informal empire there.[30]

Those higher classes were themselves the product of an empire, one of the grandest in the history of the West. In many ways, they still considered themselves a branch or at least an off-shoot of Spain. In any scheme of imperialism, their position is consequently ambiguous (see Deas, 2006 [1992]: 42–71).

Colombia and Colombians were, in the republic's first century, sometimes the object of condescension, rudeness, prejudice and bullying, from the time George IV had to have his arm twisted by Foreign Secretary Canning before he would agree to receive their envoys, 'these brown gentlemen' (cited in Stanhope, 1938: 194). That does not however add up to 'informal empire', unless the concept is to be made so broad as to cover all unequal relationships between nations. A better case might be made for more recent decades, but then the imperial power would not be Great Britain.

30   For a study of the interaction of Europeans and Colombians in the recovery of the pre-Columbian past, see Botero (2007).

8

'Literature Can Be Our Teacher': Reading Informal Empire in *El inglés de los güesos*

JENNIFER L. FRENCH

Williams College, USA

To blame or not to blame: is that the question?

In the middle of the civil war that occupies the third section of Joseph Conrad's *Nostromo* (1994 [1904]), a militant revolutionary named Gamacho stands up and makes an impassioned speech in front of the crowd that has gathered in the streets of Sulaco:

> His opinion was that war should be declared at once against France, England, Germany, and the United States, who, by introducing railways, mining enter-prises, colonization, and under such other shallow pretences aimed at robbing poor people of their lands, and with the help of these Goths and paralytics, the aristocrats would convert them into toiling and miserable slaves. (Conrad, 1994 [1904]: 332)

As anyone who has read Conrad's monumental novel about a multinational mining company and its impact on the imaginary Republic of Costaguana knows, Gamacho's diagnosis of the national condition isn't exactly wrong: by the end of Part III, conditions for working-class *Costaguaneros* are much as he predicts, while the foreign capitalists and their elite collaborators have grown very rich. But if Gamacho's insight is ultimately corroborated by more trustworthy characters, including the self-sacrificing Dr Monyham (Conrad, 1994 [1904]: 432), why does Conrad tempt us to discard it here? The speech quoted above identifies Gamacho as a rabble-rouser, inciting his compatriots to declare an absurd and hopeless multi-front war against all of Costaguana's major trading partners; the narrator also makes clear that Gamacho is corrupt, self-serving, dirty and drunk, and that the goal of his spontaneous activism is to win a share of Costaguana's treasure for himself. The scene brings to the fore the ambivalence of Conrad's vision of Latin America, including both his critique of informal empire and his profound anxiety about racial mixing and revolutionary politics. But it also functions as what Gayatri Chakravorty Spivak (2003: 22) refers to as a 'staging of rhetoricity', a narrative moment in which the reader is made to confront the formal conditions of representation and the ethical and epistemological problems they present. Do we take Gamacho for a miscreant because the narrator tells us he is? Do we question the narrator's ability to faithfully represent the scene, including the text of Gamacho's speech? By putting one of the novel's central insights about informal empire into the mouth of a racist stereotype, Conrad manages to cast doubt on Gamacho, and the narrator, and perhaps even the representational authority of the novel as a whole. But in the process, he contrasts the contextual nature of novelistic discourse with the formulaic simplifications that often characterise political speech. Almost pathologically sceptical of political activity, Conrad is here daring us to abstract the political meaning of the novel in a way that doesn't reduce the complex and shifting array of desires, perceptions and social relations *Nostromo* depicts to a set of narrow and polarising terms.

I am reminded of this scene by an essay on informal imperialism by H. S. Ferns, published posthumously in 1992:

> Much intellectual and emotional energy has been expended in Argentina in discussion and agitation about British imperialism and neo-imperialism. In fact, Britain and, particularly, the British government, has never been able to force Argentina to do anything the Argentine government and Argentine politicians have not wanted to do … If neither Argentina nor Britain is any longer in the top ten, say, in terms of wealth they have none to blame but themselves, and nothing is owed to one trying to get the better of the other. Imperialism as an explanation of the Anglo-Argentine relationship is a nonsense, and fighting each other about the Falklands/Malvinas is an irrelevant exercise in nostalgia. (Ferns, 1992b: 60)

In the aftermath of the tragic and unnecessary war between Britain and Argentina, Ferns steps back from the position taken in his earlier work and categorically dismisses the notion of informal imperialism as so much nationalist demagoguery. Rather than take issue with Ferns's conclusion, I will limit myself to pointing out that in his response the concept remains much as the other side has cast it, a simple accusation that is easy to rebut by drawing on metropolitan archives to show the complicity of the Argentinian elites and the sense of impotence experienced by foreign diplomats and capitalists when they didn't get their way. In the process, some of the risks of 'informal imperialism' as an analytical tool are made plain: its politically necessary emphasis on inequalities of wealth and power can all too easily be used to flatten out historical complexity by reducing dynamic, multiple and contradictory relations to a set of narrow and polarising terms.

As the rich and varied essays collected in this volume attest, scholars in many fields have managed to escape this logical cul-de-sac by focusing more particularly on 'informal empire' as a descriptor of Latin American realities as opposed to the ideology or policy of 'informal imperialism'. In the process, they have broadened the terms of debate and widened the field of inquiry to include subjective factors such as nationalism, class politics, identity formation, and attitudes toward gender and sexuality. In many cases, this involves looking at sources well outside the metropolitan archive in order to understand and assess the effects of British investment, technology and trade on Latin American lives. In what follows, I will explain how cultural critics have dealt with some of these issues in recent years, then return to the subject of literature to show more directly what literary analysis may offer to the discussion. My intention is not to reinscribe Conrad's radical scepticism regarding activism and political discourse, but rather to suggest ways in which careful critical reading of literary texts may help us to understand how issues of rhetoric and representation inform the way we think about localised and geopolitical inequalities. I will argue that literature is not a transparent representation of the social world, but rather an artful and subjective model for thinking about the relation between language and politics. 'Of course', as Spivak writes, 'the literary is not a blueprint to be followed in unmediated social action. But if as teachers of literature we teach reading, literature can be our teacher as well as our object of investigation' (Spivak, 2003: 23).

Post/Neo/Colonial and Dependent: Postcolonial Studies and Latin America

Any consideration of what 'informal empire' means for literary and cultural critics must begin with the emergence of postcolonial studies as an important new area of intellectual inquiry in the 1980s. Because of its methodological heterogeneity and potentially global scope, postcolonial studies almost immediately drew in scholars in a wide range of fields in the humanities and social sciences. From the beginning, it was an overtly political and self-reflexive undertaking, 'invested in the political commitment to the locational identification of its practitioners' (Young, 2001: 382). Among literary critics, the proliferation of new scholarship that followed the publication of Edward Said's *Orientalism* (1978) signalled both a distinct shift away from the Eurocentric methods of interpreting the canon that had previously dominated literary studies in the USA, and a productive new engagement between the theoretical refinements of poststructuralism and cultural critique.

For Latin Americanists, one of the most important developments was the appearance of Mary Louise Pratt's *Imperial Eyes: Travel Writing and Transculturation* (1992). Coinciding with the quincentennial anniversary of first contact, Pratt's book contributed to two significant new developments in postcolonial studies. First, it drew the Americas into the discussion of colonial discourse by comparing the cultural imaginaries created by British explorers in Africa with those of the 'capitalist vanguards' in post-Independence Spanish America. A year later, David Spurr expanded on this aspect of Pratt's study with *The Rhetoric of Empire* (1993), a systematic taxonomy of tropes and discursive modes used by metropolitan writers in their representations of colonial and postcolonial regions, including Latin America. Second, despite her principal focus on how travel writing creates 'the "domestic subject" of Euroimperialism' (Pratt, 1992: 4), Pratt's book also moves beyond the model of colonial discourse analysis established by *Orientalism* in order to demonstrate 'instances in which colonised subjects undertake to represent themselves in ways that *engage with* the coloniser's own terms' (Pratt, 1992: 7). Her chapter on 'Creole Self-fashioning', which explores some of the ways that nation-building projects of the post-Independence period responded to the hierarchical and expansionist cultures of the metropolis, formed an important and early bridge between anglo- and francophone literary studies and Latin American literary criticism.

Around the same time, a series of critiques appeared regarding the applicability of postcolonial theory to Latin American cultures and the position of Latin America itself within the field of postcolonial studies.[1] In one of the first, anthropologist Jorge Klor de Alva asserted that nearly all of the terminology taken for granted by postcolonial critics is either out of place or anachronistic when applied to Latin America:

> it is misguided to present the preindependence, *non-Indian* sectors as colonised; it is inconsistent to explain the wars of independence as anticolonial struggles; and it is misleading to characterise the Americas, following the civil wars of separation, as composed of postcolonial states. In short, the Americas, as former parts of empires which, after a series of civil wars, separated themselves politically and economically, but not culturally or socially, from their metropoles, cannot be characterised as either another Asia or Africa; Mexico is not another version of India, Brazil is not one more type of Indonesia, and Latinos in the United States – although tragically opposed by a dominant will that has sought to exclude and disempower them – are neither like Algerians in France, Pakistanis in Britain, or Palestinians in Israel. (Klor de Alva, 1995: 247)

Around the same time, literary critic Hernán Vidal warned that a long tradition of sophisticated cultural critique on the part of Latin American

---

1   See also Fernando Coronil's excellent analysis (2004) of the history and current state of the relationship between Latin American Studies and postcolonial studies.

intellectuals was being overshadowed by technological innovations developed almost exclusively in response to the experiences of colonialism and postcoloniality in India, Africa and the Middle East (Vidal, 1993). As Vidal's essay suggests, several distinct but interrelated issues were at stake in these important debates: the validity of new academic knowledge about Latin America, the marginality of Spanish and Latin American Studies relative to other fields in the US academy, the commodification of research by an increasingly market-driven scholarly publishing industry, and finally what Walter Mignolo calls 'the geopolitics of knowledge' – a sense that even within Latin American Studies, locally conditioned knowledges were being delegitimised by hegemonic metropolitan discourses (Mignolo, 2000).

Under the circumstances, it is not surprising that Vidal and others would advocate a return to some of the conceptual categories developed by dependency theorists in the 1960s and 1970s. In the aptly titled 'Can Postcoloniality Be Decolonised?', anthropologist Fernando Coronil diverges from the rigorous parsing of terms undertaken by Klor de Alva, and instead recommends that the new critical idiom be resemanticised for local use by drawing out both the ongoing economic subordination that likens Latin America to much of the global south and the historical particularities of the region, including its autochthonous intellectual tradition. He writes:

> Whether postcolonial societies emerged recently from the experience of colonization or not [...] is in my view less relevant than their continued subjection to metropolitan forces. Thus, although most of Latin America achieved its political independence early in the nineteenth century, it has remained in what many analysts consider to be a neocolonial condition; its transformation recreates colonial and dependency relations. I understand colonial and neocolonial relations as an organic linking of international and domestic relations, not as an external imposition. (Coronil, 2000: 200–201)

Like Cardoso and Faletto before him (Cardoso and Faletto, 1979), Coronil understands colonialism as a totality of metropolitan and peripheral forces, rooted in an historical identification between the interests of local elites and those of foreign capitalists. His formulation brings to the fore an important theoretical challenge in the tension between the political and moral resonance of terms such as 'colonialism' and 'neocolonialism', and the recognition that the condition to which they refer was less an 'external imposition' of the post-Independence period than a result of incomplete decolonisation after the end of Spanish rule.

Acknowledging a similar concern with the multiplicity of overarching and localised structures involved in colonial and postcolonial domination, an association of literary critics and other scholars working in the US academy formed the Latin American Subaltern Studies Group in the mid-1990s.

From its inception the group opened an important 'South–South' dialogue with Renajit Guha, Spivak and other South Asian scholars who had organised the Subaltern Studies Group a decade earlier. Founding members of the Latin American Subaltern Studies Group shared an insistence on theoretical rigour and what Ileana Rodríguez describes as 'a new humanism' born out of frustration with the collapse of Marxist narratives of national regeneration and a renewed commitment to solidarity with the poor (Rodríguez, 2001: 3). Like the South Asian Collective, the Latin American Subaltern Studies Group dedicated themselves to working within the productive tension between theory and praxis, 'to find ways of producing scholarship to demonstrate that in the failure to recognise the poor as active social, political, and heuristic agents resides the limits and thresholds of our present hermeneutical and political condition' (Rodríguez, 2001: 3). Frequently engaging with the debates about *testimonio* and Rigoberta Menchú's narrative, the Latin American Subaltern Studies Group represented a significant move away from the discursive analysis of literary texts that had dominated the first decade of postcolonial studies after Said's *Orientalism*, while retaining an important emphasis on the politics of representation manifest both within and outside the academy.[2]

'Informal Empire': Literary and Cultural Studies

It is within this rapidly evolving field of intellectual activity that we situate the work of scholars exploring the concept of 'informal empire' from the perspective of literary and cultural studies. For critics of anglophone literature continuing on the path opened by Pratt's *Imperial Eyes*, the concept of informal empire provides a useful tool to identify one of several modes of coloniality in Latin America. Unlike 'neocolonialism' and 'dependency', 'informal empire' as used by Robert D. Aguirre and Luz Elena Ramirez points towards the specifically British engagement with Latin America in the nineteenth and early twentieth centuries. Central to their work is the task of situating what Ramirez refers to as 'Americanist discourse' within the dominant ideological structures of the nineteenth-century's leading imperial power, while nevertheless taking into account the particular conditions of the British experience in Latin America, including interactions with post-Independence Latin American governments and a lack of military or diplomatic support from home when compared to the formal empire. If by definition, informal empire 'eschewed an outright model of military domination and settlement' (Aguirre, 2005:

---

2   See also Beverley (1999) and Arias (2001). Mallon (1994) offered an early critique of the Latin American Subaltern Studies Group.

xviii), one must ask to what extent the conception of imperialist ideology Edward Said develops in *Culture and Imperialism* is relevant to British attitudes towards Latin America. According to Said:

> There was a commitment [...] over and above profit, a commitment in constant circulation and recirculation, which, on the one hand, allowed decent men and women to accept the notion that distant territories and their native people *should* be subjugated, and, on the other, replenished metropolitan energies so that these decent people could think of the *imperium* as a protracted, almost metaphysical obligation to rule subordinate, inferior, or less advanced peoples. (Said, 1993: 10)

Based on different kinds of textual production, the findings of Ramirez and Aguirre attest to a heterogeneity of experiences and attitudes. Ramirez's *British Representations of Latin America* (2007), which explores literature ranging from Raleigh's *Discovery of Guiana* (1596) to Greene's *Honorary Consul* (1984), emphasises the contrast between conventional colonial discourse and 'Americanist' literature, which 'compels readers to reevaluate confidence in progress and to reconceptualise the standard geographical divisions of East and West in light of North, South, and continental contingencies' (2007: 79). For Ramirez, Americanist literature is characterised by pronounced anxieties about the fragility of British identity and an uneasy sense of having ventured perilously beyond the reach of imperial authority.

In Aguirre's work, the ideology of informal empire is an opportunistic amalgam of capitalist profiteering, civilising mission and scientific treasure-hunt. While acknowledging the practical limitations and 'improvisational', ad hoc character of British power in Latin America, *Informal Empire: Mexico and Central America in Victorian Culture* subtly shifts the emphasis from informality to imperialism through a focus on the structures of domination that permeated metropolitan science and visual culture in the nineteenth century and the specific forms they took when the object of the gaze was Latin American. Stepping outside of the 'textual universe' known to colonial discourse analysis, Aguirre instead focuses on archaeology and ethnology as instruments of power. He argues that:

> the British quest for and representation of pre-Columbian antiquities became a crucial cultural arm of the larger political and economic strategy historians call informal imperialism. Born from the difficulty of militarily dominating a newly independent Latin America as well as the strain of managing extensive colonial commitments elsewhere, British informal imperialism carved out an area of competitive advantage based largely on trade and economic policy but buttressed strongly by myriad cultural activities on the ground. The most significant of these were archaeology, which produced not only knowledge but also treasures to fill the nation's museums, and ethnology, which provided a

rationale for ranking white Europeans above dark and mixed race peoples
found across the horizon of empire. (Aguirre, 2005: xv)

The importance of archaeology and ethnology for shaping the 'domestic
subject' of informal empire is convincingly illustrated and abundantly theorised through recent work in museology and visual studies, and Aguirre's
study is of great use in examining 'the mentalities […] of the British officials
and businessmen who were primarily concerned with Latin America' (Miller,
1993: 244). Nevertheless, the question of the overall usefulness of these scientific pursuits for British economic interests they 'buttressed' (Aguirre,
2005: xv) perhaps warrants a more nuanced discussion. When Mexicans and
Central Americans appear in the fascinating narrative Aguirre relates, it is
generally to protest against what they rightly perceive as acts of imperial
plunder and to argue for their nation's legitimate legal right to retain its cultural patrimony (Aguirre, 2005: 29–33, 97–101). Given the relative lack of
political or military support for British capitalists and their reliance on the
goodwill of the local population, cultural activities that provoked outbursts
of angry nationalism on the part of Latin American leaders can hardly have
been conducive to foreign businesses operating in the region.

As I have argued elsewhere, following Tulio Halperín Donghi's discussion of the 'neo-colonial order' in *The Contemporary History of Latin America*,
informal empire was most effective when it was most invisible, unobtru-
sively blending the interests of foreign capitalists and local elites by match-
ing imported technologies, finance capital and consumer goods to Creole
desires, in order to modernise their nations according to models established
in Europe and the US (Halperín Donghi, 1993: 123–124; French, 2005: 16–19).
Mexico and Central America are undoubtedly different from the South
American countries in the attention their antiquities drew among foreigners
in the early national period as well as the importance of archaeology as a
positive feature in public articulations of national identity.[3] In South America, informal imperialists' most significant activities were trade, financial
ventures and public works such as constructing ports and railways. These
are 'cultural activities', or at the least they are economic activities with strong
cultural resonances, but they are more subtle and collaborative than the acts
of imperial plunder Aguirre describes. This is not to say that archaeology,
ethnology and scientific racism were not part of the cultural workings of informal imperialism in South America. In the Río de la Plata, for example,

---

3   In addition to Aguirre (2005), see Sara Castro-Klarén, 'The Nation in Ruins' and
     Gustavo Verdesio, 'An Amnesiac Nation', both in Castro-Klarén and Chasteen
     (2003).

national intellectuals often wielded European 'expert knowledges' in order to confirm the superiority of the ethnic elite and the necessity of 'modernising' and 'civilising' their countries, which included both technology transfer and the extermination of the indigenous (Sarmiento, 2001; Andermann, 2003; Verdesio, 2003).

From the perspective of Latin American literature, the challenge is not to understand the psychology of British capitalists who developed intense economic ties with specific Latin American countries, but rather to explain how those ties built on, transformed and reproduced pre-existent social, economic, political and cultural structures in the region. Is 'informal empire' a useful concept for getting at these relationships? To the extent that the phrase identifies the Latin American countries as subordinate elements of a nineteenth-century world order that was dominated materially and ideologically by the British Empire, yes, and it is in that sense that I refer to 'informal imperialism' and 'the invisible empire' in my 2005 book. 'Informal empire' establishes a horizontal frame of reference that is analytically useful because it helps to situate Spanish America's 'failure to decolonise' after the wars of Independence within the context of a global order that was visibly dominated by empires, especially the British. In other words, it captures the Spanish American republics' emergence from Spanish rule, internal hierarchies largely intact, into a world order that was at least as expansionist, hierarchical and racist as the old one, but ideologically driven by notions of 'modernity' and 'civilisation' emanating from the industrialised countries rather than the religious fervour of the Spanish crown. The fact that Spain had fallen behind England and France in terms of the kinds of achievements that counted in the Atlantic world in the eighteenth and nineteenth centuries – technology, science and industry – meant that the independent republics of Spanish America were always already at a disadvantage in relation to Europe and the USA.

Scholars of nineteenth-century Latin American literature have responded to some of the theoretical questions raised within postcolonial studies by attempting to elucidate the strategies that Latin American elites developed to deal with these contradictions. In recent years, critics including Julio Ramos, Carlos Alonso, Santiago Colás and Walter Mignolo have at once demystified narratives of national identity and explored the international, imperial dimensions of processes that literary studies have traditionally considered internal to the countries in question by situating them within the political, economic and epistemological asymmetries of the nineteenth-century world. Alonso in particular has focused on the ambiguous positioning of an intelligentsia that was disadvantaged with regard to the metropolis because of its association with peripheral societies, but empowered with regard to the home countries because of its

European heritage and privileged relations with the metropolis. In *The Burden of Modernity*, he refines Fredric Jameson's thesis that 'Third World' literatures 'are all in various distinct ways locked in a life-and-death struggle with first-world cultural imperialism' (Jameson, 1986: 68) by exposing the rhetorical dilemma of Latin American writers constantly at risk of being undermined by the same Eurocentric discourses of modernisation and civilisation that 'authorised' them and established their prestige (Alonso, 1998: 36). We should note that for these critics Great Britain is not of singular analytical importance, but rather is one of four imperial powers competing for dominance in various parts of the region. Mignolo's *The Idea of Latin America*, for example, discusses the emergence of the term 'Latin' America as a French manoeuvre to assert that nation's cultural affiliation with the former Iberian colonies. It was quickly adopted by Creole elites eager to assert, on the one hand, their cultural distinctness from the Anglo-Saxon countries and, on the other, their hegemony over the non-European sectors of their own nations (Mignolo, 2005: 58–59). In a cogent discussion of what he describes as 'the Creole symptom', Colás for his part describes the production of ideology in post-Independence Latin America as 'driven by the unconscious desire for the persistence of colonial relations, in terms both of dependence on the former colonial or imperial power [i.e. Europe] and of social inequality within the new nation' (Colás, 1995: 384).[4]

Benito Lynch and the Spanish-American Regional Novel

To learn from literature as these critics do is to appreciate both the modesty of its truth-claims and the significance of the conventions that regulate literary creation and interpretation, which render texts historically

---

4   My current research on the literature of the Paraguayan War (1864–1870), also working within the notion of peripheral modernity, examines the ways that European and Eurocentric colonial discourses were redirected by postcolonial elites in Argentina and Brazil towards the black, indigenous and mixed-race populations of their own countries and the Guaraní-speaking Paraguayans, all of whom were at times deemed barbaric, expendable, and even 'fated' to disappear. While distancing myself from exaggerated notions about British involvement in the conflict, most of which have been disproven by more recent empirical analysis (Bethell, 1995; Doratioto, 2002; Whigham, 2002), I nevertheless attempt to understand the war as a particularly catastrophic example of the overlapping of nation-building and coloniality, or of the regional application of the same 'principles' that rhetorically legitimated European colonialism in Africa, Asia and the Middle East and westward expansion in North America.

intelligible by establishing the grounds for improvisation and change. In the case of narrative fiction, the genre that concerns me in what follows, it is especially important to recognise 'the singularity and unverifiability of "literature as such"' (Spivak, 1999: 176), which require us to look beyond the mimetic capabilities of the text and consider the play of citation and alteration it contains, even as we locate its conditions of production in grossly uneven economic structures that cut across geographic, racial and linguistic boundaries. The final section of this chapter examines *El inglés de los güesos*, Argentinian Benito Lynch's 1924 novel about the tragic romance between an English archaeologist and the daughter of tenant farmers who shelter him during his research on the pampa. Refashioning the imported form of the scientific traveller's tale to suit Lynch's paternalistic nationalism,[5] the novel encourages us to track diverse and shifting attitudes towards European expert knowledges and the modernisation of the pampa, including a critical awareness of the complicity of local elites with the economic innovations that enriched some and impoverished others during the export booms of the 1880s and 1890s. I argue that the novel is less an allegory for informal empire than an allegory for *thinking about* informal empire, one that refuses to deal in moral absolutes of guilt and innocence, but instead models a social space in which everyone, including the reader, has some ethical involvement in what occurs.

As an example of Argentina's gauchesque novel, *El inglés de los güesos* belongs to the larger Spanish-American sub-genre known as the *novela de la tierra*, the telluric or regional novel. These narratives, produced between 1910 and 1940 by authors including Horacio Quiroga (Uruguay, 1878–1937), Rómulo Gallegos (Venezuela, 1884–1969), Benito Lynch (Argentina, 1885–1951), Ricardo Güiraldes (Argentina, 1886–1927) and José Eustasio Rivera (Colombia, 1889–1928) typically represent an agricultural or extractive industry such as logging, ranching or rubber-tapping as the primary factor

---

5 In describing the political orientation of *El inglés de los güesos* as a 'paternalistic and rural nationalism', I follow Nicolas Shumway's discussion of Argentinian nationalism as 'an ideologically messy, ill-defined, often contradictory tendency (or tendencies)' that unfolded in the nineteenth and twentieth centuries in opposition to the liberal currents associated with Bernardino Rivadavia, Domingo F. Sarmiento, Bartolomé Mitre and others (Shumway, 1991: 214). The following elements may be said to link *El inglés de los güesos* to Argentinian nationalism as Shumway defines it: (a) pride in Argentina's 'Hispanic heritage' and 'mixed ethnicity'; (b) a rejection of liberalism as elitist and anti-Argentinian; (c) a tendency to emphasise the disparate economic and political realities of Buenos Aires and the interior; (d) a belief that liberals had betrayed Argentina to British capitalists; and (e) a preference for the autochthonous in art and culture. See Shumway (1991: 291–296).

shaping the lifeways and political forms of the people who inhabit the territory in which it takes place. As I have elsewhere argued at length, distancing
myself from both the traditional view of regionalism as an 'authentic' depiction of national identity, and from the more recent, deconstructive analyses
of Alonso (1990) and González Echevarría (1985), the regionalists' collective
obsession with rural life responds to changes in land use and labour practices linked to the dramatic increase in production of primary products for
European markets in the late nineteenth and early twentieth centuries
(French, 2005: 8–30). Instead of the bucolic idylls typical of much nineteenth-century literature, the regionalists instead demonstrate the export
booms' toll on rural communities, including the expansion and capitalisa-
tion of traditional haciendas, the dissolution of common landholdings and
the development of new forms of discipline on behalf of a landowning elite
eager to maximise its profits (see Bauer, 1986: 153–186; Halperín Donghi,
1993: 118–121). Their work suggests that the overall situation Halperín
Donghi describes as 'the neo-colonial order' actually consisted of two linked
structures that, although distinct, may both be considered forms of colonialism: Latin America's external, international status as producer of raw materials for the European market, and the internal expansion of agricultural
and extractive industries at the expense of rural communities and the territories they occupied.

If the terms 'colonialism' and 'imperialism' are often used almost inter-
changeably today, the etymological root of 'colonialism' – from the Latin
colonus, meaning tiller, farmer or cultivator (Klor de Alva, 1995: 164) – establishes a peripheral and agricultural focus that is necessary to understand the aspects of informal empire that most directly concerned the
regional writers. It also gestures toward an important intertextual connection between the *novela de la tierra* and what is more commonly considered
'colonial' literature, including the work of anglophone writers such as Joseph Conrad and Rudyard Kipling. As a corpus, these texts demonstrate a
shared concern with 'thinking about, settling on, controlling land that you
do not possess, that is distant, that is lived on and controlled by others'
(Said, 1993: 5). As a result, works such as *Doña Bárbara* (Gallegos, 1929), *La
vorágine* (Rivera, 1926), and *Don Segundo Sombra* (Güiraldes, 1926) share the
basic structures of Britain's colonial adventure fiction: a young man's journey from the urban centre to the frontier of capitalist expansion, where he
must acclimatise and acculturate while participating in local struggles to
control limited human and natural resources. The difference, of course, is
that rather than follow their protagonists across wide swathes of the globe,
the Spanish-American regionalists instead map the tensions and opportunities of neocolonialism domestically, or between the 'civilised' capital and
the 'wilderness' or *desierto* of the interior.

The works that made Benito Lynch one of the most respected Argentinian novelists of his time – *Los caranchos de La Florida* (1916), *Raquela* (1918), *El inglés de los güesos* (1924) and *El romance de un gaucho* (1933) – focus on the pampa during the era of the great export booms that followed the 1879 *Conquista del Desierto*, in which Argentina's remaining pampas Indians were exterminated or driven onto reservations. While the growth of railways and steam-powered shipping made it possible to radically increase the export of wool, wheat and beef, roughly 8.5 million hectares of conquered territory passed into the hands of the 381 individuals who had financed the mission (Rock, 1986: 154). Lynch's Argentina is remarkably consistent with the situation David Rock describes during the period between 1890 and 1930:

> By 1914 and again in 1930 disparities between the littoral and the interior became more pronounced. The east was the centre of investment and consumption, and its heart, the city of Buenos Aires, an embodiment of advanced civilization. Much of the area beyond still exemplified the most backward parts of Latin America: rambling *haciendas*, an impoverished Indian or mestizo peasantry, feeble towns, inertia, and stagnation (Rock, 1986: 162).

Lynch's literary landscape is a rural Argentina of vast privately owned ranches, divided by barbed wire and dotted with the ramshackle structures where peons and tenant farmers live, deprived of the traditional mobility of the gauchos as well as the economic rewards of modernisation. Among his published work, *El inglés de los güesos* and *Plata dorada* (1909) are especially relevant to the study of informal empire because they bring together the impoverishment of rural labourers, the ostentatious modernisation of the littoral cities and the complex question of Anglo-Argentine relations. Lynch spent his early childhood on his father's cattle ranch in the province of Buenos Aires, then at the age of ten moved with the rest of the family to La Plata, where he was educated and worked for a number of years as a society columnist before beginning his literary career.

Often discarded as irrelevant to the rural fictions that followed, the semi-autobiographical *Plata dorada* satirises the upper middle class of the newly founded city for their desire to impersonate the English who went to Argentina in order to 'develop' the country. The narrator's father, suffering from 'a bad case of English-itis', sends him to an English school, encourages him to negotiate the city alone, and to take up boxing and whisky. Though primarily an urban novel, *Plata dorada* approaches the terrain that I am calling 'colonial' literature when the narrator, Williams Fernández, is hired by rich Mr Linck to operate a creamery near the Paraná River. One night while Williams and the English overseer relax outside their office, a gaucho rides up and asks permission to spend the night among their workmen. Ignoring a long-standing custom of the pampa, the overseer sends the man off to a hotel two leagues away. Williams notes that the man made little attempt to elicit his sympathy, because after years of training he is able to 'pass' as an Englishman. Then he confesses:

> It seemed to me that the man was the embodiment of my race, the sad image of my own weak race that, ejected by a gentle but firm conquest, abandoned its rights in order to sink for all time in the unfathomable mystery of nothingness ...
>
> 'These jokers think this is a ranch of gauchos' murmured Mr. Barley.
>
> And I felt cold in my heart and ashamed of myself. (Lynch, 1909: 346–347)

The scene conveys the guilty conscience of an upwardly mobile Argentinian who betrays local norms in order to improve his standing with the English and serve their mutual economic interests. As Sandra Contreras suggests, Lynch was especially concerned in his early works with Argentina's changing national identity (Contreras, 2002: 208–212); and in *Plata dorada* the narrator contrasts his father's enthusiastic identification with the British with what he himself perceives as an organic Latin American 'race'. In a move consistent with Mignolo's discussion of the discursive invention of Latin America, Williams subsumes the ethnic heterogeneity of the subcontinent into a single signifier – 'my race' – that he contrasts with the illegitimate influence of foreign capitalists operating in the region. If that 'race' is 'sad' and 'weak', Williams associates its pathetic state with a moral imperative to return to a more paternalistic social structure that is identified with the Hispanic past. As the novel concludes, the consequences of the Argentinian elites' unwillingness to disentangle themselves from British influence are figured in the premature death of Williams's fiancée. When Williams and Manuela (significantly, the daughter of Italian immigrants) are surprised in their first sexual encounter by the arrival of Mr Linck and his associates, she leaps into the river and meets a gruesome end beneath that icon of trade and material progress, the British steamer (Lynch, 1909: 380–381).

Allegories of Informal Empire in *El inglés de los güesos*

A more artful and elegant narrative, *El inglés de los güesos* reworks some of the central concerns of *Plata dorada*: Argentina's changing identity, the situation of rural workers and the responsibility of Creole elites as mediators between them and the British. It recounts the relationship between the English naturalist James Gray and sixteen-year-old Balbina Fuentes, who falls in love with Gray during his stay on the pampa and commits suicide the day after his departure. *El inglés de los güesos* occupies the intersection of several genres – comedy and tragedy, 'masculine' adventure and 'feminine' melodrama, 'foreign' travel literature and the autochthonous *novela gauchesca* – and challenges the reader's expectations of how each one performs. To understand how *El inglés de los güesos* intervenes in the ideology of informal empire we must take into account both the transnational economy represented within the text (mimesis), and the transnational economy *of* the text, by which I mean its appropriation, translation and revision of recognisable discursive models. It is by refashioning 'western machineries of representation' (Jameson, 1986: 69) that *El inglés de los güesos* becomes a 'national allegory' in the sense described by Fredric Jameson, a narrative in which literal and figurative, personal and political registers are dialectically interwoven.

As Lynch explained in a rare interview, the text was inspired by the British travellers who wrote about Argentina over the course of the nineteenth century:[6]

> Darwin, Munster, Haigh, the Robertsons? Isn't it possible that one of those amiable, erudite and vagabond English boys, who so conscientiously explored our pampa and so extensively lived among its inhabitants, had his romantic adventure with some young country girl?[7] (Petit de Murat, 1968: 48)

Lynch incorporates many of the commonplaces of his source material – the 'ignorance' of the locals, the 'simplicity' of their lives – but adjusts the perspective in ways that destabilise the authority of the metropolitan traveller. He accomplishes this most immediately by reversing the perspective of conventional travel writing so that the metropolitan traveller is now subject to the gaze of his 'travelees' (Pratt, 1992: 7) As in the title phrase, the man of science seen through the eyes of the tenant farmers is a curious and slightly comical figure:

> The arrival of Mister James, or better yet of *the Englishman of the bones*, as everyone called him, provoked the most amused curiosity and the frankest laughter among the inhabitants of the outpost known as 'La Estaca'.
>
> And with good reason: he arrived all of a sudden, there by the hollow of the lagoon, mounted on the errand-horse of 'La Estancia', more laden with gear

---

6 See Walker (1992); Welch and Figueras (1982); and Cordero (1936). Some fifteen books by British travellers were published in Argentina during the decade after the 1910 centenary celebrations.

7 '¿Darwin, Munster, Haigh, los Robertson? ¿Sería posible que esos simpáticos, ilustrados y andariegos mozos ingleses, que tan a conciencia recorrieron nuestras pampas y que tan largamente convivieron con sus habitantes no tuvieran con alguna muchachita de campo su aventura de amor?'

than the roof of a stagecoach and waving at the top of his tall silhouette, sharply contrasting with the grey background of a rainy afternoon, a large red umbrella.[8] (Lynch, 1960 [1924]: 31)

While the locals look on laughing, Gray stammers out the purpose of his visit in the macaronic Spanish that will become one of the novel's running jokes: 'Mí trabaja ... mí busca güesas antiguos ..., viejas, viejas ...' [I work ... I look for old bones ... old, old] (Lynch, 1960 [1924]: 32). Later on, Lynch's treatment of the scientific establishment becomes more satirical, suggesting that Gray's intellectual inquiry occurs within an insular circle of metropolitan researchers who draw samples and data from India, Africa and Latin America but guard the privilege of knowledge-production for themselves, as when Gray reads about 'a certain valuable anthropological donation made by a British museum to ... another British museum ...' (Lynch, 1960 [1924]: 83; ellipsis in the original). His excavation of indigenous remains will contribute to 'volume LIV of the monumental *History of the Savage Men*'. The title and volume are highly ironic, suggesting a massive will to power that effaces non-Western people's ability to construct and compile their own histories (1960 [1924]: 158).

While most of the writers collectively known as *los viajeros ingleses* gloss over the issue of communication, *El inglés de los güesos* makes Gray's pidgin Spanish an index of metropolitan provincialism, drawing attention to the linguistic complexity of rural Argentina and his own inattention to it. The agrammatical utterances that form part of the amusement of the first scene, in other words, continue long after the joke has worn thin: Gray's language skills are stagnant throughout the narrative, despite his increasing intimacy with Balbina and her family. When her mother Casiana finally asks him to lie about his imminent departure, he replies 'with arrogance': 'Mi viene esto tiera per trabaja, no per ingaña seniorito; mí un gentleman, siniora!' [I came to this land to work, not to deceive a young man, I am a gentleman, madam!] (Lynch, 1960 [1924]: 175]. The juxtaposition of Gray's insistence that he knows the rules for appropriate relations between women and men, and in fact arrived in Argentina already knowing them, with his indifference to the grammatical conventions that assign genders to almost all Spanish nouns

---

8　'La llegada de míster James, o mejor aún de *El inglés de los güesos*, como lo apodaron todos, provocó en los habitantes del puesto de "La Estaca" la más risueña curiosidad y la más franca chacota.

Y por cierto que no era para menos: apareció de repente, allá por el bajo de la laguna, jinete en el petiso de los mandados de "La Estancia", más cargado de bártulos que el imperial de una diligencia y desplegando al tope de su alta silueta, nítidamente recortada sobre el fondo gris de la tarde lluviosa, un gran paraguas rojo ...'

(not to mention the sexual connotation of the verb *engañar*) implies that perhaps something akin to 'arrogance' is afoot in his miscommunications large and small. Significantly, Balbina, whom he calls 'Babino' to the end, does learn to pronounce his name correctly, and makes an effort to learn simple phrases in English (1960 [1924]: 157). This too is ironic, since her name, pronounced correctly, is etymologically equivalent to 'Bárbara' or barbarian, the unintelligible one: *balbucear* and *balbucir* both mean to stammer or stutter, to repeat a single syllable like *bar bar bar*.

The narrator's 'standard', literary language contrasts with both Gray's agrammatical utterances and the regional speech of the tenant farmers. Lynch weaves all three together in a sophisticated narratological performance using dialogue or quoted speech, incorporated speech, free indirect discourse and interior monologues. His attention to rural speech patterns, which at first seems like another joke, becomes increasingly affirmative, as when Casiana says to Gray, 'Demasiado sé que usté no tiene la culpa! ¡Quién iba a imaginarse esta ruina, este castigo de Dios, míster "Yemes"!' [I know all too well that it isn't your fault! Who would have imagined this ruination, this divine punishment, Mr James!] 1960 [1924]: 175). Utterances like this one, in which rural speech is not only grammatical and intelligible, but rich with cultural meaning, anticipate Lynch's *Romance de un gaucho* (1933), a 500-page tragedy narrated by its eponymous protagonist. By exploring the literary potential of regional speech, crossing 'low' and 'high' registers within the text, Lynch creates a literary language that has the potential to broaden the 'imagined community' of his readers (Anderson, 1991). The narrator addresses himself to a worldly, knowing audience, one he assumes will understand references to the British university system, *spleen*, psychoanalysis, and so forth. He invites the reader to see his working-class characters, and Balbina above all, as exotic primitives, while subtly raising important questions about collective identity and responsibility.

If Lynch sets the 'European' travel narrative within the 'native' gauchesque, he re-orders the gauchesque by exposing the connection between the Argentinian interior (that inner sanctuary of 'Creole' culture and values) and the culturally and economically heterogeneous coast. As the novel sinks from comedy into tragedy we catch intermittent glimpses of the tenant farmers' material circumstances, like the 'miserable corner of a shack, delimited by a pile of sheepskins' that serves as Gray's bedroom (Lynch, 1960 [1924]: 134), and the 'ancient piece of furniture, which doña Casiana proudly called a dresser, and used to store intimate feminine garments as well as tools and produce from the garden' (Lynch, 1960 [1924]: 119). We see a lack of adequate healthcare in the family's admiration for 'the marvellous medical science of Mr James' when he cures Balbina's earache with a simple medication from his trunk (Lynch, 1960 [1924]: 82), and note

Balbina's illiteracy when she asks Mr James to decipher the letter she receives (Lynch, 1960 [1924]: 104). She and her brother, like their few peers, have no prospects for the future but to inherit the meagre living of their parents, and Buenos Aires is as remote from them as is London (Lynch, 1960 [1924]: 107).

El inglés largely avoids the business sector that occupies much of *Plata dorada* and instead introduces informal empire through the character of Don X, the rich absentee landowner who arranges Gray's visit in order to impress 'his recommender, the Minister of S.G.M., whom he saw every afternoon at the Club' (Lynch, 1960 [1924]: 144). Perhaps the most negative character in the novel, X is deferential to the Englishmen who serve his social and financial aspirations and indifferent to the well-being of his tenants. The self-indulgent life he and his wife lead in Buenos Aires is represented by a scattering of suggestive images, including his wife's 'very round little finger' pressed down upon 'the buzzer, almost disguised among complicated mouldings of mahogany wainscoting', which they use to summon the servants. He caresses Balbina's cheek during a brief visit to 'La Estaca':

> because she was merely 'her' ... and would not have dared to touch her if she had instead been Florencia Wilson, for example, another eighteen year-old virgin, whose father – a very intransigent gentleman – had presented so many obstacles fifteen years earlier when Don X applied for admission to the hermetic circle of the 'Pocker Club' [*sic*]. (Lynch, 1960 [1924]: 147)

Accustomed to harassing the servant-girls at home, X approves what he takes for a sexual liaison between James and Balbina 'with a meaningful and libertine wink' (Lynch, 1960 [1924]: 148). By including X in the narrative, even in a relatively limited role, Lynch maps the tripartite structure of the neocolonial order: rural labourers, urban Argentinian landowners, and the British.

The Englishman's presence enables Lynch to return to Sarmiento's classic formulation of 'civilization and barbarism' (Contreras, 2002: 215–217) and to juxtapose for aesthetic and ideological purposes relative extremes of centre and periphery, western science and folk knowledge, mobility and isolation. But it cannot be said to reduce neocolonialism's 'organic linking of international and domestic relations' (Coronil, 2000: 200–201) to a simple confrontation between coloniser and colonised, because Lynch's understanding of Anglo-Argentine relations was considerably more complex. Compared to Don X, James Gray is almost comically chaste: he responds to X's innuendo with the blush and gasp that will become his standard defence: 'Oh! No! Mí un *gentleman*!' Gray is not a rapist, a conqueror or even a capitalist; in fact he is the only character to become the victim of a violent crime, when he is stabbed by Balbina's rejected suitor. On the one hand, by incorporating Don

X here Lynch forces us to recognise the Creole landowner's abuse of power and his willingness to compromise the well-being of his tenants in order to advance his own interests. His motives are comparatively uncomplicated and his abdication of responsibility is clear: Don X, his name discreetly withheld, is the figure Lynch holds up to his own social class as the model of behaviour they should reject. On the other hand, it is because Lynch goes to such lengths to demonstrate that Gray's actions are not only within the law, but above board and 'gentlemanly' that I find him so compelling as an allegorical figuration of Britain's historical engagement with Argentina. The interior monologues that reveal Gray's thoughts suggest a subjectivity conditioned by a specific and identifiable ideology: he is 'a man in step with "the march of Humanity," bound by some moral obligation and who-knows-what ancestral guilt to proceed always forward, straight and methodical ...' (Lynch, 1960 [1924]: 179). Like *Nostromo*, which famously conveys Charles Gould's commitment to the dubious ideals of capitalism and the Protestant work ethic (Conrad, 1990: 100), *El inglés de los güesos* gives us a 'moral' character whose privileged position prevents him from fully recognising the negative consequences of his actions and the limited and partial nature of values he takes for universal.

In Derridean terms, Balbina is only a 'trace' of the effaced subaltern woman, the sign that remains after the exclusion of countless others whose bodies and stories might trouble the paternalistic nationalism that emerges as one of the novel's political desiderata (Derrida, 1991: 41–51). As Spivak cautions, 'The named marginal is as much a concealment as a disclosure of the margin, and where s/he discloses, s/he is singular' (Spivak, 1999: 173). Alternately known as 'Balbina' and *La Negra*, she marks the place of two groups of 'barbarians' that were removed from the national landscape in the final decades of the nineteenth century, Afro-Argentinians and the indigenous. At the same time that Lynch centres the aspects of rural life that remain marginal in his Victorian source material, most notably the labour of rural women and the sexual liaisons that everywhere developed in the context of informal empire,[9] that same act of centring nevertheless relegates countless others, victims of less sentimental wrongs, into the margins of the text. Lynch draws our attention to the question of what is missing when the narrator remarks, 'it is more than probable that if instead of Mr James it had been any other man, the savage and innocent virtue of *La Negra* would have immediately run the gravest risks' (Lynch, 1960 [1924]: 135), but he does not resist the temptation to 'other' Balbina's female neighbours by casting them in the role of malicious gossips, ugly stepsisters to her Cinderella. Put

---

9   See Louise Guenther's contribution to this volume.

bluntly, Lynch's deliberate marshalling of sympathy for Balbina, *La Negra*, serves an aesthetic and/or ideological purpose that cannot be attributed to subaltern women in general or any particular one. His is ultimately an elite project that questions the elites' willingness to make responsible decisions on behalf of other Argentinians. Like all of the twentieth-century gauche-sque novels, moreover, *El inglés de los güesos* imposes itself within a complex social and political field in which Creole elites such as Lynch confronted not only the informal influence of British capital and the impoverishment of the rural poor, but also the presence of millions of immigrants, many of whom by the 1920s were openly dissatisfied with political structures and working conditions in the cities (Rock, 1986: 199–213).

It may be too much to expect Lynch to avoid sentimentalising his tragic heroine or to cut back on the swooning descriptions of 'ebony curls and … the matte whiteness of her skin' (1960 [1924]: 81) and 'beautiful eyes, clouded over with anguish'(1960[1924]:205). While we recognise the political limita-tions of the novel's exaltation of a model of impassioned 'Latin' femininity through the figure of the beautiful working-class mestiza, it is also produc-tive to explore the narrative space that *El inglés de los güesos* opens up at the crossroads among European and Creole genres, a space that allows this idea of female and native experience to emerge from the background. Space, or more accurately place, is what ultimately undermines Gray's insistent 'anti-conquest' stance (Pratt, 1992: 7). After Casiana's confrontation with Gray, the final third of the novel records the anguished days leading up to his depar-ture, including Gray's uncertainty and his final resolution to obey the com-mand of that 'atavistic guilt' to return to his carefully plotted academic career (Lynch, 1960 [1924]: 179). The final paragraphs contrast Gray's depar-ture, enclosed in the overseer's sulky, with a rural world that is rapidly fall-ing apart. As he rides off, convinced that Balbina will soon forget him, a messenger arrives with news that the neighbourhood healer, Doña María, has died. More importantly, Casiana steps outside the following morning to find that the *desgracia* or misfortune she feared has come true: Balbina has hanged herself from a tree in the yard. Gray is already on his way to Buenos Aires, en route back to London where he will continue his career and prob-ably never return again, except in memory. What grips me in this final scene is not so much Lynch's language, which contrasts the romantic rhetoric of landscape description with the impersonality of the natural world, as the lingering idea that Gray will never know what Balbina has done – in fact, he is almost certain never to guess.

On the subject of the geopolitics of knowledge, Mignolo writes:

> I am not assuming that *only* people coming from such and such a place could
> do X. Let me insist that I am not casting the argument in deterministic terms

but in the open realm of logical possibilities, of historical circumstances and personal sensibilities. I am suggesting that for those [for] whom colonial legacies are real (i.e. they hurt), that they are more (logically, historically, and emotionally) inclined than others to theorize the past in terms of coloniality. (Mignolo, 2000: 115)

The sequence of events that closes *El inglés de los güesos* translates Mignolo's metacritical concern into the language of narrative fiction, acting as an allegory for *thinking about* informal empire. As the elementary concepts of 'point of view' and 'perspective' convey, characters' locations – Gray's absence, Casiana's presence – inform their experience and perceptions in fundamental and important ways. Without falling victim to the deterministic fallacy Mignolo defends against or the moral relativism of which postcolonial and poststructuralist theorising is often accused, we may safely point out that Gray's empirical knowledge of reality is insufficient to understand the tragedy that has happened and his own role in it. If he insists on his innocence throughout the narrative and in whatever 'afterwards' one imagines for him, it is because he judges his actions according to his own experience and expectations. But his incessantly repeated 'Mí un *gentleman*!' now sounds hollower than ever, because the reader is fully aware of the partial nature of the knowledge on which it is based and the privileges of status and mobility that make it possible. The reader, in other words, may not be the direct bearer of localised knowledge of informal empire – one of the people for whom colonialism 'hurts' in Mignolo's formulation – but our experience of reading has enabled us to see the disjunctures between metropolitan and peripheral experiences and to recognise that metropolitan sources cannot be the only or the final word on the subject. In a cross-cultural, neo- or postcolonial context, academic or otherwise, ethical thinking depends on an ability to perceive the presence of other experience and knowledge outside and beyond the dominant interpretative mechanisms, and a willingness to work in the gap between them. This, finally, is the kind of insight that *El inglés de los güesos*, and the careful, critical study of literature in general, may add to our discussion of informal empire.

9

The Artful Seductions of Informal Empire

LOUISE GUENTHER

San Francisco State University, USA

South America is so essentially a Latin continent, refusing to open the doors of her intimacies to any chance knocker ignorant of her tongues, manners, and customs. (Koebel, 1917: 528)

The encounters between British merchants and Latin Americans at the time of independence from Iberian colonial rule ranged from mutual suspicion to amusement, and occasionally amazement, with a common ground of adaptation and adjustment gradually expanding over the course of the ensuing century.[1] A close reading of primary and secondary historical sources suggests that it was a sense of generalised British *desire* that set the tone for interactions at many levels throughout the *século inglês* [British century] in Brazil (Pantaleão, 1965: 65). In the case of most of the individuals concerned, this desire was consciously directed at the promise of material wealth and its accompanying social status. However, it also shaded subtly and ambiguously into other forms, such as the desire for physical enjoyment, intellectual understanding, competitive success against peers and power to influence the surrounding environment. The Briton's impulse to engage and master this Brazilian market-territory paradoxically entailed an equally strong and opposite drive to sustain as complete as possible a physical and mental separation from that environment in daily life. As British merchants eagerly gazed upon the rich seaport markets and vast interiors of Brazil, the country's nascent forms of business, government and society, and the voluptuous womanly bodies that peopled its landscape, these separate aspects of desire subjectively and collectively merged to produce a discourse of gendered consummation, in both personal and political-economic terms. This discourse became, in fact, a

---

1   The author would like to thank fellow participants at the University of Bristol, UK conference in January 2007 for their comments on the original version of this chapter.

structuring principle in the overall experience of 'informal empire' and in the development of its historical narratives.[2]

A sensitivity to the tone of gendered desire that operated in informal-imperial relations renders certain patterns in the historiography evident and problematic. An unmistakably male need is detectable in the words of key players (as in the Koebel quote above and other quotes to follow), and is also found in the political-economic narrative storyboard, given the muscularity of the analytic language normally used to describe that historical process. The intellectual tendency to favour vital interests of male bodies when intuiting descriptive metaphors – as in penetration, expansion, decline, withdrawal – may be attributable to the shared, and thus transparent, maleness of nearly all of its authors, including dependency theorists. Nevertheless, the resulting language bias has had the effect of distorting historical understanding. It has tended to emphasise the agency of Britons as the active, that is 'male', players, and casually to downplay that of Latin Americans as the passive, that is 'female' participants.[3] The present argument does not aim to deny outright that such were the mechanics, but merely to reassess the values assigned to each gendered role. Not only were the Latin Americans as active as the British, in this commercial 'empire' lacking 'formal' controls, but their 'femaleness' also possessed its own modes of power and achievement. Such a modification in outlook will allow for a deliberate theorisation of 'informal empire' along more constructively gendered lines.

The intellectual distortion has been self-perpetuating. For all its apparent descriptive neutrality, the dominant metaphor of economic penetration subtly reifies a penetrated body, endowed with a satisfying degree of subjectivity, but denied all significant agency. To accept that penetration implies subjugation is to permeate analytic efforts with a pejorative suggestion that penetrability is an unqualified disadvantage. Subtle yet stark, this male-chauvinist bias is neither objective nor realistic, although its pedigree would stretch back to the Trojan horse. Its pervasiveness continues to shape research questions. It is practically impossible to say with a straight face that 'informal empire' was a term for the nineteenth-century economic invagination of Britain by Latin American consumers and elites, a description technically equivalent to the nineteenth-century economic penetration of Latin

---

2 For an overview of the literature and debates on the subject of British informal empire in Latin America, and conversely Latin America's dependency on Great Britain from Independence up until the First World War, see Matthew Brown's introduction to the present volume.

3 It is emphasised that these categories are referring to idealisations, not to individuals.

America by British merchants and investors; yet even this would suggest different ways of asking just what happened, how and why.[4]

Until very recently, the persistence of a male-gendered language bias in the historiography has had a way of focusing most of the serious scholarly attention on questions of successes and failures, allocation of spoils, 'survival', 'strategic' forms of 'resistance' and similar warrior-inflected concerns. It has tended to exclude or devalue female-gendered forms of desire and success that are equally natural, adult and descriptive of subjective and objective human realities in the present and past. While the distortion succeeded in screening off any untoward emotions inspired by the feminine capacity (let alone eagerness) to absorb this masculine agitation and potency and transform it inwardly into results well beyond the male ken (as Aeneas, son of Venus, emerged out of the ruins of Troy), it did so at a cost. In downplaying the fundamental importance of a universe of positive attributes that are gendered female, its ethics and aesthetics obscured the premises needed for models that would ask what it is for self and other to meet *as one*.

While masculinist themes of power through boundary violation are something of an organising principle for analysis and decision-making in a wide variety of political and economic arenas, if the image behind the scrim is illuminated, official discourses of international invasion often seem to suggest a male–male rape. This probably derives from a semi-conscious notion of the modern sovereign state as itself a sort of body that is gendered male via attributes of self-sufficiency, powers of aggression, fraternal equality with other states, external reproductive potency via colonisation of areas beyond its proper borders, and so on. It may be more characteristic of military and political narratives than of those concerning imperialistic capitalism, but the underlying plotline makes itself felt in the latter as well. In a serious but good-humoured study of how unhealthy social systems represent a collective expression of individual pathologies, Cleese and Skynner (1994: 182–183) remarked on 'the usual violence of ordinary [US] business executive language – they have an infinite number of expressions conveying the degree of violence that they intend to do to one another's bottoms'. A similar image, but on the scale of a country, even of the Cold War itself, is 'Czechoslovakia takes her knickers off to welcome capitalism' (Stoppard, 2006: 79). The substitution of a (dishonourably) willing female body for the (honourably) overpowered male has the interesting effect of rendering the image non-violent. Whereas businessmen and nation-states are aggressive among themselves, *capitalism* is not a body that can vanquish a nation-state, but rather represents an external essence whose influence can fructify over time

---

4   The idea of 'invagination' as literary satire is Lodge's (1984: 325).

if incorporated willingly into such a body. The project of restoring feminine agency to the received historical picture, both figuratively and literally, thus holds the promise of critically enhancing description and analysis on several different levels.

A *market* is more abstract than a nation-state – its boundaries are more porous, a shape changing in response to creative initiatives. Taken alone, it is less like a body, even a female body, than it is like a bed: a situation where unpredictable encounters and exchanges can lead to results that are dependent on, and independent of, their progenitors. This resonates with the 'informal empire' debate. Given the particular circumstances of the British entry into Brazil, their male-gendered motivations did not turn on ideas and sensations associated with formal mechanisms of violent conquest, but rather on those of worldly wise seduction. A quiet style of masculine self-assertion directed itself at the goal of *indirect* possession of the 'other', the femininely rendered realm of Brazil and Latin America. Britain proceeded by gradually securing permission to exploit Brazil's vast resources in return for the services, benefits and protection that her vulnerable situation required. This contrasted with the direct physical conquest and control more characteristic of the male-male military paradigms that structured the designs of formal imperialism.[5] In this chapter, I suggest that a careful study of the officially illicit, but mutually agreeable, activities that took place between British merchants/men and Latin American markets/women may assist with understanding not only the politics, economics and historiography of 'informal empire', but also the cognitive resonances that existed, in this context, between private and public forms of gendered desire.[6]

Economic historians have described the advantages accruing to elite groups in Latin America because of their role in enabling British (and later, US) capital to thrive within their respective economies. To use a familiar colloquialism referring to arrangements that are mutually advantageous but not formally recognised, 'informal empire' was a situation of British merchants, investors, and officials being 'in bed' with Latin American elites. Such alliances typically draw their effectiveness from the synergy that emerges, unregimented, from their spontaneous association. Unlike penetration language, this image leaves the vital question of which party is

---

5 On gender and British imperialism more generally, see for example Midgley (1998).

6 This project is broadly informed by the studies of gender dynamics in international/imperial politics of Stoler (1995, 2002) and Enloe (1990). The present interpretation also resonates with Matthew Brown's (2005) argument positing the Latin American wars of Independence as a staging-ground for British enactments of cultural ideals of masculinity.

playing what role at a given moment discreetly and firmly undefined, which arguably makes it a highly civilised metaphor for gender equity and cooperation. If the expression 'in bed' is examined literally, too, the concept of *legitimacy* comes much more clearly into focus. This question has not been satisfactorily considered for the case of 'informal empire', that uneasily familiar label fraught with ambivalence. It expresses the idea of a possession neither conquered nor free, dependent nor independent, appealing to inverted commas to veil the collaboration that dares not speak its name.

Brazil's alliance with Great Britain after the transfer of the Portuguese court to Rio de Janeiro in 1808 was mutually engendered almost ad hoc, for purposes of protection, profit, legitimisation and advancement. It is tempting to compare this dynamic to a socially codified partner-relationship that is neither paternal, as in the case of an imperial metropolis with formal colonial possessions, nor matrimonial, as a signed-and-sealed free-trade union with a fellow sovereign state. Even without the seductiveness impregnating the language and ideas related to it, this non-binding yet non-gentlemanly agreement already veered dangerously towards the illicit. It delineated a semi-commercial barter of favours taking place now 'in bed', now under the table, yet always under the eyes of respectably formal nineteenth-century European imperialism.[7] It sounded, in fact, rather like the unofficial and illicit sexual relationships actually enjoyed by many British merchants and Brazilian women throughout the long nineteenth century.

The early impressions recorded by British observers in Brazil illustrated a characteristically seductive attitude of lust coupled with restraint. The expressed active desire was to possess Brazil by superior skill not force. In the project of restoring female agency to the narrative of seduction, the reader

---

7   This idea of investigating the legitimacy of an empire by reference to the quality of gender relations embedded in its origin also has a classical precedent. Plutarch (c. 46–127 CE) commented on the importance of the abduction of the Sabine women for the birth of Rome. Although this story is traditionally viewed as a mass rape, it was more precisely a violent separation of the women from their fathers, followed by a much gentler seduction by their Roman captors. 'You did not come to vindicate our honour, while we were virgins, against our assailants; but do come now to force away wives from their husbands and mothers from their children' (Plutarch, 1864: 38). The Sabines' eventual concordance with the Romans' desire for matrimonial alliance, in light of the respectful treatment they received within their homes, was what granted their mutual descendants (i.e. the Roman Empire) that legitimacy that a forced conception would have lacked. Plutarch used 'female' language to drive home the connecting point: 'Nothing did more to advance the greatness of Rome, than that she did always unite and incorporate those whom she conquered into herself' (Plutarch, 1864: 35).

is asked to consider whether the power exercised by the wealth and near-attainability of Brazil upon the imagination and intention of the British could have been *equivalent yet asymmetrical* to the power of action that Britain enjoyed in this situation:

> Brazil must, in every respect, be considered as a new country. We must sow before we can expect to reap. The maturer wisdom of [Great Britain], our greater knowledge of the nature of commerce and cultivation, must suggest the means to the Portuguese inhabitants and government; and the community of interest will insure us their cordial co-operation. No country under heaven … is better suited than Brazil, both to render itself and allies great and rich. (Turnbull, 1813: 38)

> There can be no field of enterprise so magnificent in promise, so well calculated to raise sanguine hopes, so congenial to the most generous sympathies, so consistent with the best and highest interests of England as the vast continent of South America. (Brougham in Bethell, 1970: 2)

> Behold! the New World established and, if we do not throw it away, ours! (Canning cited in Bethell, 1970: 4)

The first passage was written by a British merchant who visited Brazil in 1803; the second was presented by Henry Brougham to the House of Commons in 1817; and the last was written by George Canning in 1825. There is no doubt as to the virility of the expressed desire, nor of its pervasiveness, at least among such key British agents of 'informal empire'.

Interestingly, once a sufficient number of British merchants had established themselves in Brazilian cities, their behaviours and expressed attitudes began to show that their male-gendered passion for expansive possession and control was, in practice, intimately associated with a deep fear of engulfment and loss of identity within the female-gendered territory of the host society. This is what they were there to exploit, yet they also depended upon it continuously for every aspect of economic and physical survival. This offers another means of tracing a female, 'uterine' agency of passive control operating in the 'informal empire', opposed and complementary to the male 'phallic' variety: What was initially the external *object* of desire was rendered by expatriate entry/consummation into an enveloping *place*, possessed of powers over life and death. Indeed, when their immediate Brazilian environment suddenly became hostile, as occasionally happened in reaction to British abolitionist activities, the merchants experienced extreme and persistent anxiety; they knew they were powerless to protect themselves physically from such a threat (Guenther, 2004: 43, 83–84, 160).

In daily life, the British sought protection from the surrounding dangers of otherness and nourishment for their project of mastery by deliberately establishing sharp demarcations around their micro-communities. The

question of British cultural identity performance as a means of psychological protection in the Brazilian expatriate context has been discussed at length
elsewhere (Guenther, 2004: 81–110). The key point for the present analysis is
that these boundaries of masculine self-protection apparently could not be
sustained without the presence of British women, a fact that raised the latter's status well above what it would have been in the home country: 'in
England they have not that same undivided attention paid them, but abroad
they can be little *queens* if they like' (Wetherell, 1860: 116, emphasis in original). In Bahia (Salvador) and Rio de Janeiro, the British communities' physical boundaries were drawn around the clustering of homes just beyond the
main town, serving essentially to mark off and circumscribe the presence of
British women.[8] In this way, the motherland was deliberately reified in por-
table and domesticated form, in what amounted to a psychological strategy
of fending off the uncontrolled female 'other' by the deliberate deployment
of a controlled female 'self', as it were. For British women, the effect of this
strategy was to make house-keeping comparable, if not equivalent, to gate-
keeping – and gate-keeping was fundamental for the personal and collective
survival of Britons *as* Britons, individual men enacting 'informal empire'
through their daily activities at work and at home.

To ensure its members' success, the community's primary cultural function was to prevent each member from getting too close to the surrounding environment, as defined by the likely risk of precipitating an inner
adaptation – of 'going native', losing self in willing surrender to otherness.
This need for separation extended to the local food, clothing, street life,
language, labour practices, social habits, interior design, religion, weather
and many other cultural aspects of Brazil. Above all, intimate physical
contact with Brazilian women was considered a grave danger to the cohe-
sion of the British community. Primary sources warned of the dangers of
succumbing to the physical and psychological allure of the Brazilian female, particularly those of darker complexions (Guenther, 2004: 150). Any
such act would evidently violate the integrity of the merchant's fundamental bond to his female counterpart, which in this context signified
faithfulness to the homeland itself. The merchant could not legitimately
permit himself even to dwell upon the desirability of the Brazilian female
(at least, not in print), and certainly could not indulge any such desire
openly. However, it *could* be done discreetly. Little evidence of British–
Brazilian concubinage (for lack of a better term) is to be found in the British
records, although Brazilian sources tell a very different story. The split

---

8   In Bahia, the British community comprised 120 to 150 residents at its mid-
    century height (Guenther, 2004: 62).

between ideology and practice pervaded the *mentalité* of the British in Brazil in more ways than one. For example, widespread slave ownership among expatriate merchants and financial involvement in the slave trade coexisted uneasily with British abolitionist efforts throughout the period. This was hardly mentioned by British sources, but well remarked upon by contemporary Brazilian observers. The keeping of 'native' mistresses was not very different (Guenther, 2004: 166).

This cultural prohibition against the most obvious and natural expression of the generalised British desire for the bounties of Brazil probably served to heighten and excite the merchants' awareness of the allure of local women. Illicit relationships were a fact of expatriate life, historically interesting in their own right, and relevant to the larger story insofar as their self-governed informality repeated a pattern of similarly informal practices by means of which British influence indirectly established itself throughout nineteenth-century Latin America. This analogy between the ambiguous nature of 'informal empire' as a political-economic event on the one hand, and the hidden, paradoxical and potentially vital processes of mutual influence embodied in physically intimate relationships on the other, connects the most public and most private spheres of British activity in a single interpretation.[9] The ever-present yet elusive Brazilian woman did in a sense stand in for the continent itself – its market, its mysteries and seductive dangers, and the promise of satisfaction to flow from successful mastery.

These relations between British capital ('male' agent of informal empire) and Brazilian arenas ('female' object or substance of informal empire) had to be carefully controlled in order to be sustainable over time; yet it is the nature of such desires to elude all attempts at control. While engaging in the metaphorical seduction of a newly independent state and region into the broad international network of British nodes around the world, individual merchants also wasted no time in consummating their desires for the local women directly. The proposition of a gendered reading of 'informal empire' can be seen to connect local historical fact and broad historical theory. Before sufficient numbers of British women had arrived on the scene, a British diplomat at Rio de Janeiro remarked on how 'delicate connections were soon formed, and females of the obscurest class appeared dressed in the most costly extreme of English fashion' (Mawe, 1812: 329). Around that time in Buenos Aires, a British merchant experienced 'the highly irregular living of unmarried Englishmen, during the first years of

---

9   The project of developing new historical paradigms to encompass the idea of similar patterns operating at different scales is articulated in detail by Gaddis (2002).

their settlement', and noticed how this situation 'gradually gave way to the softening and humanizing influence of [English] female society; so that in 1818 or 1819 we had sobered down to a very well conducted community' (Robertson and Robertson, 1843: 119). While this specific comment pertains to Argentina, other evidence suggests that a similar dynamic operated in Brazil (Guenther, 2004: 66–70).

The community's good British conduct served to keep them in touch with their cultural roots, but it also had positive repercussions for business, and may even have been one of the most important factors in the long-term success of 'informal empire'. In the absence of 'formal' means of economic coercion, the merchants' success depended upon convincing local clients of their trustworthiness. To the fervently Catholic population of Brazil, where for centuries Protestants had been represented as 'pagoens, bichos, e cavallos' [pagans, animals, and brutes] (Koster, 1816: 400), the British were regarded with that peculiar degree of horror and detestation with which we contemplate the Inhabitants of the Infernal Regions'.[10] Nevertheless, by the end of the century, the British reputation for honesty in business was so solid that the expression *palavra de inglês* [Englishman's word] had come to be used amongst Brazilians as an oath (Guenther, 2004: 128–129). This was no small achievement, and depended upon resolute consistency of demeanour in large and small contexts, sustained for a very considerable length of time, among compatriots who shared few bonds beyond the fact of their mutual presence in Brazil. Economic interest alone would not account for such a degree of communal devotion to reliable conduct, particularly as scrupulous honesty placed individual businessmen at a competitive disadvantage in the short run (Freyre, 1948: 179). A cultural explanation is required.

The merchants were aware that in order to affect their communal image in the eyes of Brazilians, their good conduct had to be seen to extend beyond the workplace. The need for a presentable religious centre for the community, even if Protestant, became evident early on. And, in the very act of making such a recommendation to the British community of Recife (Pernambuco), Koster (1816) indirectly chastised the merchants for violating the prime directive regarding Brazilian women:

> To these political reasons [for having a chapel] are to be added those which are of far greater importance, those to which no Christian ought to be indifferent. I well know that it is not with the merchants that the evil arises; – but enough, I will go no farther, although I could tarry long upon this subject. I wish

---

10 Letter from Charles Fraser to Viscount Castlereagh [*sic*], 14 April 1812, TNA FO 63/149.

however that I could have avoided the mention of it altogether. (Koster, 1816: 401)

The merchants were expected to deny their own involvement in the 'evil', so Koster shrugged off the expected disclaimer that only lower-class British clerks were guilty of the forbidden act, and went on declaring his deep concern for the community.[11] For the purposes of our argument, however, what is most interesting is that Koster's overall intent was itself seductive: his political objective in establishing a chapel was primarily to encourage the Brazilians to trust British merchants enough to do business with them. Concubinage, on the other hand, didn't seem to bother the Brazilians very much. In his study *Inglêses no Brasil* (1948), Gilberto Freyre referred with amusement to the strong attachment displayed by wealthy British merchants, engineers and powerful bankers towards their dark-skinned Brazilian mistresses, whom they famously kept in high style in Rio de Janeiro, Bahia and Pernambuco (Freyre, 1948: 111). Koster would have understood their attitude, because he grew up in Portugal and was himself a *senhor de engenho* [sugar plantation owner] in Pernambuco at the time of writing. Thus, if he believed that the question of illicit relationships was of 'far greater importance' to the community than even business interests, it must have been seen to pose a more basic threat to survival. According to the gendered seduction interpretation, Koster's twin recommendations were coherent: he meant to ensure that informal-imperial seduction would proceed in one direction only. The British ought to be empowered to satisfy Brazilian desires, never the other way round. He did seem to realise it was a lost cause.

The merchant communities eventually developed sustainable ways of handling this problem. Depending on the social status and discretion of the transgressing member, British men and women were capable of tacitly accepting what they felt was bound to happen from time to time, given the special powers that Brazilian women were imagined to possess (Guenther, 2004: 146–151; see also literary examples, below). If a member of the British community preferred to indulge in intimate relations with Brazilian women openly, however, degrees of social exclusion could be invoked, to the point of official erasure. 'Going native' was a label that paradoxically respected a Briton's traditional right to self-determination, while in effect excluding him from the communal British identity.

Not every form of intimate contact was forbidden, however; intermarriages did take place. Formal alliances with Brazilian families do not appear to have threatened the British merchant community's protective boundary.

---

11 See also Scully on the behaviour of British clerks (1866: 7).

Such marriages were occasionally mentioned in published primary sources, casually, without any tone of concern. The pair's equal or similar social status was probably the key factor in such cases, buttressed by the ritual power of the wedding ceremony itself, in which a 'native' (though probably light-skinned) bride was allowed to enter the British community's protective boundary in advance of physical consummation, by publicly vowing to adopt the groom's family name, religion, and other legal and cultural norms as her own for the rest of her life. This action placed her within range of social sanctions on both sides of the boundary, thus reducing the threat of cultural dilution. British women could marry into Brazilian families, too, apparently without suffering sanctions.[12] This suggests that the virginal fluidity of female social identity was never more essential for sustaining the rigidity of male self-possession than in such cultural borderlands. Women who possessed and controlled their own bodies threatened this entire edifice, as they might next take over someone else's. Brazilian seductresses of the dangerous kind tended to be in the latter category.

Once the self-similarity across scale of these two levels of British desire for Brazilian bounty is established, the next challenge is to find useful ways of narrating both histories in one frame. The result may be a bit sketchy, as a result, in part, of the dearth of reliable primary sources detailing private-life practices, especially those that were both illicit and concerned with women's lives. It is offered as an illustration for the theme of prioritising the perspective and agency of the 'passive' party in 'informal empire'. To begin with a description of Brazilian women by James Prior, a British naval officer who visited Bahia in the early 1810s:

> In full dress, the bosom and arms are liberally exposed, a singular circumstance among a people, if not jealous, at least only just escaped from jealousy; yet this passion is not an unfrequent companion to voluptuousness. Flowers and precious stones ornament the head … [Education] has done little toward ornamenting the minds of the ladies; but in the happy countries of Spain and Portugal this accomplishment is not always deemed necessary. (Prior, 1819: 104)

The image of an attractive and unsophisticated young heiress whose social background yet demanded some skill of approach is reminiscent of the

---

12 For example: 'The palace of the president of [Bahia] … was fast falling into decay until the distinguished administration of Mr Sinimbu, who repaired and renovated it, and whose refined taste, seconded by the wise judgment of his accomplished wife, a lady of English origin, who superintended its internal arrangements, has made it truly a palace' (Scully, 1866: 351).

political situation at this early stage of the 'informal empire' relationship. Although Prior's possessive drive was less pronounced than in the statements by Brougham and Canning cited above, each seemed suffused with fascination for the open display of wealth, beauty and naïveté that faced them with such equanimity. The statesmen's vision focused on the ease with which skilled British diplomacy might edge Brazil out of her bond with Portugal, while Prior spiritedly described a convent in which wives were secluded whenever their husbands were out of town (Prior, 1819: 103). Contemplating the likely meaning of this fact, and noting the ladies' combination of docile voluptuousness and mental vacuity, Prior's curiosity went beyond intellectual interest, much as Canning et al. expressed an emotional enthusiasm – exclamation marks and all – for the prospect of forging a political alliance with Brazil while her Iberian master was temporarily absent from the scene.

During the Independence struggles of the early 1820s, insecurity reigned with regard to Brazil's immediate future. The skill of William Pennell, the British consul at Bahia, in managing the uncertainty faced by the merchants during that tumultuous time was exemplary: not only did the community survive the transition to Independence, it also did so with its privileges intact, and a debt of gratitude owed to them by the new government (Guenther, 2004: 30). By remaining responsive to local conditions and attentive to all possibilities, the British were able to secure the favours they so desired:

> It was surely one of the anomalies of statesmanship that gained for England the simultaneous gratitude of Brazil and the Spanish-speaking States. She had assisted the former in her step from a royal colony to a kingdom; she had aided the latter to divest themselves of royalty and its influence by becoming republics! (Koebel, 1917: 528)

The idea of worldly wise seduction appears to fit this pattern of indirect control through self-restraint and sensitive manipulation. After Independence, British merchants turned their full attention to commercial concerns, largely a matter of seducing the locals into the habit of buying their wares and seeking cooperative ways of financing purchases and services.

As British firms grew in size and importance, so did the community. By the mid-century, many of the wealthy merchants had settled into the luxuries of mistress-keeping described by Freyre. To say that this situation repeated the pattern of British investments in Latin America by mid-century may be more of a stretch, as 'informal empire' moved along so many different paths; nevertheless, the sense of a new stability arising out of consistently sensible compromises with local realities occurs in each narrative, and these may have been mutually reinforcing.

In both stories, responsible relationships gradually grew out of the earlier frenzied desire for Brazilian booty. British merchant George Mumford wrote in his will in 1862 that he had fathered eight illegitimate children in Bahia by his Brazilian companion, Constança Ebbe. He had acknowledged each child at birth, and five were being educated in Europe at his expense when he died. However, Mumford waited until just before his death to reveal that he had also fathered an illegitimate child by another Brazilian, Balbina, who would now have rights in his estate. His property included three houses, stock in the Bahia & São Francisco Railway Company and in Banco da Bahia, and ten slaves, whose ownership was illegal by then under British law. Mumford was survived by his partner, mistress, and nine children.[13] By the early 1860s, British investments in Brazil had taken on a longer-term horizon, moving from the straightforward provision of textiles and shipping services into railways, mining and financial ventures. As these changes occurred in the world of economic and political relations, Mumford was quietly and responsibly building up a one-man 'informal empire' of his own in Bahia.

As might be expected from the length of their stay, the British presence in Brazil also affected the sphere of cultural production in both countries. Throughout the long nineteenth century, Brazilians of all classes observed with interest the appearance and behaviour of the British residents in their midst, whose eccentricities were satirised as well as emulated. Jokes and plays were animated by the familiar stereotype of the *inglês* (Guenther, 2004: 127, 130). Of particular interest for the purposes of this comparison is a drawing-room comedy from 1842 by playwright Martins Pena, *Os dous, ou o inglês maquinista* [*The machine-making Englishman*]. This was a light farce and a comment on the British government's treatment of Brazil at the height of British abolitionism, in which Brazil was represented as the beautiful widow Clemência, and Britain as a greedy merchant who had designs on her fortune. Mister Gainer, whose amorous attentions to Dona Clemência had nothing to do with her personal attractions, was a villain-buffoon. His awful Portuguese and crass behaviour, as rendered by Martins Pena, put the British in their place within the social structure of Brazil, where commerce was not considered an especially honourable vocation. Gainer used social calls to solicit investments for a new machine that he declared could transform an ox into roast beef, polished boots, hair-combs, sugar, sweets and even almonds within 30 minutes (Martins Pena, 1960 [1842]: 115). He bristled at a teasing

---

13   Arquivo do Estado da Bahia: Seção Judiciária: Testamento 7-3048-0-2, George Mumford, 12 February 1862.

suggestion by a Brazilian character that his operations were enriching himself rather more than Brazil:

> *Felício*: How unkind men are! To call you, the most philanthropic and disinterested and most excellent friend of Brazil, a speculator who uses others' capital, and many other names ...
>
> *Gainer*: What! That is libel! I am driving myself into the poorhouse with my projects, for the good of Brazil![14]

At the end of the play, Gainer had just gained the widow's acceptance when her rightful husband, mistakenly presumed dead at the hands of rebels in the southern province of Rio Grande do Sul, leapt from behind a curtain and pounced on Gainer to avenge his audacity. During a tense time in diplomatic relations between Brazil and Great Britain, this play re-asserted national pride, but did not sacrifice civility: the British character was humbled without being humiliated. His last action on stage was to deliver a knockout punch to a secondary character, Negreiro (literally 'slave trader') before running away, his empty jacket still clasped in the latter's hand (Martins Pena, 1960 [1842]: 132).

A certain fascination with the British has persisted throughout the period of US ascendancy which succeeded British hegemony in the region. Prominent Brazilian humorist Jô Soares chose as the theme for his mystery novel, *O Xangô de Baker Street* (1995), the premise that Sherlock Holmes secretly went to Rio de Janeiro in 1886 at the request of Emperor Pedro II, who needed an effective and discreet investigation into the question of a stolen Stradivarius belonging to his mistress. The novel was translated into English as *A Samba for Sherlock* (Soares, 1997), and later made into a successful film (Faria, 2001; see Figure 1).

To recreate the setting for his story, Soares thoroughly researched nineteenth-century Rio de Janeiro – the text includes a five-page bibliography – and added several what-ifs, including a justification for Holmes's surprising knowledge of Portuguese and Dr Watson's inadvertent invention of the *caipirinha* cocktail, Brazil's national drink (Soares, 1995: 106, 229–231). The main interest of the novel, however, lies less in the effect that Sherlock Holmes had on Rio de Janeiro than in that which Rio de Janeiro had upon Sherlock Holmes. In this Brazilian re-imagining of an English fictional character,

---

14 'Felício: Mas veja como os homens são maus. Chamarem ao senhor, que é o homem o mais filantrópico e desenteressado e amicíssimo do Brasil, especulador de dinheiros alheios e outros nomes mais... Gainer: Eu rica! Que calúnia! Eu rica? Eu está pobre com minhas projetos pra bem do Brasil!' (Martins Pena, 1960 [1842]: 116).

Figure 1.   Thalma de Freitas and Joaquim de Almeida in *The Xango of Baker Street* (Faria, 2001) http://adorocinema.cidadeinternet.com.br/filmes/xango-de-baker-street/xango-de-baker-street.asp

Holmes fell in love with Anna Candelária, an actress whose father was a priest, in the very act of saving her from a fiendish killer. The beautiful green-eyed *mestiça* warmly returned his feelings. At the moment of truth, however, a deeper mystery was discovered: following the Brazilian stereo-type of the *inglês,* at the age of 32, Sherlock Holmes remained a virgin. The romance gently ended when Anna turned down his invitation to become Anna Candelária Scott Holmes and live with him in England. The dejected detective returned to London with Dr Watson and the recovered Stradivarius, given to him by the Emperor as a souvenir of his tropical adventure.

While Brazilians were developing their own stereotypes about British merchants, the latter developed many of their own regarding Brazilians. Predictably, the attitude within expatriate enclaves was to reinforce the cul-tural imperative of self-segregation at every turn (Guenther, 2004: 111–123). However, ideas of another sort were steadily seeping into British minds across the Atlantic, leaving detectable traces in the cultural production of authors who never set foot in Latin America. This imagery emphasised the uncontrollably passionate and dangerous nature of beautiful Latin Ameri-can women, who were often identified in some way with the region's cli-mate and vegetation, as imagined by the authors. One of the best examples of this imagery, the significance of which for the present argument will soon become apparent, comes from Sir Arthur Conan Doyle himself. He pub-lished a story in 1927 about a Brazilian beauty who had accompanied her husband to England, and there met a cruel end. 'The Problem of Thor Bridge' was published in *The Case Book of Sherlock Holmes* (1927), the final volume of the detective's adventures.

In 'Thor Bridge', a brash American tycoon named Gibson but known as the Gold King met his wife, Maria Pinto, while prospecting in the Brazilian jungle. Maria, the daughter of a government official at Manaus, was 'rare and wonderful in her beauty' and possessed 'a deep rich nature, too, passionate, whole-hearted, tropical, ill-balanced'. Gibson explains to Holmes that:

> it was only when the romance had passed ..: that I realized that we had nothing – absolutely nothing – in common. My love faded ... but nothing changed her. She adored me in those English woods as she had adored me twenty years ago on the banks of the Amazon. (Conan Doyle, 2003 [1927]: 589)

The force-of-nature intensity of Maria's passion was repeatedly stressed:

> she was a creature of the tropics ... a child of the sun and of passion. She had loved him as such women can love, but when her own physical charms had faded ... there was nothing to hold him. (Conan Doyle, 2003 [1927]: 585)

Gibson treated his wife harshly, yet when her body was found, all suspicions pointed to the family's young English governess, Miss Dunbar.

Gibson hired Holmes to help clear her of the murder charges: 'there is no doubt that my wife was bitterly jealous ... she was crazy with hatred, and the heat of the Amazon was always in her blood'. She had 'poured her whole wild fury out in burning and horrible words' to the governess. In Miss Dunbar's words:

> She hated me, Mr. Holmes. She hated me with all the fervour of her tropical nature. She was a woman who would do nothing by halves, and the measure of her love for her husband was the measure also of her hatred for me ... she loved so vividly in a physical sense that she could hardly understand the mental, and even spiritual, tie which held her husband to me. (Conan Doyle, 2003 [1927]: 595)

At their first sight of Miss Dunbar, both Holmes and Watson were gripped with an unshakeable trust in her good nature:

> it was no wonder that even the masterful millionaire had found in her something more powerful than himself – something which could control and guide him ... an innate nobility of character which would make her influence always for the good. (Conan Doyle, 2003 [1927]: 594)

Curiously, this closely reflected the traditional role of British women in the expatriate merchant enclaves: to forestall the corruption(s) of male desire by tightening the bond to the homeland-self, as conceived spiritually, culturally and physically. Soon afterwards, Holmes was able to deduce that Maria had actually faked her own murder to punish Miss Dunbar for winning her husband's affections. This rather excessive form of revenge reflected the trope of 'female' Latin America: a subtle threat of extreme and irrational violence linked British perceptions of Latin American women's temperament, on the one hand, and British perceptions of the continent's rich natural environment, with its unpredictable tempests and vast, unmapped jungles of disturbing flora and dangerous fauna, on the other.

This emotional and gendered vision of Latin American nature persists almost to the present day. In *The Open House* (1972), one of the many popular mystery novels written by Oxford English Literature don J. I. M. Stewart and published under the pen name Michael Innes, many of the same tropes are evoked as in Conan Doyle half a century earlier. For example, a large greenhouse inside an English country home, owned by a family whose fortunes were linked to their long-term involvement in Latin American affairs, is described as follows:

> They were tropical trees: writhing, with unnaturally large and waxen foliage, dropping thick tendrils like hangman's ropes from their upper branches, showing here and there enormous red blossoms, like gouts of blood on wounded dinosaurs ... he didn't like them, or the rank warm odour of rotting vegetation upon which they seemed to batten, at all ... It was uncommonly hot and sticky. From somewhere came an alarming hissing sound, so that Appleby for a moment expected the appearance of fauna among the flora in the form of snakes and serpents hastening forward to enfold him in their mortal coils. (Innes, 1972: 113–114)

In constructions such as these, the feminine poise and placidity of real Brazilian women, so often admired by nineteenth-century visitors, may secretly have been feared to mask a violent sexuality smouldering treacherously within ill-disciplined female minds. Travel narratives had long publicised the idea that Brazilian women's lustful appetites verged on depravity (Augel, 1980: 222). In this context, to remove such a creature from her natural environment was to invite disaster. In 'The Problem of Thor Bridge', Holmes observed how 'the workings of this unhappy woman's mind were deep and subtle ... she blamed this innocent lady [Dunbar] for all those harsh dealings and unkind words with which her husband tried to repel her too demonstrative affection', pensively noting that 'I do not think that in our adventures we have ever come across a stranger example of what perverted love can bring about' (Conan Doyle, 2003 [1927]: 599).

Yet such examples did exist. The idea of the unhinged Latin American temptress may even have carved out a place in the heart of English literature during the highpoint of 'informal empire'. In Charlotte Brontë's *Jane Eyre*

(1847), Mr Rochester's first wife was Latin American – a voracious madwoman confined to an attic until she leapt from the roof after setting his house on fire. Bertha Antoinetta Mason was born to a wealthy British merchant and his native wife in Spanish Town, Jamaica (Brontë, 1954 [1847]: 258), and brought to England by her husband.[15] The novel's lavish descriptions of her belligerent insanity are too extensive to quote fully, but resolve into a similar question of tropical blood and physical appetite: 'Bertha Mason, the true daughter of an infamous mother, dragged me through all the hideous and degrading agonies which must attend a man bound to a wife at once intemperate and unchaste' (Brontë, 1954 [1847]: 273). Rochester made it clear to Jane that 'it is not because she is mad I hate her' (Brontë, 1954 [1847]: 268). After a few years of living with Bertha, the hero 'longed only for what suited me – for the antipodes of the Creole' (Brontë, 1954 [1847]: 278); so he, too, turned to his demure and self-controlled English governess, who bore more than a passing resemblance to Miss Dunbar.

It is tempting to conjecture that Conan Doyle modelled Maria Pinto on Bertha Mason, who was (in Rochester's words):

> the boast of Spanish Town for her beauty ... a fine woman ... tall, dark, and majestic. Her family wished to secure me because I was of a good race; and so did she ... my senses were excited; and being ignorant, raw, and inexperienced, I thought I loved her. (Brontë, 1954 [1847]: 271–272)

But Conan Doyle made Maria Pinto a Brazilian. He had studied the Amazon for his novel *The Lost World* (1912), and later published a short story entitled 'The Brazilian Cat' in *Tales of Terror and Mystery* (1922). This story, which predated 'The Problem of Thor Bridge', possessed significant similarities to it, including a rich villain called King, here an aristocratic Englishman who had 'spent an adventurous life in Brazil'; and his Brazilian wife, said to hate 'that anyone – male or female – should for an instant come between us. Her ideal is a desert island and an eternal *tête-à-tête*. That gives you the clue to her actions, which are ... not very far removed from mania' (Conan Doyle, 1977 [1922]: 92). To this familiar scenario, Conan Doyle added a highly dangerous but stunningly beautiful giant cat, 'one of the most absolutely treacherous and bloodthirsty creatures upon earth' (Conan Doyle, 1977 [1922]: 93), raised by King from a kitten, and kept under his control in a special cage built in a separate wing of his mansion. Many of Conan Doyle's descriptions of the animal resembled Brontë's images of Bertha in action, save for the helpless

---

15 I am indebted to Prof. Henry Mayr-Harting for his observation regarding Bertha's ancestry.

fascination expressed by the narrator even as he contemplated his predicament. Compare Conan Doyle:

> I knew then that [the cat] meant to kill me. Yet I found myself even at that moment admiring the sinuous grace of the devilish thing, its long, undulating, rippling movements, the gloss of its beautiful flanks, the vivid, palpitating scarlet of the glistening tongue which hung from the jet-black muzzle. And all the time that deep, threatening growl was rising and rising in an unbroken crescendo. I knew that the crisis was at hand (Conan Doyle, 1977 [1922]: 102).

with Brontë:

> The lunatic sprang and grappled his throat viciously, and laid her teeth to his cheek: they struggled. She was a big woman, in stature almost equalling her husband, and corpulent besides: she showed virile force in the contest – more than once she almost throttled him, athletic as he was. He could have settled her with a well-planted blow; but he would not strike: he would only wrestle (Brontë, 1954 [1847]: 261).

These Englishmen survived their Latin American ordeals by a very narrow margin: Rochester lost a hand and was blinded in the fire, although his sight was restored after marrying Jane (Brontë, 1954 [1847]: 405). Conan Doyle's narrator had to 'carry a stick as a sign of my night with the Brazilian cat' for the rest of his life (Conan Doyle, 1977 [1922]: 105). However, King's jealous wife turned out to be herself a prisoner of the man who had devised the cage; and after the cat had eaten him alive, 'with what remained from her husband's property she went back to her native land, and ... took the veil at Pernambuco' (Conan Doyle, 1977 [1922]: 106).

Stories such as these seemed to stand as a warning to those who would imagine that a passionately female Latin American 'nature' could be induced to combine with the masculine British climate of 'civilised' self-restraint without inviting disaster. Such a perception chimed with the prohibition on expatriate British merchants from intermingling too closely with the women around them, alluring as they were. It is argued that whatever its sources, or the tensions it caused, in practice this prohibition worked to preserve the integrity and boost the effectiveness of British commerce in Latin America generally, by creating and sustaining affiliative cultural enclaves that contained the agents of 'informal empire' and protected their masculine prowess from neutralisation and 'uterine' absorption by the host environment, which was gendered female. An interesting consequence of the social relations that developed historically out of this situation was that disturbing ideas about Latin American women's sexuality succeeded in making inroads into the British mind as deep and lasting as those made by the merchants' capital into the economy of Latin America.

By contrast, encounters between Brazilian women and British men have been remembered by Brazilians without any comparable sense of danger. Soares's Anna Candelária realised that it would be dangerous for her to wander too far from home, but her reaction was far more temperate than the British characters or authors might have expected: 'Darling, try to understand. In London, I would be like a fish out of water. How long would this love last? I have my work, and am too independent to be just a wife' (Soares, 1995: 333).[16] No signs of uncontrollable tropical rage edged the physical appeal of Anna, just as Martins Pena endowed Dona Clemência with good sense, good looks, and a complete lack of malice.

It is not easy to document the history of real women in such contexts for purposes of meaningful comparison, but an anecdotal comparison can be useful. At mid-century, in the British enclave of Bahia, British merchant Andrew Comber recorded the death of his Brazilian wife, Maria Emilia Freitas Comber (1814–1845), and praised her 'exemplary and faithful discharge of her various duties as daughter, sister, wife and mother'. He added, in a touching postscript, that she had 'died at the age of 28 years 9 months & 14 days', which suggests that Maria was well loved by her husband.[17] At almost the same time, in Yorkshire, a clergyman's daughter – and former English governess – wrote the words, 'when *my wife* is prompted by her familiar to burn people in their beds at night, to stab them, to bite their flesh from their bones, and so on – ' (Brontë, 1954 [1847]: 268, emphasis in original). Whatever Latin American women may have been in real life, the insatiable Sycoraxes were very much constructs of British creation, built out of culturally and racially inflected ideas dating back to the earliest days of 'informal empire'.

After a hard day's work in the tropics, expatriate merchants gratefully repaired to the serene reassurance of their British wives' embraces, believing these to provide vital protection of their essential selves from the unnerving otherness that enveloped them on every side. The community's social practices *would* be more intelligible if the overall process of 'informal empire' were understood as the slow, undesired invagination of British merchants by the Latin American host environment *simultaneously* with the desired penetration of it, which is already the thrust of the traditional narrative. The

---

16 'Procura entender, querido. Em Londres eu ficaria como um peixe fora d'água. Quanto tempo duraria o nosso amor em meio a uma terra estranha? ... Tenho minha profissão, sou independente demais para ser apenas uma esposa'.
17 Baptism and Burial Records, Igreja Episcopal Anglicana do Brasil, Salvador, Bahia; tombstone inscriptions, The British Cemetery at Bahia; Guenther (2004: 139).

boundaries of the expatriate enclave existed specifically to protect the British, sustaining them for continued survival inside the body in which they lived, uneasily connected in practice but independent in principle, for the duration of the long nineteenth century.

To conclude, the debate around 'informal empire' will benefit from the recognition that historical questions of commercial and military might are already closely related to those of the cultural turn. Mainstream economists have recently reincorporated the role of emotions into formal models (Sent, 2004: 750), realising in the process that Adam Smith's *Theory of Moral Sentiments* (1759) anticipated much of the emerging field of 'behavioural economics' (Ashraf, Camerer and Loewenstein, 2005: 132). The role of darker psychological drives in motivating larger economic events, including 'informal empire', is acknowledged in principle. In practice, it has shaped the story as well as the telling.

Broad historical patterns represent the collective results of daily relationships sustained between particular persons over long periods of time, through micro-level decisions influenced by ideas and interpretations of the *other*. With limited personal experience of their foreign environment, the British merchants of nineteenth-century Latin America had to improvise, relying heavily on their familiar cultural practices and standards to survive as an identifiable group. As time passed, the experiences and impressions of these merchants were communicated back to the home country, and there evolved into cultural stereotypes of surprising potency that strengthened the sense of difference that had originally produced them. The displacement of ideas regarding gender, sexuality and desire onto external objects played an important role in the British understanding and experience of 'informal empire', and can formally be recognised as a motivating factor. In the project of narrating anew the history of adventurous economic advances by European capital and capitalists into the alluring lands and markets of nineteenth-century Latin America, the incorporation of private histories and needs into the broader pattern of materially driven motivations and outcomes will result in a more complex understanding of the whole.

10

Afterword: Informal Empire: Past, Present and Future

ANDREW THOMPSON

University of Leeds, UK

I

The concept of 'informal empire' can be traced back at least as far as C.R. Fay's *Cambridge History of the British Empire* (1940). But whatever its origins, Jack Gallagher and Ronald Robinson are rightly regarded as its leading exponents.[1] Their 1953 essay, which is justly acclaimed as a landmark in the study of British overseas expansion, put 'informal empire' into the Imperial historian's phrase book, in which it has since remained. Robinson and Gallagher portrayed the nineteenth century as a period of relentless expansion, taking many different forms, whereby Victorian governments worked to establish British paramountcy by whatever means seemed locally most appropriate. The preferred mode of expansion was *informal*, resulting from the forces of economic and cultural attraction; the actual annexation of overseas territory (*formal empire*) was always a last resort – a departure from the normal pattern of securing British interests in the wider world, undertaken not in response to organised opinion or electoral pressures, but in response to the perceptions of a policy-making elite (the *official* or *collective* mind).

For proponents of the concept of 'informal empire', Latin America has always been held integral. Of course, in Latin America itself, 'informal empire' came hard on the heels of dependency theory. The ideological underpinnings of these two concepts were diametrically imposed – the former intended as a refutation of Marxist historical writing, the latter inspired by it. They did share common ground, however, in so far as they both regarded the nature of Latin America's external relations as key to understanding the continent's internal development. Dependency theory portrayed those relations in overwhelmingly negative terms; 'informal empire', meanwhile, was

---

1 For further reflection on the significance of their work, see Thompson (2004).

much more reticent on the question of whether Latin America pursued export-led development to its profit or detriment.[2]

Quite a lot of water has passed under the bridge since scholars first debated 'dependency theory' and 'informal empire' in the generation after the Second World War. Yet whereas scholars of British expansion continue to grapple with the question of what model might best explain Britain's relationships with the world's weaker nations and economies, Latin Americanists tend nowadays to be more attracted by new currents of postcolonial theory (e.g. Thurner and Guerrero, 2003). 'Indigeneity' (as a way of understanding the relations between settlers and 'first' or 'aboriginal' peoples), 'cultural agency', 'network theory' and 'tans-nationalism' (as a way of understanding how colonial and neocolonial spaces were joined together and knowledge, people and goods circulated around them), and 'globalisation' (as a way of understanding the forces that circumvented or circumscribed nation states) are all cases in point (e.g. Sommer, 2006; Pratt, 2007). As David Rock and Alan Knight show in this volume, the importance of culture in shaping encounters between peoples is increasingly recognised by scholars. Other contributors, such as Louise Guenther, go further, arguing that both the 'political' and the 'economic' spheres of informal empire were culturally constructed. The foregrounding of these debates as to the relative weight of commerce, capital and culture in configuring informal empire is one of this book's most important themes.

The return to informal empire sits neatly alongside other historiographical trends of recent years. Researchers studying the British empire and Latin America have both been lured by the 'Atlantic world' as an analytic framework – not only scholars of black slavery but white slavery, too, especially those writing about prostitution and organised crime (see here Van Onselen, 2000, 2007, which tells the chilling story of the trafficking of prostitutes, and related criminal activity, from Britain and France to the USA, Southern Africa, Argentina and Chile, replete as it is with episodes of seduction, rape, deception, extortion, burglary and murder; and Londres, 1928). In that sense, it might be argued that 'informal empire' is now a concept for which the Imperial historian has greater need than the Latin Americanist. To say this is not to disparage 'informal empire'. Rather it is to recognise the differing demands placed on the concept by two distinct historiographical traditions.

---

2   Even then, it must be recognised that dependency theory was the much more influential of the two concepts. As David Rock and Paul Garner observed at the University of Bristol conference in January 2007, the dispute between Robinson and Gallagher and Platt had little impact in Latin America itself: it was predominantly an Anglo-Centric affair.

This book demonstrates that many of the main issues relating to informal empire remain a matter of ongoing debate. The amount of influence exerted by Britain in Latin America is either questioned or emphasised by all the contributors. Louise Guenther's spirited intervention argues for the markedly gendered nature of the concept itself, and of the nature of British 'intervention' in the continent. Fernanda Peñaloza's chapter deconstructs the links between travel writing, imperial projects and the anxieties of the self in its encounters with the sublime. Charles Jones and Jennifer French further blur the boundaries by showing how different aspects of informal empire were combined in the lives, career trajectories and writings of key protagonists who had origins, affiliations and dreams on both sides of the Atlantic. In sum, the book shows that there is much life left in the traditional political–economic–diplomatic understanding of informal empire – the 'Commerce and Capital' of the book's title – but also roundly demonstrates that interpretations grounded in cultural studies and cultural history are re-orientating the research agenda.

In this Afterword, I want to reflect further on the chapters in this volume and to propose two things. First, that Imperial history must hold on to the concept of informal empire, but that, if it is to do so, the concept needs to be refashioned. An interdisciplinary scope, as displayed in this volume, is essential to such a project. The aim of this refashioning should be to give the concept greater analytical precision, as well as to relate it to the 'new' Imperial history and postcolonial studies – both of which have brought other concepts and theories in their train. Second, whether or not one sees the concept of informal empire as capturing the essence of Britain's relations with Latin America during the 'long' nineteenth century, it is clear from the chapters in this volume that it does nonetheless throw into sharp relief several of the more salient historical questions and problems thrown up by the exposure of Latin American societies to the industrialising economies of Western Europe and the USA – this is a further reason why, half a century after it was first elaborated, informal empire is still worth debating.

II

The 'devil' of informal empire, it might be said, lies less in the detail than in the definition. Several of the essays in this volume underline the need for greater conceptual clarity. The essence of the problem, as recognised by participants at the University of Bristol conference in January 2007, has been the tendency to construct informal empire as a *category* (analytically distinct from the formal empire) rather than as a *continuum* (along which regions of both formal and informal rule can then be positioned, according to the nature of their relationship with Britain at any one point in time). Constructing informal empire as a category risks homogenising it. Indeed, it is worth emphasising in this context that even the formal empire was far from uniform. There were in fact a variety of levels and mechanisms of formal control. For example, the self-governing dominions, or 'neo-Britains' as they have lately been called (Belich, 2005), enjoyed a substantial measure of autonomy by the turn of the twentieth century, so much so that they were arguably less subject to British interference than parts of the informal empire at this time. Hence, concepts of informal *and* formal empire need to be able to accommodate the variety and complexity of Europe's colonial and semi-colonial presences.

The logic of a continuum, therefore, is to recognise that issues of 'coercion', 'agency', 'sustained pressure' and 'asymmetrical power' are (and have to be) present in imperial relationships, but that, according to time and place, they are exercised in differing ways and exist to differing degrees.[3] Yet to recognise this still leaves a big question begging, namely, as Leslie Bethell enquired at the Bristol conference, 'what is a sufficient condition for the concept of informal empire to be fulfilled?' One way of responding to Bethell's question would be to say that there has to be conscious exploitation in the relationship, or that the economic benefits stemming from it have to accrue unevenly in Britain's favour.[4] As Alan Knight suggests in his chapter, 'exploitation' is itself a normative term, yet the question *cui bono?* remains pertinent for the historian. This interpretation of 'informal empire' is frequently found in the literature, although it has often led scholars to conclude that the concept is difficult empirically to sustain.

Another way of thinking about informal empire would be in terms of the exercise of sovereignty – the capacity to act independently, or to take decisions of one's own (see Hopkins, 1994; Sen, 2002; Blom Hansen and Stepputat, 2005).[5] In this case, for a Latin American state to be considered part of Britain's imperial domain, its sovereignty would have to be seriously compromised over a sustained period of time (drawing on Beloff, 1968; Thomas, 1985). Of course, formal sovereign independence was an established fact across Latin America by 1830. The question here is whether this sovereignty

---

3   See, for example the chapters in this volume by Rock and Knight.
4   This issue is skilfully treated in Colin Lewis's chapter in this volume; see, especially, his precisely phrased conclusion that: 'there was a balance of mutual (not necessarily equal) benefit in the relationship'.
5   Hopkins's (1994) response to my own essay in *JLAS* (1992) was very suggestive on the concept of sovereignty and its relevance to debates about informal empire, even if we disagreed on the detail of the Anglo-Argentine case. See also Cain and Hopkins (2002), cited in the Introduction to this volume, 7, p.18.

was substantive, and whether economic controls, political power or cultural influence were wielded from outside in such a way as to materially constrain the freedom of manoeuvre of Latin American societies and states (see Holton, 2005). The answer provided (albeit tentatively) by the chapters in this volume seems to be that something akin to this state of affairs was true of Argentina in the 1930s (following French and Rock) or Brazil in the mid-1880s (following Guenther). Conversely, informal empire appears to have been weakest in Colombia (following Deas) and other areas such as Ecuador and Bolivia.

The issue of sovereignty can also be explored by disaggregating the impact of the things most likely to undermine it: commerce, capital and, less obviously but no less importantly, culture. In this respect, the geography of informal empire in Latin America is worth considering further. How far were external commercial influences primarily the domain of the Atlantic seaboard? How far did the influence of foreign capital make itself felt mainly along railway lines and in capital and/or port cities? And how far were immigrants (from southern and eastern Europe) the key vector of external cultural influences (and thus a counterweight to power exercised by Britain)? These are questions that rarely explicitly feature in the literature on informal empire in Latin America, but which help us to better compare the impact of foreign influence and interventions across its states and regions.

What, then, might be the advantages of reformulating the concept of 'informal empire' around sovereignty? First, it could help to convey how, as David Rock suggests, imperialism in Latin America was less a 'fact' or 'accomplishment' than 'an aspiration'. As Rock rightly insists, we need to explore the exercise of British power in the region in a more nuanced fashion. Key points to take on board here are that sovereignty can be exercised over a range of aspects of statehood – economic, military, diplomatic, for example – and that it can be diminished by degrees. Hence, it was possible for sovereignty to be eroded in some spheres, while potentially left intact in others (Hinsley, 1986), for it to be partially as well as wholly constrained, and for it to be voluntarily relinquished as well as forcibly removed. Significantly, it could also be recovered after having been lost.

Second, sovereignty, by its very nature, is performative – states need not only to possess it, but *to be seen* to possess it. In Latin America, different groups have evinced varied perspectives on the possession of sovereignty. Infringed sovereignty, or at least the belief, however exaggerated or contrived, that it had been infringed, became a key element of nationalist discourse, as the introduction to this volume has already shown (p. 5). Approached in this way, the concept of sovereignty can also help to capture two key features of Britain's relationship with many Latin American states during the 'long' nineteenth century. On the one hand, the fact that newly independent Latin American states were asserting a 'fledgling sovereignty' (MacLean, 1995: 199) for much of this period needs to be emphasised. It meant that the prospect of being absorbed into Britain's 'informal empire' was never far removed. But, on the other hand, the limits on British power were equally real and palpable. They resulted from the lack of a strong military presence to back up diplomatic negotiations or commercial and financial pressure (the blockades of the Royal Navy were always a rather blunt instrument here), as well as from the skill and resourcefulness shown by Latin American states in defending their interests and pursuing their ambitions.

Third, refracting imperial power through the optic of sovereignty provides a way of connecting an older literature on informal empire to newer literatures on the role of empires in developing transnational ideas and institutions (examples of this new literature include Bashford, 2004; Grant, Levine and Trentmann, 2007). Of particular interest here is how the existence and unity of empires were made possible by supranational connections, and how empires fostered networks that cut across national boundaries (Hopkins, 1999: 205; Lester, 2001). In an essay on the relationship between empires, networks and discourses, the Africanist, Cooper (2001: 23) argues powerfully for the value of the network concept in analysing with greater precision long-distance connections over extensive periods of time. However, as soon as we begin to re-imagine imperial geographies along networked lines, we are faced with the tricky question of where power spatially resided.[6] In particular, if we are to conceive of empires as interconnected zones constituted by multiple points of contact and complex circuits of exchange (as in Lester 2001; Proudfoot and Roche, 2006) this in turn has implications for how we think about the diffusion of imperial power. For the logic of a 'networked' or 'decentred' approach to studying empires is that metropole and colony acted and reacted upon each other in complex ways, and that sovereignty in the colonies (formal or informal), far from being static or stable, was subject to constant negotiation and renegotiation by a variety of settler and non-settler groups. Robinson and Gallagher's version of 'informal empire', carrying as it does the implication that one power (A) determined the 'rules of the game' in which another power (B) then had to operate, perhaps leaves insufficient scope for such reciprocity and interdependence.

---

6   See, for example Daniels and Kennedy (2002) which argues for peripheries occupying a more central position in the early modern colonial world, and carrying more power in relation to metropolitan centres than scholars have often allowed.

III

Which aspects of Latin America's history might a refashioned concept of 'informal empire' serve to illuminate? The chapters in this volume draw at least three to the reader's attention. First, there is considerable scope to improve our knowledge of the British who settled in Buenos Aires, Montevideo, Rio de Janeiro, Mexico, Lima, Havana and elsewhere. For too long these 'mini-Britains' – which also include treaty port China, occupied Egypt and highland Kenya, as well as parts of Latin America – have been overshadowed in the historiography (for a commendable effort to redress the balance, see Bickers, forthcoming). We need to better understand the forms that settler projects took outside formal settlement schemes. What, for example was the frame of reference of the British in Latin America? Did they feel part of a wider, global British community or civilisation, and think of themselves, and their struggles, in relation to expatriates and settlers elsewhere? Or, conversely, as Louise Guenther suggests in her contribution to this volume, did they take on a more cosmopolitan outlook by forming partnerships, intermingling and even intermarrying with merchants and professionals from other European nations or from Latin America itself? (see also Jones, 1987: 69–79). How many of the expatriate British in Latin America came from Britain, and how many had moved on there from elsewhere in the empire – from the Caribbean or Australia, for instance? What status did they enjoy in Latin America, and how far were their children able to carve a social niche for themselves? Jennifer French's contribution to this volume provides a captivating insight into the role that literature played in revealing the hidden secrets of intimate Anglo-Argentine relationships, for example. Yet as French herself argues, there is much more work to be done here. What were the attitudes of the British to the society around them, and how far did the views they formed of 'indigenous' Latin Americans resemble the views that settlers elsewhere in the British empire formed of 'first' peoples in their midst? We also need to establish what place the British in Latin America occupied in the 'settler hierarchy' or 'diaspora'. How effective were they in mobilising special interests or wider electoral support back home? And how far were officials and ministers in London persuaded by British residents in Latin America that they could 'provide a local infrastructure into which imperial power could readily be injected' by means of the 'colonial bridgehead'? (Darwin, 1997: 641).

Second, if informal empire is about the exercise of power in international relations, it is clear that much of the literature focuses upon political and economic forms of power. But what of power's other registers? How far did ties of culture and kinship, as opposed to commerce and finance, bind Britain to Latin America? And how were cultural influences mediated from

Europe (and the USA) to Latin America and, for that matter, vice-versa? Matthew Brown rightly remarks in his introduction upon how the 'new' Imperial history, with its emphasis upon knowledge-based forms of power, remains remarkably silent on Latin America. The chapters in this volume, and the papers delivered at the Bristol conference, show how we need to study cultural influences from Britain in conjunction with those from elsewhere in Europe (France, Italy and Spain, especially, but also the Russian and Polish Jews sucked in from the Tsarist empire – at the high point of the inflow, in 1910, an estimated 5 per cent of Argentina's immigrants were Jewish) as well as the USA, and how these evolved alongside what Martínez (2001) has called 'cosmopolitan nationalism'. They also raise the tricky question of whether the aping or emulating of European culture by Latin American elites is better read as a sign of their self-assurance or their subordination. Beyond that, they point to the possibilities of relating 'culture' to 'economy', and, in particular, of exploring how far the strength of cultural ties drew strength from economic interests, or, conversely, how far culture, in the form of new patterns of consumption or foreign technology transfer through migration, for example, underpinned economic activity and behaviour (as in Martínez-Fernández, 1994). Of course, this is potentially a huge research agenda, but recent writing on the social and economic life of the Cornish in Latin America (Schwartz, 2005) suggests some ways in which it might profitably be taken forward.

Third, the chapters in this volume draw the reader's attention to a long-standing concern of Latin Americanists – the ways in which class relations have been embedded in capitalist structures. To be sure, there is a danger of exaggerating the effects of export-led development on the alignment of social forces in Latin American societies as they integrated into the global economy. Nevertheless, there is something to be said for placing Latin American elites in a broader 'British world' context (see Bridge and Fedorowich, 2003). The Argentine landed elite's emulation of the technocratic, modernising elites of Britain, France and the USA is of particular interest here. There are potential parallels with the political elites of Australia, New Zealand and Canada who saw themselves not so much as reproducing metropolitan society but as building '*better* Britains' o'er the seas. A recent, albeit controversial essay by Gott (2007) makes precisely this point. Gott cautions against setting Latin America conveniently apart from the rest of the world. Instead he suggests that the continent should be considered 'as a white settler society' alongside Australia, South Africa and Canada, and included in the general histories of the global expansion of migrant populations from all over Europe. One of the attractions of 'informal empire' as a concept in Latin American history is that it encourages us to think comparatively.

The fact that the wealth of Latin American elites was derived in such a large measure from the export sector, and therefore from their willingness to enter into an economic partnership with Britain, must also merit further consideration. It affected how external relations were understood, as well as how elites were themselves perceived by their own societies. On both fronts, and especially in Argentina and Mexico, there were signs of rising discontent by 1914 (as discussed in Charles Jones's contribution to this volume, and in Hora, 2001). The dominance of British capital, and the uneven distribution of the gains arising from it, served to foment political opposition, labour militancy and economic nationalism. Getting to grips with the last of these concepts – 'economic nationalism' – is vitally important, therefore. Indeed, it is central to our understanding of the social cleavages opened up by participation in the international economy. Such participation was, of course, a *sine qua non* of the rapidly rising wealth of societies such as Argentina in the quarter century before the First World War (O'Rourke and Williamson, 1999). But, compared to 'informal empire', 'economic nationalism' is arguably under-theorised, and Miller's (2006) dissection of it into rhetorical, retributive and regulatory strands is a very useful way of thinking about how and why Latin Americans reacted against British economic involvement. Of course, Latin American presidents – Hugo Chavez especially – continue to remobilise older anti-imperialist traditions today in their fight against neoliberalism. This, however, seems to be a largely rhetorical exercise, devoid of any real substance or significance beyond that of evoking a sense of past injustices and aggressions. Indeed, as a recent special issue of the *Bulletin of Latin American Research* shows, the discussion of Latin American nationalism is currently taking new directions. Goebel (2007), especially, argues for an understanding of nationalist ideology and discourse framed less around the issue of foreign influence or intervention and more around local and national processes. In so far as he draws attention to the 'transnational dynamics of nationalism' it is in terms of wider Spanish and Latin American solidarities rather than (perceived) states of semi-colonialism or foreign exploitation.

IV

Among the main consequences of the expansion of British power in the world in the generation before the First World War was the creation of a group of settler societies with distinctive economic characteristics. Hitherto sparsely populated regions such as the Argentine pampas occupied a privileged position in the first 'global economy' constructed by British free traders in the nineteenth century. With an abundance of fertile land, yet a lack of capital and labour, they had an almost magnetic attraction for British investors and European emigrants. By building modern transport infra-structures, and by exporting a narrow range of 'staple' commodities (mainly foods and raw materials), they were able to achieve impressive levels of growth and high per capita incomes. They tend to be referred to as 'regions of recent settlement', 'temperate colonies', or 'white' dominions. Australia, Canada, New Zealand and Argentina (as an 'honorary dominion') are usu-ally the centrepiece of comparative studies of their economies, which may or may not also include South Africa and Uruguay.

The importance of external economic relationships in explaining the dis-tinctive evolution of settler societies was first recognised by 'staples theory', although its advocates tended to focus on particular societies rather than look at them comparatively (Innis, 1956, 1995; Schevdin, 1990). The pioneer of the *comparative* study of dominion capitalism is Donald Denoon (1979, 1983). His ambitious analysis of six settler societies (Australia, New Zea-land, South Africa, Argentina, Chile and Uruguay), while allowing for dif-fering responses to world economic conditions, nonetheless places them in a distinct category of development and attributes to them 'powerful strands of commonality' requiring a generalised explanation. Denoon argues that settler capitalists, separated from Europe by large distances and yet self-consciously European in their attitudes and aspirations, pursued export-led growth to considerable material advantage. They were, of course, depen-dent on Britain for capital and for markets. However, Denoon sees this state of 'unforced dependence' as perfectly compatible with 'wide autonomy', even if it dissipated the energies of some groups who might have driven these societies toward greater self-reliance (see also Kubicek, 1999, who sug-gests that 'peripheral autonomy' rather than 'peripheral dependence' best captures the situation of Australia, Canada and South Africa by 1911).

Yet, as more recent writing suggests, we must continue to be mindful of the differences between Latin America and other parts of the British impe-rial world. As Mathew Brown states in the introduction to this volume, Brit-ish informal empire in Latin America 'existed in the shadow of several empires and competing projects', in particular, from the beginning of the twentieth century, the emergent empire of the USA (see also, Magee and Thompson, forthcoming). Moreover, as several contributors to the Bristol conference highlighted, differences in political tradition, religious affiliation and the origins of immigrants were significant here (see also Platt and Di Tella, 1985: 2–17). In particular, it bears reiterating that, in key respects, the nature of migration to Latin America can be sharply contrasted to migration within the 'British world'. Take, for instance, the Italians who moved to Ar-gentina in increasing numbers in the early twentieth century. The employ-ment of Italian men was marginal throughout British overseas territories. The dominions did not welcome Catholic or Jewish immigrants (in fact,

Australia and Canada both restricted migration from Italy at times); skilled labour tended to be recruited from Britain itself, and contract labour from Britain's own colonies (principally India) and its commercial sphere in south China. By contrast, in Argentina, Italy accounted for 50 per cent of all immigrants before 1914 (see Gabaccia, 2000: 179 and Chapter 4 more generally for comparisons between Italian settlements in Latin America, the USA and the neo-Britains). Many of these immigrants were temporary or seasonal workers, leasing pampean land on short-term contracts, or selling their labour during harvest. This diminished risk and avoided the burden of fixed investments, while allowing them to accumulate considerable amounts of capital to remit home.[7] The situation was quite different for migrants to the Canadian prairies from Eastern Canada, the USA and the British Isles, who made landownership their main goal. They moved with an eye to setting up permanent enterprises, and their preference was for self-employment rather than selling their labour (Adelman, 1994: 1–5, 260–263; also Platt and Di Tella, 1985: 5). While a part of the explanation for this difference rests in prevailing property relations (common-property commutation favoured large owners in Argentina, and smallholders in Canada), settler ideology also comes into play. Within the British world of the later nineteenth and early twentieth centuries, a 'secular utopianism' entered into the emigrant creed; it was premised on the myth (or promise) of the yeoman freehold, and vigorously propagated by a plethora of British emigrant literature (Belich, 2005). Within Latin America such an ideology had less purchase, and was orientated more towards so-called 'internal colonisation' of hitherto neglected regions such as Antioquia in Colombia (Parsons, 1979; Brew, 2000) and La Plata in Argentina (see French in this volume).

Migration may also help to explain why, within British society, Latin America was rarely, if ever, referred to as a part of a 'Greater Britain'. That is not to say that Latin America never stirred public interest. Aguirre (2005) has recently shown how objects of Mesoamerican culture were avidly collected, catalogued, and displayed by the British in the nineteenth century.[8] But the shifting languages of imperialism, especially in the political sphere, focused preponderantly on British settler societies, and neglected formal regions of authoritarian rule (Thompson, 1997). In the former, Britishness was conceived of as a broad church, capable of accommodating a variety of

---

7   For example, we know that between 1889/1890 and 1913/1914, Italian migrants in Argentina remitted 7,386,869 lira or, at 1913 exchange rates, around £288,367 back home (Dean, 1974: 3).

8   See also Forman (2000a) which, *inter alia*, suggests that the attention of the British public was from time to time attracted to British interventions overseas by newspaper reporting, cartoons, novels, poetry, and plays.

settler and non-settler groups. Smaller expatriate British communities in societies such as Argentina, Uruguay, Brazil, Mexico or Chile figured far less prominently in discussions of the relationship between the British at home and the overseas British. Malcolm Deas has persuasively argued in this volume that the British community in Colombia was small and lacking in influence.

All this is not to say that Latin America should not be factored into the emerging academic debate about 'imperial Britain'. Existing studies of the empire's effects on, and significance for, the metropole rarely make mention of it (see Hall, 2002, Porter, 2004b; Thompson, 2005). But recent research points to possible influences and connections. Among the merchant banks of the City of London, in regions with a high degree of skilled labour mobility (e.g. Cornwall), and in provincial railway engineering companies (not least in my own city of Leeds), there would almost certainly have been a degree of consciousness of Latin America, albeit a highly selective one. Beyond that, one might point to the development of the international diamond trade from the early to mid-nineteenth century. Before the discoveries in Kimberley in South Africa around 1870, approximately 90 per cent of rough diamonds traded came from Brazil. The promulgation of knowledge about diamond gems and mining, under the auspices of the increasingly professionalised disciplines of chemistry, physics, geology and mineralogy, became centred on Britain (see Kinsey, forthcoming). Museum exhibits, travelogues, public lectures, and scientific publications were all vectors for creating a consciousness of diamonds among (elite) British consumers, and, in the process, drawing their attention to the main source of production in Brazil. The question of consumer consciousness could further be extended to the steep rise in exports from Latin America to Britain at the turn of the nineteenth and twentieth centuries. By the late 1890s, imported frozen beef from Argentina – made possible by the introduction of refrigeration on steamships – was making noticeable inroads into the British market (see Winstanley, 1983). How far the British consumer was actually aware of this is a moot point, but one perhaps worth exploring.[9] And, of course, there are the Welsh emigrants to Patagonia, once famously described by David Lloyd George as a 'little Wales across the sea'. They were not large in number – a few thousand in all – but probably had a disproportionate impact in terms of the awareness they generated back in Wales of this piece of Argentine-owned territory, the suzerainty of which was disputed with

---

9   Groot (2006) has recently, and engagingly, revisited the links between everyday consumption, colonial goods and the British market, albeit she only refers in passing to products exported from Latin America.

Chile; many Welsh settlers in fact eventually returned from Patagonia because of their growing dislike of living under an 'alien flag' as well as the tensions caused by the growth of non-Welsh (mainly Italian) colonisation (see Williams, 1975; Owen, 1977).

V

Within Latin America, the use of models such as 'dependency', 'neocolonialism' and 'informal empire' has to be set against a backdrop of the continent's 'history wars' – ideologically motivated exchanges between so-called radical-nationalist, conservative-nationalist and liberal schools (for the term 'history wars' and its application in Australia, see MacIntyre and Clark, 2003, and for Argentina, see Lewis and Rock, both in this volume). The attraction of each of these models is more limited today, as new political concerns have emerged around the treatment of 'first' or 'indigenous' peoples, the impact of immigration and the effects of globalisation on the economy and the environment. These concerns are likely to be reflected in the future study of the history of British involvement in Latin America, which, if the latest publications are anything to go by, is already adopting comparative, transregional and transnational frameworks, in order to explore issues of loyalty and identity in fresh and interesting ways (Brown, 2006), and to rethink aspects of economic history such as the anatomy of financial crises (see, e.g. Kindleberger and Aliber, 2005 on the ramifications of the 1890 Baring Crisis for capital markets in South Africa, Australia, the USA and the rest of Latin America). It may even be that, in returning to 'informal empire' again, the lasting impact of the chapters in this volume – several of which, it has to be said, evince some scepticism toward the concept – will be to open up new approaches to studying imperialism globally and comparatively, approaches that can help us to make sense of a continent that, no sooner had it freed itself from the shackles of Spanish and Portuguese power, found itself falling prey to the 'designs' of Britain (and the USA). Precisely how such designs are best characterised, and how far they were ever fulfilled, is a subject that remains worthy of our attention.

11

References

Abel, C. G. and Lewis, C. M. (eds.) (1985) *Latin America, Economic Imperialism and the State: The Political Economy of the External Connection from Independence to the Present*. Institute of Latin American Studies: London.

Acevedo Díaz, M. (1978) *La culebra pico de oro*. Instituto Colombiano de Cultura: Bogotá.

Acton, L. (1975) *Lectures on Modern History*. Peter Smith: Gloucester.

Adelman, J. (1994) *Frontier Development: Land, Labour and Capital on the Wheatlands of Argentina and Canada, 1890–1914*. Oxford University Press: Oxford.

Adelman, J. (1999) *Republic of Capital: Buenos Aires and the Legal Transformation of the Atlantic World*. University of California: Stanford.

Adelman, J. (2006) *Sovereignty and Revolution in the Iberian Atlantic*. Princeton University Press: Princeton.

Agassiz, Elizabeth Cary (1872) 'The Hassler Glacier in the Straits of Magellan', *Atlantic Monthly* **30** (October): 472–478.

Agassiz, Elizabeth Cary (1873) 'In the Straits of Magellan', *Atlantic Monthly* **31** (January): 89–95.

Aguilar, G. (2003) 'The National Opera: A Migrant Genre of Imperial Expansion'. *Journal of Latin American Cultural Studies* **12**(1): 83–94.

Aguirre, R. (2005) *Informal Empire. Mexico and Central America in Victorian Culture*. University of Minnesota Press: Minnesota.

Alberdi, J. B. (1852) *'Bases y puntos de partida para la organización política de la República Argentina'*, in J. M. Mayer (ed.) *Las Bases de Alberdi*. Editorial Sudamericana: Buenos Aires (1969 edition).

Albert, B. (1988) *South America and the First World War. The Impact of the War on Brazil, Argentina, Peru and Chile*. Cambridge University Press: Cambridge.

Alhadeff, P. (1985) 'Dependency, Historiography and Objections to the Roca Pact', in C. Abel and C. Lewis (eds.) *Latin America, Economic Imperialism and the State: The Political Economy of External Connections from Independence to the Present*. The Athlone Press: London, 367–378.

Alonso, C. J. (1990) *The Spanish American Regional Novel: Modernity and Autochthony*. Cambridge University Press: Cambridge.

Alonso, C. J. (1998) *The Burden of Modernity: The Rhetoric of Cultural Discourse in Spanish America*. Oxford University Press: Oxford.

Alonso, P. (2000) *Between Revolution and the Ballot Box: The Origins of the Argentine Radical Party in the 1890s*. Cambridge University Press: Cambridge.

Amaral, S. E. (1998) *The Rise of Capitalism on the Pampas: The Estancias of Buenos Aires, 1785–1870*. Cambridge University Press: Cambridge.

Amunátegui Solar, D. (1895) *El sistema de Lancaster en Chile, i en otros paises sudamericanos*. Imprenta Cervantes: Santiago de Chile.

Andermann, J. (2003) 'Fronteras: la conquista del desierto y la economía de la violencia', in F. Schmidt-Welle (ed.) *Ficciones y silencios fundacionales*. Iberoamericana: Madrid, 117–135.

Anderson, B. (1991) *Imagined Communities: Reflections on the Origin and Spread of Nationalism*. Verso: London.

Anderson, G. L. (1977) 'The Social Economy of Late-Victorian Clerks', in G. Crossick (ed.) *The Lower Middle Class in Britain, 1870–1914*. Croom Helm: London, 113–133.

Anderson, M. (2006) *Women and the Politics of Travel, 1870–1914*. Associated University Presses: Cranberry.

Appiah, K. A. (2006) *Cosmopolitanism: Ethics in a World of Strangers*. W.W. Norton: New York.

Archetti, E. (1999) *Masculinities: Football, Polo and the Tango in Argentina*. Berg: New York.

Arias, A. (2001) *The Rigoberta Menchú Controversy*. University of Minnesota: Minneapolis.

Arnold, C. and Frost, F. J. (1909) *The American Egypt: A Record of Travels in Yucatán*. Hutchinson: London.

Ashraf, N., Camerer, C. F. and Loewenstein, G. (2005) 'Adam Smith, Behavioral Economist'. *Journal of Economic Perspectives* **19**(3): 131–145.

Augel, M. P. (1980) *Visitantes estrangeiros na Bahia oitocentista*. Editora Cultrix: São Paulo.

Avella Gómez, M. (2003) 'Antecedentes históricos de la deuda externa colombiana. La paz británica'. *Revista de Economía Institucional* **5**(9) [WWW document]. URL http://www.banrep.gov.co/docum/ftp/borra239.pdf [accessed 1 April 2007].

Barres, F. (1944) 'Reseña de los ferrocarriles argentinos', *Boletin de la Asociación International Permanente del Congreso Panamericano de Ferrocarriles* **28**(86): 31–85.

Bartlett, R. (1994) *The Making of Europe. Conquest, Colonization and Cultural Change, 950–1350*. Penguin Books: Harmondsworth.

Bashford, A. (2004) *Imperial Hygiene: A Critical History of Colonialism, Nationalism and Public Health*. Palgrave MacMillan: Basingstoke.

Bauer, A. (1986) 'Rural Spanish America, 1870–1930', in L. Bethell (ed.) *The Cambridge History of Latin America*, Vol. 4. Cambridge University Press: Cambridge, 153–186.

Bauer, A. (2001) *Goods, Power, History: Latin America's Material Culture*. Cambridge University Press: Cambridge.

Bayly, C. A. (1989) *Imperial Meridian: British Empire & the World, 1780–1830*. Longman: London.

Bayly, C. A. (2004) *The Birth of the Modern World, 1789–1914, Global Connections and Comparisons*. Blackwell: Oxford.

Belich, J. (2005) 'The Rise of the Angloworld: Settlement in North America and Australasia, 1784–1918', in P. Buckner and R. Douglas Francis (eds.) *Rediscovering the British World*. University of Calgary Press: Calgary, 39–57.

Bell, P. L. (1921) *Colombia, A Commercial and Industrial Handbook*. US Government Publications: Washington.

Bello, A. (1832) *Derecho de gentes*. Santiago de Chile Imprenta de la opinión.

Bello, A. (1984) *Obras Completas: Vol. 25, Epistolario*. Fundación de la Casa de Bello: Caracas.

Beloff, M. (1968) 'Reflections on Intervention'. *Journal of International Affairs*, **22**: 198–207.

Bethell, L. (1970) *The Abolition of the Brazilian Slave Trade: Britain, Brazil and the Slave Trade Question, 1807–1869*. Cambridge University Press: Cambridge.

Bethell, L. (1995) 'O imperialismo britânico e a Guerra do Paraguai', in M. E. Castro Magalhães Marques (ed.) *A Guerra do Paraguai 130 anos depois*. Relume Dumará: Rio de Janeiro, 133–150.

Beverley, J. (1999) *Subalternity and Representation: Arguments in Cultural Theory*. Duke University Press: Durham.

Beverley, J. (2003) '*Adiós*: A National Allegory (Some Reflections on Latin American Cultural Studies)', in S. Hart and R. Young (eds.) *Contemporary Latin American Cultural Studies*. Arnold: London, 48–60.

Bickers, R. (ed.) (forthcoming) *Settler and Expatriate Societies*. Oxford University Press: Oxford.

Black, J. (1997) *Maps and Politics*. Reaktion Books: London.

Blackwood's (1825) *Blackwood's Edinburgh Journal*. Blackwood: Edinburgh.

Blom Hansen, T. and Stepputat, F. (2005) *Sovereign Bodies: Citizens, Migrants and States in the Postcolonial World*. Princeton University Press: Princeton.

Bolívar, S. (1830) 'Letter to Juan José Flores, 9 November 1830, Barranquilla, translated into English by F. H. Fornoff', in D. Bushnell (ed.) *El Libertador: Writings of Simón Bolívar*. Oxford University Press: Oxford, 146.

BOLSA. *Archives of the Bank of London and South America*. University College London: Special Collections. (Archives unpublished).

Botero, C. I. (2007) *El redescubrimiento del pasado prehispánico de Colombia: viajeros, arqueólogos y coleccionistas, 1820–1940*. Instituto Colombiano de Antropología e Historia/Universidad de los Andes: Bogotá.

Box, B. (2003) *South American Handbook 2004*. Footprint: Bath.

Boyle, V. (ed.) (1999) *Letters from George Reid 1867–1870*. Valerie Boyle: London.

Brew, R. (2000) *El desarollo económico de Antioquia desde la independencia hasta 1920*. Editorial Clio: Medellín.

Bridge, C. and Fedorowich, K. (eds.) (2003) *The British World: Diaspora, Culture and Identity*. Frank Cass: London.

Briones, C. and Lanata, J. L. (eds.) (2002) *Archaeological and Anthropological Perspectives on the Native Peoples of Pampa, Patagonia, and Tierra del Fuego to the Nineteenth Century*. Bergin & Garvey: Westport.

British and Foreign Bible Society (1811–1829) *Annual Report of the British and Foreign Bible Society*, Vols. 7–25 (cited as ARBFBS). British and Forign Bible Society: London.

Brontë, C. (1954 [1847]) *Jane Eyre*. The Literary Guild of America, Inc.: Garden City.

Brown, J. C. (1994) 'Revival of the Rural Economy and Society in Buenos Aires', in M. D. Szuchman and J. C. Brown (eds.) *Revolution and Restoration: The Rearrangement of Power in Argentina, 1776–1860*. University of Nebraska Press: Lincoln, 240–272.

Brown, M. (2005) 'Adventurers, Foreign Women and Masculinity in the Colombian Wars of Independence'. *Feminist Review* **79**: 36–51.

Brown, M. (2006) *Adventuring through Spanish Colonies: Simón Bolívar, Foreign Mercenaries and the Birth of New Nations*. Liverpool University Press: Liverpool.

Browning, J. E. (1921) 'Joseph Lancaster, James Thomson, and the Lancasterian System of Mutual Instruction, with Special Reference to Hispanic America'. *Hispanic American Historical Review* **4**(1): 49–98.

Bunge, A. (1918) *Ferrocariles argentinos: contribución al estudio del patrimonio nacional*. Imprenta Mercatali: Buenos Aires.

Burke, E. (1757) *A Philosophical Enquiry into the Sublime and Beautiful*. Penguin: London (1998 edition).

Burton, A. (ed.) (2003) *After the Imperial Turn: Thinking with and through the Nation*. Duke University Press: Durham.

Burton, R. F. (1870) *Letters from the Battlefields of Paraguay*. Tinsley Brothers: London.

Bushnell, D. (1956) 'Two Stages in Colombian Tariff Policy, The Radical Era and the Return to Protection, 1861–1885'. *Inter-American Economic Affairs* 9: 3–23.

Butterfield, H. (1951 [1931]) *The Whig Interpretation of History*. G. Bell and Sons: London.

Cain, P. J. (2006) 'Foreword' in B. Bush, *Imperialism and Postcolonialism*. Lonon: Longman.

Cain, P. J. and Harrison, M. (eds.) (2001) *Imperialism. Critical Concepts in Historical Studies*. Routledge: London.

Cain, P. and Hopkins, A. G. (1986) 'Gentlemanly Capitalism and British Expansion Overseas, I: The Old Colonial System, 1688–1850'. *Economic History Review* 39(4): 501–524.

Cain, P. and Hopkins, A. G. (2002) *British Imperialism: Innovation and Expansion, 1688–1914*. Longman: London.

Calvert, P. A. R. (1968) *The Mexican Revolution, 1910–14. The Diplomacy of Anglo-American Conflict*. Cambridge University Press: Cambridge.

Cardoso, F. H. and Faletto, E. (1979) *Dependency and Development in Latin America* (trans. M. Mattingly Urquidi). University of California Press: Berkeley.

Cassirer, E. (1951) *The Philosophy of the Enlightenment*. Princeton University Press: Princeton.

Castro, C. (1902) 'Proclama de ante el bloqueo extranjero', 9 December, Caracas [WWW document]. URL http://analitica.com/Bitblio/ccastro/planta_insolente.asp. [accessed 4 December 2007].

Castro-Klarén, S. (2003) 'The Nation in Ruins: Archaeology and the Rise of the Nation', in S. Castro-Klarén and J. C. Chasteen (eds.) *Beyond Imagined Communities: Reading and Writing the Nation in Nineteenth-Century Latin America*. Woodrow Wilson Center Press: Washington, DC Johns Hopkins University Press: Baltimore, 161–195.

Cavallo, D., Domenech, R. and Mundlak, Y. (1999) *Agriculture and Economic Growth in Argentina, 1913–1984*. International Food Policy Research Institute: Washington, DC.

Chasteen, J. C. and Castro-Klarén, S. (eds.) (2003) *Beyond Imagined Communities: Reading and Writing the Nation in Nineteenth-Century Latin America*. Woodrow Wilson Center Press and Johns Hopkins University Press: Baltimore.

Chatwin, B. (1977) *In Patagonia*. Picador: London.

Chavez, H. (2007) Interview with Canal 7, 9 March, Argentina [WWW document]. URL http://www.hemisferio.org/al-eeuu/boletin_chavez/pdf/argentina/documento_11.pdf [accessed 20 August 2000].

Cleese, J. and Skynner, R. (1994) *Life and How to Survive It*. W.W. Norton & Co.: London and New York.

Clemente, I. (2005) *The Foreign Policy of Colombia in the Caribbean Basin, 1832–1904*. Unpublished doctoral dissertation, University of London, London.

Coatsworth, J. H. (1998) 'Economic and Institutional Trajectories in Nineteenth-Century Latin America' In J. H. Coatsworth and A. M. Taylor (eds.) *Latin*

America and the World Economy since 1800. Harvard University Press: Cambridge, Mass, 24–27.

Colás, S. (1995) 'Of Creole Symptoms, Cuban Fantasies, and Other Latin American Postcolonial Ideologies'. *PMLA* **110**(3): 382–396.

Colley, L. (2002a) 'What is Imperial History?', in D. Cannadine (ed.) *What is History Now?* Palgrave Macmillan: London, 132–147.

Colley, L. (2002b) *Captives. Britain, Empire, and the World, 1600–1850.* New York: Pantheon Books.

Collier, D. and Mahon, J. (1993) 'Conceptual Stretching Revisited: Adapting Categories in Comparative Analysis'. *American Political Science Review* **87**(4): 845–855.

Comaroff, J. L. and Comaroff, J. (1991) *Of Revelation and Revolution: Christianity, Colonialism and Consciousness in South Africa.* University of Chicago Press: Chicago.

Comaroff, J. L. and Comaroff, J. (1992) *Ethnography and the Historical Imagination.* Westview: Boulder.

Conaghan, C. M. (2005) *Fujimori's Peru: Deception in the Public Sphere.* University of Pittsburgh Press: Pittsburgh.

Conan Doyle, A. (1977 [1922]) 'The Brazilian Cat', in *Tales of Terror and Mystery.* Doubleday: Garden City, 88–107.

Conan Doyle, A. (2003 [1927]) 'The Problem of Thor Bridge', in G. State (ed.) *The Complete Sherlock Holmes*, Vol. 2. Barnes & Noble Classics: New York, 582–600.

Congreso Nacional (1891) *Diario de Sesiones de la Cámara de Diputados.* Congreso Nacional de Argentina: Buenos Aires.

Conrad, J. (1994 [1904]) *Nostromo: Or, a Tale of the Seaboard.* World's Classics: Oxford.

Contreras, S. (2002) 'El campo de Benito Lynch: del realismo a la novela sentimental', in M.T. Gramuglio (ed.) *El imperio realista, Historia crítica de la literatura Argentina*, Vol. 6, series editor, Noé Jitrik. Emecé: Buenos Aires, 201–223.

Cooper, F. (2001) 'Networks, Moral Discourse, and History', in T. M. Callaghy, R. Kassimir and R. Latham (eds.) *Intervention and Transnationalism in Africa.* Cambridge University Press: Cambridge, 23–46.

Cooper, F. (2005) *Colonialism in Question: Theory, Knowledge, History.* University of California Press: Berkeley.

Cooper, J. F. (1992 [1826]) *The Last of the Mohicans.* Penguin Books: London.

Cordero, C. J. (1936) *Los relatos de los viajeros extranjeros posteriores a la Revolución de Mayo como fuentes de la historia argentina: ensayo de sistematización bibliográfica.* Coni: Buenos Aires.

Coronil, F. (1998) 'Foreword', in G. M. Joseph, C. C. LeGrand and R. D. Salvatore (eds.) *Close Encounters of Empire: Writing the Cultural History of US – Latin American Relations.* Duke University Press: London and Chapel Hill, ix–xii.

Coronil, F. (2000) 'Can Postcoloniality Be Decolonized?', in D. Brydon (ed.) *Postcolonialism: Critical Concepts*, Vol. 1. Routledge: London, 190–206.

Coronil, F. (2004) 'Latin American Postcolonial Studies and Global Decolonization', in N. Lazarus (ed.) *Postcolonial Literary Studies*, 221–240.

Cortés Conde, R. (1974) *The First Stages of Modernization in Spanish America.* Harper & Row: New York.

Cortés Conde, R. (1979) *El progreso argentino, 1880–1914*. Editorial Sudamericana: Buenos Aires.

Costeloe, M. (2003) *Bonds and Bondholders: British Investors and Mexico's Foreign Debt 1824–1888*, Praeger: Greenwood Press.

Crabtree, J. (2005) *Patterns of Protest: Politics and Social Movements in Bolivia*. Latin American Bureau: London.

Crafts, N. (2003) *Steam as a General Purpose Technology: A Growth Accounting Approach*. Working Paper No. 73/02. LSE Department of Economic History: London.

Cronon, W. (1995) *Uncommon Ground: Toward Reinventing Nature*. W.W. Norton: New York.

Crosby, A. W. (1996) *Ecological Imperialism*. Cambridge University Press: Cambridge.

Cussen, A. (1992) *Bello and Bolívar: Poetry and Politics in the Spanish American Revolution*. Cambridge University Press: Cambridge.

Daniels, C. and Kennedy, M. V. (eds.) (2002) *Negotiated Empires: Centres and Peripheries in the Americas, 1500–1820*. Routledge: New York.

Darwin, C. (1989) *Voyage of the Beagle* (eds., J. Brown and M. Neve). Penguin: London.

Darwin, C. (2001) *Charles Darwin's Beagle Diary* (ed. R. Darwin Keynes). Cambridge University Press: Cambridge.

Darwin, C. (2002) *Autobiographies* (eds. M. Neve and S. Messenger). Penguin: London.

Darwin, J. (1997) 'Imperialism and the Victorians: The Dynamics of Territorial Expansion'. *English Historical Review* 112(447): 614–642.

Darwin, J. (forthcoming) 'Orphans of Empire', in R. Bickers (ed.) *Settler and Expatriate Societies*. Oxford University Press: Oxford.

Dávila, C. and Miller, R. M. (eds.) (1999) *Business History in Latin America: The Experience of Seven Countries*. Liverpool University Press: Liverpool.

Davis, D. (ed.) (2006) *Beyond Slavery: The Multifaceted Legacy of Africans in Latin America*. Rowman & Littlefield: Lanham.

Davis, L. (1999) 'The Late Nineteenth-Century British Imperialist: Specification, Quantification and Controlled Conjectures', in R. E. Dumett (ed.) *Gentlemanly Capitalism and British Imperialism*. Longman: London, 82–112.

Dawson, F. G. (1990) *The First Latin American Debt Crisis: The City of London and the 1822–25 Loan Bubble*. Yale University Press: New Haven.

de Bolla, P. (1989) *The Discourse of the Sublime: Readings in History, Aesthetics, and the Subject*. Basil Blackwell: Oxford.

Dealtry, W. (1810) *A Letter to the Reverend Dr Wordsworth*. Hatchard: London.

Dean, W. (1974) *Remittances of Italian Immigrants from Brazil, Argentina, Uruguay and the USA*. New York University: New York.

Deas, M. (1982) 'The Fiscal Problems of Nineteenth-Century Colombia'. *Journal of Latin American Studies* 14(2): 287–328.

Deas, M. (1992) 'Miguel Antonio Caro and Friends: Power and Grammar in Colombia'. *History Workshop* 34: 42–71.

Deas, M. (1994) *Vida y opiniones de William Wills*, 2 vols. Banco de la República: Bogotá.

Deas, M. (2004) 'John Diston Powles', in H. C. G. Matthew and B. Harrison (eds.) *Oxford Dictionary of National Biography: From the Earliest Times to the Year 2000*. Oxford University Press: Oxford.

Deas, M. (2006 [1993]) *Del poder y la gramática: y otros ensayos sobre historia, política y literatura colombianas*, 3rd edn. Tercer Mundo Editores: Bogotá.

Deas, M. and Sánchez, E. (eds.) (1991) *Santander y los ingleses, 1832–1840*, 2 vols. Fundación para la conmemoración del Bicentenario del Natalicio y el Sesquicentenario de la muerte del General Francisco de la Paula Santander: Bogotá.

Dehne, P. (2005) 'From "Business as Usual" to a More Global War: The British Decision to Attack Germans in South America During the First World War'. *Journal of British Studies* **44**(3): 516–535.

della Paolera, G. and Taylor, A. M. (2003) *Straining at the Anchor: The Argentine Currency Board and the Search for Macroeconomic Stability, 1880–1935*. Chicago University Press: Chicago.

Denoon, D. (1979) 'Understanding Settler Societies'. *Historical Studies* **18**: 511–527.

Denoon, D. (1983) *Settler Capitalism. The Dynamics of Dependent Development in the Southern Hemisphere*. Oxford University Press: Oxford.

Derrida, J. (1991) 'Of Grammatology (trans. G. Chakravorty Spivak)', in P. Kamuf (ed.) *A Derrida Reader: Between the Blinds*. Columbia University: New York, 31–58.

Dewey, C. (1978) 'The End of the Imperialism of Free Trade: The Eclipse of the Lancashire Lobby and the Concession of Fiscal Autonomy to India', in C. Dewey and A. G. Hopkins (eds.) *The Imperial Impact: Studies in the Economic History of Africa and India*. Athlone Press for the Institute of Commonwealth Studies: London, 35–67.

DGFFCC (Dirección General de Ferrocarriles, República Argentina, Ministerio de Obras Públicas) (1913, 1938, 1947). *Estadísticas de Ferrocarriles en Explotación*. Imprenta Nacional: Buenos Aires.

Díaz Alejandro, C. F. (1970) *Essays on the Economic History of the Argentine Republic*. Yale University Press: New Haven.

Díaz-Andreu, M. (2008) *A World History of Nineteenth-Century Archaeology. Nationalism, Colonialism and the Past*. Oxford University Press: Oxford.

Dirks, N. B. (ed.) (1992) *Colonialism and Culture*. University of Michigan Press: Ann Arbor.

Dixie, F. (1881) *Across Patagonia*. R. Worthington: New York (first published in London: Bentley and Son, 1880).

Domínguez, J. (1978) *Cuba. Order and Revolution*. Harvard University Press: Cambridge, MA.

Doratioto, F. (2002) *Maldita guerra: nova historia da Guerra do Paraguai*. Companhia das Letras: São Paulo.

d'Orbigny, A. (1835) *Voyage dans l'Amerique meridionale, 1826–1833*. Pitois-Levrault: Paris.

Dorfman, A. (1983) *Cincuenta años de de industrialización en la Argentina, 1930–80: desarrollo y perspectivas*. Solar: Buenos Aires.

Doyle, M. W. (1986) *Empires*. Cornell University Press: Ithaca.

Dumett, R. E. (1999) 'Introduction: Exploring the Cain/Hopkins Paradigm: Issues for Debate and Topics for New Research', in R. E. Dumett (ed.) *Gentlemanly Capitalism and British Imperialism. The New Debate on Empire*. Harlow, Addison Wesley Longman: London.

Dunch, R. (2002) 'Beyond Cultural Imperialism: Cultural Theory, Christian Missions and Global Modernity'. *History and Theory* **41**(3): 301–325.

Eckalbar, J. C. (1979) 'The Saint-Simonians in Industry and Economic Development'. *American Journal of Economics and Sociology* **38**(1): 83–96.

Elliott, J. H. (2006) *Empires of the Atlantic World: Britain and Spain in America 1492–1830*. Yale University Press: New Haven.

Elton, G. (1960) *The Tudor Constitution: Documents and Commentary*. Cambridge University Press: Cambridge.

Enloe, C. (1990) *Bananas, Beaches and Bases: Making Feminist Sense of International Politics*. University of California Press: Berkeley.

Escudé, C. (1988) 'Argentine Territorial Nationalism'. *Journal of Latin American Studies* **20**(1): 139–165.

Every, E. F. (1933) *South America. Memories of Thirty Years*. Society for Promoting Christian Knowledge: London.

Fair, J. (1899) *Some Notes on My Early Connection with the Buenos Ayres Great Southern Railway*. Bright's: Bournemouth.

Falkoff, M. (1981) 'Argentine Dependency in a Conservative Mirror: Alejandro Bunge and the Argentine frustration, 1919–43'. *Inter-American Economic Affairs* **35**: 57–75.

Faria, M., Jr. (dir.) (2001) *The Xango of Baker Street*. Film produced by MGN Filmes and Skylight Cinema.

Fay, C. R. (1940) *Cambridge History of the British Empire*. Cambridge University Press: Cambridge.

Ferguson, F. (1992) *Solitude and the Sublime: Romanticism and the Aesthetics of Individuation*. Routledge: New York and London.

Ferguson, N. (2004a) *Empire. How Britain Made the Modern World*. Penguin Books: London.

Ferguson, N. (2004b) *Colossus. The Price of America's Empire*. Penguin Books: London.

Fernández Armesto, F. (2002) 'Epilogue: What is History *Now*?', in D. Cannadine (ed.) *What is History Now?* Palgrave Macmillan: London, 148–161.

Ferns, H. S. (1960) *Britain and Argentina in the Nineteenth Century*. Oxford University Press: Oxford.

Ferns, H. S. (1992a) 'The Baring Crisis Revisited'. *Journal of Latin American Studies*, **24**(2): 241–273.

Ferns, H. S. (1992b) 'Argentina: Part of an Informal Empire?', in A. Hennessy and J. King (eds.) *The Land England Lost: Agentina and Britain: A special Relationship*. British Academic Press: London, 49–61.

Ferrer, A. (1967) *The Argentine Economy*. University of California Press: Berkeley.

Fleming, W. J. (1977) 'Mendoza y el desarrollo de la red ferroviaria nacional entre 1854 y 1886'. *Investigaciones y Ensayos* **23**: 365–393.

Fodor, J. (1986) 'The Origins of Argentina's Sterling Balances, 1939–43', in G. Di Tella and D. C. M. Platt (eds.) *The Political Economy of Argentina, 1880–1946*. St. Martin's Press: New York, 154–182.

Fogel, R. W. and Engerman, S. L. (1976) *Time on the Cross. Evidence and Methods*, Vol. 2. Wildwood House: London.

Fogarty, J. Gallo, E. and Diéguez, H. (1979) *Argentina y Australia*. Instituto Torcuato di Tella: Buenos Aires.

Fontana, J. (1979) *La crisis del antiguo régimen, 1808–1833*. Crítica: Barcelona.

Ford, A. G. (1962) *The Gold Standard, 1880–1914. Britain and Argentina*. The Clarendon Press: Oxford.

Forman, R. (2000a) 'Harbouring Discontent: British Imperialism through Brazilian Eyes in the Christie Affair', in M. Hewitt (ed.) *An Age of Equipoise. Reassessing Mid-Victorian Britain*. Ashgate: Aldershot, 225–243.

Forman, R. (2000b) 'When Britons Brave Brazil: British Imperialism and the Adventure Tale in Latin America, 1850–1918'. *Victorian Studies* **42**(3): 455–487.

Fowler, W. (2004) 'Joseph Welsh: A British *Santanista* (Mexico, 1832)'. *Journal of Latin American Studies* **36**(1): 29–56.

Fradera, J. M. (2005) *Colonias para después de un imperio*. Edicions Bellaterra: Barcelona.

French, J. (2005) *Nature, Neo-Colonialism, and the Spanish American Regional Writers*. Dartmouth/University Press of New England: Hanover N. H. and London.

Freyre, G. (1948) *Inglêses no Brasil: aspectos da influência britânica sobre a vida, a paisagem e a cultura do Brasil*. José Olympio: Rio de Janeiro.

Gabaccia, D. R. (2000) *Italy's Many Diasporas*. UCL Press: London.

Gaddis, J. L. (2002) *The Landscape of History: How Historians Map the Past*. Oxford University Press: Oxford and New York.

Galasso, N. (1985) *Raúl Scalabrini Oritz y la lucha contra la dominación inglesa*. Ediciones del Pensamiento Naiconal: Buenos Aires.

Gallagher, J. and Robinson, R. (1953) 'The Imperialism of Free Trade'. *Economic History Review* **VI**(1): 1–15.

Gallagher, J. and Robinson, R. with Denny, A. (1961) *Africa and the Victorians: The Official Mind of Imperialism*. Macmillan: London.

Gallardo, G. (1962) *La política religiosa de Rivadavia*. Ediciones Theoria: Buenos Aires.

Gallegos, R. (1992) *Doña Bárbara*, D. Miliana (ed.). Catedra: Madrid.

Gallo, K. (2001a) *Anticipating Independence: The Origins of British-Argentine Relations, 1780–1806*. Paper presented for the Second Annual Argentina Conference, St Antony's College, Oxford, 14–15 May.

Gallo, K. (2001b) *Great Britain and Argentina: From Invasion to Recognition, 1806–26*. Palgrave: New York.

Gallo, K. (2004) *Las invasiones inglesas*. Eudeba: Buenos Aires.

García Estrada, R. de J. (2006) *Los extranjeros en Colombia: su aporte a la construcción de la nación*. Planeta: Bogotá.

Gartner, A. (2005) *Los místeres de las minas*. A. Gartner: Manizales.

Gerchunoff, P. and Llach, L. (2003) *El ciclo de la ilusión y el desencanto: un siglo de políticas económicas argentinas*. Ariel: Buenos Aires.

Goebel, M. (2007) 'Nationalism, the Left and Hegemony in Latin America'. *Bulletin of Latin American Research* **26**(3): 311–318.

Golinger, E. (2007) *The Chávez Code: Cracking US Intervention in Venezuela*. Pluto Press: London.

González Echevarría, R. (1985) *The Voice of the Masters: Writing and Authority in Spanish American Literature*. Cambridge University Press: Cambridge.

Goodwin, P. B. (1977) 'The Central Argentine Railway and the Economic Development of Argentina, 1854–1881'. *Hispanic American Historical Review* **57**(4): 613–632.

Gootenberg, P. (1989) *Between Silver and Guano: Commercial Policy and the State in Postindependence Peru*. Princeton University Press: Princeton.

Gott, R. (2007) 'The SLAS 2006 Lecture: Latin America as a White Settler Society'. *Bulletin of Latin American Research* **26**(2): 269–289.

Gough, B. (1999) 'Profit and Power: Informal Empire, the Navy and Latin America', in R. E. Durnett (ed.) *Gentlemanly Capitalism and British Imperialism: The New Debate on Empire*. Addison Wesley Longman: London, 68–82.

Graham-Yooll, A. (2002) *Imperial Skirmishes. War and Gunboat Diplomacy in Latin America*. Signal Books: Oxford.

Grant, K., Levine, P. and Trentmann, F. (eds.) (2007) *Empire and Transnationalism, c. 1880–1950*. Palgrave MacMillan: Basingstoke.

Gravil, R. (1985) *The Anglo-Argentine Connection, 1900–1939*. Westview Press: Boulder.

Gravil, R. and Rooth, T. (1978) 'A Time of Acute Dependence: Argentina in the 1930s'. *Journal of European Economic History* 7(3): 337–378.

Gregory, D. (1992) *Brute New World. The Rediscovery of Latin America in the Early Nineteenth Century*. British Academic Press: London.

Groot, J. de (2006) 'Metropolitan Desires and Colonial Connections: Reflections on Consumption and Empire', in C. Hall and S. Rose (eds.) *At Home with the Empire. Metropolitan Culture and the Imperial World*. Cambridge University Press: Cambridge, 166–190.

Guenther, L. H. (2004) *British Merchants in Nineteenth-Century Brazil: Business, Culture, and Identity in Bahia, 1808–50*. Centre for Brazilian Studies of the University of Oxford: Oxford.

Güiraldes, R. (1978) *Don Segundo Sombra* S. M. Saz (ed.). Catedra: Madrid.

Haber, S. (ed.) (1990) *How Latin America Fell Behind: Essays on the Economic Histories of Brazil and Mexico, 1800–1914*. Stanford University Press: Stanford.

Hall, C. (ed.) (2000) *Cultures of Empire: Colonizers in Britain and the Empire in the Nineteenth and Twentieth Centuries. A Reader*. Manchester University Press: Manchester.

Hall, C. (2002) *Civilising Subjects: Metropole and Colony in the English Imagination 1830–1867*. Polity Press: London.

Halperín Donghi, T. (1970) *El revisionismo historico argentino*. Siglo Veintinno Editors: Mexico, 75–76, 84–92.

Halperín Donghi, T. (1980) 'La historiografía: treinta años enbusca de un rumbo', in G. Ferrari and E. Gallo (eds.) *La Argentina del ochenta al centenario*. Sudamericana: Buenos Aires, 829–840.

Halperín Donghi, T. (1986) 'The Argentine Export Economy: Intimations of Mortality, 1894–1930', in G. Di Tella and D. C. M. Platt (eds.) *The Political Economy of Argentina, 1880–1946*. Macmillan: London, 25–37.

Halperín Donghi, T. (1987) 'El liberalismo argentino y el liberalismo mexicano: dos destinos divergentes', in T. Halperín Donghi (ed.) *El espejo de la historia*. Buenos Aires: Sudamericana, 141–166.

Halperín Donghi T. (1989) 'La apertura mercantil en el Rio de la Plata: impacto global y desigualdades regionales, 1800–1850' in R. Liehr (ed.) *América Latina en la época de Simón Bolivar: La formación de las economias nacionales y los intereses económicos europeos, 1800–1850*. Colloquium Verlag: Berlin, 115–138.

Halperín Donghi, T. (1993) *The Contemporary History of Latin America* (ed. and trans. J. C. Chasteen). Duke University Press: Durham.

Hamilton Thom, J. (ed.) (1845) *The Life of Joseph Blanco White, Written by Himself; with Portions of his Correspondence*. John Chapman: London.

Hechter, M. (1975) *Internal Colonialism: The Celtic Fringe in British National Development, 1536–1966*. RKP: London.

Hennessy, A. (1992) 'Argentines, Anglo-Argentines and Others', in A. Hennessy and J. King (eds.), *The Land that England Lost: Argentina and Britain, A Special Relationship*. British Academic Press: London, 9–48.

Hennessy, A. (2000) 'Ramiro de Maetzu: *Hispanidad* and the Search for a Surrogate Imperialism', in J. Harrison and A. Hoyle (eds.) *Spain's 1898 Crisis: Regeneration, Modernism, Post-colonialism*. Manchester University Press: Manchester, 105–117.

Hennessy, A. and King, J. (eds.) (1992) *The Land England Lost: Argentina and Britain: A Special Relationship*. British Academic Press: London.

Herwig, H. H. (1986) *Germany's Vision of Empire in Venezuela, 1871–1914*. Princeton University Press: Princeton.

Herzog, T. (2003) *Defining Nations: Immigrants and Citizens in Early Modern Spain and Spanish America*. Yale University Press: New Haven.

Hexter, J. H. (1979) *On Historians*. Harvard University Press: Cambridge, M. A.

Hiatt, W. (2007) 'Flying "Cholo": Incas, Airplanes, and the Construction of Andean Modernity in 1920s Cuzco, Peru'. *The Americas* **63**(3): 327–358.

Hinchliff, T. W. (1863) *South American Sketches; or A Visit to Rio de Janeiro, the Organ Mountains, La Plata, and the Paraná*. Longman: London.

Hinsley, F. H. (1986) *Sovereignty*, 2nd edn. Cambridge University Press: Cambridge.

Hobsbawm, E. J. (1969) *Industry and Empire: From 1750 to the Present Day*. Penguin: Harmondsworth.

Hobson, J. A. (1902) *Imperialism: A Study*. George Allen & Unwin: London.

Holton, R. (2005) 'The Inclusion of the Non-European World in International Society, 1870s–1920s: Evidence from Global Networks'. *Global Networks* **5**(3): 239–259.

Hopkins, A. G. (1994) 'Informal Empire in Argentine: An Alternative View'. *Journal of Latin American Studies* **26**(2): 469–484.

Hopkins, A. G. (1999) 'Back to the Future. From National History to Imperial History'. *Past & Present* **164**: 198–243.

Hood, M. (1977) *Gunboat Dipomacy: Great Power Pressure in Venezuela, 1895–1905*. A.S. Barnes & Co.: Cranbury, NJ.

Hora, R. (2001) *The Landowners of the Argentine Pampas. A Social and Political History, 1860–1945*. Oxford University Press: Oxford.

Hora, R. (2005) 'Britain, the British Landed Class and the Argentine Landowners'. *Canadian Journal of Latin American and Caribbean Studies* **3**(9): 9–54.

Hosne, R. (2001) *Patagonia: Myths and Legends* (trans. C. Duggan). Duggan-Webster: Buenos Aires.

Howe, S. (2000) *Ireland and Empire: Colonial Legacies in Irish History and Culture*. Oxford University Press: Oxford.

Howe, S. (2001) 'The Slow Death and Strange ReBirths of Imperial History'. *Journal of Imperial and Commonwealth History* **29**(2): 131–141.

Howe, S. (2002) *Empire: A Very Short Introduction*. Oxford University Press: Oxford.

Hudson, W. H. (1893) *Idle Days in Patagonia*. Chapman and Hall: London.

Hulme, P. (1986) *Colonial Encounters: Europe and the Native Caribbean, 1492–1797*. Metheun: London and New York.

Hunt, L. (1988) *The New Cultural History*. University of California Press: Berkeley.

Huntington, S. P. (2004) *Who Are We? America's Great Debate*. Simon and Schuster: London.

Ingenieros, J. (1961) *La evolución de las ideas argentineas*. El futuro: Buenos Aires.

Innes, M. (1972) *The Open House*. Dodd, Mead, & Co.: New York.

Innis, H. (1956) *Essays in Canadian Economic History*. University of Toronto Press: Toronto.

Innis, H. (1995) *Staples, Markets and Cultural Change: Selected Essays* (ed. D. Drache). McGill-Queen's University Press: Montreal.

Irazusta, J. (1934 and 1963) *La influencia británica en el Río de la Plata*. EUDEBA: Buenos Aires.

Irazusta, R. and Irazusta, J. (1934) *La Argentina y el imperialismo británico: los eslabones de una cadena, 1806–1933*. Tor: Buenos Aires.

Irisarri, A. J. de (1833) *Empréstito de Chile*. Imprenta de la Opinión: Santiago de Chile.

Jaksic, I. (ed) 2001) *Andrés Bello: Scholarship and Nation-Building in Nineteenth-Century Latin America*. Cambridge University Press: Cambridge.

Jameson, F. (1986) 'Third-World Literature in the Era of Multinational Capitalism'. *Social Text* **15**(Autumn): 65–88.

Jones, C. A. (1973) *British Financial Institutions in Argentina, 1860–1914*. Unpublished doctoral dissertation, University of Cambridge, Cambridge.

Jones, C. A. (1980) 'Business Imperialism' and Argentina, 1875–1900: A Theoretical Note'. *Journal of Latin American Studies* **12**(2): 437–444.

Jones, C. A. (1983) *The North–South Dialogue: A Brief History*. Pinter: London.

Jones, C. A. (1987) *International Business in the Nineteenth Century. The Rise and Fall of a Cosmopolitan Bourgeoisie*. Wheatsheaf: Brighton.

Jones, C. A. (1992) *El Reino Unido y América: Inversiones e influencia económica*. MAPFRE: Madrid.

Jones, G. (1986–1987) *The History of the British Bank of the Middle East*, Vol. 1. Cambridge University Press: Cambridge.

Jones, K. L. (1986) 'Nineteenth Century British Travel Accounts of Argentina'. *Ethnohistory* **33**(2): 195–221.

Joseph, G. M. (1998) 'Towards a Cultural History of US-Latin American Relations', in G. M. Joseph, C. C. LeGrand and R. D. Salvatore (eds.) *Close Encounters of Empire: Writing the Cultural History of US – Latin American Relations*. Duke University Press: London and Chapel Hill, 3–46.

Joseph, G. M., LeGrand, C. C. and Salvatore. R. D. (eds.) (1998) *Close Encounters of Empire: Writing the Cultural History of US – Latin American Relations*. Duke University Press: London and Chapel Hill.

Joslin, D. (1963) *A Century of Banking in Latin America*. Oxford University Press: London and New York.

Junguito, R. (1995) *La deuda externa en el siglo XIX. Cien años de incumplimiento*. Tercer Mundo Editores: Bogotá.

Kant, I. (1978) *The Critique of Judgement* (trans. J. Creed Meredith). Clarendon Press: Oxford.

Kennedy, D. (1996) 'Imperial History and Post-Colonial Theory'. *Journal of Imperial and Commonwealth History* **24**(3): 345–363.

Kennedy, D. (2002) *Britain and Empire: 1880–1945*. Longman: London.

Keohane, R. O. (1984) *After Hegemony. Cooperation and Discord in the World Economy*. Princeton University Press: Princeton.

Kindleberger, C. P. and Aliber, R. Z. (2005) *Manias, Panics and Crashes. A History of Financial Crises*. Palgrave MacMillan: Basingstoke.

King, F. H. H. with King, C. E. and King, D. J. S. (1987) *The History of the Hongkong and Shanghai Banking Corporation. Volume 1: The Hongkong Bank in Late Imperial China, 1864–1902: On an Even Keel*. Cambridge University Press: Cambridge.

Kinsey, D. (forthcoming) 'Mapping the Diamond World: Mineralogy, Geology, and the Material Culture of Empire' Unpublished doctoral dissertation, University of Illinois at Urbana-Champaign.

Klor de Alva, J. (1995) 'The Postcolonization of the (Latin) American Experience: A Reconsideration of "Colonialism," "Postcolonialism," and "Mestizaje"', in G. Prakash (ed.) *After Colonialism: Imperial Histories and Postcolonial Displacements*. Princeton University Press: Princeton, 241–275.

Knight, A. (1986) *The Mexican Revolution*, 2 vols. Cambridge University Press: Cambridge.

Knight, A. (1995) 'British Attitudes Towards the Mexican Revolution', in W. R. Louis (ed.) *Adventures with Britannia. Personalities, Politics and Culture in Britain*. I.B. Tauris: London, 273–290.

Knight, A. (1999) 'Britain and Latin America', in A. Porter (ed.) *The Oxford History of the British Empire, Vol. 3. The Nineteenth Century*. Oxford University Press: Oxford, 122–144.

Knight, A. (2006) 'Patterns and Prescriptions in Mexican Historiography'. *Bulletin of Latin American Research* 25(3): 340–366.

Knight, A. (forthcoming) 'US Hegemony in Latin America', in F. Rosen (ed.) *Hegemony and Resistance in Latin America*. Duke Univeristy Press: Durham.

Koebel, W. H. (1917) *British Exploits in South America: A History of British Activities in Exploration, Military Adventure, Diplomacy, Science, and Trade in Latin America*. The Century Co.: New York.

Koebner, R. (1965) *Empire*. Grosset and Dunlap: New York.

Koster, H. (1816) *Travels in Brazil*. Longman, Hurst, Rees, Orme, and Brown: London.

Kubicek, R. (1999) 'Economic Power at the Periphery: Canada, Australia and South Africa, 1850–1914', in R. E. Dumett (ed.) *Gentlemanly Capitalism and British Imperialism: The New Debate*, Longman: London, 113–126.

Lal, D. (2004) *In Praise of Empires: Globalization and Order*. Palgrave MacMillan: New York.

Lamas, A., López, V. F. and Gutierrez, J. M. (1871–1874) *Revista del Rio de la Plata: periódico mensual de historia y literature de América, Buenos Alies*.

Lambert, D. and Lester, A. (eds.) (2006) *Colonial Lives Across the British Empire: Imperial Careering in the Long Nineteenth-Century*. Cambridge University Press: Cambridge.

Lancaster, J. (1833) *Epitome of Some of the Chief Events and Transactions in the Life of Joseph Lancaster, Containing an Account of the Rise and Progress of the Lancasterian System of Education* …. Baldwin & Peck: New Haven.

Langford, P. (1989) *A Polite and Commercial People. England 1727–1783*. Oxford University Press: Oxford.

Leask, N. (2002) *Curiosity and the Aesthetics of Travel Writing, 1770–1840: 'From an Antique Land'*. Oxford University Press: Oxford.

Lemaitre, E. (1974) *La bolsa o la vida: cuatro agresiones imperialistas contra Colombia*. Banco de la República: Bogotá.

Lemaitre, E. (1980) *Panamá y su separación de Colombia*. Banco Popular: Bogotá.

Lenin, V. I. (1920) 'Imperialism, The Highest Stage of Capitalism (A Popular Outline)', in *Selected Works*. Lawrence & Wishart: London, 169–263 (1969 edition.)

Lenz, M. H. (2004) *Crescimento econômico e crise na Argentina de 1870 a 1930: a 'Belle Époque'*. Editora da UFRGS: Porto Alegre.

Lester, A. (2001) *Imperial Networks, Creating Identities in Nineteenth-Century South Africa and Britain*. Routledge: London.

Lewis, C. M. (1968) 'Problems of Railway Development in Argentina, 1857–1890'. *Inter-American Economic Affairs* **22**(2): 55–75, 73–74.

Lewis, C. M. (1977) 'British Railway Companies and the Argentine Government', in D. C. M. Platt (ed.) *Business Imperialism, 1840–1930: An Inquiry Based on British Experience in Latin America*. Clarendon: Oxford.

Lewis, C. M. (1983) *British Railways in Argentina, 1857–1914: A Case Study of Foreign Investment*. Athlone: London.

Lewis, C. M. (1985) 'Railways and Industrialisation: Argentina and Brazil, 1870–1929' in C. Abel and C. M. Lewis (eds) *Latin America: Economic Imperialism and the State*. Athlone: London, 199–230.

Lindsey-Poland, J. (2004) 'US Military Bases in Latin America and the Caribbean'. *Foreign Policy* **9**(3): 1–4.

Lipsey, R. G., Bekar, C. and Carlaw, K. (1998) 'What Requires Explanation?', in E. Helpman (ed.) *General Purpose Technologies and Economic Growth*. MIT Press: Cambridge, MA, 15–54.

Lloyd, R. (ed.) (1911) *Twentieth Century Impressions of Argentina*. Lloyd's Bank: London.

Lodge, D. (1984) *Small World: An Academic Romance*. Penguin: New York.

Londres, A. (1928) *The Road to Buenos Aires: The White Slave Traffic*. Constable & Co.: London.

Loomba, A. (2000) *Colonialism/Postcolonialism*. Routledge: New York.

Lopez, M. J. (1971) Historia de los ferrocarriles de la provincia de Buenos Aims, 1857–1886. Lumiere: Buenos Aims, 37.

López, M. J. (1994) *Historia de los ferrocarriles nacionales, 1866–1886*. Lumiere: Buenos Aires.

López, M. J. (2000a) *Ferrocarriles, deuda y crisis: historia de los ferrocarriles and la Argentina de 1887 a 1896*. Editorial de Belgrano: Buenos Aires.

López, M. J. (2000b) *Historia de los ferrocarriles de la provincia de Buenos Aires, 1857–1886*. Lumiere: Buenos Aires.

López, S. (2003) *Representaciones de la Patagonia: colonos, científicos y políticos (1870–1914)*. Ediciones al Margen: La Plata.

López, V. F. (1846) *Manual de la historia de Chile*. Impr. Del Progreso: Santiago de Chile.

López, V. F. (1871) *Les races aryennes du Perou: leur langue, leur religion, leur histoire*. A. Frank: Paris; the author: Montevideo.

López, V. F. (1881) *Historia de la Revolución Argentina de sus precedentes coloniales hasta el derrocamiento de la tiranía en 1852*. Impr. de mayo: Buenos Aires.

López, V. F. (1907) *Manual de la historia Argentina*. A.V. Lopez: Buenos Aires.

López, V. F. (1913) *Historia de la República Argentina: su origen, su revolución y su desarollo político*, 10 Vols. Impr. de G Kraft: Buenos Aires.

López, V. F. (1917) *La novia del hereje o la inquisición de Lima*. La cultura argentina: Buenos Aires.

López, V. F. (1929) *Evocaciones históricos: autobiografía – la gran semana de 1810, etc.* El Ateneo: Buenos Aires.

López, V. F. (2000c [n.d.]) *La loca de la guardia*. Biblioteca Virtual Miguel de Cervantes [WWW document]. URL www.cervantesvirtual.com [accessed December 2006].

López Domínguez, L. H. (ed.) (1990) *Administraciones de Santander*, Vol. 3/6, 1831–1833. Fundación para la conmemoración del Bicentenario del Natalicio y el Sesquicentenario de la muerte del General Francisco de la Paula Santander: Bogotá.

Louis, W. R. (1976) *Imperialism: The Robinson and Gallagher Controversy*. New Viewpoints: New York.

Love, T. (1942) *Un inglés. Cinco años en Buenos Aires 1820–1825 por 'un ingles', con un prologo de A.B. Gonzalez Garaño*. Ediciones Argentinas 'El Solar': Buenos Aires.

Lynch, B. (1909) *Plata dorada*. Rodríguez Giles: Buenos Aires.

Lynch, B. (1960 [1924]) *El inglés de los güesos*. Troquel: Buenos Aires.

Lynch, J. (2001) *Masacre en las pampas. La matanza de inmigrantes en Tandil, 1872*. Emecé Editores: Buenos Aires.

Lynch, J. (2001) *Caudillos in Spanish America 1800–1850*. The Clarendon Press: Oxford.

Lynn, M. (1999) 'British Policy, Trade, and Informal Empire in the Mid-Nineteenth Century', in A. Porter (ed.) *The Oxford History of the British Empire, Vol. 3. The Nineteenth Century*. Oxford University Press: Oxford, 101–121.

MacDonald, C. (1992) 'End of Empire: The Decline of the Anglo-Argentine Connection, 1918–1951', in A. Hennessy and J. King (eds.), *The Land Engalnd Lost*. Longman: London 79–92.

MacIntyre, S. and Clark, A. (2003) *The History Wars*. Melbourne University Press: Melbourne.

Maddison, A. (2001) *The World Economy: A Millennial Perspective*. OECD: Paris.

Magee, G. and Thompson, A. S. (eds.) (forthcoming) *Empire and Globalisation: A Cultural Economy of the British World, c. 1840–1914*. Cambridge University Press: Cambridge.

Makdisi, U. (1997) 'Reclaiming the Land of the Bible: Missionary Secularism and Evangelical Modernism'. *American Historical Review* **1020**(3): 680–713.

Mallon, F. E. (1994) 'The Promise and Dilemma of Subaltern Studies: Perspectives from Latin American History'. *American Historical Review* **99**(5): 1491–1515.

Manchester, A. K. (1933) *British Preëminence in Brazil: Its Rise and Decline*. University of North Carolina Press: Chapel Hill.

Maradona, D. (2005) 'In Conversation on the Tren del Alba', published in *La Jornada*, 6 November (cited by Sandra Russo of *Página 12*) [WWW document]. URL http://www.jornada.unam.mx/2005/11/06/006n1eco.php [20 August 2007].

Marcos, S. (2007) 'La guerra de conquista', 31 March [WWW document]. URL http://vulcano.wordpress.com/2007/03/31/la-guerra-de-conquista-subcomandante-marcos/ [20 August 2007].

Marichal, C. (1989) *A Century of Debt Crises in Latin America*. Princeton University Press: Princeton.

Marshall, O. (2005) *English, Irish and Irish-American Pioneer Settlers in Nineteenth-Century Brazil*. Centre for Brazilian Studies: Oxford.

Martínez, F. (2001) *El nacionalismo cosmopolita. La referencia europea en la construcción nacional en Colombia, 1845–1900*. Banco de la República, Instituto Francés de Estudios Andinos: Bogotá.

Martínez-Fernández, L. (1994) *Torn between Empires: Economy, Society and Patterns of Political Thought in the Hispanic Caribbean, 1840–1878*. University of Georgia Press: Athens.

Martins Pena, L. C. (1966) *Os dous, ou o inglês maquinista*, in D. Damasceno (ed.) *Comédias de Martins Pena*. Edições de Ouro: São Paulo, 104–135.

Mawe, J. (1812) *Travels in the Interior of Brazil, Particularly in the Gold and Diamond Districts of that Country, by Authority of the Prince Regent of Portugal*. Longman, Hurst Rees, Orme, and Brown: London.

McBeth, B. S. (2001) *Gunboats, Corruption, and Claims: Foreign Intervention in Venezuela, 1899–1908*. Greenwood Press: Westport.

McClintock, A. (1992) 'The Angel of Progress: Pitfalls of the Term "Post-colonialism"'. *Social Text* **31–32**: 84–98.

McCloskey, D. N. (1981) *Enterprise and Trade in Victorian Britain*. Allen and Unwin: London.

McCullough, D. (1977) *The Path between the Seas: The Creation of the Panama Canal, 1870–1914*. Simon and Schuster: New York.

McFarlane, A. (1994) *The British in the Americas, 1480–1815*. Longman: London.

McLean, D. (1995) *War, Diplomacy and Informal Empire. Britain and the Republics of La Plata, 1836–53*. British Academic Press: London.

McLynn, F. (1991) *From the Sierras to the Pampas. Richard Burton's Travels in the Americas, 1860–69*. Century: London.

Mehta, U. S. (1996) 'Liberal Strategies of Exclusion', in F. Cooper and A. L. Stoler (eds.) *Tensions of Empire. Colonial Cultures in a Bourgeois World*. University of California Press: Berkeley, 59–86.

Midgley, C. (ed.) (1998) *Gender and Imperialism*. Manchester University Press: Manchester.

Mignolo, W. (2000) *Local Histories/Global Designs*. Princeton University Press: Princeton.

Mignolo, W. (2005) *The Idea of Latin America*. Blackwell: Oxford.

Míguez, E. J. (1985) *Las tierras delos ingelses en la Argenitna 1870–1914*. Editorial Belgrano: Buenos Aires.

Mills, S. (2003) 'Gender and Colonial Space', in R. Lewis and S. Mills (eds.) *Feminist Postcolonial Theory. A Reader*. Routledge: New York, 692–719.

Miller, R. M. (1993) *Britain and Latin America in the Nineteenth and Twentieth Centuries*. Longman: London.

Miller, R. M. (2001) 'Informal Empire in Latin America', in R. Louis (ed.) *The Oxford History of the British Empire, Vol. 5. Historiography*. Oxford University Press: Oxford, 437–448.

Miller, R. M. (2006) *British Firms and Populist Nationalism in Post-War Latin America*. Paper presented to International Economic History Congress, Helsinki, 2006 [WWW document]. URL http://www.helsinki.fi/iehc2006/papers3/Miller.pdf [20 August 2007].

Mitre, B. (1947 [1857]) *Historia de Belgrano y de la independencia Argentina*. Estrada: Buenos Aires.

Mommsen, W. J. (1980) *Theories of Imperialism* (trans. P.S. Falla). Random House: New York.

Monroe, J. (1823) 'Seventh Annual Message to Congress', 2 December 1823, in *A Century of Lawmaking for a New Nation: U.S. Congressional Documents and Debates, 1774–1875*. Library of Congress: Washington.

Moreno, F. P. (2001) *Viaje a la Patagonia Austral*. El Elefante Blanco: Buenos Aires.

Moreno Alonso, M. (1998) *Blanco White, la obsesión de España*. Alfar: Sevilla.

Moreyra, B. I. (2003) 'La historiografía', in *Academia Nacional de la Historia Nueva Historia de la nación Argentina: Tomo X: la Argentina del siglo XX*. Planeta: Buenos Aires, 67–110.

Morgan, E. (1907) *Hacia los Andes* (trans. I. Hughes de Jones). El Regional: Rawson (1982 edition).

Morris, R. J. (1983) 'Voluntary Societies and British Urban Elites, 1780–1850: An Analysis'. *The Historical Journal* **26**(1): 95–118.

Moyes, J. (1829) El Evangilo de Jesus Cristo Segun San Lucas en aymara y espanol. London.

Mulhall, M. G. and Mulhall, E. T. (1863) *The River Plate Handbook, Guide, Directory and Almanac for 1863, Comprising the City and Province of Buenos Aires, the Other Argentina Provinces, Montevideo etc*. Buenos Aires: Mulhall.

Murphy, M. (1989) *Blanco White: Self-Banished Spaniard*. Yale University Press: New Haven.

Murray, E. (2004) *Devenir irlandés: narrativas íntimas de la emigración irlandesa a la Argentina*. Eudeba: Buenos Aires.

Nandy, A. (1983) *The Intimate Enemy. Loss and Recovery of Self under Colonialism*. Oxford University Press: Delhi.

Naregal, V. (2001) *Language Politics, Elites, and the Public Sphere. Western India under Colonialism*. Anthem Press: London.

Naro, N. (ed.) (2003) *Blacks, Coloureds and National Identity in Nineteenth-Century Latin America*. Institute of Latin American Studies: London.

Naylor, S. (2001) 'Discovering nature, rediscovering the self: natural historians and the landscapes of Argentina'. *Environment and Planning D: Society and Space* **19**: 227–247.

Northrup, D. (1995) *Labour in the Age of Imperialism, 1834–1922*. Cambridge University Press: Cambridge.

Nowell-Smith, P. H. (1961) *Ethics*. Penguin: Harmondsworth.

Nunn, F. M. (1983) *Yesterday's Soldiers: European Military Professionalism in South America, 1890–1940*. University of Nebraska Press: Lincoln and London.

O'Brien, P. K. (1988) 'The Costs and Benefits of British Imperialism, 1846–1914'. *Past and Present* **120**: 163–200.

O'Connell, A. (1986) 'Free Trade in One (Primary Producing) Country: The Case of Argentina in the 1920s', in G. Di Tella and D. C. M. Platt (eds.) *The Political Economy of Argentina*. St. Martin's Press: New York, 74–94.

O'Phelan Godoy, S. (2002) 'Una doble inserción. Los irlandeses bajo los Borbones: del puerto de Cádiz al Perú', in S. O'Phelan Godoy and C. Salazar-Soler (eds.) *Passeurs, mediadores culturales y agentes de la primera globalisación en el Mundo Ibérico, siglos XVI-XIX*. Pontificia Universidad Católica del Perú, Instituto Riva-Agüero, Instituto Francés de Estudios Andinos: Lima.

O'Rourke, K. and Williamson, G. (1999) *Globalization in History: The Evolution of a Nineteenth Century Atlantic Economy*. MIT Press: Cambridge, MA.

Ortiz, R. M. (1958) *El farrocarril en al economia argentina*. Cátedra Lisando de la Torre: Buenos Aires, 19–36.

Oszlak, O. (1982) *La formación del estado argentino*. Editorial Belgrano: Buenos Aires.

Ottino, M. (2003) *Asociación Argentina de Cultura Inglesa. Su gente. Su historia*. AACI: Buenos Aires.

Owen, G. D. (1977) *Crisis in Chubut. A Chapter in the History of the Welsh Colony in Patagonia*. Christopher Davies: Swansea.

Palmerston, L. (1832) Speech to Parliament, 16 April. *Parliamentary Papers*, 3rd Series, Vol. 12, 561 (cited in Smith 1978: 17).

Palmerston, L. (1841) Letter to Auckland (cited in D.C.M. Platt 1968: 297).

Palmerston, L. (1850) Memorandum, 29 September 1850 (cited in R. Hyam (1983). *Britain's Imperial Century 1815–1914: A Study of Empire and Expansion*. Macmillan: London, 119).

Pantaleão, O. (1965) 'A presença inglesa', in S. B. de Hollanda (ed.) *História geral da civilização brasileira*, II/1. Difusão Européia do Livro: São Paulo, 64–99.

Parish, W. (1839) *Buenos Ayres, and the Provinces of Rio de la Plata; their Present State, Trade, and Debt; with Some Account from Original Documents of the Progress of Geographical Discovery in Those Parts of South America during the Last Sixty Years*. John Murray: London.

Parry, B. (2004) 'The Institutionalisation of Postcolonial Studies', in N. Lazarus (ed.) *The Cambridge Companion to Postcolonial Literary Studies*. Cambridge University Press: Cambridge, 66–80.

Parry, J. H. (1965) *Report of the Committee on Latin American Studies* (chairman: J. H. Parry; known as the Parry Report). HMSO: London.

Parsons, J. J. (1979) *La colonización en el occidente de Colombia*. Carlos Valencia Editores: Bogotá.

Payró, R. J. (1898) *La Australia Argentina: excursión periodística a las costas patagónicas, Tierra del Fuego e Islas de los Estados*. Imprenta de la Nación: Buenos Aires.

Pearce, A. (2007) *Before 'Informal Empire'?: The Hope-Barings and Gordon & Murphy Contracts, 1805–1808*. Paper presented to 'Informal Empire?' Conference, University of Bristol, UK, 27 January 2007.

Peñaloza, F. (2004a) *Ethnographic Curiosity and the Aesthetics of Othering: Nineteenth-Century British Representations of Argentine Patagonia*. Unpublished doctoral dissertation, University of Exeter, UK.

Peñaloza, F. (2004b) 'A Sublime Journey to the Barren Plains: Lady Florence Dixie's *Across Patagonia* (1880)'. *Limina* **10**: 81–97.

Petit de Murat, U. (1968) *Genio y figura de Benito Lynch*. Editorial Universitaria: Buenos Aires.

Pinilla, N. (1943) *La polémica del romanticismo en 1842*. Editorial Americalee: Buenos Aires.

Pi Sunyer, C. (1978) *Patriótas americanos en Londres: Miranda, Bello y otras figuras*. Monte Ávila Editores SA: Caracas.

Platt, D. C. M. (1965) 'The British in South America – An Archive Report'. *Bulletin of the Institute of Historical Research* **38**: 172–191.

Platt, D. C. M. (1967) 'British Diplomacy in Latin America Since the Emancipation'. *Inter-American Economic Affairs* **21**(1): 21–41.

Platt, D. C. M. (1968a) 'The Imperialism of Free Trade: Some Reservations'. *Economic History Review* **21**(2): 296–306.

Platt, D. C. M. (1968b) *Finance, Trade and Politics in British Foreign Policy, 1815–1914*. The Clarendon Press: Oxford.

Platt, D. C. M. (1972) *Latin America and British Trade 1806–1914*. Black: London.

Platt, D. C. M. (1973) 'Further Objections to an "Imperialism of Free Trade"'. *Economic History Review* **26**(1): 77–91.

Platt, D. C. M. (1977) *Business Imperialism, 1840–1930: An Inquiry Based on British Experience in Latin America*. Clarendon: Oxford.

Platt, D. C. M. and Di Tella, G. (eds.) (1985) *Argentina, Australia and Canada: Studies in Comparative Development, 1870–1965*. MacMillan: London.

Plutarch (1864) 'Romulus', in *The Lives of the Noble Grecians and Romans* (trans. J. Dryden and rev. A. H. Clough). The Modern Library: New York, 24–45.

Pons, A. (2006) *Blanco White y América*. Instituto Feijóo de Estudios del Siglo XVIII: Oviedo.

Pope, A. (1763) 'An Essay on Man', in M. Mack (ed.) *The Poems of Alexander Pope*, Vol. III, Part I. Methuen & Co.: London.

Porter, A. (1985) 'Commerce and Christianity: The Rise and Fall of a Nineteenth Century Missionary Slogan'. *The Historical Journal* **28**(3): 597–621.

Porter, A. (2004a) *Religion versus Empire? British Protestant Missionaries and Overseas Expansion, 1700-1914*. Manchester University Press: Manchester.

Porter, B. (2004b) *The Absent-Minded Imperialists: Empire, Society, and Culture in Britain*. Oxford University Press: Oxford.

Pratt, M. L. (1992) *Imperial Eyes: Travel Writing and Transculturation*. Routledge: London.

Pratt, M. L. (2007) 'Planetary Plottings: *Indigeneity* versus *neoliberalism*', keynote lecture given at *Parallel Lines, Parallel Lives? Comparative Approaches and Dialogues in Postcolonial Studies, with a Specific Focus on Relations between Africa and the Americas*. Institute of Colonial and Postcolonial Studies, University of Leeds, Leeds, 15–16 February.

Price, R. (2006) 'One Big Thing: Britain, Its Empire, and Their Imperial Culture'. *Journal of British Studies* **45**(3): 602–627.

Prieto, A. (1996) *Los viajeros ingleses y la emergencia de la literatura argentina 1820–1850*. Editorial Sudamericana: Buenos Aires.

Prior, J. (1819) *Voyage Along the Eastern Coast of Africa to Mozambique, Johanna and Quiloa to St. Helena, Rio de Janeiro, Bahia, and Pernambuco in Brazil, in the Nisus Frigate*. Sir Richard Phillips & Co.: London.

Proudfoot, L. and Roche, M. (eds.) (2006) *(Dis)placing Empire. Renegotiating British Colonial Geographies*. Ashgate: Aldershot.

Quarterly Review (1810) *The Quarterly Review.*, 4(1810): 68–80.

Quarterly Review (1821–1827) *The Quarterly Review.*, **25(48)–36(72).**

Quijano, A. (2001) *Colonialidad del poder: globalización y democracia*. Sociedad y Política Ediciones: Lima.

Racine, K. (1996) *Imagining Independence: London's Spanish American Community 1790–1829*. Unpublished doctoral dissertation, Tulane University, USA.

Raffo, V. (2004) *El origin británico del deporte argentino. Atletismo, cricket, fútbol, polo, remo y rugby durante las presidencias de Mitre, Sarmiento y Avellaneda*. Victor Raffo: Buenos Aires.

Ramirez, L. E. (2007) *British Representations of Latin America*. University Press of Florida: Gainesville.

Ramos Mexía, E. (1936) *Mis Memorias 1853–1935*. Editorial La Facultad: Buenos Aires.

Rapoport, M. (1981) *Gran Bretaña, Estados Unidos y las clases dirigentes argentines*. Ed. Belgrano: Buenos Aires.

Rapoport, M. (1988) 'El Modelo agroexportador argentino, 1880–1914' in M. Rapoport (ed.) *Economia e historia: Contribuciones a la historia e eonómica argentina*. Tesis: Buenos Aires,179–182.

Rapoport, M. (2000) *Historia económica, política y social de la Argentina, 1880–2000*. Ediciones Macchi: Buenos Aires.

Reber, V. B. (1979) *British Mercantile Houses in Buenos Aires, 1810–1880*. Harvard University Press: Cambridge, MA.

Regalsky, A. (1989) 'Foreign Capital, Local Interests and Railways Development in Argentina: French Investment in Railways, 1900–1914'. *Journal of Latin American Studies* 21(3): 425–452.

Regalsky, A. (2002) *Mercados, inversores y élites: la inversiones franceses en la Argentina, 1880–1914*. Editorial de la Universidad Nacional de Tres de Febrero: Buenos Aires.

Restrepo, J. M. (1956) *Diario político y militar*, 4 vols. Ministerio de Educación Nacional: Bogotá.

Restrepo, V. (1885) *Estudio sobre las minas de oro y plata en Colombia*, 5th edn., 1979. FAES: Medellín.

Rheinheimer, H. P. (1988) *Topo: The Story of a Scottish Colony Near Caracas 1825–1827*. Scottish Academic Press: Edinburgh.

Rivadavia, B. (1817) 'Letter to J. M. de Pueyrredón, 22 March 1817', published in *Comisión de Bernardino Rivadavia*, Vol. 1, Universidad de Buenos Aires, 196–214 (cited in Gallo, K. (2006) *The Struggle for an Enlightened Republic: Buenos Aires and Rivadavia*. Institute for Latin American Studies: London, 17).

Rivera, J. E. (1995) *La Vorágine* M. Ordóñez (ed.). Catedra: Madrid.

Rivière, P. (1995) *Absent-Minded Imperialism: Britain and the Expansion of Empire in Nineteenth-Century Brazil*. Tauris: London.

Robertson, J. P. and Robertson, W. P. (1843) *Letters on South America*, 3 vols. John Murray: London.

Robinson, R. (1972) 'Non-European Foundations of European Imperialism: Sketch for a Theory of Collaboration', in R. Owen and B. Sutcliffe (eds.) *Studies in the Theory of Imperialism*. Longman: London, 117–142.

Robinson, R. (1986) 'The Excentric Idea of Imperialism, with or without Empire', in W. J. Mommsen and J. Osterhammel (eds.) *Imperialism and After: Continuities and Discontinuities*. Allen and Unwin: London, 267–289.

Rocafuerte, V. (1831) *Ensayo sobre la tolerancia religiosa*. M. Rivera: Mexico.

Roccatagliata, J. (1987) *Los ferrocarriles en la Argentina: un enfoque geográfico*. EUDEBA: Buenos Aires.

Rocchi, F. (2001) *Britain versus Newcomers: The Struggle for the Argentine Market, 1890–1914*. Paper presented at the 'British-Argentine Relations, 1780–1914' Conference, St Antony's College, Oxford, May.

Rocchi, F. (2006) *Chimneys in the Desert: Industrialisation in Argentina during the Export Boom Years, 1870–1930*. Stanford University press: Stanford, 135–143.

Rock, D. (1975) *Politics in Argentina, 1890–1930. The Rise and Fall of Radicalism.* Cambridge University Press: Cambridge.

Rock, D. (1986) *Argentina, 1516–1982: From Spanish Colonization to the Falklands War.* I. B. Tauris: London.

Rock, D. (2002) *State Formation and Political Movements in Argentina, 1860–1916.* Stanford University Press: Stanford.

Rock, D. (forthcoming) 'The British Community in Argentina, 1806–1960', in R. Bickers (ed.) *Settlers Over the Seas.*

Rodríguez, I. (ed.) (2001) *The Latin American Subaltern Studies Reader.* Duke University Press: Durham and London.

Rodríguez, O. J. (1975) *The Emergence of Spanish America: Vicente Rocafuerte and Spanish Americanism 1808–1832.* University of California Press: Berkeley and Los Angeles.

Rodríguez, M. (1964) *A Palmerstonian Diplomat in Central America: Frederick Chatfield Esq.* University of Arizona Press: Tuscon.

Roldán Vera, E. (2001) 'Reading in Questions and Answers: The Catechism as an Educational Genre in Early Independent Spanish America'. *Book History* 4: 17–48.

Roldán Vera, E. (2003) *The British Book Trade and Spanish American Independence: Education and Knowledge Transmission in Transcontinental Perspective.* Ashgate: Aldershot.

Rooth, T. (1993) *British Protectionism and the International Economy: Overseas Commercial Policy in the 1930s.* Cambridge University Press: Cambridge.

Rumbold, H. (1890) *The Great Silver River. Notes of a Residence in Buenos Ayres in 1880 and 1881,* 2nd edn. John Murray: London.

Rumbold, H. (1904) *Further Recollections of a Diplomatist.* Edward Arnold: London.

Sabato, H. (1990) *Agrarian Capitalism and the World Market: Buenos Aires in the Pastoral Age, 1840-1890.* University of New Mexico Press: Albuquerque.

Safford, F. (1965) *Commerce and Enterprise in Central Colombia, 1821–1870.* Unpublished doctoral dissertation, Columbia University, USA

Safford, F. (1988) 'The Emergence of Economic Liberalism in Colombia', in J. Love and N. Jacobsen (eds.) *Guiding the Invisible Hand: Economic Liberalism and the State in Latin America.* Praeger: New York, 35–63.

Said, E. W. (1978) *Orientalism.* Routledge and Kegan Paul: London.

Said, E. W. (1993) *Culture and Imperialism.* Alfred A. Knopf: New York.

Salvatore, R. D. (1998) 'The Enterprise of Knowledge: Representational Machines of Informal Empire', in G. M. Joseph, C. C. LeGrand and R. D. Salvatore (eds.) *Close Encounters* Duke University Press: London and Chapel Hill, 69–104.

Salvatore, R. D. (2003) 'Reflections on Hiram Bingham and the Yale Peruvian Expedition'. *Nepantla: Views from South* 4(1): 67–80.

Salvatore, R. D. and Newland, C. (2003) 'Between Independence and the Golden Age: The Early Argentine Economy', in G. della Paolera and A. M. Taylor (eds.) *A New Economic History of Argentina.* Cambridge University Press: Cambridge, 19–45.

Samson, J. (2007) 'Review of Norman Etherington, ed. *Missions and Empire.* Oxford History of the British Empire Companion Series. Oxford: Oxford University Press, 2005'. H-Net: Humanities & Social Sciences Online, July.

Sarmiento, D. F. (1868) *Life in the Argentine Republic in the Days of the Tyrants; or, Civilization and Barbarism*. Sampson, Low, Son & Marston: London [a translation of the first Spanish edition, Santiago de Chile, 1845].

Sarmiento, D. F. (2001) *Conflicto y armonías de las razas en América. Obras Completas*, Vol. 37. Universidad de La Matanza: Buenos Aires.

Scalabrini Ortiz, R. (1958) *Historia de los ferrocarriles argentinos*. Editorial Devenir: Buenos Aires, 19–36.

Schevdin, C. B. (1990) 'Staples and Regions of Pax Britannics'. *Economic History Review* **43**: 533–559.

Schmidt-Nowara, C. and Nieto-Phillips, J. M. (eds.) (2006) *Interpreting Spanish Colonialism: Empires, Nations and Legends*. University of New Mexico Press: Albuquerque.

Schwartz, S. P. (2005) 'Migration Networks and the Transnationalisation of Social Capital: Cornish Migration to Latin America'. *Cornish Studies*, **13**: 256–287.

Scully, W. (1866) *Brazil, Its Provinces and Chief Cities, the Manners and Customs of the People, Agricultural, Commercial and Other Statistics Taken by the Latest Official Documents With a Variety of Useful and Entertaining Knowledge, Both for the Merchant and the Emigrant*. John Murray: London.

Sen, S. (2000) *Distant Sovereignty: National Imperialism and the Origins of British India*. Routledge: New York.

Sent, E. M. (2004) 'Behavioral Economics: How Psychology Made Its (Limited) Way Back into Economics'. *History of Political Economy* **36**(4): 734–760.

Seymour, R. A. (1869) *Pioneering in the Pampas or the First Four Years of a Settler's Experience in the La Plata Camps*. Longmans, Green and Co: London.

Sheinin, D. and Mayo, C. A. (eds.) (1997) *Es igual pero distinto: Essays in the History of Canada and Argentina*. The Frost Centre: Peterborough, Ontario.

Shumway, N. (1991) *The Invention of Argentina*. University of California Press: Berkeley.

Smith, J. (1978) 'New World Diplomacy: A Reappraisal of British Policy Towards Latin America, 1823–1850'. *Inter-American Economic Affairs* **32**(2): 3–24.

Smith, J. (1979) *Illusions of Conflict: Anglo-American Diplomacy Towards Latin America, 1865–1896*. University of Pittsburgh Press: Pittsburgh.

Smith, T. (1981) *The Pattern of Imperialism. The United States, Great Britain and the Late Industrializing World since 1815*. Cambridge University Press: Cambridge.

Soares, J. E. (1995) *O Xangô de Baker Street*. Companhia das Letras: São Paulo.

Soares, J. E. (1997) *A Samba for Sherlock* (trans. C. E. Landers). Pantheon: New York.

Solberg, C. E. (1987) *The Prairies and the Pampas. Agrarian Policy in Canada and Argentina, 1880–1930*. Stanford University Press: Stanford.

Sommer, D. (ed.) (2006) *Cultural Agency in the Americas*. Duke University Press: Durham.

Spivak, G. C. (1999) *A Critique of Postcolonial Reason: Toward a History of the Vanishing Present*. Harvard University Press: Cambridge, MA.

Spivak, G. C. (2003) *Death of a Discipline*. Columbia University Press: New York.

Spurr, D. (1993) *The Rhetoric of Empire: Colonial Discourse in Journalism, Travel Writing, and Imperial Administration*. Duke University Press: Durham and London.

Stanhope, H. P. and Earl, V. (1938) *Notes of Conversations with the Duke of Wellington, 1831–1851*, 2nd edn. Oxford University Press: Oxford.

Stevenson, J. T. (1936) *The History of St. George's College, Quilmes, Argentina*. Society for Promoting Christian Knowledge: London.

Stoler, A. L. (1995) *Race and the Education of Desire: Foucault's History of Sexuality and the Colonial Order of Things*. Duke University Press: Durham.

Stoler, A. L. (2002) *Carnal Knowledge and Imperial Power: Race and the Intimate in Colonial Rule*. University of California Press: Berkeley.

Stoler, A. L. (2006a) 'On Degrees of Imperial Sovereignty'. *Public Culture* **18**(1): 125–146.

Stoler, A. L. (ed.) (2006b) *Haunted by Empire: Geographies of Intimacy in North American History*. Duke University Press: Chapel Hill.

Stoppard, T. (2006) *Rock 'n' Roll*. Faber and Faber: London.

Strange, S. (1988) *States and Markets*. Pinter: London.

Street, J. (1953) 'Lord Strangford and the Río de la Plata'. *Hispanic American Historical Review* **33**: 477–510.

Suescun Pozas, M. del C. (1998) 'From Reading to Seeing: Doing and Undoing Imperialism in the Visual Arts', in G. M. Joseph, C. C. LeGrand and R. D. Salvatore (eds.) *Close Encounters*, Duke University Press: London Chapel Hills 525–555.

Summerhill, W. R. (2006) 'The Development of Infrastructure', in V. Bulmer-Thomas, J. H. Coatsworth and R. Cortés Conde (eds.) *The Cambridge Economic History of Latin America: Vol. II: The Long Twentieth Century*. Cambridge University Press: Cambridge, 293–326.

Suskind, R. (2004) 'Without A Doubt'. *New York Times Magazine,* 17 October.

Sutch, R. (2003) *Towards a Unified Approach to the Economic History of Settler Economies*. Keynote Address, Conference of the Asociación Uruguaya de Historia Económica, Montevideo.

Tacitus (1964) *On Britain and Germany*. Penguin Books: Harmondsworth.

Taylor, A. J. P. (1976) 'The Meanings of Imperialism', in W. R. Louis (ed.) *Imperialism*Newviewpoints: New York, 197–199.

Taylor, A. M. (1997) *Argentina and the World Capital Market: Savings, Investment and International Capital Mobility in the Twentieth Century*. Unpublished article.

Taylor, A. M. (2003) 'Capital Accumulation', in G. della Paolera and A. M. Taylor (eds.) *A New Economic History of Argentina*. Cambridge University Press: Cambridge, 170–196.

Teignmouth, L. (1818) *A Letter to the Rev. Christopher Wordsworth D.D. in Reply to his Strictures*. Hatchard: London.

Thomas, C. (1985) *New States, Sovereignty and Intervention*. Gower: Aldershot.

Thompson, A. S. (1992) 'Informal Empire? An Exploration in the History of AngloArgentine Relations, 1810–1914'. *Journal of Latin American Studies* **24**(2): 419–436.

Thompson, A. S. (1997) 'The Languages of Imperialism and the Meanings of Empire: Imperial Discourse in British Politics, 1895–1914'. *Journal of British Studies* **36**(2): 147–177.

Thompson, A. S. (2004) 'Ronald Robinson and John Gallagher', in H. C. G. Matthew and B. Harrison (eds.) *Oxford Dictionary of National Biography: From the Earliest Times to the Year 2000*. Oxford University Press: Oxford.

Thompson, A. S. (2005) *The Empire Strikes Back? The Impact of Imperialism on Britain from the Mid-Nineteenth Century.* Harlow: Pearson Education.

Thomson, J. (1827) *Letters on the Moral and Religious State of South America.* James Nisbet: London.

Thurner, T. and Guerrero, A. (eds.) (2003) *After Spanish Rule: Postcolonial Predicaments of the Americas.* Duke University Press: Durham.

Tornquist, E. (1919) *The Economic Development of the Argentine Republic in the Last Fifty Years.* Banco Tornquist: Buenos Aires.

Turnbull, J. (1813) *A Voyage Round the World, in the Years 1800, 1801, 1802, 1803, and 1804, in Which the Author Visited Madeira, the Brazils, Cape of Good Hope, the English Settlement of Botany Bay and Norfolk Island and the Principal Islands in the Pacific Ocean.* Maxwell: London.

Turner, T. A. (1892) *Argentina and the Argentines: Notes and Impressions of a Five Years' Sojourn in the Argentine Republic, 1885–1890.* S. Sonnenschein & Co: London.

Van Onselen, C. (2000) 'Jewish Marginality in the Atlantic World: Organised Crime in the Era of the Great Migrations, 1880–1914'. *South African Historical Journal* **43**: 96–137.

Van Onselen, C. (2007) *The Fox and the Flies. The World of Joseph Silver, Racketeer and Psychopath.* Jonathan Cape: London.

Vargas García, E. (2006) 'Imperio informal? La política británica hacia América Latina en el siglo XIX'. *Foro Internacional* **184** 46(2): 353–385.

Vaughan, E. (1987) *Joseph Lancaster en Caracas, 1824–1827.* Ediciones del Ministerio de Educación: Caracas.

Vázquez-Presedo, V. (1971) *El caso argentino: migración de factores, comercio exterior y desarrollo, 1875–1914.* EUDEBA: Buenos Aires.

Verdesio, G. (2003) 'An Amnesiac Nation: The Erasure of Indigenous Pasts By Uruguayan Expert Knowledges', in J. C. Chasteen and S. Castro-Klarén (eds.) *Beyond Imagined Communities,* Woodrow Wilson Centre Press: Washington DC, 196–224.

Vidal, H. (1993) 'The Concept of Colonial and Postcolonial Discourse: A Perspective from Literary Criticism'. *Latin American Research Review* **28**(3): 113–119.

Vieira, E. R. P. (1999) 'Postcolonialisms and the Latin Americas'. *Interventions* **1**(2): 273–281.

Vitelli, G. (1999) *Los dos siglos de la Argentina: historia económica comparada.* Prendergast: Buenos Aires.

von Humboldt, A. (1850) *Views of Nature* (trans. E. C. Otte and H. G. Bohns). Henry G. Bohn: London.

Walker, J. (1992) 'British Travel Writing and Argentina', in A. Hennessey and J. King (eds.) *The Land That England Lost.* British Academic Press: London, 183–200.

Walton, W. (1810) *Present State of the Spanish Colonies,* 2 vols. Longman, Hurst, Rees, Orme and Brown: London.

Ward, S. (2003) 'Transcending the Nation: A Global Imperial History?', in A. Burton (ed.) *After the Imperial Turn,* Duke University Press: Durham 44–56.

Welch, T. L. and Figueras, M. (1982) *Travel Accounts and Descriptions of Latin America and the Caribbean, 1800–1920: A Selected Bibliography.* Columbus Memorial Library: Washington, D.C.

Wetherell, J. (1860) *Brazil: Stray Notes from Bahia: Being Extracts from Letters, &c., During a Residence of Fifteen Years.* Webb and Hunt: Liverpool.

Whigham, T. L. (2002) *The Paraguayan War, Vol. 1: Causes and Early Conduct*. University of Nebraska: Lincoln.

Whitehead, L. (1994) 'State Organization in Latin America Since 1930', in L. Bethell (ed.) *Cambridge History of Latin America*, Vol. 6. Cambridge University Press: Cambridge, 3–95.

Wilde, J. A. (1960) *Buenos Aires setenta años atrás*. EUDEBA: Buenos Aires.

Williams, G. (1975) *The Desert and the Dream. A Study of Welsh Colonisation in Chubut, 1865–95*. University of Wales Press: Cardiff.

Williams, G. (1991) *The Welsh in Patagonia: The State and the Ethnic Community*. University of Wales Press: Cardiff.

Williams, R. (1961) *Culture and Society 1780–1950*. Harmondsworth: Penguin.

Winchester, S. (2006) *A Crack in the Edge of the World*. Penguin Books: London.

Winn, P. (1976) 'Britain's Informal Empire in Uruguay in the Nineteenth Century'. *Past and Present* **73**: 100–126.

Winograd, C. and Véganzonès, M.-A. (1997) *Argentina in the Twentieth Century: An Account of Long-Awaited Growth*. OECD: Paris.

Winstanley, M. (1983) *The Shopkeeper's World 1830–1914*. Manchester University Press: Manchester.

Wordsworth, D. D. and Rev. C. (1810) *Reasons for Declining to become a Subscriber to the British and Foreign Bible Society*. Rivington: London.

Wordsworth, D. D. and Rev. C. (1818) *A Letter to the Right Hon. Lord Teignmouth, in Vindication of his 'Reasons for Declining…'*. Rivington: London.

Yaben, J. R. (1938) *Biografías Argentinas y Sudamericanas*. Editorial 'Metropolis': Buenos Aires.

Young, R. J. C. (1990) *White Mythologies: Writing History and the West*. Routledge: London.

Young, R. J. C. (1995) *Colonial Desire: Hybridity in Theory, Culture and Race*. Routledge: London.

Young, R. J. C. (2001) *Postcolonialism. An Historical Introduction*. Blackwell: Oxford.

Young, R. J. C. (2003) *Postcolonialism. A Very Short Introduction*. Oxford University Press: Oxford.

Zaldneno, E. A. (1975) *Libras y rieles: las inversiones británicaś para el desarrollo de los ferrocarriles in Argentina, Brasil, Canadá e india durante el siglo XIX*. Editorial El Coloquio: Buenos Aires, 44.

Index